Confederate Generals in the Western Theater

Confederate Generals in the Western Theater

VOLUME 4

Essays on America's Civil War

Edited by Lawrence Lee Hewitt and Thomas E. Schott
With a Foreword by Wiley Sword

The Western Theater in the Civil War • Gary D. Joiner, Series Editor

The University of Tennessee Press / Knoxville

The Western Theater in the Civil War series seeks to emphasize an emerging trend in the historiography of the nation's greatest conflict: a more general recognition that events in the West, far from being a sideshow to storied campaigns in the East, were, in many ways, even more decisive in the outcome of the war. Among the works that will be produced are scholarly monographs, biographies of leaders who need reconsideration, and edited collections that present up-to-date scholarship in this rapidly developing field.

First Edition.

Library of Congress Cataloging-in-Publication Data

Confederate generals in the western theater: volume 4: essays on America's Civil War / edited by Lawrence Lee Hewitt and Thomas E. Schott; with a foreword by Wiley Sword. — 1st ed.
p. cm. — (The western theater in the Civil War)
Includes bibliographical references and index.

ISBN-13: 978-1-62190-290-4 (hardcover)

1. Generals—Confederate States of America—History.
2. Generals—Confederate States of America—Biography.
3. Mississippi River Valley—History—Civil War, 1861–1865—Campaigns.
4. United States—History—Civil War, 1861–1865—Campaigns.
5. Command of troops—History—19th century.
6. Military art and science—Confederate States of America—History.

I. Hewitt, Lawrence L.
II. Schott, Thomas E.

E467.C773 2010
973.7092'2—dc22
2009051917

For
Arthur W. Bergeron Jr.,
Nathaniel Cheairs Hughes Jr.,
and
Wiley Sword

Contents

Illustrations

Figures

Maps

Foreword

AT FIRST GLANCE IT MAY SEEM THAT VOLUME 4 OF *CONFEDERATE GENERALS IN THE Western Theater* features many commanders of a less than stellar reputation or significance. Some have been maligned, misunderstood, or relegated to an inferior status.

Yet humanity is vastly complex. Early accounts from the pre-centennial era often embraced popular history, some being rather simplistic, obscuring the truth and reality prevalent with even the most controversial figures. Because the South ultimately suffered a gruesome defeat, those leaders and commanders who attempted but notably failed have been especially demeaned in the traditionally assessed aftermath.

In our era of expanded electronic research and the availability of vast quantities of data, the performance of many Civil War individuals is now being subjected to great scrutiny. Failures or successes of military leaders are rarely overlooked by present-day historians, although judgments about their abilities often remain controversial. The Civil War had heroes and goats aplenty among those who led, and not a few of them still exist in a shroud of mystery and with a fog of uncertainty about them.

Readers will find interesting new information and interpretations about several fascinating if often overlooked figures in this volume. These include Brigadier General Felix Kirk Zollicoffer, who is revealed by C. David Dalton as a victim of disadvantages and discrepancies at Mill Springs, from weaponry to a lack of command communications. Both his infirmities and bad luck proved key factors as well. Roger S. Durham tells us of General Robert E. Lee's unique plans for defending the coastal areas in the Carolinas during late 1861 to early 1862. Lee's reasoning incorporated antebellum perspectives about the security of well-constructed brick and masonry fortifications such as Fort Pulaski, which proved invalid under shelling by vastly improved "modern" artillery such as Parrott rifles and Columbiad guns. And his inconsistent troop dispositions in relation to actual needs—dispersing them to defend coastal areas such as Savannah—left most of them idle following Lee's departure for other assignments. Stuart W. Sanders's essay on

Benjamin Hardin Helm will be compelling to many based upon his relationship with the Lincolns, and in the aftermath of Helm's death, the furor that occurred with Helm's wife inside the White House. Michael R. Bradley gives us a well-informed insight into Bushrod Rust Johnson, whose unremarkable career was highlighted by occasional spurts of brilliance that garnered significant results. Brian S. Wills reminds us of Abraham Buford and his behind-the-scenes contributions to Nathan Bedford Forrest's great litany of accomplishments. Buford's contributions were often obscured by factors beyond the public notice, yet many witnesses of the actual events noted and appreciated his talents. Gideon J. Pillow, a prominent politician-general at the outbreak of the war, proved lacking as a military commander when given the opportunity. Yet, he was an able administrator, and the late Nathaniel Cheairs Hughes Jr. provides us insight into Pillow's contributions and failings in a well-crafted essay that serves as a farewell message from a prominent historian. James M. Prichard's treatise on John Hunt Morgan presents an uncommon perspective on the "Last Kentucky Raid," including the controversies over the famous cavalryman's leadership and activities. Stewart L. Bennett's essay on William H. T. Walker is a fine commentary on the career of a highly irascible but gifted personality, who dared confront adversity and discord with his own ideas, but suffered greatly in the rendering. Keith S. Bohannon's essay on Edward C. Walthall illustrates how competence and ability were not always rewarded with rank or prestige, although according to some, Walthall was slated to become a lieutenant general at the war's end—that is, when there was a vacancy. Walthall's role in the aftermath of the Franklin-Nashville debacle illustrates just how competently he performed in a crisis. Last, but not least, Chris E. Fonvielle Jr. gives us a detailed insight into Braxton Bragg's war-ending operations at Wilmington, North Carolina: how Bragg, worn to a frazzle by disasters, was "virtually ignored" and could but "mourn over the sad spectacle hourly presented of disorganization, demoralization, and destruction." Though due in large measure to his own actions, Bragg said he would bear them and his "mortifying and humiliating" position "with resignation."

The distinguished historians of these essays have often provided a new and welcome view that redefines the personalities and events involved. From chiefs such as Braxton Bragg to underlings like Gideon J. Pillow, the authors' new considerations and revised assessments will doubtless reshape our understanding and broaden our perspectives on these leaders. The enlightened and sophisticated examination of Civil War history represented here provides fresh material—new food for thought that perhaps will help stave off the emotional and disproportionate history often accorded to both the giants and lesser lights alike. And it will remind us again that we are all a combination of the positive and negative events of our lives, and always subject to capricious fortune and the luck that shapes our existence. So too were the Confederate commanders in their era.

Enjoy the many new insights, as I know you will, and keep the essence of our great Civil War heritage in mind. The results as defined by both good and bad may be controversial, but even as we strive for a broader view, we realize that the entire story will never be fully written—except by Our Creator.

Wiley Sword
September 10, 2015

Preface

Over ten years ago, Art Bergeron and Larry Hewitt, wanting to work together on another book, came up with the idea of a collection of essays on Confederate generals who served in the Western Theater. What started out to be a single volume containing both original and previously published essays quickly turned into a multi-volume project. *Confederate Generals in the Western Theater*, volume one, *Classic Essays on America's Civil War*, which contained articles that had first appeared in various historical journals, sadly did not appear in print until two weeks after Art's untimely death in 2010. Tom Schott promptly donned Art's mantle, and together we have pressed on with the project, in no small part to honor our friend's memory.

Since the conception of this series, several seminal works on Civil War history have appeared. None of those, unfortunately, broke with the continuing historiographical trend that the Confederacy lost the war on the home front. While we agree with virtually every professional historian that the Confederacy had a chance to achieve its independence, the question remains why did it fail? We contend that the fledging nation lost on the battlefields of the Western Theater, and further, that responsibility for those defeats lay more with the Confederate generals than their opponents. Only by studying these men can we better understand how the Civil War ended as it did.

The ten essays in this, the final book of the series under our editorship, offer the usual variety of content: some essays present full biographies, while others focus on a single campaign. The subjects include two full generals, four major generals (including one who exercised corps command), and four brigadiers. In terms of pre-war military experience, they range from West Point graduates and career officers to rank neophytes. Geographically, two essays focus on Kentucky and two on the Atlantic coast, while the balance cover multiple states in the Western Theater. The essays are in chronological order, focused on the subject's service as a general officer or on a particular campaign. One stark difference distinguishes this group of generals from those of the previous volumes—four of the ten were killed in action.

"'He Died on the Field of Glory': Felix Kirk Zollicoffer and the Confederate Defeat at Mill Springs," the first contribution to this series by C. David Dalton focuses on one of these. A newspaper editor, politician, and former Unionist without any military experience, Zollicoffer received his brigadier general's commission, first in the Army of Tennessee and then in the Provisional Army of the Confederate States, to placate the ex-Whigs and "Know-Nothings" in Tennessee. Assigned to defend the Memphis & Charleston Railroad and Cumberland Gap in East Tennessee, Zollicoffer quickly moved troops into Kentucky when that state ended its neutrality and declared for the Union. His deployment north of the Cumberland River forced his superior, Major General George B. Crittenden, to fight an unwanted battle that resulted in the first breech of the Confederate line across the Bluegrass State. Zollicoffer died a hero; the survivors, notably Crittenden, got the blame.

"Robert E. Lee's Lost Campaign" is by another first-time contributor, Roger S. Durham. His essay covers the most neglected part of the career of the Confederacy's greatest general: his service as commander of the Department of South Carolina, Georgia, and East Florida from November 8, 1861–March 3, 1862. Readers unfamiliar with the series might be surprised at the inclusion of essays dealing with the Atlantic coast, but the National Park Service's American Battlefield Protection Program deems everything south and west of Virginia and east of the Mississippi River as the Western Theater. And most Confederate Army of Tennessee veterans would probably have agreed. Nonetheless this region of the war might easily be dismissed in Lee's case because not a single noteworthy engagement occurred during his tenure as commander. Lee manifestly changed the area, however, relocating the Confederate defensive line from the coastal islands well inland. This provided a more mobile defense for the railroad running between Charleston and Savannah and prevented the senseless capture of troops and heavy ordnance preceding Lee's command of the department. Time would prove the wisdom of his strategy, but contemporaries severely criticized him for abandoning territory to the enemy without a fight.

Our most prolific contributor, Stuart W. Sanders's third offering is "'I Have Gone in for the War': Benjamin Hardin Helm." After graduating from West Point and serving in the 2nd U.S. Cavalry in Texas, "inflammatory rheumatism" forced Helm to give up the military. Returning to Kentucky, he became a successful attorney and politician, and in 1856, married Emilie Todd, Mary Todd Lincoln's half-sister. Turning down Lincoln's offer of a major's commission and a position as paymaster in the U.S. Army in March 1861, he worked instead to maintain Kentucky's neutrality. When that ended, he entered Confederate service as colonel of the 1st Kentucky Cavalry Regiment. As a brigadier general in the spring of 1862, Helm took charge of an infantry brigade. He was transferred to the Army of Tennessee early in 1863 and given command of the "Orphan Brigade," which he led until his death seven months later at Chickamauga.

That bloody battle provided unbelievable good fortune to another brigadier. "From Hoover's Gap to Chickamauga: Bushrod Rust Johnson's Best Three Months of the War" is Michael R. Bradley's first contribution to the series. A native of Ohio, Johnson was a Quaker and, at least as a young man, an abolitionist. A military career that began with his graduation from West Point quickly ended in resignation to avoid court-martial. When war erupted in 1861, Johnson, a widower with a learning disabled child who was struggling to make a living teaching at a military school in Tennessee, cast his lot with the South. His Confederate career also took odd turns, from personal misfortunes following Fort Donelson and Little Sailor's Creek to earning promotion to major general for his defense of Petersburg. All but forgotten is the fact that Johnson's ad hoc division, and not the veterans of the Army of Northern Virginia, spearheaded James Longstreet's celebrated breakthrough at Chickamauga.

In "'Hellraising' Abraham Buford: Nathan Bedford Forrest's Dependable Lieutenant," Brian S. Wills provides what for now is the definitive biography of this Confederate brigadier general. Though a West Point graduate and longtime professional soldier, the Kentucky-born Buford was slow to choose sides when war came. As an advocate of state's rights but an opponent of secession, he supported Kentucky's neutrality in 1861, and even when that ended, Buford remained on the sideline. Not until the Confederates returned to the Bluegrass State in force in September 1862 did Buford cast his lot with the South. President Jefferson Davis rewarded him with a brigadier's commission for quickly recruiting several regiments of Kentuckians for the Confederate army. He led a cavalry brigade in Tennessee and an infantry brigade in Louisiana and Mississippi before taking command of a division of cavalry under Nathan Bedford Forrest in the spring of 1864. The quintessential Kentucky gentleman who loved bourbon, fast women, and faster horses, Buford lived life to the fullest only to die penniless and by his own hand.

One of only three historians to contribute to the *Classics* volume of this series and a subsequent one, Nathaniel Cheairs Hughes Jr. died before completing his final revision of "Unwept, Unhonored, and Unsung: Gideon J. Pillow." Fortunately for us, the text was complete, as was his *The Life and Wars of Gideon J. Pillow*—currently available from the University of Tennessee Press—which he cowrote in 1993 with Roy P. Stonesifer Jr. Pillow's abandonment of his men at Fort Donelson (along with fellow general John B. Floyd) has all but blotted out his subsequent contributions to the Confederate war effort. He returned to field duty in time to take charge of a brigade at the Battle of Murfreesboro. Afterward he did a superb job rounding up conscripts and returning deserters to the ranks before being assigned to the cavalry in 1864. His only engagement as an independent commander occurred at LaFayette, Georgia, the focal point of the essay. Relieved from field command for his failure there, Pillow served a stint as Commissary General for Prisoners before the war ended.

Best remembered for his raid north of the Ohio River and the successes that preceded his capture in Ohio, John Hunt Morgan's career following his escape from prison is largely unknown and misunderstood. In "Banner in the Dust: John Hunt Morgan's Last Kentucky Raid," James M. Prichard analyzes Morgan's final campaign, which culminated in his defeat near Cynthiana and the rout of his command. Morgan managed to escape, tainted by crimes committed by his subordinates and leaving his banner in enemy hands. His death ten weeks later brought an end to the investigation of him for banditry.

In "A Ghost on Horseback: The Many Wounds and Curious Death of William H. T. Walker," Stewart L. Bennett focuses on the injuries and illnesses of a man who earned the nickname "Old Shot Pouch" for multiple wounds sustained while fighting Seminoles and Mexicans. He sheds considerable light on conflicting accounts of Walker's death during the Battle of Atlanta in July 1864. A West Point graduate, Walker managed to have a successful career in both the U.S. and Confederate armies despite resigning from both early on and having a divisive relationship with President Jefferson Davis.

In his essay "'He Exhibited the Highest Soldierly Qualities': Edward C. Walthall," Keith S. Bohannon examines the Confederate career of Walthall, a man who brought but the barest modicum of military experience to his participation in the war. But his performance in positions of increasing responsibility—company, regimental, and then brigade command at Chickamauga and the battles around Chattanooga—merited praise and promotion. He assumed command of a division during the Atlanta Campaign and soon thereafter was promoted to major general where he performed outstandingly at the subsequent battles of Peachtree Creek and Ezra Church. Following John Bell Hood's catastrophic invasion of Tennessee, Walthall took command of eight used up infantry brigades and, with Major General Nathan Bedford Forrest, performed yeoman service as Hood's rear guard during the retreat. It's hard to contest Bohannon's contention that Walthall was one of the best Confederate generals in any theater.

Fittingly, the volume's final essay addresses the last field campaign of General Braxton Bragg. In "Unlucky in War: Braxton Bragg's Return to Field Duty at Wilmington, North Carolina," Chris E. Fonvielle Jr. recounts the doleful tale of the fall of Fort Fisher and with it Wilmington, North Carolina, the last surviving Confederate port and sole entrepôt for war material and supplies for Lee's army in Virginia. Bragg, a dubious appointment on the face of it, replaced Major General William Henry Chase Whiting as commander of the Wilmington defenses in late 1864, when threats against the city, which Whiting had warned about for months, appeared real. Fort Fisher withstood the greatest naval bombardment in history on December 24–25, 1864, for which Bragg took credit. But on January 15, 1865, a combined Federal force succeeded in capturing the vital fort, a defeat which can be attributed to Bragg's negligence as much to as to any other cause.

Our thanks to the University of Tennessee Press for permitting us to retain traditional editorial practices in this volume, whereby military ranks are always capitalized and unit designations use numerals. Most importantly, Confederate brigades, divisions, and corps are always referred to by their commander's name. While the Union army numbered all of these units throughout the war, the Confederacy never adopted a uniform standard, an inconsistency that has proven troublesome for historians and confusing for readers.

A Confederate corps might be named (Reserve), numbered (I, First, or 1st), designated as a wing (Left or Right), or referred to by the last name of its commander. The latter practice was more common for brigades and divisions, though occasionally they would be numbered as well. Several brigades were identified by nickname during the war, a trend that historians have continued. "Hood's Texas Brigade" or simply the "Texas Brigade" of the Army of Northern Virginia is probably the best known example, but only the Stonewall Brigade had a government sanctioned nickname.

The brigade in the Western Theater most frequently referred to by sobriquet was Kentucky's famed "Orphan Brigade." Between the spring of 1862 and the fall of 1863, this unit went by a host of "official" names, the last of which was Lewis's Brigade, Breckinridge's Division, Breckinridge's corps, Army of Tennessee. This designation illustrates a second problem inherent in the Confederacy's designation system. Major General John C. Breckinridge was given command of a corps during the siege of Chattanooga, but President Davis never submitted his nomination for promotion to lieutenant general. Consequently, the division he formally commanded officially remained Breckinridge's Division, even though it was under the temporary command of Brigadier General William B. Bate. Only later, after Bate was promoted to major general and the War Department permanently assigned him to command, did it become known as Bate's Division.

Anything that enables the reader to more easily track the ever-changing Confederate high command in the Western Theater is helpful. Knowing if a brigade, division, or corps entered a battle under a temporary commander fits this category. And because our subject is the generals themselves, rather than clutter the text with obscure numbers or confuse readers about who was in command at a given time, we have made one exception to strict historical accuracy. Confederate units are designated by the name of their official commander throughout the volume: for example, "Vaughan's Brigade," "Major General John C. Breckinridge's Division," and "Lieutenant General Hardee's Corps." Occasionally, references such as "Reserve Corps" in the case of Major General William H. T. Walker during the Chickamauga Campaign also appear. If, however, "brigade," "division," or "corps" appears in lowercase, it means that the commanding officer is only temporary. Readers will therefore immediately know that "Hardee's Corps" means that Lieutenant General William J. Hardee is present with his troops and "Vaughan's brigade" means that Alfred J. Vaughan is only in temporary command at that moment.

Lastly, the reader will find that Edmund Kirby Smith has the last name "Kirby Smith" in this volume. That was how he himself wanted it rendered, but the government bureaucracy saw it differently. Kirby Smith's children added a hyphen to solve the problem, as did Louisiana State University when it named its largest dorm Kirby-Smith Hall. We have honored the general's wishes.

Lawrence Lee Hewitt
Thomas E. Schott

Acknowledgments

We wish to thank our authors for their contributions, as well as Wiley Sword, Gary D. Joiner, Scot Danforth, and everyone at the University of Tennessee Press who assisted in the publication of this volume. We also wish to express our gratitude to the following for providing illustrations: Tennessee State Library and Archives, Savas Publishing Company, Kennesaw Mountain Historical Association, Chris E. Fonvielle Jr., David Friedrichs, Dave Powell, Tim Smith, and Stewart Bennett.

Brigadier General Felix Kirk Zollicoffer. Library of Congress.

"He Died on the Field of Glory": Felix Kirk Zollicoffer and the Confederate Defeat at Mill Springs

C. David Dalton

As the morning of January 19, 1862, dawned, the first major Civil War engagement in Kentucky was underway just north of Mill Springs, a small community on the Cumberland River in the southeastern part of the state. The battle was being fought without the benefit of sunlight, as rain clouds hovered overhead and patches of fog passed across the battlefield. With the added pollution of musket and artillery smoke, visibility was poor, at best. Confederate Brigadier General William Henry Carroll commented that "the eye could distinguish objects only a short distance."[1] Despite these conditions but needing to determine the course of the action, Confederate Brigadier General Felix Kirk Zollicoffer decided to ride to his left, while at about the same time Union Colonel Speed Fry rode to his right, along the rail fence behind which he had been fighting. As Fry neared the Mill Springs road, he encountered what seemed to be an officer riding calmly toward his lines. The officer's uniform was concealed by a raincoat, but the placid manner of his approach and his proximity to the Union lines convinced Fry that he was a newly arrived Federal officer. Fry rode up to his side, so close that their knees touched. The unidentified officer, nodding his head to the left, spoke first: "We must not shoot our own men. Those are our men." Fry responded, "Of course not. I would not do so intentionally." The conversation ended, and Fry started back to his regiment.[2]

As Fry approached his men, another mounted officer emerged from the trees where the brief meeting had just occurred, firing his pistol into Union ranks and striking Fry's horse. Somewhat confused but acting on instinct, Fry returned fire, as did his men. It suddenly dawned on Fry that his conversation only minutes earlier had not been with a new Federal officer but a displaced Confederate. Amidst pistol and musket shots, the second Confederate officer fled unharmed, but the one with whom Fry had just spoken, fell from his mount, killed instantly. Upon viewing the body, there was no doubt as the identity: it was Brigadier General Felix Kirk Zollicoffer.

Born on the family farm near Bigbyville, Tennessee, on May 11, 1812, Zollicoffer was the son of John Jacob Zollicoffer and Martha Kirk. His great-grandfather, Baron Jacob Christopher Zollicoffer, had emigrated from Switzerland to America, eventually settling in North Carolina. His grandfather, Captain George Zollicoffer, fought in the Revolutionary War and, as a result of his service, received several hundred acres of land in Maury County, Tennessee.[3] Growing up in a rural area did not afford much of an opportunity for formal education, but young Felix had an appetite for the written word and attended log cabin "field schools" for eight years until he entered the newly created Jackson College in Columbia. His stay was brief, though, lasting only one year. Taking a position as apprentice to A. O. P. Nicholson, a local Columbia printer, Zollicoffer found the newspaper business to his liking. Subsequent jobs took him from Paris in the northwestern part of Tennessee to Knoxville in the eastern part of the state. He eventually returned home to become editor of the *Columbia Observer* in 1834 and the following year was named state printer for Tennessee.[4]

With his star rising in business, Zollicoffer next turned his attention to Louisa Pocahontas Gordon, whom he married in September 1835.[5] Perhaps sensing an obligation to continue the family military tradition, Zollicoffer volunteered to fight with his fellow Tennesseans in the Second Seminole War, serving with the rank of lieutenant. He returned to Columbia in 1837, resuming his editorship of the *Observer* until an opportunity arose that would thrust him into the political arena. The *Nashville Republican Banner,* the most influential Whig newspaper in the state, tendered Zollicoffer the position of associate editor, which he accepted. Despite the dominance of Jacksonian Democrats, Zollicoffer quickly gained a reputation for his fiery editorials, which had the added benefit of name recognition at the polls. He served as Tennessee state adjutant general and comptroller from 1846–49, as state senator from 1849–52, and as U.S. Representative from 1853–59.[6]

During his first congressional election, Zollicoffer's political barbs led to a duel with John L. Marling, editor of the *Nashville Union,* which supported Democratic presidential candidate Franklin Pierce. Zollicoffer's Whiggish pen ridiculed Pierce on a host of issues. Marling responded that the *Republican Banner* had intentionally misrepresented Pierce's position on abolitionism and slavery, even stooping to personal attacks on his character. "Now, we say this is *believing* General Pierce. We use the word in all its length and breadth. It is shameless misrepresentation. . . . It is a course unworthy of an honorable man." Soon after the editorial's publication, Zollicoffer sent word that he would meet Marling in front of the *Union* office for satisfaction. Although accounts vary slightly, it seems that Marling fired first, but the shot missed. Zollicoffer's derringer then misfired, and while retrieving another cap, Marling fired a second time, striking Zollicoffer's right hand. Unfazed, Zollicoffer returned fire, striking Marling in the face, below his eye. Although Marling survived his wounds and the two men later reconciled, Zollicoffer's fiery temperament and editorial influence helped carry Tennessee for the Whig candidate, Winfield Scott, in 1852.[7]

Politically, Zollicoffer resembled many other Southern Whigs—a Unionist supporter of state rights. He railed against the disunionist talk emanating from the Nashville Convention in 1850 but supported the Kansas-Nebraska Act in 1854 which put Illinois Senator Stephen A. Douglas's "popular sovereignty" doctrine to the test in that territory. In a speech before Congress, he stated: "We are one people, living under the same Constitution, and entitled in all the Territories to equal privileges of occupancy and settlement."[8] Like many Whigs of both sections, he found himself without a party when the Whigs disintegrated after the 1852 election. So he became a member of the short-lived American Party, more commonly referred to as "Know-Nothings," since they avoided taking a stand on the divisive issue of slavery. During the 1856 presidential election, Zollicoffer stated: "[I] thank Heaven, there is a third great party in the field, composed of national men, North and South, who have united . . . to preserve the Union, to calm the popular exasperation, and to restore, once more, peace, confidence, and good will between the great sections."[9] Once again desperately trying to avoid the toxic slavery issue, he helped form the Constitutional Union Party four years later whose presidential candidate was John Bell, a fellow Tennessean. But when Republican Abraham Lincoln swept the northern electoral vote to victory, Zollicoffer wrote to his brother Frederick that:

> It is melancholy to contemplate, that such a government as ours, the wisest and most just ever created, cannot stand. . . . I trust the catastrophe may yet be averted; but I am not blind to the danger, or insensible to the just grievances of the Southern States. . . . I am truly devoted to the constitutional rights of the slave-holding states. If disunion comes, I trust they will all stand together, but I hope they will not act precipitously. . . . I think immediate secession for present causes is not the wisest and best remedy for the evils complained of or feared. What is to be done should be done coolly, slowly, deliberately, and after free consultation among the slave-holding States. . . . Let them firmly but respectfully demand a repeal of the State acts, annulling the fugitive slave law. Let them demand a guarantee that the Federal Government shall

> never interfere to abolish slavery in the States. If these things are denied us, I am for resorting to any means which the wisdom and patriotism of the South may devise to protect ourselves against existing and anticipated injuries and wrongs.[10]

Despite having retired from national politics, Zollicoffer represented Tennessee at the ill-fated Washington Peace Conference in February 1861. Even after the firing on Fort Sumter, Zollicoffer hoped the nation could avoid war. He was holding a peace rally in Nashville when news arrived that Lincoln had called for seventy-five thousand volunteers to put down the rebellion in South Carolina. In his mind, as in many others throughout the South, Lincoln's action amounted to a declaration of war, and in the weeks prior to Tennessee's withdrawal from the Union, Zollicoffer volunteered his services, and meager military experience, to his state.[11]

On May 9, 1861, Tennessee's Governor Isham G. Harris commissioned Zollicoffer as brigadier general in the Provisional Army of Tennessee. His early service comprised receiving, organizing, and training recruits in the Nashville area. When the army was transferred to Confederate control, Major General Leonidas Polk recommended that Zollicoffer be sent to the eastern part of the state to secure the Memphis & Charleston Railroad as well as to challenge the pro-Unionist sentiment so prevalent in the region. Confederate President Jefferson Davis assigned Zollicoffer to command the District of East Tennessee with three simple orders: "Preserve peace, protect the railroad, and repel invasion."[12]

Confederate authorities believed that the Federal "Home Guards" at Camp Dick Robinson in Kentucky could, at any moment, invade East Tennessee and control the strategic Cumberland Gap. On August 29, 1861, Zollicoffer telegraphed Confederate Adjutant and Inspector General Samuel Cooper in Richmond that Camp Dick Robinson had at least four thousand well-armed men, with new recruits arriving daily. Many Unionists from East Tennessee, he added, had been and were crossing over into Kentucky to get arms from the Union camp, all of which made for a potentially explosive situation.[13]

However, the eastern Kentucky-Tennessee area was not the scene of the first clash in the Bluegrass State. The western region along the Mississippi River would claim that distinction. On September 4, 1861, Polk disregarded Kentucky's self-proclaimed neutrality and occupied Columbus, a strategic town on the eastern bank of the Mississippi River. Union leaders condemned Polk's move, saying it rivaled the firing on Fort Sumter, but Davis defended the action as "absolutely necessary" for the security of secessionists in southwestern Kentucky. Perhaps the *Woodford (KY) Pennant* summed up the entire incident best: "The rubicon is crossed."[14]

With Kentucky's neutrality broken, both Union and Confederate forces sought to occupy key locations throughout the state. Confederate commanding general in the West, Albert Sidney Johnston, met briefly with Zollicoffer in Knoxville in early September and approved his advancing into Kentucky by way of Cumberland Gap.[15] Zollicoffer's command consisted of seven infantry regiments and four cavalry battalions, most of them composed of Tennesseans.[16] He left two regiments at Knoxville and one at Cumberland Gap, while sending a battery of guns and the remaining troops fifteen miles into southeastern Kentucky to Cumberland Ford, renamed Camp Buckner. By mid-September, Zollicoffer took up a northern trek towards Barboursville, in Knox County. When his advance force of eight hundred men entered the town at daylight on September 19, they encountered three hundred Union soldiers, apparently unaware of the Confederate movement. After a brief skirmish the Confederates drove the surprised Federals from the town. Casualty reports showed twelve Union soldiers killed and two captured, with an unknown number wounded. Of Zollicoffer's soldiers, only two were killed and three wounded.[17]

At Camp Dick Robinson, Brigadier General George H. Thomas received reports of the advance, but the Union commander was not overly concerned with the movement, confident that Zollicoffer would retreat to Cumberland Gap if confronted by a superior Union force. The lack of supplies in Barboursville temporarily suspended any thoughts Zollicoffer had for moving into the heartland of Kentucky. On September 24 he noted the lack of even one day's ration of bread in the entire camp. But when foraging parties returned with enough provisions for a week, Zollicoffer decided to continue his movement deeper into Kentucky. He noted: "It is probable our best defense of East Tennessee is an onward movement toward those who threaten invasion." His actions were premature, though, as Johnston had written Zollicoffer the previous day that "a forward movement from your present position at this time cannot be made."[18] The message did not reach Zollicoffer until he was two days on the march.

At 4:00 A.M. on September 25, Colonel James Rains led his 11th Tennessee Infantry Regiment to Laurel Bridge on the London road. Three cavalry companies and a section of artillery accompanied Rains, as well as a battalion of Colonel Winfield S. Statham's 15th Mississippi Infantry Regiment. A second wave of Zollicoffer's forces, Colonel David H. Cummings's 19th Tennessee Infantry Regiment, two cavalry companies, and several empty wagons headed towards the Goose Creek salt mines in Clay County, seventeen miles to the east. To divert attention away from the move on valuable salt works, the Confederates planned to surprise the several hundred Union soldiers encamped at Laurel Bridge, fifty miles south of Camp Dick Robinson. The diversion succeeded splendidly as Federal pickets surrounding Laurel

Bridge were quickly driven in, and the Confederates captured three prisoners along with eight thousand cartridges, twenty-five thousand caps, three kegs of powder, six barrels of salt, two wagons and teams, three other horses, twenty-five pairs of shoes, and several guns. The force sent to the salt works returned to Camp Buckner without incident, along with two hundred barrels of the badly needed food preservative.[19]

By October 1861, Lincoln had devised several plans of attack upon the South, one of which involved eastern Kentucky. Simultaneous with a coastal movement on the Carolinas, Lincoln proposed an attack on Cumberland Gap and western Virginia in order to rid those areas of Confederates. In fact, on October 1, Zollicoffer received word that 2,500 "Lincolnites" had assembled near Louisa, in Lawrence County of northeastern Kentucky, and were threatening to invade and control the vital Sandy Valley. Troops from Camp Dick Robinson were reported moving on Cumberland Gap, with two regiments already encamped between London and the Rockcastle River.[20]

Zollicoffer asked Johnston's permission to go forth and meet the Union troops from Camp Dick Robinson. "Exercise your own discretion in attacking the enemy," Johnston replied.[21] Obviously, the Confederate effort in eastern Kentucky could not afford a disastrous defeat and forfeiture of Cumberland Gap, but if Zollicoffer could check the Union offensive by active defensive maneuvers, he might buy additional time for the arrival of badly needed men and equipment. But lack of sufficient provisions and adequate transportation for 4,500 men delayed Zollicoffer's advance for several days. Finally, at midnight on October 7, Union scouts informed Thomas that Zollicoffer had begun an advance towards central Kentucky.[22] Three days later, a forward party of Confederates established a temporary camp on a hill nine miles north of London in Rockcastle County. The hill would become a battlefield less than a week later.

As Zollicoffer passed through London, a small skirmish between pickets occurred, with only nominal casualties on each side. The fight, however, served notice to the Confederate commander that he was nearing Rockcastle Hills where Brigadier General Albin Schoepf, Colonel Theophilus Garrard, and four thousand Union troops from Camp Dick Robinson were entrenched on Wildcat Mountain. Zollicoffer, upon a first glance at the Federal position, called it "a natural fortification, almost inaccessible," but it did not deter his plan of attack.[23]

On October 21, Zollicoffer cautiously approached Camp Wildcat, the Union position in the Rockcastle Hills. A dense forest encircling the area concealed his advance for the most part. Colonel Tazewell W. Newman's 17th Tennessee and Colonel Cummings's 19th Tennessee infantry regiments prepared for a frontal assault, while ten additional companies moved to the left. Newman's men closed to within eighty yards of the Federal position when their ranks were riddled by a heavy Union volley. They continued moving forward, albeit slower, without firing a shot, groping for protection from the galling rifle and musket fire. When they were within fifty yards of the Union lines, the Confederates fired a volley and intense gunfire continued for over half an hour. With the battle raging, Newman, showing no fear, led four companies gallantly up the steep hillside. Some of the men reached the Federal works but, being destitute of cartridges and coming under increasing fire, they were forced to fall back and regroup.[24]

Intermittent firing continued throughout the day until Zollicoffer realized that the hilltop Federal position could not be taken without a heavy loss of Confederate life. Reluctantly, he decided to fall back to Cumberland Ford. The Confederates lost eleven killed and forty-two wounded, while Union casualties were listed at four killed and eighteen wounded. By October 25, Zollicoffer had returned to Camp Buckner, having failed in his first battlefield effort, though the Battle of Camp Wildcat or Rockcastle Hills was more of a reconnaissance in force than a pitched battle. Zollicoffer could only wait and see if his active defensive gestures would slow the planned Union advance upon Cumberland Gap.[25]

Zollicoffer's repulse at Rockcastle Hills demonstrated the difficulties of conducting operations in eastern Kentucky. With numerous mountains to traverse, some often insurmountable, the key to victory resided with obtaining an advantageous defensive position, awaiting the attack, and repulsing it. Furthermore, provisions in the area were scarce, and the farther north Zollicoffer tried to move, the longer his supply line became, with the entire route in hostile Unionist territory. Yet, if Zollicoffer chose to remain in the Cumberland Gap area, he lost the tactical offensive advantage of surprise, an important tool in the early months of the war.

Following the Confederate retreat, rumors circulated that Zollicoffer would be replaced. Because of the immense importance that Cumberland Gap played in Southern strategy, only one name was mentioned repeatedly as his replacement—General Robert E. Lee. Union leaders feared that Lee would be sent to Kentucky with a powerful army and sweep through the entire state, a view echoed by the *New York Times*.[26] However, if such a change were seriously contemplated, it did not materialize, and Zollicoffer remained in command at Cumberland Gap. He did, however, become alarmed that the Federals might counterattack before additional men could be sent forward to strengthen his army. So to protect this vital area, Johnston ordered Brigadier Generals Leroy P. Walker and William Carroll with their respective troops to Knoxville to bolster the defenses of Cumberland Gap and the various mountain passes in the area.

The arrival of additional men and supplies strengthened Zollicoffer's defenses at Cumberland Gap, but many more mountain passes penetrating into East Tennessee existed than he could possibly defend. So he scattered four cavalry companies to the west to ascertain whether the Federals would try to outflank him.[27] The effort soon succeeded when those troopers captured a Federal spy who confessed that it was indeed the Federal plan to send two or three regiments against Cumberland Gap, hoping to draw Zollicoffer out for a fight, while the principal Union force would move through a different pass and outflank the Confederates. The spy estimated the total Union force at twenty thousand.[28] Zollicoffer now dispatched several regiments to the west thus shifting the scene of fighting from eastern Kentucky to East Tennessee.

Residents of the Volunteer State were genuinely concerned for the safety of their region. After the Confederate advance into central Kentucky had been repulsed, they feared a massive Union counterattack upon Zollicoffer to seize the East Tennessee & Virginia Railroad, the vital communication link with the east. Zollicoffer sent urgent appeals for additional men and artillery to strengthen his position in the mountains, while at the same time ordering four infantry regiments to fortify the passes where he expected the Union assaults. This rapid and substantial movement of men westward resulted in alarming reports to Thomas that Zollicoffer had been reinforced to not less than twenty thousand men.[29] Although he regarded that report as inaccurate, Thomas displayed his conservative approach to warfare and recalled his advanced troops to Camp Dick Robinson. Even if Zollicoffer had only half that number, Thomas could ill afford to be caught in a fight with several of his units dispersed in eastern Kentucky. He would wait for a better opportunity to strike.

Confederate scouting reports confirmed the Union withdrawal, and by November 4, Zollicoffer realized that the suspected Union attack had dissipated. He then proposed to Johnston that his force be more closely aligned with that of Brigadier General Simon Bolivar Buckner at Bowling Green:

> If therefore it should meet with your approval, I will as rapidly as possible, endeavor to so fortify the Cumberland Gap that the smallest possible force will be necessary there; will simultaneously endeavor to fortify or thoroughly blockade the passes near Jacksborough . . . and concentrate them [troops] upon some point in the open country near Jamestown, with the view of advancing towards Danville.[30]

Zollicoffer was again considering an offensive into Kentucky. He left the regiments of Colonels James Rains and William Churchwell at Cumberland Gap to complete the breastworks, while he led five regiments, a battery of artillery, and a small group of cavalry northward. By November 7, he acquired four additional regiments as well as news that a small force of three to four hundred Federals were encamped just east of Monticello, the only known Yankees south of the Cumberland River.[31]

But on November 11, 1861, the Adjutant and Inspector General's Office in Richmond issued Special Order No. 216, placing George B. Crittenden in command of the troops in the District of East Tennessee. A West Point graduate, Crittenden served in both the Black Hawk and Mexican Wars, and by 1856 held the rank of lieutenant colonel in the U.S. Army. With the outbreak of civil war, however, he resigned his commission and accepted the rank of brigadier; he was later promoted to major general in the Confederate army.[32]

Crittenden's appointment to the District of East Tennessee was due in large part to personal intervention by President Davis. It was no coincidence that when news reached Richmond of Zollicoffer's defeat at Rockcastle Hills, Davis sent an "unofficial" inquiry to Crittenden to gauge his interest in commanding an army to invade his native Kentucky. Davis hoped to revive the state's waning support of the Confederacy by offering Crittenden, whose family name was widely recognized throughout the state, command of the Confederate forces at Cumberland Gap for an advance into the Commonwealth.[33]

Johnston, unaware of the change of command made in Richmond, had meanwhile approved a plan whereby Zollicoffer, with his four thousand men, would establish a camp at Mill Springs, Kentucky, and, if not threatened by the enemy during the winter months ahead, launch a spring offensive into the central part of the state.[34] Zollicoffer proposed "to take and strengthen a position between Monticello and Somerset, giving us facilities for commanding the Cumberland River, the coal region supplying Nashville. If I can clear the banks of the Cumberland of our enemies, supplies may this winter be furnished us by boats from Nashville."[35] He reiterated this goal less than two weeks later when he added that if the region north of the Cumberland could be cleared of the enemy, it would provide him an opportunity to draw supplies from Nashville, via water, rather than from Knoxville over poor roads.[36]

Major General George B. Crittenden. Courtesy of Lawrence Lee Hewitt.

On November 29, Zollicoffer arrived at Mill Springs, a small community on the southern bank of the Cumberland River. This vast and winding river was the key to the entire area which also had an abundance of crops, forage, and even a large grist mill, hence the name Mill Springs. These elements, combined with the formidable bluffs edging the southern bank of the river, afforded Zollicoffer an excellent location for establishing winter quarters for his troops, while also presenting the Union command with an offensive threat to central Kentucky.[37] But to be a real threat, Zollicoffer had to put men across the Cumberland River. On the last day of November, he wrote Johnston that he was preparing to cross the river: "The lumber and the saw mill here will materially aid in constructing boats. . . . As soon as it is possible I will cross the river in force." Two days later, he repeated his plans to cross the Cumberland once transports could be built.[38]

At Louisville, Brigadier General Don Carlos Buell, Union commander of the Department of the Ohio, doubted that Zollicoffer would cross the river. He expected, rather, that Zollicoffer would attempt no more than a reconnaissance in force and certainly not risk a major engagement. Many in Buell's camp disagreed about Zollicoffer's intentions, however, since he had already outsmarted the Union commanders by leaving Cumberland Gap and establishing a fortified position on the Cumberland River. Zollicoffer's active defense would relieve pressure on Johnston in Bowling Green by occupying the full attention of the troops from Camp Dick Robinson. At the same time, it also secured additional time for men and supplies to be sent to Mill Springs from Nashville.[39]

Zollicoffer's position at Mill Springs changed the entire nature of operations in central and eastern Kentucky. If his first plan of action included an attack on Camp Dick Robinson, his second was surely to hold his own position on the Cumberland River, for Johnston desired Zollicoffer to continue observing the enemy until such time as he could reinforce his army.[40] Johnston planned to establish a strong Confederate line of defense across southern Kentucky, from the Mississippi River through Bowling Green to Mill Springs, ending at Cumberland Gap.

In early December, Schoepf was sent to watch Zollicoffer and prevent his crossing the Cumberland in force. After reconnoitering, Schoepf wrote Thomas, overestimating the Confederate army at nine thousand strong. But before he could finish the letter, Confederate artillery atop the southern bluffs of the Cumberland opened fire on the advanced Union forces. Zollicoffer also reported the clash to Johnston, the first of several offensive displays. Zollicoffer's actions pleased Johnston: "Every move is entirely approved," he wrote on December 4. But he also warned that Zollicoffer should safeguard the Monticello-Somerset road, on the southern side of the Cumberland River, the most practical road the enemy could use to advance on

Mill Springs. But he acquiesced to Zollicoffer's more thorough knowledge of the country.[41] It was vintage Johnston to rely on his subordinate's decisions as to what was best when he himself did not know an area.

While Schoepf kept his vigil on Zollicoffer, rumors circulated of a Confederate attack on central Kentucky. A black man crossed over to the northern side of the Cumberland and told Schoepf on December 4 that the Confederates had constructed a large number of boats and were, at any moment, contemplating an attack. When the expected Confederate offensive did not materialize, Buell, attempting to downplay the significance of the Southern force, wrote that Zollicoffer was making only harmless demonstrations. "He will do no great harm."[42]

But on December 9, Confederate advance forces were thrown across the Cumberland River, much to the surprise and despair of the retreating Yankees. A few days of inactivity had lulled Schoepf into a false sense of security, and the Confederates easily put five infantry regiments, seven cavalry companies, and four pieces of artillery across the river. Zollicoffer's new position, which he immediately fortified, was at Beech Grove, directly across the Cumberland from Mill Springs. Zollicoffer described Beech Grove as a "naturally strong" defensive position.[43]

Following this bold move, Zollicoffer received Johnston's letter of December 4 about the importance of the Monticello–Somerset road, which he answered immediately. Zollicoffer inferred that Johnston wanted him to remain at Mill Springs guarding the road. But with Schoepf receiving reinforcements from Camp Dick Robinson and with limited transportation for a rapid removal, Zollicoffer felt it impossible to recross the Cumberland at that particular time. He tried to bolster support for his move by praising his current position. He cited the protection the river afforded both flanks and rear—the camp resembled a horseshoe—as well as its suitability as an excellent springboard for operations into central Kentucky. He believed Beech Grove "a much stronger natural position for defense than that on the south bank. I think it should be held at all hazards."[44]

In fact, the northern bank was not a better natural location. There was a marked difference in elevation between the two river banks, with the southern cliffs dominating the entire area while the opposite shoreline only gradually rose to the north. Moreover, in the view of several historians, having a river in their rear, trapped rather than protected the Confederates.[45] However, Zollicoffer had mentioned the key word "defense," for by mid-December he had not received the necessary men and supplies for an immediate offensive into central Kentucky. Consequently, he was contemplating the second phase of his plan—a defensive stand in winter quarters at Beech Grove. He updated Davis on December 14 of his recent activities, and at the end of the communication, Zollicoffer added, almost casually, that the

Plot of rebel fortifications at Mill Springs, drawn by James Hartwell Henson, Company D, 20th Tennessee Volunteers, December 1861. Courtesy of the Tennessee State Library and Archives, Nashville.

Federals had eight to ten infantry regiments at Somerset and another five at Columbia, whereas he himself had four and a half regiments at Beech Grove and two across the river at Mill Springs.[46] With his recent successful forward movements, taking the initiative and surprising the Federals, Zollicoffer hoped for an opportunity to redeem himself to Richmond authorities who still thought him unqualified for active command.

Such was not to be the case. On December 15, Crittenden arrived in Knoxville and assumed overall command of the Confederate forces in the area.[47] The next day, without sufficient knowledge of the area and without communicating with Zollicoffer concerning the reasons for his crossing the Cumberland, Crittenden ordered Zollicoffer to recross the river to Mill Springs.[48] The order seems to be based on Zollicoffer's acknowledgment that his force was not only outnumbered by the enemy but divided by the river. "General Zollicoffer is threatened by a much superior force in front and one nearly equal on his left flank," Crittenden wrote Davis. "He has been ordered by me to recross the river."[49] Zollicoffer's correspondence had mentioned no such threat, however, and he did not comply with the message. Instead, he maintained his defensive stand at Beech Grove.

Why Zollicoffer chose to disobey a superior's command has been an object of controversy. First, Bennett H. Young wrote that Zollicoffer's move to the northern shore of the Cumberland was without Johnston's approval.[50] This is erroneous, however, since Johnston had approved all of Zollicoffer's actions preceding his move to Beech Grove and left the matter of guarding the Monticello–Somerset road to Zollicoffer's discretion. Later, when Zollicoffer informed Johnston on December 9 that he had crossed to the northern bank, Johnston did not countermand the move.

Second, Crittenden's order to recross the Cumberland has never been found. It exists only in statements Crittenden made to Johnston and Davis. A close examination of these remarks does not make clear if the order was, in fact, written. Perhaps, the order had been a hasty verbal command based upon Crittenden's assumption that Zollicoffer's force faced immediate peril.[51] Despite Zollicoffer's limited military experience, it is almost inconceivable that a general officer would completely disregard a superior's written command and risk charges of insubordination and neglect of duty.

Third, Zollicoffer wrote to Crittenden on December 26: "Your letters of 15th and 17th inst. reached me together this evening."[52] It has been speculated that one of these letters contained the order to recross, but neither of these communications has been found, so such speculations are merely that.[53] Crittenden's documented correspondence with Davis and Johnston regarding the order to recross was on neither December 15 nor 17, but were in fact dated December 16. It seems plausible that if Crittenden were so concerned about Zollicoffer's divided position that he would have written to him immediately upon assuming command on December 15. It also can be assumed that Crittenden would have also written immediately to his superiors informing them of his directive rather than wait a day to do so.

Fourth, Zollicoffer's letter to Crittenden on December 26 makes no mention whatsoever of the order to recross. Zollicoffer acknowledged the arrival of a battalion of Colonel William B. Wood's 16th Alabama Infantry Regiment and Captain Hugh McClung's Tennessee battery of two guns, but then states "a swell in the Cumberland has rendered it imfordable [*sic*]."[54] Such a comment implies that the newly arrived troops were still at Mill Springs and could not cross the river due to a lack of reliable transportation rather than deliberate disobedience of a direct order to recross.

Fifth, Zollicoffer believed that his crossing of the Cumberland River had created consternation among Union generals. The *New York Tribune* reflected as much, declaring that Zollicoffer's move to Beech Grove "showed an unusual enterprise and energy on his part," as surprised Union generals readily admitted. "His subsequent selection of a position for entrenched encampments on both banks of the river . . . proved him to be possessed of a good strategical eye."[55] As long as he remained on the Cumberland's southern shore, Zollicoffer posed no credible offensive threat. But from his position at Beech Grove, Zollicoffer could, if the opportunity arose, strike at scattered Union columns, something that could not be done from south of the river. At Beech Grove, he presented an active threat to the Union forces in the area.

Sixth, as mentioned previously, historians have criticized Zollicoffer for dividing his army and hemming part of it against the Cumberland. But the river trapped the Confederates only if they were confronted by a superior Union force. Zollicoffer must have realized this possibility and reasoned that such an attack would not be forthcoming in the winter months or that the rugged terrain on the northern shore, his extensive fortification of Beech Grove, as well as his artillery perched atop the southern cliffs, protected him. By fortifying the northern bank, controlling the area with artillery from the opposite shore, and absent written orders, Zollicoffer remained at Beech Grove.

Throughout December, rumors of Zollicoffer's advance into Kentucky continued to spread, and Schoepf performed an extended reconnaissance of the Rebel entrenchments, concluding that Zollicoffer's new position could not be overrun without heavy loss of life. Beech Grove's broken and hilly terrain made it difficult to place artillery in a commanding position without being exposed to Confederate batteries on the heights across the Cumberland River. "Under these circumstances," Schoepf concluded, "I hardly know what move is best to be made."[56]

But without additional men and supplies for an advance, Zollicoffer remained in his fortified position at Beech Grove as the year drew to a close, convincing Schoepf and others that he was going into winter quarters. On December 21, Schoepf wrote to Thomas: "Enemy remains quiet. . . . I have no information to induce me to think that he mediates an attack." A week later, Schoepf indicated a "strong probability that he [Zollicoffer] has no intention of moving from the vicinity of Mill Springs." With his earthworks nearing completion, Zollicoffer felt confident that the Yankees would not attack his strong position, and he allowed his men to protect themselves from the winter elements by constructing 150 log and mud huts as Christmas approached.[57]

January 1862 brought with it not only a change in military events but in the weather as well. December had been most unseasonable, with warm days, cool nights, and only occasional blasts of cold air. A journal from a family in Lebanon, Kentucky, about sixty miles from Mill Springs, listed adjectives such as warm, pleasant, Indian summer, and moderate to describe the weather and recorded only four days of rainfall for the month. But in January the weather turned rapidly from moderate to seasonal as wind, rain, snow, and frigid temperatures engulfed the area. With living quarters already erected at Beech Grove, Zollicoffer decided to forgo any further offensive intentions and remain within his fortifications for the winter. He did not expect an attack during the inclement weather, and if one did occur, he considered his chances of success greater than those of the Federal invaders. One thing he did expect was the arrival of Crittenden and some reinforcements.[58]

On January 3, Crittenden finally arrived at Mill Springs. Surprised to find troops still at Beech Grove, he questioned Zollicoffer about the order to withdraw across the river. Crittenden recalled after the war that Zollicoffer explained that the messenger had lost several days in returning to camp, that he had expected Crittenden to arrive at any time, and that the recent bad weather had caused a substantial rise in the river, thus increasing the risk involved in recrossing.[59] It was apparent, however, that Crittenden disagreed with Zollicoffer over his decision to remain at Beech Grove, as he immediately began raft construction, and four days later the small stern-wheel steamer, *Noble Ellis*, arrived at Mill Springs to aid in transporting the army back across the river. However, the weather remained bad, and the work on the rafts progressed slowly.

Crittenden's arrival at Mill Springs heightened Union fears of a burgeoning Confederate force, and Schoepf, in a detailed study of the Confederate position, vowed it would take a force of ten thousand men to dislodge the Southerners from Beech Grove. Zollicoffer had felled timber for nearly a mile in front of his entrenchments to prevent a surprise frontal attack, while the river rendered a flanking movement impossible. Schoepf concluded that only with a force of at least double that of the enemy could the Union troops entertain any hope of carrying Beech Grove and driving the Confederates into the Cumberland. Thomas, however, was dubious the Confederate position was impregnable. Schoepf would not say positively that such was the case, but he did say that an attack upon Beech Grove would result in heavy Union losses.[60]

Apprehension was not confined to the Union ranks, however, as evidence of growing Confederate concern for their position emerged as January entered its second week. On January 12, Assistant Adjutant General William W. Mackall replied to a transfer request made by Colonel Statham of the 15th Mississippi, who had grown impatient of Zollicoffer's defensive stand. Eager for a fight, he applied for transfer to Bowling Green, an area he thought had more potential for action. "The position of General Zollicoffer is too important and too exposed to permit any reduction of force," Mackall replied, "particularly so great a reduction as the removal of your regiment would be." General Johnston, he continued, "is satisfied that you will soon have an opportunity under General Zollicoffer of contributing to turn back the invaders of the South."[61] Johnston was correct in his assessment. Buell ordered Thomas's four brigades toward Logan's Cross Roads, ten miles north of Beech Grove, where they arrived on January 17. Schoepf's brigade, moving west from Somerset to join Thomas, was greatly delayed by recent rains and was unable to reach the rendezvous before hostilities commenced.[62]

January 18 brought with it another steady drench of rain, increasing the possibility of floods on the Cumberland and its tributaries. The same day, Crittenden received advice from an area resident that two Federal regiments had been cut off by the flooding of Fishing Creek to the east.[63] This was Schoepf's force, and if Crittenden sought an opportunity to attack before the Union armies could combine, the rain seemed a blessing in disguise. "I am threatened by a superior force of the enemy in front," he messaged Bowling Green, "and finding it impossible to cross the river, I will have to make the fight on the ground I now occupy. If you can do so, I would ask that a diversion be made in my favor."[64]

Late that evening, Crittenden called a council of his subordinate officers and informed them that a Union army of superior strength was approaching. Their options were two. The recent rains had divided the enemy, providing an opportunity for the Confederates to leave their trenches and strike Thomas, an attack he would surely not be expecting, given the weather and Zollicoffer's recent inactivity. Or they could remain within their fortifications and await the anticipated Union attack. According to Crittenden's personal account of the conference several years later, the officers agreed unanimously to go on the attack. "There was not one of them who did not concur with me in that Thomas must be attacked immediately, and, if possible, by surprise."[65]

But others disagreed. James G. M. Ramsey, a prominent Tennessee politician, wrote to Johnston on January 24, 1862, that Zollicoffer's advance was "against his own earnest protest." The *Tuscumbia (AL) Constitution* reported that Zollicoffer protested the offensive, as he thought the Federals should be forced to attack him within his own breastworks.[66] It is true that during December, with the prospect of receiving men and supplies, Zollicoffer seriously considered an advance, but by mid-January he had decisively changed his mind. Since his arrival on the northern shore of the Cumberland, he had maintained a defensive stand at Beech Grove, except for occasional forage raiding parties. He had built winter quarters for his men and was satisfied to remain within his fortifications and await better weather for an offensive or, the alternative, an ill-fated Union attack.

Furthermore, Crittenden's explanation for the attack revealed another purpose: simply repulsing an attack "would probably give us time to cross the Cumberland with artillery and wagons" on the boats then being built.[67] So Crittenden's referral to it being "impossible to cross the river" in his letter to Johnston on January 18 was with all his military apparatus. Crittenden had the services of the *Noble Ellis* as well as several flatboats to carry men across the Cumberland, no matter how high the water level. In fact, that same day Crittenden ferried the 17th and 28th Tennessee infantry regiments from Mill Springs to Beech Grove to bolster his force.

Though a West Point graduate and career army officer, many perceived Crittenden's appointment as political. A successful advance by a "political" general would vindicate not only him but Jefferson Davis as well. The decision to attack, therefore, cannot be attributed in whole or in part to Zollicoffer. Major General George B. Crittenden, the commanding officer of the Confederate forces at Mill Springs and Beech Grove, ordered the Southerners out of their strong defensive position to attack the Union force encamped at Logan's Cross Roads.[68]

The Confederates were awakened at midnight, January 19, during a dreary, continuous rain to begin the march northward. Zollicoffer's Brigade of four infantry regiments, two cavalry companies, and an artillery battery assumed the lead position in the march to the field of battle. Brigadier General Carroll followed close behind with three infantry regiments and a smaller battery of guns. A regiment of infantry and two cavalry battalions were held in reserve.[69]

Streaks of lightning blazed across the clouded sky, adding only momentary light to an otherwise dark night. The constant rainfall further impaired the vision of the soldiers as they trudged along a hilly, barely visible path, alert to the sound of mud choking the shoes of troops in front to guide them. After six hours, the Confederates had covered only ten miles and as the gloom of dawn emerged on this Sabbath morning, January 19, 1862, a crackle of gunfire sounded in the distance; advance cavalry had met Union pickets. Zollicoffer's troops rapidly threw out skirmish lines and advanced along the Mill Springs road, expecting resistance to appear momentarily on the dim horizon. They were correct. The soggy road had cost the Southerners valuable time. They had anticipated being in position for attack before dawn, but their arrival roughly corresponded with early breakfast for the Union troops, who, though surprised, were awake and soon ready to give battle.[70]

After the Union pickets were driven in, Crittenden ordered three infantry regiments to lead the frontal attack: the 19th Tennessee, under the command of Colonel Cummings, the 15th Mississippi, temporarily commanded by Lieutenant Colonel Edward C. Walthall, and the 20th Tennessee, led by Colonel Joel A. Battle. Colonel Frank Wolford's 1st Kentucky Cavalry Regiment was the only Federal unit to oppose the early Confederate advance, and it presented only nominal resistance. Colonel Mahlon D. Manson, commander of Thomas's Second Brigade, sent forward two infantry regiments,

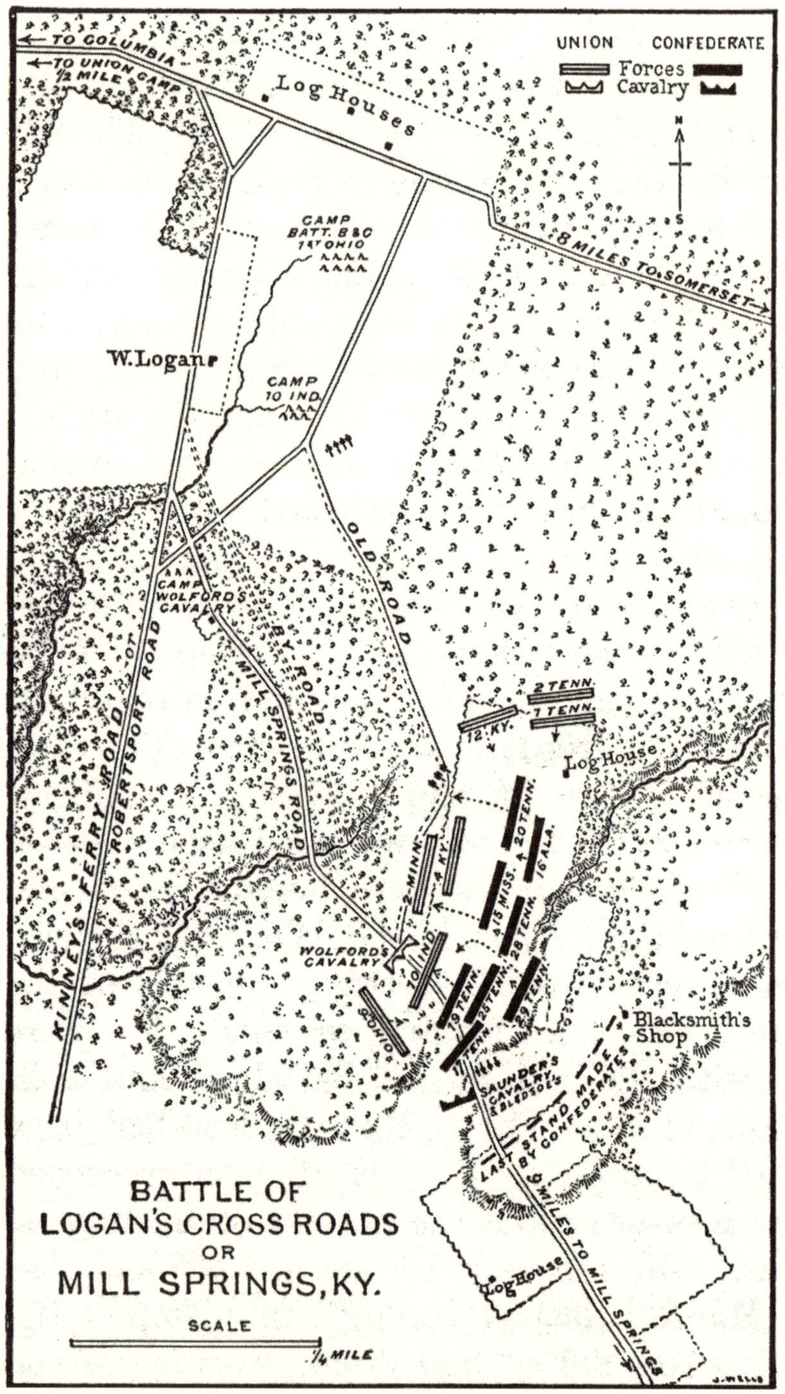

Battle of Mill Springs. From Johnson and Buel, *Battles and Leaders of the Civil War* (1884–88).

the 10th Indiana under the command of Lieutenant Colonel William C. Kise and the 4th Kentucky under Colonel Speed Fry, to extend the Union line to the east. Manson then called personally on Thomas to report the unexpected Confederate advance and his dispersion of troops.[71]

The early intermittent gunfire quickened its pace as Zollicoffer's Brigade prevailed in the early fighting, but the Confederates could not break through the loosely constructed Union line. Crittenden placed Carroll's Brigade immediately behind Zollicoffer's front-line troops to act as reserve or to give the appearance of a concentrated attack on the center with more troops than actually engaged. To counter, Thomas hurried forward the 2nd Minnesota Infantry Regiment, under the command of Colonel Horatio P. Van Cleve, to support the Union center. The 4th Kentucky, upon arriving at the scene of battle, had no specific orders on placement, but Fry positioned his men along a rail fence in the edge of a wooded area along the Mill Springs road. Battle's 20th Tennessee and Walthall's 15th Mississippi were leading a spirited advance through a corn field adjacent to the road, and, much to Fry's chagrin, a deep ravine penetrated the field 250 yards in front of his position. From its cover, the Confederates were able to keep up a galling fire. Thus thwarted, Fry climbed atop the rail fence and defied the enemy to stand up and fight like men. For no apparent reason, Fry's futile gesture seemed to cause a lull in the fighting during which the tide of battle turned.[72]

Somehow in the confusion of battle compounded by poor visibility, Zollicoffer rode from the protection of his army into the Union ranks. Though his action is often attributed to his suffering from myopia, the general's inability to detect Union soldiers was actually due to the fact that many of Crittenden's Confederates wore remnants of blue uniforms—a common practice in the early days of the Civil War.[73] When Zollicoffer rode into the ranks of Fry's 4th Kentucky, he apparently thought it was Walthall's 15th Mississippi. Zollicoffer's remarks to Fry indicated that he believed the 4th Kentucky was a Confederate unit firing on another Confederate unit. He fell from his mount about twenty yards from where the fateful conversation took place.[74] The second unidentified officer who fired into Union ranks was Zollicoffer's aide, who belatedly realized that his general had ridden into the proverbial lion's den and tried brashly to correct the error. Assuming that Zollicoffer would realize his mistake and possibly escape unharmed, he chose to fire at Fry as he rode away, but it was Lieutenant Henry Fogg who escaped, not Brigadier General Zollicoffer.[75]

Who killed Zollicoffer? Tradition attributes Zollicoffer's death to Fry. Indeed, he is the most obvious answer since he was the closest to Zollicoffer and fired the first shot in that direction. Many of the official accounts of the battle as well as varying newspapers credited Fry.[76] But Fry, himself, refused the accolades and in his official report to Thomas did not even use

Battle near Mill Springs, Ky.—Death of Gen. Zollicoffer. From Robert Tomes and Benjamin G. Smith, *The War with the South: A History of the Great American Rebellion* (1862).

Zollicoffer's name, suggesting that he had been duped by the Confederate officer as to his identity. In an 1887 history of Kentucky, Fry supplied details concerning the death of Zollicoffer: he did fire the first shot, he said, but he did not know if his was the fatal one.[77] Regardless of who actually killed the Tennessean, he died, as one chronicler put it, "under peculiar circumstances," and his loss was a staggering blow to the morale of the Confederate troops engaged in battle, a disaster from which they never recovered.[78]

News of Zollicoffer's death, at 9:20 A.M., spread like wildfire through the Confederate ranks. With the battle raging, Crittenden sought to rally his stunned men and break through the Union center. Walthall's and Battle's regiments charged across the field with bayonets fixed, but Fry's men stood their ground and poured volley after volley into their ranks. The fence Fry used earlier to issue his oratorical decree became the only object separating the two armies. Hand-to-hand combat raged along its length, as bayonets thrust through the rail fence, and arms wrested away on both sides.[79]

Meanwhile, Thomas had arrived to direct the Federal troops, after a delay attributed by some to his inability to get into his new uniform.[80]

He immediately regrouped the 10th Indiana and ordered a bayonet charge upon the Confederates by the Mill Springs road. He then sent forward the 9th Ohio Infantry Regiment, under the command of Major Gustavus Kammerling, to support the Indiana troops trying to neutralize the Confederate left and possibly turn their flank. Thomas then rode over to Fry's troops in the center. Upon viewing the 4th Kentucky's determined stand, he sent Van Cleve's 2nd Minnesota forward to occupy a gap between Fry and Kise. Thomas's last maneuver was placing a battery of guns and bringing up three additional infantry regiments to extend the Union line—the 12th Kentucky, under the command of Colonel William A. Haskins, and the 1st and 2nd Tennessee under Colonels Robert Byrd and James P. T. Carter, respectively. The newly arrived Union troops took up a position on the extreme eastern edge of the battlefield and applied pressure on the Confederate right flank. Crittenden tried to counter the Federal artillery by ordering Captain Arthur M. Rutledge forward with two guns along the road, but the artillery on both sides proved wholly ineffective.[81]

Momentum shifted upon Thomas's arrival, and the Yankees started a spirited charge. The Confederate left wing, though reinforced by the 17th Tennessee led by Lieutenant Colonel T. C. H. Miller, could not resist the push of the 10th Indiana and the 9th Ohio through the woods, and it collapsed. Panic and confusion gripped the entire Confederate line, which first wavered and then fell back, its resistance spent. It was a few minutes after noon.[82]

Crittenden tried to regroup his men but confusion, disorder, and chaos had engulfed them. Union troops found haversacks filled with corn and bacon, discarded by the panic-stricken Confederates along the Mill Springs road.[83] The 29th Tennessee Infantry Regiment, under the command of Colonel Samuel Powell made one last valiant stand. After Powell was wounded, that line collapsed as well, and the Yankees took up pursuit of the fleeing Southerners. Union casualties were 39 killed and 297 wounded, while the Confederates lost 125 killed, 309 wounded, and 99 missing.[84] The brunt of the Confederate offensive had been borne by Walthall's and Battle's regiments, which sustained 287 casualties, almost half of the Confederate total.

Although the Confederates actually engaged more men than the Federals in a concentrated attack upon the Union center, they failed to break through the Federal ranks. Zollicoffer's death may have contributed, but perhaps the most telling factor was the armaments of the opposing sides. The great majority of Southern troops carried flintlock muskets, while others had only percussion squirrel rifles or double-barrel shotguns. In a continuous mist, these flintlocks discharged only sporadically or could not be fired at all. On the other hand, Thomas's men for the most part carried Enfield, Sharps, or Spencer rifles, more modern weapons which could carry shot at least a half mile. The superiority of arms proved to be a decided advantage for the Union side. Another element was Thomas's several Kentucky regiments, which defended their own soil, while Crittenden's "invaders" were composed of units from throughout the South.[85]

Crittenden and the remnants of his army returned to Beech Grove late in the afternoon over the same muddy road they had trudged only hours earlier. Thomas followed close behind but was unable to reach the Confederate entrenchments and organize his men for a final assault before darkness fell. Crittenden correctly sized up his situation. Given the dispirited morale of the troops and the loss of all the cooked rations, he "deemed an immediate crossing of the Cumberland necessary."[86]

He ordered two flatboats tied to the *Noble Ellis* and under the cover of darkness, the Confederates withdrew to the southern bank in the span of six hours, midnight to dawn. The 15th Mississippi was the first regiment to cross, at about 11:30 P.M.[87] Crittenden had written Johnston the day before explaining the need for battle because the river could not be crossed. But, in fact, he successfully ferried a defeated, demoralized army across the flooded Cumberland at night. So apparently the river was passable for men, and Crittenden could have moved back to Mill Springs whenever he wished, avoiding the resounding defeat.

As daylight neared, panic once again swept through the Confederate forces still at Beech Grove. They abandoned everything: still-standing tents, blankets, clothes, cooking utensils, wagons, horses, artillery, and many of the wounded. They were not even able to destroy their papers, some of which indicated the disagreement emerging from Crittenden's council of war.[88]

Soldiers of the 17th Tennessee, the last regiment at Beech Grove, crammed onto the already overloaded flatboats while others tried to swim the flooded Cumberland. With the first light of January 20 emerging on the horizon, Thomas's Parrott rifled cannons opened fire on the *Noble Ellis*, making its last trip to Mill Springs. Crittenden watched from the southern bank as the remnants of his nine infantry regiments, four battalions and two companies of cavalry, and portions of two artillery companies retreated southward; the rest of his command had been lost.[89]

Although the Yankees had achieved a brilliant victory at Mill Springs, the most disastrous defeat the Confederacy had yet experienced, it was nevertheless inconclusive, since Crittenden escaped into Tennessee with the majority of his force. Thomas, when asked by Fry why he did not demand a surrender from Crittenden the night before, replied, "Hang it Fry, I never once thought of it." Thomas reasoned that given Kentucky's still somewhat divided sentiments regarding the Union or Confederacy, the complete dispersion of Southern troops from Kentucky soil was the best method of securing the state for the Union.[90]

Accounts of the Battle of Mill Springs soon filled newspapers across America, with the *New York Times* calling the engagement "The Most Brilliant Victory of the War."[91] In fact, Johnston first learned of the disastrous defeat by reading a January 22 issue of the *Louisville (KY) Courier.* Various newspaper accounts raised pertinent questions concerning Zollicoffer's position at Beech Grove and Crittenden's futile attack on Thomas. The *Louisville (KY) Daily Journal* published a letter from Union Colonel Green Clay declaring Zollicoffer's camp a strong position, whose entrenchments could have held off thirty thousand troops, and Beech Grove's winter quarters sufficient for fifteen thousand men. The *New York Times* reported that Beech Grove was "beautifully entrenched" with excellent winter quarters. "Why then the attack?" it wondered.[92] But Crittenden, the commanding general, believed a successful attack not only in the best interests of his men but his own, too. For it would thrust him into a prominent position. Instead he became the object of severe criticism throughout the South.

After his defeat, Crittenden was blasted by a torrent of scathing denunciations. Thomas R. R. Cobb, a prominent Georgian Congressman, wrote to his wife on January 24, 1862: "We are all depressed this morning over the disaster at Somerset last Sunday. It is attributed entirely to a drunken, Godless General, who in a spree on Sunday morning led our troops to their destruction. Zollicoffer was a noble man and a fine officer. In the effort to redeem the day, I doubt not, he lost his life."[93]

Tennessee newspaper editors, obviously distressed by the death of one of their former colleagues, focused on rumors of Crittenden's sobriety. But the most recent and detailed assessment of the battle has concluded that although he drank on the night preceding the attack and again once across the river, Crittenden was sober for the battle, and his drinking had no effect on the battle's outcome.[94]

Nevertheless, letters poured into Richmond excoriating the Kentuckian. James Ramsey wrote President Davis on January 24 describing the Confederate force as "perfectly demoralized" and "refusing to serve under him." Ramsey redeemed Zollicoffer by focusing criticism on Crittenden, for "had Zollicoffer not been ordered to make that unwise advance all would now have been alright. The only salvation of the defeated army is to recall Crittenden and replace him." Landon Hayes wrote Davis declaring Crittenden's army as "utterly routed and demoralized. . . . Confidence is gone in the ranks and among the people. It must be restored. I am confident it cannot be done under Generals Crittenden and Carroll." Governor Harris opined that "Crittenden can never rally troops [in] east Tennessee. Some other general must be sent there."[95]

In defense of his actions, Crittenden attributed the loss of the battle to the inferiority of arms and the untimely death of the highly esteemed Zollicoffer. Crittenden reiterated that his actions had been taken out of necessity, noting: "I ought not be held responsible for that necessity. As to how I managed it, I have nothing further to say."[96]

Davis, in his memoirs, supported Crittenden's explanation. He further speculated that if all the troops had been in position at dawn, a concerted attack would have probably resulted in victory. He thought the strategy "not only defensible but commendable, and the affair to be ranked with one of the many brilliant conceptions of the war." Davis also refrained from chastising Zollicoffer's decision to divide his forces along the Cumberland: "General Zollicoffer may have well believed that he could better resist the crossing of the Cumberland by removing to the right bank rather than removing to the left."[97]

Major General Buell called Mill Springs one of the most important battles of the Civil War, the first large-scale Union victory. Indeed, it opened a gap in Johnston's line of Confederate defense across southern Kentucky that would eventually collapse following defeats at Forts Henry and Donelson in mid-February. By then Zollicoffer's body had been viewed by thousands of mourners as he lay in state in the Hall of Representatives in Nashville before being buried in the Old City Cemetery.[98]

On May 19, 1910, in the house where Zollicoffer lived while a resident of Nashville, a marble tablet was dedicated to honor his birthday. His four daughters as well as several local dignitaries attended, including the managing editor of the general's former newspaper, the *Nashville Republican Banner.* During the ceremony, Miss Susie Gentry read a poem dedicated to Brigadier General Felix Kirk Zollicoffer:

First in the fight and first in the arms
Of the white-winged angels of glory,
With the heart of the South at the feet of God,
And his wounds to tell the story;

And the blood that flowed from his hero heart
On the spot where he nobly perished
Was drunk by the earth as a sacrament
In the holy cause he cherished.

In heaven a home with the brave and blessed,
And for his soul's sustaining
The apocalyptic eyes of Christ—
And nothing on earth remaining

But a handful of dust in the land of his choice,
A name in song and story,
And Fame to shout with her braven voice:
He died on the field of Glory![99]

Notes

1. U.S. War Department, *The War of the Rebellion: A Compilation of the Official Records of the Union and Confederate Armies,* 128 vols. (Washington, DC, 1880–1901), ser. 1, vol. 7:112 (hereafter cited as *OR*; all references are to series 1 unless otherwise indicated).
2. Raymond E. Myers, *The Zollie Tree* (Louisville, KY, 1964), 122–23.
3. The family plantation, which eventually included close to a thousand acres, was just south of present-day Columbia, Tennessee. Edd Winfield Parks, "Zollicoffer: Southern Whig," *Tennessee Historical Quarterly* 11 (Dec. 1952): 347–48.
4. Some of the biographical information was submitted by Craig Hopkins, great-great-grandson of Frederick Zollicoffer, the brother of Felix Kirk Zollicoffer, and can be found at http://www.rootsweb.ancestry.com/~tnmaury/biotext.htm. A. O. P. Nicholson was actually an older cousin who, in addition to being a newspaper editor, also served as chief justice of the Tennessee Supreme Court and as U.S. Senator. Myers, *The Zollie Tree,* 11.
5. Zollicoffer and wife Louisa had a total of fourteen children, but all six sons and two daughters died in infancy. See Audrey June (Denny) Lambert, "General Felix K. Zollicoffer," accessed Apr. 27, 2015, http://www.ajlambert.com/history/zollicof.pdf.
6. Myers, *The Zollie Tree,* 26; James C. Stamper, "Felix K. Zollicoffer: Tennessee Editor and Politician," *Tennessee Historical Quarterly* 28 (Winter 1969): 356.
7. Particulars on the duel differ. Myers states it resulted from a disagreement over the construction of a new bridge (*The Zollie Tree,* 24–25); Parks states that after the duel, Zollicoffer went to a local barber shop to have the bullet removed from his hand ("Zollicoffer: Southern Whig," 352); and E. Thomas Wood says Zollicoffer's pistol did not misfire, and that Marling was struck in the face as he was discharging his second shot ("Nashville Now and Then: Fightin' Words," accessed May 12, 2015, http://www.nashvillepost.com/home/article/20401180/nashville-now-and-then-fightin-words).
8. Stamper, "Felix K. Zollicoffer," 373. Popular sovereignty aimed to solve the problem of territorial slavery by putting the question to the settlers in the territory. Although theoretically defensible, it proved a practical disaster. The bill was fiercely opposed by many in the North, and its passage gave rise to the Republican Party.
9. Ibid.
10. Felix Kirk Zollicoffer to Frederick Zollicoffer, Nov. 21, 1860, in Myers, *The Zollie Tree,* 43–44. Frederick, a physician, lived in Mississippi.
11. Parks, "Zollicoffer: Southern Whig," 354.

12. *OR*, vol. 4:378, 374.

13. Ibid., 397.

14. Jefferson Davis, *The Rise and Fall of Confederate Government*, 2 vols. (New York, 1881), 1:396; *Woodford (KY) Pennant* [n.d.], quoted in Wilson P. Shortridge, "Kentucky Neutrality in 1861," *Mississippi Valley Historical Review* 9 (Mar. 1923): 287n20.

15. William Preston Johnston, *The Life of General Albert Sidney Johnston: Embracing His Services in the Armies of the United States, the Republic of Texas, and the Confederate States* (New York, 1879), 306.

16. *OR*, vol. 4:409.

17. Ibid., 199.

18. Ibid., 423–26, 429.

19. Ibid., 202.

20. Abraham Lincoln, *Collected Works of Lincoln*, ed. Roy Basler, 8 vols. (New Brunswick, NJ, 1953), 4:542, 545; *OR*, vol. 4:433–34, 201.

21. *OR*, vol. 4:435.

22. Ibid., 309, 462–63.

23. Ibid., 210.

24. Ibid., 213–14.

25. Ibid., 205, 210; Frank Moore, ed., *The Rebellion Record: A Diary of American Events with Documents*, Narratives, Illustrative Incidents, Poetry, Etc. 12 vols. (New York, 1861–68), 3:226–31. Various newspaper reports of the battle are also contained within *The Rebellion Record.*

26. *OR*, vol. 4:206; *New York Times*, Oct. 29, 1861.

27. *OR*, vol. 4:487.

28. Ibid., 490.

29. Ibid., 328, 496, 502.

30. Ibid., 516–17.

31. Ibid., 232-33, 527.

32. Ibid., 533, 538. Confederate Secretary of War Judah P. Benjamin stated that Crittenden's appointment as major general was required due to the increasing size of Confederate forces in the region. Dumas Malone, ed., *Dictionary of American Biography*, 20 vols. (New York, 1926–36), 4:545–46.

33. *OR*, vol. 4:473; *OR*, vol. 52, pt. 2:185. Crittenden was the son of John J. Crittenden who served in both houses of Congress, as U.S. attorney general, and as the seventeenth governor of Kentucky.

34. Johnston, *Life of General Johnston*, 357; *OR*, vol. 7:687.

35. *OR*, vol. 4:244.

36. *OR*, vol. 7:706, 715.

37. *OR*, vol. 4:243; *OR*, vol. 7:687, 697, 713.

38. *OR*, vol. 7:10, 725.

39. Ibid., 458; Thomas L. Connelly, *Army of the Heartland: The Army of Tennessee, 1861–1862* (Baton Rouge, LA, 1967), 87, 89.

40. Johnston, *Life of General Johnston*, 395.

41. *OR*, vol. 7:7–8, 734.

42. Ibid., 473, 477.

43. Ibid., 10, 12.

44. Ibid., 753; Marcus J. Wright, "Sketch of General Felix K. Zollicoffer," *Southern Bivouac* 2 (July 1884): 490. In a recent article, it has been speculated that "this dispatch [December 4] may have also contained an order for Zollicoffer to move his men back across the river. Unfortunately the dispatch no longer exists." Ron Nicholas, "Mill Springs: The First Battle for Kentucky," in *The Civil War in Kentucky: Battle for the Bluegrass State*, ed. Kent Masterson Brown (Mason City, IA, 2000), 54.

45. C. David Dalton, "Zollicoffer, Crittenden, and the Mill Springs Campaign: Some Persistent Questions," *Filson Club History Quarterly* 60 (Oct. 1986): 463.

46. *OR*, vol. 7:12.

47. From mid-November to mid-December, Zollicoffer continued to correspond with both Johnston in Bowling Green and Davis in Richmond rather than Crittenden, who travelled from Knoxville and Richmond on several occasions seeking additional troops, which made communications with his superior officer problematic. Kenneth A. Hafendorfer, *Mill Springs: Campaign and Battle of Mill Springs, Kentucky* (Louisville, KY, 2001), 110.

48. *OR*, vol. 7:769; *OR*, vol. 52, pt. 2:239.

49. *OR*, vol. 7:769–70.

50. Bennett H. Young, "Zollicoffer's Oak," *Southern Historical Society Papers* 31 (1903): 166.

51. *OR*, vol. 7:769–70; Davis, *Rise and Fall*, 2:19–20. Crittenden also stated that he had "sent a courier post haste" ordering Zollicoffer to recross. Johnston, *Life of General Johnston*, 399.

52. Zollicoffer to Crittenden, Dec. 26, 1861, Archives and Manuscripts, Chicago History Museum.

53. Hafendorfer, *Mill Springs*, 133.

54. Zollicoffer to Crittenden, Dec. 26, 1861.

55. *New York Tribune*, n.d., quoted in Myers, *The Zollie Tree*, 72.

56. *OR,* vol. 7:506.

57. *OR,* vol. 52, pt. 2:243. Even Zollicoffer's regimental commanders believed they were going into winter quarters. *OR,* vol. 7:10, 516, 526–27. General Orders No. 43 from Zollicoffer, Dec. 20, 1861, stated: "The time has come when huts must be constructed to protect the forces of the Brigade against inclement weather." General and Special Orders Book, Aug. 21, 1861—Jan. 2, 1862, Manuscripts Department, Eleanor S. Brockenbrough Library, Museum of the Confederacy, Richmond, VA (hereafter cited as General and Special Orders Book). A copy of Zollicoffer's order book is on file in Mill Springs National Battlefield Museum, Nancy, KY. *OR,* vol. 7:797; R. Gerald McMurtry, "Zollicoffer and the Battle of Mill Springs," *Filson Club History Quarterly* 29 (Oct. 1955): 306.

58. Maria I. Knott, Diary, Dec. 15, 1861—Jan. 25, 1862, Knott Collection, Manuscripts Division, Kentucky Library, Western Kentucky University, Bowling Green; *OR,* vol. 7:797; General Orders No. 47, Dec. 31, 1861, General and Special Orders Book.

59. Davis, *Rise and Fall,* 2:19–20; Crittenden's recollection of Zollicoffer's explanation does not bear up to scrutiny: "No measureable amount of rain had fallen in the region between the 26th of December and the 2nd of January." Hafendorfer, *Mill Springs,* 133. In fact, Zollicoffer wrote Johnston on December 26 that the Cumberland River was so low that boats from Nashville could not reach him. *OR,* vol. 7:797; Zollicoffer to Crittenden, Dec. 26, 1861. On the other hand, Nicholas states that "wet weather had turned the Cumberland River into a torrent that destroyed most of the rafts and barges the Confederates had used to make the crossing." Nicholas, "Mill Springs," 55–56.

60. *OR,* vol. 7:536, 542, 545.

61. Ibid., 828.

62. Ibid., 558. Logan's Cross Roads was named for a local landowner, William Logan. It is in Pulaski County, near Nancy, Kentucky.

63. Wright, "Sketch of Zollicoffer," 491. Reportedly two widows who lived on Fishing Creek kept Zollicoffer informed of Federal troop movements. They reported "by grapevine telegraph" that Fishing Creek was so high that it could not be crossed. John W. Simpson, "A Boy's Story of the Battle of Fishing Creek and Other Incidents of the Civil War" (unpublished manuscript in the Mill Springs National Battlefield Library, Nancy, Kentucky). A substantially condensed version was later published in *Confederate Veteran* 18, no. 7 (July 1910): 335–36.

64. *OR,* vol. 7:103.

65. Davis, *Rise and Fall,* 2:20. A *Louisville (KY) Courier* correspondent also agreed that there was unanimous agreement. Moore, *Rebellion Record,* 4:45.

66. *OR*, vol. 52, pt. 2:257; Moore, *Rebellion Record*, 4:47.

67. Davis, *Rise and Fall*, 2:20.

68. *OR*, vol. 7:105.

69. Ibid., 82, 106.

70. Knott Diary, Jan. 20, 1862. On this date, the entry read: "Had another storm last night and considerable thunder and rain this morning. Cloudy all day." The initial clash was along Timmy's Branch, a little over a mile south of the Union encampment.

71. *OR*, vol. 7:79, 84, 90, 106.

72. Ibid., 80, 87, 106; Lowell H. Harrison, *The Civil War in Kentucky* (Lexington, KY, 1975), 26.

73. The earliest reference to Zollicoffer suffering from myopia as an explanation for his wandering into Union ranks seems to be Johnston, *Life of General Johnston*, 403. The most recent examination of the battle also supports the claim, but does so by citing the Johnston work. See Stuart Sanders, *The Battle of Mill Springs Kentucky* (Charleston, SC, 2013), 14, 77. On the other hand, Hafendorfer's *Mill Springs*, the most extensive work on the battle, mentions his nearsightedness (287) but later concludes that "being nearsighted indicates only a difficulty seeing a distant object," which was impossible on that fateful morning due to the fog and smoke drifting across the battlefield (573). Myers, Zollicoffer's only biographer, does not even mention the condition in *The Zollie Tree.*

74. His body was later discovered by Union troops and placed under a tree. Several buttons and pieces of clothing were taken as souvenirs until Brigadier General George H. Thomas ordered a guard to protect the body until it could be returned to the Confederates. Hafendorfer, *Mill Springs*, 289; Nicholas, "Mill Springs," 70–71.

75. One recent study believes that Zollicoffer realized his mistake and the conversation with Fry was an attempt to bluff his way out of the situation. Hafendorfer, *Mill Springs*, 288.

76. Several newspapers—*New York Times*, *Cincinnati Commercial*, and *Louisville Journal*—credited Fry with Zollicoffer's death. Moore, *Rebellion Record*, 4:47.

77. W. H. Perrin, J. H. Battle, and G. C. Kniffin, *Kentucky, A History of the State* (Louisville, KY, 1887), 393. Two wounds were found on the body: the fatal one was from a minié ball that passed through his heart and the other from a pistol. Therefore, Fry should not have been credited. Wright, "Sketch of Zollicoffer," 492; McMurtry, "Zollicoffer," 309. For detailed descriptions of the conflicting accounts, see Hafendorfer, *Mill Springs*, 569–81, and Geoffrey R. Walden, "Death of Gen. Felix K. Zollicoffer" accessed Apr. 1, 2008, http://www.oocities.org/pentagon/quarters/1864/zolldeath.htm.

78. Mark M. Boatner III, *The Civil War Dictionary* (New York, 1959), 319.

79. Hafendorfer, *Mill Springs*, 290; *OR*, vol. 7:107.

80. McMurtry, "Zollicoffer," 308.

81. *OR*, vol. 7:90–91, 93–97.

82. The most detailed account of the battle is Hafendorfer, *Mill Springs*, 181–420.

83. R. M. Kelly, "Holding Kentucky for the Union," in *Battles and Leaders of the Civil War: Being for the Most Part Contributions by Union and Confederate Officers Based upon "The Century War Series,"* ed. Robert Underwood Johnson and Clarence Clough Buel, 4 vols. (1884–88; repr., New York, 1956), 1:390.

84. *OR*, vol. 7:82, 108.

85. Ibid.; Young, "Zollicoffer's Oak," 166–68: Hafendorfer, *Mill Springs*, 421; McMurtry, "Zollicoffer," 312; Myers, *Zollie Tree*, 73; Thomas Speed, *The Union Cause in Kentucky, 1860–1865* (New York, 1907), 195.

86. *OR*, vol. 7:109.

87. Hafendorfer, *Mill Springs*, 459–60, 465. The author states that it took approximately 15–20 minutes to cross the river.

88. Journal of Alfred Pirtle, 1859–62, Jan. 24, 1862. Special Collections, The Filson Historical Society, Louisville, KY; *Cincinnati Commercial*, Jan. 20, 1862, quoted in Moore, *Rebellion Record*, 4:44; *OR*, vol. 7:76.

89. *OR*, vol. 7:110. John Simpson wrote that the Confederates burned the *Noble Ellis* after the last crossing and then retreated. He called it "the saddest day I had ever seen." Simpson, "A Boy's Story."

90. Kelly, "Holding Kentucky for the Union," 391; Myers, *Zollie Tree*, 110.

91. *New York Times*, Jan. 22, 1862. Accounts of the battle from the *Cincinnati Commercial, Louisville Courier, Nashville Banner,* and *Tuscumbia Constitution* are quoted in Moore, *Rebellion Record*, 4:34–49.

92. *Louisville (KY) Daily Journal*, Jan. 23, 1862; *Frankfort (KY) Tri-Weekly Yeoman*, Jan. 25, 1862; *New York Times*, Jan. 26, 1862.

93. Thomas R. R. Cobb, "Extracts from Letters to his Wife, February 3, 1861–December 10, 1862," *Southern Historical Society Papers* 28 (1900): 290. Numerous reports circulated that Crittenden was not sober on the day of the battle.

94. Hafendorfer, *Mill Springs*, 539.

95. *OR*, vol. 52, pt. 2:256–57; *OR* vol. 7:849; Grady McWhiney, "Controversy in Kentucky: Braxton Bragg's Campaign of 1862," *Civil War History* 6 (Mar. 1960): 7. Bragg specifically named Crittenden as unqualified for command.

96. Davis, *Rise and Fall*, 2:21.

97. Ibid., 2:21–23. Davis stated that he was dissatisfied with the outcome but could not fault Crittenden's motives.

98. *OR*, vol. 16, pt. 1:25; Don Carlos Buell, Statement of Major General Buell in *Review of the Evidence before the Military Commission Appointed by the War Department* (Washington, DC, 1863), 3. Zollicoffer was buried on February 2, 1862.

99. The four surviving daughters were Virginia Wilson, Octavia Bond, Felicia Metcalf, and Loulie Sansom; the managing editor was M. B. Morton; the poet was Henry Lynden Flash. "Dedication of the Gen. Zollicoffer Tablet," *Confederate Veteran* 18, no. 7 (July 1910): 335.

General Robert E. Lee. Library of Congress.

Robert E. Lee's Lost Campaign

Roger S. Durham

> "The whole training of an officer seeks to accomplish one purpose–to instill in him the ability to take over in battle in time of crisis."
>
> —General Matthew B. Ridgway

General Robert E. Lee's connection to Virginia and the Army of Northern Virginia is so strongly established that few people would connect him with service outside the Eastern Theater. However, Lee did spend four months as a department commander in the Western Theater early in the war, and while this service has generally been looked at as nothing more than a footnote to his Confederate service, it was actually a significant period of time in his development and for that department. It was a turning point for Lee in several ways, and this essay will seek to examine how Lee handled what was a difficult challenge for him and how he learned from it.

As is well known, after Lee followed Virginia out of the Union, he offered his services to the state and was soon involved in administrative details in Richmond. In late July 1861, he was sent to western Virginia to take command of Confederate forces operating there. However, the situation was far from ideal. Mountainous terrain, bad weather, disease among his troops, and problems with his subordinate commanders all combined to doom his efforts there. His forces were ultimately defeated, and in September, Lee found himself criticized for his performance.

From the Allegheny Mountains, he was ordered to the Atlantic coast to take command of the newly established Department of South Carolina, Georgia, and East Florida. Whether this assignment was a promotion for Lee or a punishment is still debated. Regardless, Lee found himself plunged into another difficult situation, and to understand that situation one must first examine the events that transpired up to the point Lee arrived on the scene. The war had been going on for six months, and the South was trying desperately to organize its government and its military forces and to defend against Northern operations directed against them. Serious questions about the necessary logistics of providing for military forces and their organization needed addressing. There were plenty of volunteers but precious little of the military hardware, weaponry, and accoutrements required for them, and the states looked to the Confederate government to provide it. The Confederate government was trying to establish a national army with the expectation that the vast number of local militia and state defense forces would step up and take enlistment in that army. However, the governors of several states objected to giving up troops that had been raised for state defense for fear they would be ordered out of the state and not returned if the state was threatened. Enlistments also presented an issue. Early enlistments were for only a few months. The Confederate government was asking for enlistments "for the war," but few were stepping up.[1]

For many of the residents of the southeast coast, the war had been something distant. The blockade had affected cities like Charleston and Savannah, but it was little more than a token effort at best. When the authorities looked at defending their coastline, they merely had to examine their history since many past military operations had come from the sea, and this would also be the obvious route of approach used by their enemy. The southeast coast, including a network of barrier islands off the coast with smaller islands inland surrounded by marshes and waterways, offered numerous access points.

The initial Southern plan of defense relied on the concept of providing earthen fortifications at the northern and southern ends of every major barrier island off the coast. These forts were meant to deny their enemy access to the inland waterways of their coast. This plan was put into motion throughout the summer of 1861 with many batteries being built, armed, and manned on the barrier islands, with existing forts such as Fort Pulaski on the Georgia-South Carolina border and Fort Clinch on the Georgia–Florida border serving as anchors and strong points on the northern and southern ends of the Georgia coastline.

While Lee had been involved in western Virginia, the U.S. Navy blockade board had been laying out a strategy to strengthen the blockade of the southeast coast and construct a support base for operations in that area. A massive invasion fleet of warships, gunboats, and supply and troop transports was assembled to implement this plan, with selected targets of Port Royal Sound and Hilton Head Island, South Carolina. Port Royal Sound offered a good anchorage, and Hilton Head Island sat strategically between the cities of Charleston and Savannah, both potential targets for offensive operations. The operation was under the command of Flag Officer Samuel F. Du Pont.

Du Pont's plan to implement the blockade and establish enforcement was simple:

1. Establish a base of operations at Port Royal Sound
2. Close down shipping at major ports
3. Take possession of Federal lighthouses
4. Close down access to the major sounds
5. Open up the intra-coastal waterway.

Once Du Pont occupied Hilton Head Island and established his base there, he could then release his fleet of gunboats to cruise the coast and investigate while other gunboats would work from assigned stations located along the coast.[2]

In early November 1861, Lee was traveling south to Charleston to take up the responsibilities of his new assignment. Simultaneously, Du Pont's invasion fleet was also traveling south, bound for Port Royal Sound. These ships would give General Lee a welcome that he did not expect. The fleet arrived off the coast of South Carolina on November 4–5. Port Royal Sound at this time was defended by a large earthen fortification on the north end of Hilton Head Island and another one on the south end of St. Phillips Island, across the sound. The Union naval forces skirmished with Confederate gunboats, but the defenders were ready.[3]

On November 7, Du Pont's warships steamed into Port Royal Sound and engaged the Confederate defenses on Hilton Head and St. Phillips Islands. Within a matter of hours, the Southerners had been driven from their fortifications, and only through a stroke of good fortune were they able to escape from the islands. By the end of the day, Federal troops were being brought ashore, and Du Pont was on his way to establishing his base of operations. The Southerners had confidently expected a victory, and their defeat sowed uncertainty and fear far beyond the immediate coastal area.[4]

Lee arrived on the scene almost simultaneously with Du Pont's attack. On the evening of November 7, while en route to the site, he met Brigadier General Roswell S. Ripley, who reported the day's events. The two discussed the available resources, troop dispositions, and logistics. Ripley, who had been promoted to brigadier general a few months before, had held nominal command of the area and somewhat resented Lee's arrival on the scene. Already questions of whose authority was superior had arisen. The situation was critical. Lee found himself responsible for defending over two hundred miles of coastline with limited logistical support; his troops were scattered, poorly organized, and equipped; and he was facing a large, aggressive enemy that had mobility and the initiative. The question of command authority only aggravated his substantial problems.[5]

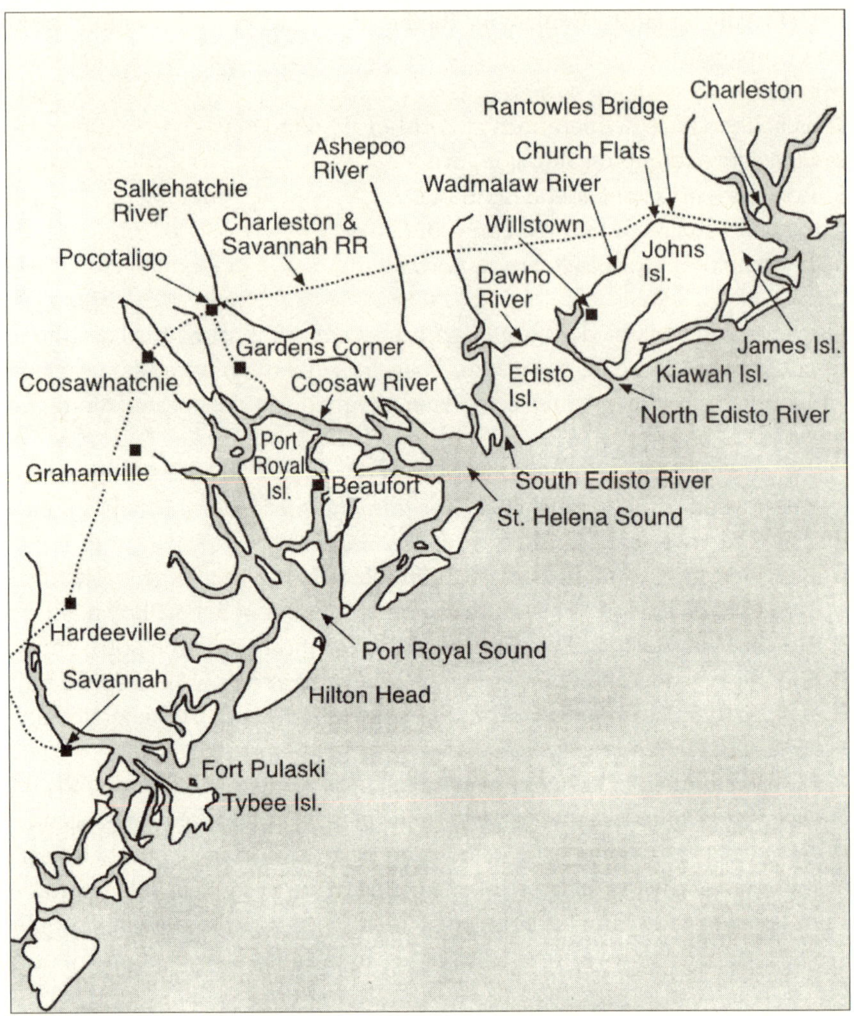

Atlantic Seaboard, 1862. Courtesy of the Savas Publishing Company.

The following day, Lee assumed command and established his headquarters at the small community of Coosawhatchie, located on the Charleston & Savannah Railroad. This allowed him access to both of those cities and provided a transportation link that ran parallel to his line of defense; it was one of his biggest assets for communication and the transportation of troops and supplies. His experience in western Virginia that summer—when he'd seen Confederate troops moved from Harper's Ferry to Manassas and Norfolk in April and July—had demonstrated the value of a railroad to move troops. Naturally, this railroad was also a target for the Federals. The war was only a few months old and the Confederacy not much older, and Lee did not yet have his signature white beard. He still wore his blue U.S. Army uniform. Second Lieutenant Gabriel E. Manigault, adjutant of the 4th South Carolina Cavalry Regiment noted: "He wore then the blue uniform of the U.S. Army with the conical shaped soft hat of the officers, the only part of his beard which was unshaven being a grey moustache."[6]

Since Lee's adversary was operating on the offshore islands and in the waterways and had troops occupying Hilton Head Island and the nearby community of Beaufort, it was difficult for him to obtain accurate intelligence on the Federals' operations and intentions. Lee could not do more than observe what could be seen from points on the mainland. He first tried to ensure that his immediate defenses were sufficient before examining the defenses further down the coast. Charleston was adjudged adequately defended for the present, but the coast south of that city lay dangerously exposed, and his forces there had been scattered and disorganized by the events of November 7.[7]

On November 9, Lee wrote to Secretary of War Judah P. Benjamin to report on the status of affairs following the loss of Hilton Head Island:

> The troops were got over [from Hilton Head Island] during the night, but their tents, clothing, and provisions were mostly lost, and all the guns left in the batteries. . . . General Drayton reports he has but 955 men with him, and no field battery, the troops from Georgia that were on the island returned to Savannah without orders. Colonel [John] Dunovant's regiment is in as destitute a condition as General Drayton's command, as they were obliged to leave everything behind, and number between 600 and 700 men. . . . At present I am endeavoring to collect troops to defend the line of railroad and to push forward the defenses of Charleston and Savannah. . . .
>
> I fear there are but few State troops ready for the field. The garrisons of the forts at Charleston and Savannah and on the coast cannot be removed from the batteries while ignorant of the designs of the enemy.[8]

That same day, Lee inspected the defenses in the vicinity of Pocotaligo. The railroad between Savannah and Charleston crossed four rivers, and each wooden trestle was vulnerable to destruction by U.S. forces that might ascend the waterways and come within range of these crossings. The destruction of even one of these bridges could have disastrous consequences, so it was imperative that adequate defenses and troops be provided to protect them. Following his inspection, Lee then traveled to Savannah to examine the status of affairs at that city. He inspected Savannah on November 10 and found it too vulnerable, since early thinking had considered that defenses built on the offshore islands would be sufficient. The events of November 7 clearly illustrated how exposed Savannah really was. The city was approachable by five major water routes, and a vast, intricate system of defenses would be required to protect it. Work began immediately to block river approaches and construct defenses at all of the water approaches to the city. Lee likewise ordered defenses constructed to link into those being built in South Carolina; these would create a protective perimeter running parallel to the coast designed to protect railroad and communication links between Charleston and Savannah. He also ordered all of the offshore islands in the vicinity abandoned and their ordnance, supplies, and troops relocated to support defenses on the mainland.[9]

On November 11, Lee visited Fort Pulaski, situated to protect the mouth of the Savannah River; during its initial construction, this fort was the scene of his earliest service as a young lieutenant of engineers fresh from West Point. Much was expected of the fort's ability to withstand the enemy's operations against Savannah. From Fort Pulaski, the new commander could clearly see numerous U.S. Navy ships at anchor offshore. He returned to Charleston shortly after.

On the night of November 12, the blockade-runner *Fingal* arrived off the coast, filled with arms, ordnance, and military equipment purchased by the Confederate government. The *Fingal*'s crew, unaware of recent events along the southeast coast, still managed to slip into the Savannah River, past Fort Pulaski, and successfully docked at Savannah's waterfront. The ship brought plentiful and much needed military stores: eleven thousand Enfield rifles, twenty-four thousand pounds of gunpowder, five hundred sabers, half a million cartridges, over a million percussion caps, four artillery pieces, seven tons of artillery ammunition, medicine, uniforms, clothing, and blankets. But its arrival also set off a considerable amount of heated debate among several state governors and the Confederate government about who would receive this material. Once again, Lee would be in the middle of the contentious discussion, but he was able to issue five thousand Enfield rifles to Georgia and South Carolina troops in his department and sent two of the artillery pieces to Fort Pulaski.[10]

Lee remained in Charleston November 13–16, dealing with the myriad issues brought to him over lack of equipment, enlistments, questions of authority, and priorities. Not until November 19 did Secretary of War Benjamin determine just how the *Fingal*'s cargo would be divided up and who got what.[11]

The arrival of the *Fingal* and the distribution of its cargo did much to relieve the problems of arms and supplies for Lee's troops, but the threat posed by the Federal forces operating offshore did not abate. Lee insisted on the construction of new defenses and the strengthening of existing ones. This involved huge amounts of labor, and while slaves performed much of this work, many troops were also put to the task. The use of both labor pools created unique problems of their own. Using slaves to work on defenses oftentimes placed them close to the front lines, and many of them seized the opportunity to flee to the Federals offshore. The loss of these laborers was one thing, but their intimate knowledge of the coast and familiarity with military dispositions also meant that the enemy would gain valuable intelligence to use against the Southerners. On the other hand, using the white troops for this labor tended to create discontent because many of them were not necessarily used to hard, manual labor, and in any case they resented doing work regarded as fit only for slaves. Lee was soon known as the "King of Spades."[12]

Lee returned to the lower coast to inspect the defenses extending from Savannah to Fernandina, Florida, noting that removing ordnance and supplies from the islands and relocating them at strategic points on the mainland progressed, although much work remained. He returned to Savannah on November 21 and filed his report to Adjutant and Inspector General Samuel Cooper in Richmond, noting his concern about the lack of artillery ammunition, trained artillerists, and qualified officers to teach them. Before returning to his Coosawhatchie headquarters, he inspected the progress being made on Savannah's defenses.[13]

While Lee struggled with his own problems of sorting out these issues, the Federal forces were busy implementing their agenda. Du Pont's gunboats fanned out along the coast patrolling for blockade-runners. Before the attack on Hilton Head Island, the blockade had consisted primarily of a cordon of vessels that attempted to close down major ports such as Charleston and Savannah. Now that Du Pont had a large contingent of gunboats, he established an offshore ring of ships that tried to interdict any maritime traffic approaching the coast. Charleston was an obvious target for offensive operations, but Savannah was also tempting. On the night of November 24, three Federal gunboats shelled Tybee Island driving off the remaining Confederate forces. The following afternoon, Federal troops landed and occupied the island. Following this the gunboats scouted Wassaw and Ossabaw Sounds to the south of Tybee Island and landed troops on the north end of Wassaw Island.[14]

Since Fort Pulaski stood firm in the mouth of the Savannah River, the Federal commanders made plans to investigate the waterways around the fort to find a bypass and enter the Savannah River behind it. North of Fort Pulaski, a stream called Wright River paralleled the Savannah River. Its course took it near the New River in South Carolina, and before the war,

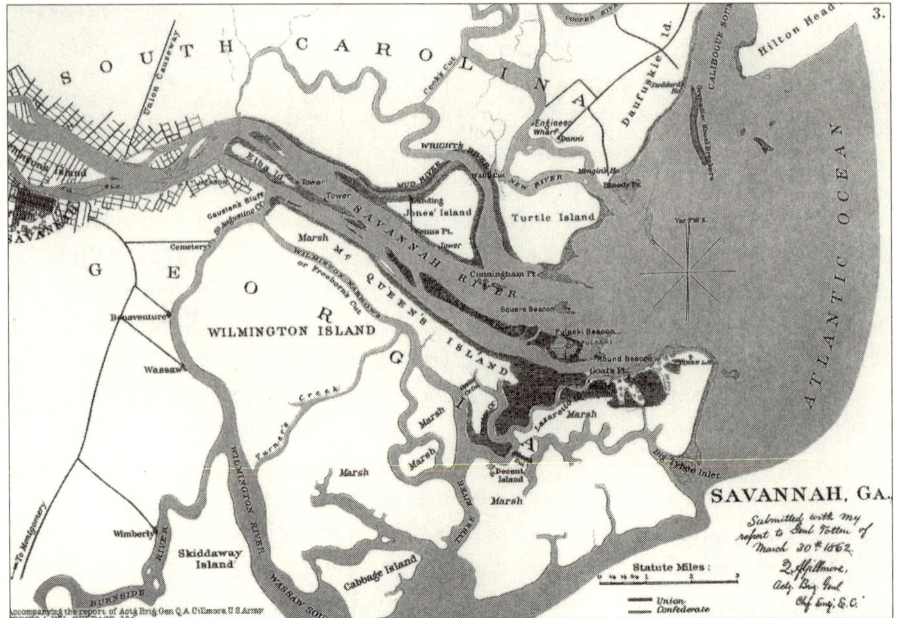

Waterways around Fort Pulaski. From *Atlas to Accompany the Official Records of the Union and Confederate Armies* (1891–95), plate LXXXIII, no. 3.

a channel known as Wall's Cut had been dug to connect this route to the Wright River so that the Savannah would became part of a water route leading into Port Royal Sound. The Southerners had obstructed the entrance to Wall's Cut by sinking pilings as well as a large vessel in the river there, but the Federals began quietly working to remove the obstacles and clear the route. A tributary called Mud Creek fed into Wright River, but it ended short of entering the Savannah River. With Wall's Cut cleared, the Federals began dredging operations to open Mud Creek into the Savannah River behind Fort Pulaski, thus bypassing it entirely. All of this activity in the Savannah area greatly concerned Lee as he considered the possibility that the Federals were either planning a major offensive or establishing a ruse to divert Southern resources from the intended target area.[15]

While Lee had been occupied with establishing a new defensive line on the coast, Governor Andrew Pickens of South Carolina had been writing to Confederate President Jefferson Davis complaining about personnel problems with some of the commanders as well as other issues. Davis reiterated his support of Lee and ordered Brigadier General John C. Pemberton to the department to assist Lee.[16] With the situation at Savannah worsening daily, Lee recognized the impossibility of focusing his undivided attention on the entire coast. So he decided to break the area up into five districts under the command of officers who would oversee the operations in their areas and report directly to him. This would allow him to delegate routine matters to these officers while he focused on the larger strategic issues.[17]

On December 2 Lee made a trip up the Broad River to organize a light force to deal with marauding Federals. Three days later he traveled to Palmetto Point from where he could view the Federal fleet. Returning to Charleston on December 11, he intended to examine the city's defenses but arrived to find the business district threatened by a large fire east of King

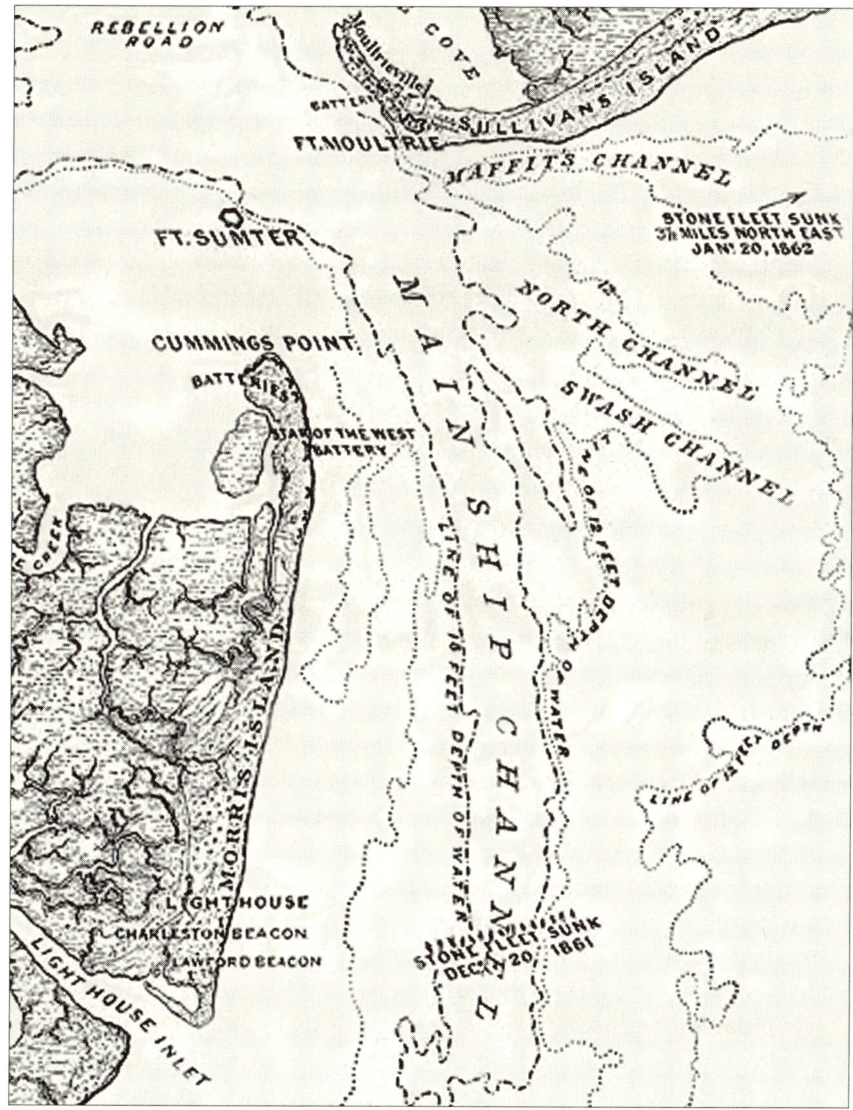

Entrance to Charleston Harbor. From *Battles and Leaders of the Civil War: People's Pictorial Edition* (New York: Century and De Vinne, 1894), 10.

Street and near the Cooper River. Clearly the Yankees were not the only danger Charlestonians faced. While imminent threats appeared at Savannah, Federal operations also targeted Charleston. The two cities presented different defensive challenges: Charleston sat on the coast, approachable by limited, already defended water routes. Savannah on the other hand was situated inland but vulnerable via numerous waterways, most of which had yet to be adequately secured. The urgency there was highlighted by the increasing attention that Federal forces were giving to exploring the waterways and occupying the offshore islands.

But Charleston was still an attractive target for the Federals, and if they were not yet ready to launch an assault on the city, they were interested in cutting off its access to the outside world. One project underway for a period of time involved collecting old whaling ships and other derelicts, loading them with rocks, bringing them to the southeast coast, and sinking them in the entrances to Charleston Harbor, aiming to close it to ship traffic. On December 20, the first anniversary of South Carolina's secession from the Union, the "Stone Fleet," as it had been dubbed, appeared off the city. The old ships were scuttled to block the south channel off Morris Island and the north channel near Rattlesnake Shoals, but these actions only partially succeeded since other access points remained open.[18]

As 1861 drew to a close, Lee was still consumed by a host of issues: increasing his troop strength, convincing units to enlist in the Confederate service rather than state service, securing crops and property, and finding enough artillery and weapons to arm the troops he did have. In some units many soldiers still carried outdated flintlock muskets.[19]

Although the recent arrival of troops from Tennessee was one positive development, the number of men available in the department still concerned Lee. On December 27, he wrote to Governor Pickens of South Carolina: "The strength of the enemy, as far as I am able to judge, exceeds the whole force we have in this State. It can be thrown . . . against any point and far outnumbers any force we can bring against it in the field." To General Cooper, Lee noted: "I am aware that we must fight against great odds, and I always trust that the spirit of our soldiers will be an overmatch to the numbers of our opponents. Our works are not yet finished; their progress is slow; guns are required for their armament, and I have not received as many troops from South Carolina and Georgia as I at first expected." The outcome of the year's events had clearly not been what the Southerners had anticipated when they embarked upon their quest for independence.[20]

The dawning of January 1862 still found the Federals busily occupied with attempting to clear the obstructions from Wall's Cut north of the Savannah River and building up strength in warships and troops off of Fort Pulaski and on the nearby barrier islands. It was clear to Lee that the Federals were up to something, and in early January, he returned to Savannah to inspect the defensive progress there. On January 6, he inspected Fort Pulaski and was dismayed to find it ill-prepared to repel a determined assault or even a siege. With the number of waterways located in the area, he was well aware that the possibility of the fort being cut off was substantial, and he ordered that the fort be adequately provisioned to withstand a prolonged siege.[21]

Due to the situation in the Savannah area, Lee transferred his headquarters there, and during the second week of January, once again traveled down the coast to examine the progress of defensive preparations at Brunswick, Georgia, and Fernandina, Florida. On the return trip from Fernandina, Lee took advantage of the opportunity to stop at Cumberland Island to visit Dungeness, where his father was buried after his death there on March 25, 1818. His father, Revolutionary War hero Henry "Light Horse Harry" Lee III, had served under General Nathanael Greene and earned great renown for pursuing Lord Charles Cornwallis out of the Carolinas. This was the only time Lee *ever* visited the site. He returned to Savannah and remained there for the balance of his time commanding the department.[22]

The activity of the Federal forces on the Georgia coast continued to concern Lee. The enemy had increased their strength on Tybee and Wassaw Islands, and naval reconnaissance down the coast indicated their interest in Fernandina as well. Word arrived of a blockading vessel scouting the sounds off of Brunswick and patrolling the offshore waters. Apparently they were up to something on Tybee Island as well, but there was no definite information. Unknown to Lee, the Federal forces were busily constructing masked batteries along the island's northeastern shore for emplacing artillery to reduce Fort Pulaski. For the time being the work was being hidden, although the garrison of the fort suspected something was going on.[23]

Although the threat to Savannah and the lower Georgia coast was clear, Lee had no good intelligence on his adversary's intentions. And the Federals were still bedeviling Charleston: on January 20 they sunk another fleet of hulks in the harbor entrance channel to obstruct access for blockade-runners.[24]

Meanwhile, the Federals also cleared access to Wall's Cut and continued dredging a channel through Mud Creek to reach the Savannah River from the north bank. They organized an expedition to scout alternate water approaches to the river. A force of six gunboats had been stationed in the Wright River by way of Wall's Cut, and on January 27, another flotilla of seven shallow draft gunboats south of the Savannah River, slipped up the Tybee River, passing Fort Pulaski under cover of darkness, and the following day passed upriver to a point where only a single row of pilings obstructed the channel. A reconnaissance in small boats up the channel past the pilings showed that access to St. Augustine Creek could easily be gained and from there so could the Savannah. The expedition remained in the Tybee River that night planning to withdraw the following day.[25]

Federal interest in the Wright River concerned Lee enough that he ordered Commodore Josiah Tattnall to escort two supply vessels to Fort Pulaski to ensure that additional supplies were stockpiled there. On the morning of January 28, Tattnall's squadron of three ships—the *Savannah,* the *Resolute,* and the *Sampson*—convoyed the two supply ships down the river. Immediately detected, the Federal gunboats opened fire when they came into range. Tattnall received fire from north and south of the river and attempted to respond. Considering the positions of the enemy gunboats, he feared they might gain access to the river behind him and cut him off. As a result, he withdrew *Savannah* and *Resolute,* while *Sampson* escorted the two supply vessels to Fort Pulaski. Once the supplies were delivered, the three vessels once again ran the gauntlet of fire to return to Savannah.[26]

On January 29, the Federal gunboats retired downstream. On the same day, Lee traveled down the Savannah River with Brigadier General Alexander W. Lawton and Colonel George P. Harrison to visit Fort Jackson, from which he could observe the approaches to the city. The threat presented by the Federal operations intending to bypass Fort Pulaski meant that, if they succeeded, Fort Jackson would be the next point from which a defense would be mounted; therefore, Lee made a number of visits and paid special attention to the preparations there. Two days later, on January 31, he returned to Fort Jackson and spent a good part of the day laying out the location for a new earthen battery he wanted constructed just downstream and adjacent to the fort. Fort Jackson was a masonry fort that dated from the War of 1812; it was woefully unprepared to meet a determined naval assault from downriver. The new battery, named Battery Lee, would augment Fort Jackson and offer a much better defense. Construction began immediately, and a team of more than two hundred laborers began clearing the site. A railroad spur was ultimately built to haul sand in order to build its thick, earthen walls. Lee returned four days later on February 4 with Lawton to inspect the progress of construction. Armament for the battery was already arriving, and on this day a mortar arrived.[27]

Defensive measures moved forward everywhere, spurred on by the recent engagement in the rivers east of the city. With many of the offshore islands being abandoned, additional heavy guns were relocated to augment existing defenses and to arm newly built ones. A short distance southeast of Fort Jackson stood Causten's Bluff, a rise of high ground on St. Augustine Creek. One of Savannah's "keystone" defensive fortifications was constructed here to control river traffic and access to the Savannah River from the waterways to the south and to guard the rear of Fort Jackson. This earthwork was eventually named Fort Bartow in honor of Colonel Francis Bartow,

Georgia's first martyr to the cause, who had been killed while leading Georgia troops at the Battle of Bull Run on July 21, 1861.[28]

During one of Lee's inspection trips around the Savannah defenses, he visited Causten's Bluff where he witnessed the firing of a newly mounted cannon. It almost turned out to be a fatal event for Lee. William W. Mackall, a youngster at the time, witnessed the event. He wrote in later years:

> I had the high privilege as a boy of meeting for the first time General Robert E. Lee. . . . It was in the early stage of the war and my mother and her children were visiting father, Mr. Francis Sorrel of Savannah. At that time General Lee was in command of the Coast defenses of South Carolina and Georgia, and happened to be in Savannah on an inspection trip during our sojourn there. He was pleasantly acquainted with my grandfather and a very close friend of my father. . . . The Ordnance Department of the Confederacy had recently turned out a huge cannon, which was supposed to have the capacity of throwing a cannon ball a distance of five miles. This gun had been mounted at Causten's Bluff and General Lee invited my grandfather to drive out to the Bluff with him and witness the discharge of the gun and he asked permission of my grandfather to take with him also my brother and myself. . . .
>
> We made the trip by carriage and [upon] arriving took our stand possibly with some others on a mound from which we could see the cannon and also have a view of the marshes. At the first attempt to fire there was no ignition, but at the second attempt, the cannon split wide open, the upper half, rising into the air and passing over our heads, buried itself in the swamp some three or four hundred yards inland, and the lower half remained stationary, while the ball shot out into space. A few soldiers were slightly injured by flying splinters of iron, but otherwise there were no serious casualties.[29]

One can only wonder at how the course of the war would have changed had Lee been killed or injured by the bursting of this gun.

By this time Lee was well on his way to growing the white beard that would be part of his signature appearance. When he had arrived in Charleston in November 1861, he only wore a moustache, but through the weeks of traveling along the coast he had let his beard grow. In February 1862, he would also acquire something else that would always be associated with him: his renowned horse, Traveller.

Lee first crossed paths with the horse when he was serving in western Virginia in the fall of 1861. At that time, the horse belonged to Major Thomas L.

Broun and his brother, Captain Joseph Broun, quartermaster of the Wise Legion. When Lee took command of the Wise Legion and Brigadier General John B. Floyd's Brigade, he saw the horse in camp and took a great liking to it. Lee spoke to Captain Broun about the horse and indicated his interest in purchasing it. But before a bargain could be struck, events took Lee from western Virginia to the southeast coast where he became immersed in his job there. Shortly after his arrival, however, the third regiment of the Wise Legion, officially known as the 60th Virginia Infantry, was transferred to the South Carolina coast where once again Lee crossed paths with the horse.[30]

Major Broun later recalled:

> Upon seeing my brother on this horse near Pocotaligo, in South Carolina, General Lee at once recognized the horse, and again inquired of him pleasantly about *'his colt.'*
>
> My brother then offered him the horse as a gift, which the General promptly declined, and at the same time remarked: "If you will *willingly* sell me the horse, I will gladly use it for a week or so to learn its qualities." Thereupon my brother had the horse sent to General Lee's stable. In about a week the horse was returned to my brother, with a note from General Lee stating that the animal suited him, but that he could not longer use so valuable a horse in such times, unless it was his own; that if he (my brother) would not sell, please to keep the horse, with many thanks. This was in February 1862. . . .
>
> My brother wrote to me of General Lee's desire to have the horse, and asked me what he should do. I replied at once: 'If he will not accept it, then sell it to him at what it cost me.' He then sold the horse to General Lee for $200 in currency, the sum of $25 having been added by General Lee to the price I paid for the horse in September 1861, to make up for the depreciation in our currency from September 1861, to February 1862.[31]

Lee was still extremely concerned about an attack against Savannah; however, events occurring elsewhere would eventually impact Lee's operations to defend the southeastern coast. While Lee had been occupied in Georgia and South Carolina, the Confederate garrison of Fort Henry in Tennessee surrendered on February 6, opening the Tennessee River to Union gunboats. Then Federal troops under Major General Ulysses S. Grant invested nearby Fort Donelson on the Cumberland River, and it appeared that the Confederate garrison would be forced to capitulate. The news of Fort Henry's fall became but one event in a string of bad news arriving at Lee's headquarters. Two days later there was word of the capture of Roanoke Island off the coast of North Carolina. The enemy seemed active everywhere, and the fortunes of the Southern states only receded.[32]

Though undoubtedly concerned about the Confederacy's military setbacks, Lee had plenty to occupy his attentions on the southeast coast, such as the Federal blockade of Brunswick. Georgia Governor Joseph E. Brown wrote Lee in dismay at the possibility of the town being abandoned. Lee had to point out the military necessity of such a move and the difficulty of risking troops to defend such an isolated position. Brown also worried about whether Lee intended to burn the city or not.[33]

While Lee had been occupied in overseeing the construction of the earthen battery adjacent to Fort Jackson, the Federals had also been toiling a short way downstream constructing a six-gun battery of their own. They located the battery on a mud island in the Savannah River on ground the Southerners had deemed impractical for fortifications. This emplacement, dubbed Battery Vulcan, was situated on Venus Point on Jones Island and commanded the approaches downriver from the city—as the steamer *Ida,* bound for Fort Pulaski, discovered when it was unexpectedly fired on by the hidden battery. The vessel successfully made the run to the fort and returned no worse for wear, but the existence of the battery at Venus Point greatly irked the Southerners. The Federals constructed another six-gun emplacement, Battery Hamilton, a few days later on Bird Island. This pair of Federal batteries all but closed off any further steamer traffic to Fort Pulaski.[34]

Lee met with his staff and discussed taking some kind of offensive action against these two batteries, but in the end it was decided not to attempt any such operation because of the difficulty involved and the fact that even if they succeeded, the Confederates would not be able to hold the batteries. So Fort Pulaski was essentially cut off from any assistance coming from Savannah. Henceforth, only small boats navigating the shallow waterways through the marsh would be able to reach the fort.[35]

The build up of Federal operations and the steadily growing fleet of Union warships anchored off Tybee Island obviously portended some major offensive in the works, but Lee had no idea where the enemy would strike. All indications pointed to Savannah, and all Lee could do was shift his forces from the many islands back to the mainland and the city. No matter where the Federals struck, the potential for disaster was great. There were even discussions of abandoning Savannah and Brunswick, and the necessity of burning the former if it were evacuated.[36]

News of enemy operations elsewhere was also discouraging. On February 16, Fort Donelson fell in Tennessee, another disaster for the Confederates that would ultimately impact Lee's plans in Georgia. On the seventeenth, he paid another visit to Fort Jackson to inspect the progress on the new battery going up adjacent to the fort. The following day, Secretary of War Benjamin ordered Lee to "withdraw all forces from the islands in your department to the main-land, taking proper measures to save the artillery and munitions of war." Lee had anticipated this move and had already initiated steps to remove the troops and material from many of the islands. The troops from St. Simons and Jekyll Islands had been moved to Brunswick, and efforts were underway to transport the ordnance and material to Savannah. The new orders meant that Brunswick would have to be evacuated. Lee had intended to destroy the town to deny its use to the enemy; however, he would not do so without the approval of Governor Brown. Understanding the dire situation regarding Brunswick, the governor responded to Lee's letter on the matter of burning Brunswick: "I have to say that if my own house were in Brunswick I would certainly set fire to it, when driven from it by the enemy, rather than see it used by them as a shelter. We should destroy whatever the military necessities require . . . private property and private rights must yield to the great public interests now at stake." In the end, the wharves, the lighthouse, and the hotel were all that was burned, to deny their use by the Federals. On February 19, Lee issued orders to abandon all of the offshore islands as far south as Amelia Island in north Florida.[37]

The abandonment of the islands required a great deal of work in packing up material, supplies, and ordnance and transporting it to points on the mainland, from whence it had to be sent either to Savannah or to new defensive points along the coast. The returning garrisons also had to be transported to bolster the defenses around Savannah and other posts on the mainland. And all of this work had to be done with the greatest amount of caution lest the Federals catch them at a vulnerable moment. Lee fretted that whatever offensive operation his enemy planned might begin during these evacuation and reorganization operations along the coast.

The loss of Fort Donelson affected Lee's plans in ways he may or may not have anticipated. On February 24, Secretary of War Benjamin wrote him explaining that because of events at Fort Donelson, remaining Confederate forces in Tennessee were being withdrawn further south to defend the railroad from Memphis to Richmond. However, the necessity of augmenting the troops there required the transfer of troops from other departments. So Lee was ordered to "withdraw all such forces as are now employed in the defense of the seaboard of Florida . . . and to send forward the troops to Tennessee . . . by the most expeditious route." This could have hardly been a welcome development, but Lee responded by sending the 23rd Mississippi Infantry and a regiment of cavalry to Tennessee.[38]

That same day Lee, accompanied by Brigadier Generals Lawton, Hugh W. Mercer, and William H. T. Walker, visited Fort Jackson to examine the progress on Battery Lee. The atmosphere was thick with tension. Even more Federal gunboats and transports lay at anchor in Tybee Roads and Wassaw

Sound. At this point, Savannah appeared the obvious target to any observer, and preparations to meet the inevitable attack moved forward at a feverish pace. As ordnance and troops arrived from the abandoned islands, they were immediately emplaced to strengthen the city's defenses. Events were quickly moving to a momentous conclusion.[39]

On February 27, Battery Lee was nearly complete, mounting seven guns and three mortars with two companies of men to garrison it. In conjunction with old Fort Jackson and similar earthen batteries built across the river, this point was intended to be the rock that stopped any enemy naval assault up the river. All eyes anxiously watched the growing fleet of enemy ships collecting off the coast; however, when the sun rose on the morning of March 1, they were all gone, having sailed off during the night much to the surprise and chagrin of the Southern defenders. Where they had gone was a mystery, but it was clear that Savannah was not their intended target.[40]

So much enemy activity had been going on around Savannah that everyone anticipated an attack on the city, but now the fleet and the enemy troops camped on Wassaw Island had disappeared. Lee could not know for certain whether the enemy was moving against another point on the coast or conducting a feint in order to draw Confederate defenders away from Savannah. That afternoon he traveled out to Fort Jackson to examine the state of things at Battery Lee and the other fortifications on both sides of the river at this point. He found no sign of the enemy anywhere: either coming up the river or any of the other water approaches east of the city.[41]

While Lee pondered what his enemy was up to, the missing fleet of transports, gunboats, and warships was well on its way down the coast. Although Du Pont was unaware that Cumberland Island, Amelia Island, and the town of Fernandina, Florida, were being abandoned, Amelia Island was the target of this operation, and the fleet came to anchor off the southern end of Jekyll Island around 3:00 P.M. while gunboats scouted the neighboring islands and sounds. They found the Confederate fortifications empty of guns and soldiers: everything appeared abandoned. This discovery encouraged Du Pont, so at 4:30 P.M. the shallow draft gunboats entered St. Andrew's Sound and were staged to continue down the inland waterway behind Cumberland Island. The heavier warships and transports proceeded offshore to approach Amelia Island from the Atlantic side. The plan was for the gunboats to work their way through the inland passage and to enter the St. Mary's River behind Fort Clinch on the north point of Amelia Island, while the heavier warships approached from seaward to engage the fort. It was a good plan, but the falling tide complicated the passage of the gunboats.[42]

The Confederate forces on Amelia Island and in the city of Fernandina, unaware of the approach of their enemy, were just completing their final efforts to evacuate the men and material from the island. When they did discover Du Pont's approach, they were obviously unprepared to make a defense and quickly evacuated to the mainland. The island fell with virtually no resistance.

Lee's greatest test was at hand. The enemy had stolen a march on him, pressing an attack where he did not expect it and where his orders had left his forces ill-prepared to meet it. But how he would have dealt with this situation was quickly rendered academic by the arrival of a telegram from President Davis on March 3: "If circumstances will, in your judgment, warrant your leaving, I wish to see you here with the least delay."[43]

While the loss of Amelia Island had not been totally unexpected, Lee met with his staff and pressed forward with defensive preparations for Savannah and Fort Pulaski, still the most significant area on the Georgia coast, which the enemy had not forgotten. Lee departed Savannah by train that evening, and command of the department devolved onto Brigadier General Pemberton.[44]

Lee was faced with a host of new challenges in Richmond as he took up duties as military advisor to President Davis, but he continued to send correspondence and instructions to subordinates still dealing with the situation on the southeast coast. It was soon quite clear that Lee would not be returning to Georgia, and on March 14, Pemberton was officially assigned as commander of the Department of South Carolina, Georgia, and East Florida.[45]

While Lee had faced a difficult challenge during his tenure on the southeast coast, he had left the area much better prepared to meet an attack than it had been when he arrived four months earlier. At that time, the command was in disarray, everything was disorganized, and there were problems across the spectrum, from enlistments to armaments and defensive preparations. Lee had managed to develop and implement a cohesive defensive plan for more than two hundred miles of the southeast coast that incorporated the entire coast and created strong points at places like Charleston and Savannah. Although he had been forced to relinquish the offshore islands, he had little choice. To attempt to defend them would have only sacrificed men and material that could have been better used on the mainland. However, by giving up the islands he also gave his enemy access to areas and facilities that would support their blockading operations, and in the instance of Fort Pulaski, the loss of Tybee Island gave the Federals a land platform from which to shell the fort with newly developed rifled artillery. The loss of Tybee all but guaranteed the fall of the fort, which was taken by the Federals on April 11 after Lee's departure.

As an engineer, Lee understood the need for effective fortifications, and his program to build these defenses around Charleston and Savannah and along the coast did not endear him to his soldiers. But it did create an effective barrier to enemy attack. When he arrived on the coast, Savannah was sorely unprepared for a determined attack from the sea, and the loss of Hilton Head Island only emphasized that fact. Only the want of aggressiveness by the Federal forces and Lee's insistence on constructing a strong defensive barrier saved Savannah. In the end Savannah, like Charleston, fairly bristled with fortifications and artillery along every water approach to the city. It obviously would not be taken without great effort and bloodshed, and that the Federals ultimately chose not to test those defenses shows they were not willing to pay that price. Their goal, after all, was not to possess the real estate but rather to tie down as many Confederate defenders as possible manning the city's defenses. Capturing the city would be a hollow victory. Already blockaded, its effectiveness as a port was negated, and if the city were taken, the Confederate forces defending it would be freed for use elsewhere while Federal troops would be tied down garrisoning it.

Lee brought some semblance of order and organization to the department in the four months he commanded it. He had created a functioning operation where there had only been confusion and chaos. He did not contribute a great military victory, but he provided a solid foundation upon which his successors would continue to build. Lee's contribution early in the war was ultimately overshadowed by the service he would provide to the Confederacy in Virginia. He brought with him a greater knowledge in dealing with difficult situations and people, and these experiences would serve him well. He also brought with him a new persona, his signature white beard, and his mount, Traveller. Both would contribute to the iconic image of Lee that we have come to know today. Shortly after his arrival in Richmond, he was in a position from which he would be tapped to step into the spotlight and lead an army to glory.

Notes

1. U.S. War Department, *The War of the Rebellion: A Compilation of the Official Records of the Union and Confederate Armies,* 128 vols. (Washington, DC, 1880–1901), ser. 1, vol. 6:310–15, 318–19, 320–21, 335, 340, 376 (hereafter cited as *OR;* all references are to series 1 unless otherwise indicated).

2. U. S. Navy War Records Office, *Official Records of the Union and Confederate Navies in the War of the Rebellion,* 31 vols. (Washington, DC, 1894–1927), ser. 1, vol. 12:524–25 (hereafter cited as *ORN;* all references are to series 1 unless otherwise indicated); *OR,* vol. 6:350–61, 369, 370–400.

3. *ORN,* vol. 12:277–78, 280–85, 350–55.

4. Ibid.; William D. Dixon, Diary, Nov. 8, 1861, Georgia Historical Society, Savannah; Joseph Jones to Rev. C. C. Jones, Nov. 7, 1861, Joseph Jones Collection, and Charles C. Jones Jr. to Rev. and Mrs. C. C. Jones, Nov. 8, 1861,

C. C. Jones Collection, both in the Manuscripts Division, Howard-Tilton Memorial Library, Tulane University, New Orleans.

5. *OR*, vol. 6:334, 366.

6. Ibid., 311–12; Douglas S. Freeman, *R. E. Lee: A Biography*, 4 vols. (New York, 1949), 1:611–12; Gabriel Manigault, "Memoirs," South Carolina Historical Society, Charleston.

7. *OR*, vol. 6:346–47.

8. Ibid., 312–13.

9. Charles C. Jones Jr. to Rev. and Mrs. C. C. Jones, Nov. 9, 1861, Rev. C. C. Jones Papers, Hargrett Rare Book and Manuscript Library, University of Georgia, Athens; Daniel J. Crooks Jr., *Lee in the Low Country, Defending Charleston and Savannah 1861–1862* (Charleston, SC, 2008), 68; Samuel Francis Du Pont, *Samuel Francis Du Pont, a Selection from His Civil War Letters,* ed. John D. Hayes, 3 vols. (Ithaca, NY, 1969), 1:347–50; Charles C. Jones Jr., *Historical Sketch of the Chatham Artillery during the Confederate Struggle for Independence* (Albany, NY, 1867), 33–36; Charles C. Jones Jr., *The Siege of Savannah in December 1864 and the Confederate Operations in the Third Military District of South Carolina during General Sherman's March to the Sea* (Albany, NY, 1874), 51, 63; Alexander A. Lawrence, *A Present for Mr. Lincoln: The Story of Savannah from Secession to Sherman* (Macon, GA, 1961), 4; Robert Manson Myers, ed., *The Children of Pride: A True Story of Georgia and the Civil War* (New Haven, CT, 1972), 763; *ORN*, vol. 12:93; *OR*, vol. 6:23, 312.

10. *OR*, vol. 6:318–19, 322–27.

11. Ibid., 327.

12. Ibid., 331.

13. Ibid., 327–329; Dixon Diary, Nov. 21, 1861.

14. Dixon Diary, Nov. 24 and 25, 1861; *OR*, vol. 6:32–33, 192–93; *ORN*, vol. 12:359–60, 364.

15. *ORN*, vol. 12:492–95, 523; Myers, *Children of Pride*, 847; *OR*, vol. 6:85–87.

16. *OR*, vol. 6:334, 344, 347.

17. Ibid., 344–45.

18. Ibid., 42–43; Freeman, *R. E. Lee*, 1:611.

19. *OR*, vol. 6:339–40, 346, 348, 358, 362.

20. Ibid., 347, 357, 367 (quotes); *ORN*, vol. 12:494, 523–28.

21. *OR*, vol. 6:84.

22. Crooks, *Lee in the Low Country*, 101–4.

23. *OR*, vol. 6:368.

24. Ibid., 42–44; E. B. Long, *The Civil War Day By Day, An Almanac 1861–1865* (Garden City, NY, 1971), 162.

25. *OR*, vol. 6:83–87.

26. *ORN*, vol. 12:524–25.

27. Dixon Diary, Jan. 29, 31, Feb. 4, 6, 1862.

28. Jones, *The Siege of Savannah*, 102; Lawrence, *A Present for Mr. Lincoln*, 75; Derek Smith, *Civil War Savannah* (Savannah, GA, 1997), 89.

29. William W. Mackall, *A Son's Recollection of His Father* (New York, 1930), 222–23.

30. Thomas L. Broun, "General R. E. Lee's War-Horses, Traveller and Lucy Long," *Southern Historical Society Papers* 18 (1890): 388–91; Thomas L. Broun, "General R. E. Lee's War Horses," *Southern Historical Society Papers* 19 (1891): 333–35.

31. Broun, "General R. E. Lee's War Horses," 333–35.

32. *OR*, vol. 6:168, 367; Long, *Civil War Day by Day*, 167, 171–72.

33. *OR*, vol. 6:168, 367; Long, *Civil War Day by Day*, 167, 171–72; *ORN*, vol. 12:377, 379, 386–87, 390–91.

34. *OR* vol. 6:90–91, 144; *ORN*, vol. 12:500, 555–56; *ORN*, vol. 14:323.

35. Smith, *Civil War Savannah*, 65–66.

36. Du Pont, *Samuel Francis Du Pont*, 1:347–50; Jones, *Historical Sketch of the Chatham Artillery*, 55–65; *ORN*, vol. 12:386, 390–91.

37. Dixon Diary, Feb. 17, 1862; *OR*, vol. 6:91, 390 (quote), 391–93, 394; Crooks, *Lee in the Low Country*, 108.

38. *OR*, vol. 6:398, 400.

39. Dixon Diary, Feb. 24, 1862.

40. Ibid., Feb. 27, 1862.

41. Ibid., Mar. 1, 1862.

42. *ORN*, vol. 12:523, 572, 576–77; *OR*, vol. 6:95.

43. *OR*, vol. 6:400.

44. Ibid., 401–2.

45. Ibid., 406–7.

Brigadier General Benjamin Hardin Helm. Courtesy of the Kentucky Digital Library.

"I Have Gone in for the War": Benjamin Hardin Helm

Stuart W. Sanders

On September 22, 1863, U.S. Supreme Court Justice David Davis visited the White House to see his friend, President Abraham Lincoln. Davis found the commander-in-chief in intense grief. "Davis," Lincoln said, "I feel as David of old did when he was told of the death of Absalom." Two days earlier, Lincoln's brother-in-law, the Kentucky-born Confederate Brigadier General Benjamin Hardin Helm, had been mortally wounded at the Battle of Chickamauga. "I never saw Mr. Lincoln more moved," Davis wrote. "I saw how grief-stricken he was so I closed the door and left him alone."[1]

Best known for being the Rebel brother-in-law of the Union president, Helm's military career was one of missed opportunities. Therefore, he became a noted casualty that well-summarized the fratricidal conflict. The circumstances of his life, notably untimely injuries that kept him out of major battles, make assessing his wartime career difficult. His marriage, however, to Mary Todd Lincoln's half-sister and the adoration of his troops makes his life worthy of closer examination.[2]

Kentucky governor Beriah Magoffin once said that "some of the best blood of Ky. flows in [Helm's] veins." He was born in Bardstown, Kentucky, on June 2, 1831, at "Edgewood," a home built by his maternal grandfather and namesake, noted attorney Ben Hardin. He was the oldest of twelve children born to John Larue Helm and Lucinda Barbour Hardin Helm, and his family was closely tied to Kentucky's pioneer settlement. His great-grandfather, Captain Thomas Helm, had moved to the area in 1780, while a maternal relative, Revolutionary War veteran John Hardin, had settled near Bardstown in 1786. Helm's family later moved to Elizabethtown in Hardin County (named for John Hardin), and his father eventually served two terms as Kentucky's governor.[3]

Helm—who was often addressed by his middle name Hardin—was first educated locally. In 1846, he enrolled in the Kentucky Military Institute in Frankfort but, after a few months, entered the U.S. Military Academy at West Point. Upon graduating in 1851, Helm, six feet tall with brown hair and blue eyes, ranked ninth out of forty-two cadets. He was brevetted a second lieutenant in the 2nd United States Cavalry and was stationed at Carlisle Barracks, Pennsylvania, before being posted to Fort Lincoln, Texas. After six months on the frontier, he contracted "inflammatory rheumatism" and returned to Kentucky. His father, a prominent attorney, urged Hardin to study law, and, in the autumn of 1852, he resigned his commission.[4]

After studying with his father, Hardin graduated from the University of Louisville law school in 1853. He then attended a specialized law program at Harvard, where he gave serious thought to his career. He wrote his sister that "a lawyer's business is no child's play if he attends to it properly," and added that "when unengaged in his office business his leisure time should be devoted to his profession." Upon returning to Elizabethtown, he practiced with his father before partnering with his cousin, Martin Hardin Cofer. They worked together for two years, and, like Helm, Cofer became a Confederate officer.[5]

With a military education, a stint as a cavalryman, and a promising legal career, the next step for Helm as he met the familial and social expectations was a political career. In 1855, he was elected to represent Hardin County in the Kentucky legislature. Like his father, Hardin was a Whig, but he entered politics as that party disappeared. In the Kentucky House, however, Helm supported Whig policies like internal improvements and served on the judiciary committee. Much of his legislative focus revolved around the judiciary, and he worked to reorganize Kentucky's courts and judicial districts. He introduced a bill "to promote internal improvement and common school education," pushed for new railroad charters, and sponsored bills supporting railroads, especially the Louisville & Nashville Railroad, which ran through Elizabethtown. Notably, Helm's father was president of the Louisville & Nashville during this period.

Although Helm voted for resolutions supporting the fugitive slave law and introduced "a bill providing for the better security of negro property," he voted against legislation proscribing the death penalty for those who helped slaves escape. The Kentucky legislature debated the Kansas-Nebraska Act, and, on February 8, 1855, Helm voted for a resolution that supported slavery in the territories. Illustrating Helm's move to the American Party, or "Know-Nothings," the resolution also urged slowing immigration. At least two of his fellow legislators—Roger Hanson and Horatio W. Bruce—played important roles in his life. During the Civil War, Helm assumed command of the 1st Kentucky Brigade after Hanson's death. Bruce, a future Confederate congressman, became Helm's law partner and brother-in-law, marrying Helm's sister when he and Helm were both legislators.[6]

Helm's legislative experience included more than bills, committee meetings, and political wrangling. He also met Emilie Todd, the beautiful daughter of Robert S. Todd, a Lexington merchant. In addition to their family backgrounds, with both of them descended from noted Kentucky pioneers, Helm and Emilie were well-educated, she having attended private schools in Lexington as well as a music conservatory in Cincinnati. Emilie was also the half-sister of Mary Todd Lincoln, eighteen years her senior. On March 20, 1856, Hardin and Emilie were married in Frankfort and celebrated with a reception held at Buena Vista, the Todd family retreat outside of the capital. Their marriage was blessed with three children, but Helm was killed shortly after his eldest child turned six years old.[7]

Theirs was not a marriage of convenience but of love. Throughout the summer of 1856, while stumping on behalf of American Party presidential candidate Millard Fillmore, Helm wrote loving letters to his wife. "But Emma I *can't keep* your image out of my mind, all the time, nearly," he wrote. In another letter he chided her: "Dear Emma, do take care of yourself, for if you should contract ill-health I would be miserable. I could never see one I love so devotedly, prostrated with disease, and be happy. I beg you then Emma for my sake to do nothing to injure your health."[8]

Emilie Todd Helm. Courtesy of the Kentucky Digital Library.

In August 1856, Helm became the Commonwealth's attorney for Kentucky's third judicial district. During that time, he traveled to Springfield, Illinois, for a legal case, where he stayed with his in-laws, Abraham and Mary Lincoln. Helm and Lincoln had much in common. In addition to both being attorneys, Lincoln's father had lived in Elizabethtown, and Lincoln had been born in nearby Hodgenville. Both also had limited military experiences, with Helm's short tenure as a cavalryman and Lincoln's service during the Black Hawk War. They became fast friends, and Hardin was "one of Lincoln's favorite in-laws."[9]

Continually seeking opportunities, Helm resigned as Commonwealth's attorney in 1858 and moved to Louisville, where he formed a partnership with his brother-in-law,

Horatio W. Bruce. With the sectional crisis peaking, Helm joined the Kentucky State Guard, the commonwealth's pre-war militia. On March 30, 1860, Helm was sworn in as a colonel and assistant inspector general. That same year, Helm's brother-in-law, Abraham Lincoln, won the presidency. Helm, who had become a States Rights Democrat, did not support Lincoln. Neither, however, did many of Lincoln's in-laws. In Fayette County, the home of the Todds, Lincoln received only five votes.[10]

Despite Helm's lack of support, Lincoln looked to his brother-in-law when the Civil War erupted. In April 1861, as more Southern states seceded, Lincoln asked Helm to visit him at the White House and offered him the position of paymaster, with the rank of major. Mary hoped that this offer would pull her sister to Washington. "Emilie will be a belle at the White House receptions and we will be so proud of her," she told Helm, "and we need handsome, scholarly, dignified young men like yourself to ornament our army." Lincoln gave Helm a sealed envelope, containing the commission. "Ben, here is something for you," he said. "Think it over by yourself, and let me know what you will do." Helm replied: "You have been kind and generous to me beyond anything I have known. I have no claim on you for I opposed your candidacy and did what I could for the election of another, but with no unkindly feelings toward you. I wish I could see my way–I will try to do what is right. You shall have my answer in a few days."

As Helm departed for Kentucky, Mary said: "We hope very soon to see you both in Washington."[11]

Helm recognized that this was a rare opportunity, noting:

> The ideal career was before me. The highest positions in the profession for which I was educated were opened to me in one day. I would not only be the youngest officer of my rank in the army, but could have transferred at the earliest possible moment to one of the cavalry regiments. With the changes occurring in them by [Southern resignations], I would certainly have been a full colonel within the year. I had a bitter struggle with myself; such an opportunity rarely offers itself in a lifetime. The most painful moment of my life was when I declined the generous offer of my brother-in-law.[12]

After leaving the White House, Helm encountered Robert E. Lee, who had just resigned from the U. S. Army to cast his lot with Virginia. "Are you feeling well, Colonel Lee?" Helm asked. "Well in body but not in mind," Lee replied. "In the prime of life I quit a service in which were all my hopes and expectations in this world." Helm told Lee about Lincoln's offer, and Lee replied, "My mind is too much disturbed to give you any advice." Lee, however, said that "there must be a great war" and told Helm to "do as your conscience and honor bid."[13]

Conscience and honor led Helm southward. In May 1861, he traveled to the Confederate capital, then at Montgomery, Alabama, and met with President Jefferson Davis. Helm offered his services, and Davis told Helm to return to the Bluegrass State to work for Kentucky's secession. Without a Confederate commission, Helm went home and focused his energies on the Kentucky State Guard. While Unionists complained that the Kentucky State Guard was pro-Confederate, its commander, Simon Bolivar Buckner, along with Helm and others, actually worked for Kentucky's neutrality. When neutrality ended, however, Helm sought advice from several friends and decided to join the Confederate army. Emilie recalled that her husband "had to follow his conscience and that for weal or woe he felt he must side with his own people." Familial considerations burdened his decision. Helm's father, who served his first term as Kentucky's governor in the 1850s, "although a large slave owner, was a strong Union man at the beginning of the war" and supported Kentucky's neutrality. The governor owned sixty slaves, and Helm's daughter wrote that her father "feared [that] the freeing of the slaves would ruin the South." Therefore, Helm donned Rebel gray, and soon he and Cofer were seen as the Confederates' primary contacts in Elizabethtown. Buckner told Southern officers to look to them "in relation to [the] destruction of bridges and [the] organization of troops." On September 21, 1861, Buckner ordered Helm to unite with other pro-Confederate Kentuckians to destroy locks and a dam at Rochester, Kentucky.[14]

Reviving his dream of fighting from the saddle, Helm recruited the 1st Kentucky Cavalry Regiment. Equipped by their families, the troopers hailed from thirteen counties. "This regiment was composed of the flower of the youth of Kentucky," remarked one nineteenth-century writer. "It was a beautiful sight when this gallant band of Confederates were marching or on parade." Many of the officers were mounted on their own Kentucky thoroughbreds with their black servants mounted on extra horses.[15]

Despite its aristocratic bent, Helm worked the regiment hard and drilled them often. "Theirs was a rigid discipline," wrote historian William C. Davis. "Company drill in the morning, regimental drill in the afternoon, brigade drill on Friday, inspection on Saturday, and leisure hours occupied with saber drill and fatigue and guard duty." From Bowling Green on October 10, Helm wrote Emilie that his recruiting efforts had succeeded. "I am getting up my regiment very rapidly, I think. I will soon be in the field again." He added, "this separation I sincerely hope will not continue long—but dear one I have gone in for the war. And if God spares my life I expect to battle to the end of it. I feel that I am fighting for our civil liberty." Helm's efforts were soon recognized, and on October 19, 1861, he was commissioned colonel of the regiment.[16]

Helm's men, familiar with the region, became valuable scouts. Confederate General Albert Sidney Johnston had established a defensive line across southern Kentucky, with his headquarters at Bowling Green. In December, Helm's cavalry reconnoitered near Scottsville and Glasgow, watching for Federal movements toward Woodsonville and Columbia. Johnston told Secretary of War Judah P. Benjamin that if Union soldiers advanced, Helm would burn bridges to hinder their march.[17]

In early January 1862, Helm reported Federals moving from Columbia toward Burkesville to block Confederate Brigadier General Felix Kirk Zollicoffer, who was operating near Somerset. One week later, Zollicoffer clashed with Unionists near Mill Springs. The Confederates were repulsed, Zollicoffer killed, the eastern wing of Johnston's defensive line collapsed, and Johnston abandoned Bowling Green. As the Southerners retreated toward Nashville, Helm guarded the rear, burning bridges along the way. Reaching Nashville, the regiment guarded stores in the abandoned town. By March, Helm was operating around Florence and Tuscumbia, Alabama, guarding bridges and eyeing Union Major General Don Carlos Buell's Army of the Ohio.[18]

Although Helm successfully scouted Yankees before the Battle of Mill Springs, he made a significant blunder in early April 1862. Supposedly watching Buell's army, Helm incorrectly reported him moving on Decatur, Alabama, rather than joining Union Major General Ulysses S. Grant's army at Pittsburg Landing, Tennessee. There, on April 6 and 7, Johnston's army clashed with Grant, who was reinforced by Buell, at the Battle of Shiloh. Historian Larry J. Daniel remarked that Helm's cavalry "had detected only Ormsby Mitchell's division marching toward Alabama. The balance of Buell's army had continued toward Pittsburg Landing." Johnston was killed on the first day, and Buell's arrival tipped the balance in favor of the Federals, who shoved the Rebels from the field. Confederate General Pierre G. T. Beauregard, who assumed command after Johnston was killed, later claimed he ignored Helm's inaccurate report. The shock of Johnston's death and the fact that many could share blame for the loss kept Helm's reputation intact. Shiloh hit Helm particularly hard, however. Emilie's brother, Samuel Todd, was killed in action—"shot through the body in [his regiment's] first charge," he died the next day.[19]

There was no time to mourn the loss. On April 14, Helm scouted near Tuscumbia and told Beauregard that the Federals were expecting reinforcements near Decatur. Skirmishes increased, and Helm worried about holding a key bridge over the Tennessee River at Florence. He relayed additional fears to his wife, telling Emilie he "felt great uneasiness" about not hearing from her. However, the bridge at Florence no longer concerned him. "I have since burned that magnificent structure," he wrote. "I regret deeply that it became my duty to destroy it. But as a soldier I know nothing but to obey orders."[20]

Helm's earlier reconnaissance failure had not damaged his reputation. On April 17, he was promoted to brigadier general, to rank from March 14. Sent to Major General John C. Breckinridge, a Todd family friend who had served as U.S. vice president, Helm was given brigade command. He was happy with the promotion but wanted Bluegrass soldiers. "I was very sorry I could not get with the Kentucky troops," he wrote Emilie. "I want to identify my destiny with them." Although his men were not Kentuckians, he could appoint Bluegrass soldiers to his staff. Emilie's youngest brother, Alexander Todd, became his aide-de-camp.[21]

In Corinth that May, Helm commanded Arkansas, Mississippi, and Missouri regiments in Breckinridge's Reserve Corps. That month he took a leave of absence following "surgery for hemorrhoids and an anal fissure" but returned to duty on July 8. During his absence, Breckinridge's men reinforced Vicksburg, Mississippi. Facing a Union gunboat fleet, the troops endured bombardments and supported artillery batteries to defend the city from Federal landings. Once healed, on July 8 Helm was assigned command of a brigade that included Kentucky troops: the 4th and 9th Kentucky Infantry Regiments, plus the 4th Alabama Infantry Battalion, 31st Alabama and 31st Mississippi Infantry Regiments, and the Pettus Flying Artillery (Mississippi) Battery. Helm's Brigade protected the city and supported the *Arkansas*, an ironclad ram.[22]

With Vicksburg temporarily secure, Confederate Major General Earl Van Dorn sent Breckinridge's division of four thousand men to Camp Moore, near Tangipahoa, Louisiana, close to the New Orleans, Jackson & Great Northern Railroad. On July 30, the Confederates—many of them sick—marched for Baton Rouge, fifty miles away. Working in concert with the *Arkansas*, Breckinridge hoped to drive off Federal troops there. But with few supplies and racked with illnesses caused by bad water, the Rebels' numbers had dwindled to fewer than 2,600 men when they neared Baton Rouge. On August 3, the Southerners reached the Comite River, ten miles from Baton Rouge. There, Breckinridge referred to Helm's troops as "my brave, noble, ragged Kentuckians." These men, as Private Gervis Granger of the 6th Kentucky Infantry Regiment explained, "feared a rattlesnake more than the bluecoats." Soon, however, they met the latter in force.[23]

At 11:00 P.M. on August 4, Helm's Brigade led the advance. "It was a rather dark, starlit night," one Confederate remarked. After crawling forward for two hours, the tired, sick, and jittery Confederates halted less than two miles from the Union lines. Soon the clattering of horses' hooves broke through the night. According to Lieutenant John Pirtle, one of Helm's aides, "we had no information that any of our friends were in our front, and when suddenly there came galloping down on us at full speed what seemed to be a regiment of cavalry, we naturally supposed it was an attack of the enemy." Confederate troops, including mounted partisan rangers led by Lieutenant Colonel Thomas Shields, had engaged Federal pickets before bolting back to the Rebel lines. Mistaking them for Union cavalry, Helm's men opened fire and chaos erupted. Men rode into trees, artillery overturned, and several soldiers fell from friendly fire. Helm rode forward to calm the troops, and a bullet struck his horse. The mount reared and fell, rolling over the general's leg, crushing it. Sadly, First Lieutenant Alexander Todd, Helm's twenty-three-year-old brother-in-law and aide-de-camp, was shot and killed.[24]

Aleck's death was yet another blow to the family. Samuel Todd had fallen four months earlier, and now the youngest Todd sibling had been killed by friendly fire. Helm wrote Emilie, "Aleck was killed at Baton Rouge. I am slightly wounded. Will be up in a few days. Remain where you are until you hear from me again." The news struck Mary Todd Lincoln particularly hard. "Oh little Aleck, why had you to die?" she cried at the news. "Sister Mary's heart is particular sore over the death of Alec," Emilie later wrote. "He was so young, so loving, so impetuous, our dear, red-headed baby brother!" Federal officers also learned about the incident. Union Major General William S. Rosecrans reported, "B. H. Helm was knocked over, confused by their running cavalry; Captain Todd, Mrs. Lincoln's brother, was killed."[25]

Helm's leg was broken, and according to his surgeon, he had a bad "contusion of his right thigh." On August 8, he requested a leave of absence for "being unfit for military duty on account of an injury received from the fall of my horse." He did, however, remain useful to the service. Major General Samuel Jones told Helm that he needed "an officer of your rank and experience to command at Chattanooga." Jones added: "In the present state of your health you are hardly able, I should think, to perform active duty in the field, and would be all the better for a month or so of service at a post such as Chattanooga." According to Confederate General Braxton Bragg, Helm was "not likely to return to field duty for months." Therefore, Helm took command of the vital railroad junction, but after several months, he was reassigned to command of the Eastern District of the Department of the Gulf, headquartered at Pollard, Alabama.[26]

On December 31, 1862, and January 2, 1863, Union and Confederate forces clashed in a major battle near Murfreesboro, Tennessee. Helm's two Kentucky regiments had rejoined other Bluegrass troops to form the 1st Kentucky Brigade, which came to be known as the "Orphan Brigade." At Murfreesboro, the unit was torn apart by massed artillery and their commander, Helm's former legislative colleague Brigadier General Roger Hanson, was mortally wounded. Although twenty-five of the brigade's officers asked for Colonel Thomas H. Hunt to be placed in command, Confederate authorities looked to Helm, who was "relieved from duty in the District of the Gulf" and given the Orphan Brigade. Helm arrived near Manchester, Tennessee, on February 16, 1863, and took command of the 2nd, 4th, 6th, and 9th Kentucky infantry regiments, the 41st Alabama Infantry Regiment, and Captain Robert Cobb's Kentucky battery. Among the brigade's officers were several friends, including his cousin, Martin Hardin Cofer.[27]

Hanson's discipline and the ardor of campaigning had already whipped the brigade into shape. Recognized for their precision on the drill field, Helm continued to stress its training. According to Private John S. Jackman, once Helm took command, "the boys had a good deal of drilling to do." The work paid off. Within a month, Colonel William Preston Johnston reviewed the brigade. "Their performance was rapid," he reported, "yet precise, their appearance tough and active, and they will compare for efficiency with any brigade in the Confederate army." Helm was also a disciplinarian. When one sergeant left his post, the general busted him to private and gave him hard labor for a month. Helm became, however, a beloved leader. As Peter Cozzens wrote: "No brigade in the Army of Tennessee loved its commander more." Private Johnny Green of the 9th Kentucky Infantry remarked that Helm "soon became the Idol of his men."[28]

By mid-April, Helm told Emilie that his division might go to Kentucky. He, however, did "not believe it, [for] it cannot be spared from the army." He was correct. On April 22, they moved on Federals near Manchester and McMinnville. Two days later, they scouted toward Hoover's Gap before going toward Murfreesboro. Occasionally commanding Breckinridge's Division, by late May he was in Wartrace with the brigade, which numbered 2,282 officers and men.[29]

Kentucky would remain far away. On May 24, Breckinridge's Division, including Helm's Brigade, Brigadier General Daniel Adams's Brigade, and Brigadier General Marcellus Stovall's Brigade (formerly William Preston's), was ordered to Jackson, Mississippi. Confederate authorities had asked Bragg to send troops there to relieve besieged Vicksburg, and Bragg sent Breckinridge, his bitter enemy. The Orphan Brigade left Wartrace and traveling through Atlanta and Montgomery to Jackson, arrived near there on May 31. Helm was ordered to press ahead rapidly and limited to "only ordnance stores, cooking utensils, and six tents or flies to every 70 men . . . with the smallest quantity of personal baggage." He rushed to Jackson with his 2,018 officers and men, and by June 5, they guarded roads leading out of town.[30]

Helm was war-weary. On June 20, he wrote Emilie: "I am getting very tired of this climate and that I will soon get away from here but I see no hope of leaving soon especially if Vicksburg should fall." If, he hoped, the "war would only cease, I think I could be perfectly happy with you & the children in any kind of home how humble it might be." He added, "excuse me for giving way to the bitter [utterances], it is not often I permit such feelings to take possession of me." He missed his wife; his leg probably bothered him; and he may have felt guilt about the death of Alexander Todd, the kinsman left in his charge.[31]

Helm had little time for bitter feelings. On July 1, the Confederates moved from Jackson toward Vicksburg. Suffering from sickness and poor water, several men also fell from sunstroke, and straggling mounted along with losses. Helm's Brigade dropped to 1,945 men. On July 4, Breckinridge received the warning that "Vicksburg has fallen, and the enemy is threatening an immediate advance." The Confederates hustled back to Jackson with Helm's Brigade guarding the rear. "The march back to Jackson was very trying owing to the intense heat & lack of water," Green wrote, "but we beat [Grant] there & immediately began entrenching." After some skirmishing, the Federals sent a three-brigade "reconnaissance in force" to test the Southern lines. The Confederates pushed back what Green called "a furious attack," and he added, "the slaughter was dreadful." Helm's troops were relatively unscathed, suffering two killed and eleven wounded. But the Union dead lay unburied for days, and Green commented, "the stench has become terrible."[32]

When the Federals began encircling the city, the Confederates withdrew, with Helm's men again covering the rear. Marching east toward Morton, Mississippi, they camped at "Camp Hurricane," where sickness and sunstroke continued to plague them. Helm's mood continued to darken. "As usual, we are on a grand retreat," he wrote, "the sufferings of which, so far as I am personally concerned, are unparalleled in the war. We have to drink water that, in ordinary times, you wouldn't offer your horse; and I have hardly slept out of a swamp since we left Jackson." Helm added that "I do not think that Grant is making much of a pursuit." The Yankees "are glad enough to get rid of us on any terms."[33]

Illness, not Northerners, dwindled the ranks. By July 15, 1863, Helm's Brigade consisted of 175 officers and 1,752 men. By late August, the unit numbered 122 officers and 1,611 soldiers. The troops were ecstatic when orders arrived to return to Bragg's army, and, by August 31, they were near Chattanooga.[34]

Breckinridge's entire division reached Chattanooga on September 2, but Bragg quickly abandoned the city to strike Rosecrans's army as it moved through several mountain passes to the south. By September 18, after moving from Catlett's Gap, Breckinridge's Division was at Glass Mill, on the east bank of Chickamauga Creek. There, they formed the far left flank of Bragg's line. Federals had reached the area, and Helm sent the 2nd Kentucky Infantry Regiment across the creek to find the Union line, placing the 6th Kentucky Infantry Regiment on a nearby ridge for support. Lieutenant

Colonel James Moss noted that the 2nd Kentucky moved forward "to feel the enemy's position." Soon, they exchanged fire with enemy troops. The spattering musketry continued until dark.[35]

When the sun rose on September 19, Helm had 159 officers and 1,260 men. Breckinridge sent the entire brigade across the creek to reconnoiter the enemy position. Once the infantry crossed, Helm sent Cobb over with a 12-pounder Napoleon and a 12-pounder howitzer. Helm's Kentuckians faced some Unionist Bluegrass troops, including the 15th Kentucky Infantry Regiment. Members of the brigade likely knew some of these enemy Kentuckians, who were recruited from Bullitt and Jefferson Counties.[36]

Helm told Cobb to fire upon "a house in an open field," five hundred yards away, to drive off enemy skirmishers. Union artillery nine hundred yards behind the house responded. The artillery duel intensified, and four more Confederate guns appeared and drove off the Federal artillery. Colonel Joseph Lewis of the 6th Kentucky reported: "About 9 A.M. a shot from [Cobb's] battery into a house about five hundred yards off, where the enemy's skirmishers were concealed, elicited an immediate response from the enemy farther to the right, followed soon after by a spirited artillery duel." The exchange lasted about forty minutes, and Lieutenant General Daniel Harvey Hill remarked that "an examination of the ground subsequently showed that our fire was unusually accurate and fatal. The ground was still strewed with unburied men, and 11 horses lay near the position of the Yankee battery." Union Brigadier General John Beatty simply called it "a sharp artillery fight."[37]

The Federal fire was also accurate and memorable. One Kentuckian wrote: "We had to lay flat down and spread out like Cuban adders on the ground. . . . Shells cut the young trees, and limbs from the larger ones, and they fell promiscuously over and around us. These terrible missiles would also plough the ground and burst in our midst, making sad havoc. Fourteen of our brigade were killed here before we received orders to recross the river." Green remarked that "the enemys [*sic*] shells played great havoc in our ranks. One shell killed one man next on my left & the man on the other side of me." He added that "the men at my elbow on each side of me had both been killed by the same shot." Lieutenant Lot D. Young of Helm's Brigade noted that it was "one of the fiercest artillery duels it was my pleasure to witness during the war," while Private Jackman commented that it was "the wickedest artillery duel . . . I ever saw." Finally, Helm's infantry pushed back several Union regiments. Steady skirmishing continued until mid-afternoon, when Helm's Brigade was called back across the creek, having lost between 14 to 22 men.[38]

That afternoon, Breckinridge's Division began marching northward to close up with the troops on their right. After passing the vicinity of Lee and

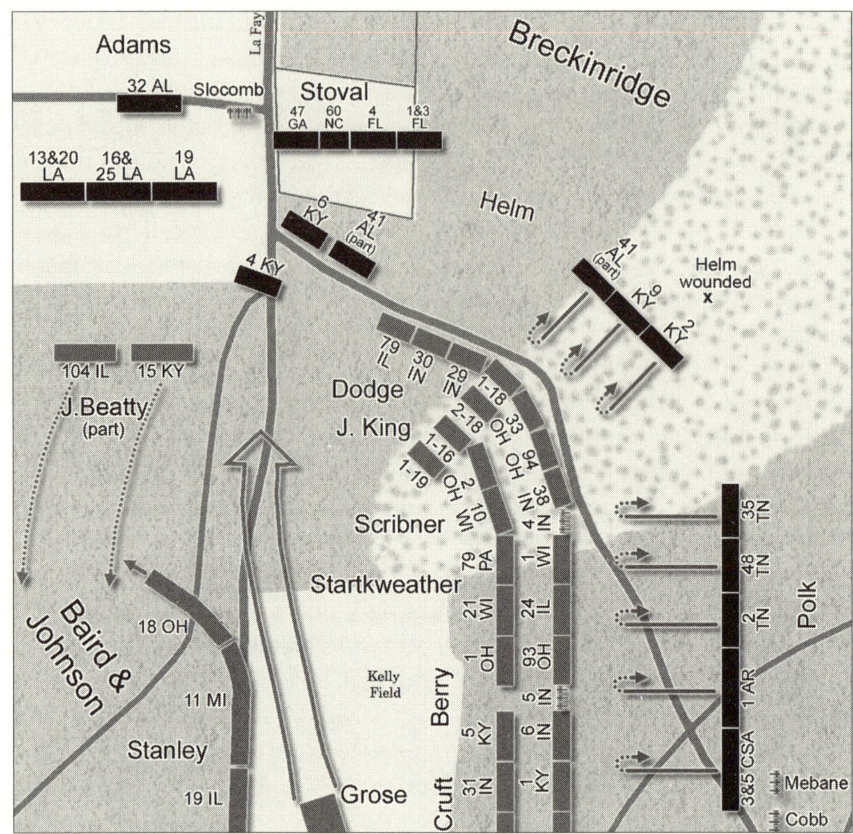

Battle of Chickamauga, September 20, 1863. From *The Maps of Chickamauga* by David Powell and David Friedrichs (New York: Savas Beatie, 2009), 151. Used with permission.

Gordon's Mill, the men were moving behind the line of the entire Confederate army to the far Confederate right flank. Heavy fighting had raged during the day, and that night both sides rearranged their positions. Breckinridge's men crossed the Chickamauga at Alexander's Bridge, and between 9:00 and 10:00 P.M. they camped near Confederate Lieutenant General Leonidas Polk's headquarters. Jackman wrote, "not far from [Alexander's Bridge] we stopped in an old field for the night. We built a large fire, yet not having any blankets with me, I did not sleep any. The night was very cold." Helm's men could hear the cries of the wounded; it was a freezing, restless night.[39]

The Rebels also heard Union troops chopping trees and building breastworks. The Federals strengthened their defenses at a critical bend in their line. In the morning, Helm's men would strike that angle. In fact, Hill noted, Breckinridge had been placed on the far right to outflank the Federals and "turn the log breastworks which the Yankees could be heard working at from the close of the action until after daylight."[40]

Early on the morning of September 20, Polk ordered Breckinridge to move farther to the right to extend the Confederate flank. His division formed to the right of Major General Patrick Cleburne's Division. Helm's Brigade deployed between 3:00 and 4:00 A.M., and immediately before sunrise, moved into a line of battle on the left side of Breckinridge's Division. Stovall's Brigade was to Helm's right, forming the center of Breckinridge's Division, while Adams's Brigade comprised Breckinridge's right. Helm's Brigade now numbered 152 officers and 1,252 men. At 7:00 A.M., Helm sent the 4th Kentucky Infantry forward as skirmishers. The regiment quickly became "hotly engaged," driving a group of Federals from a ridge and severely wounding their commander, Colonel Joseph P. Nuckols.[41]

Neither Breckinridge nor Helm was familiar with the terrain, but, shortly after daylight, the entire brigade was ordered to advance. Bragg had wanted a dawn assault, but the attack was delayed by several hours. Cleburne also worried about the Federals' position. Having heard the Yankees cutting trees, Hill noted to Polk: "General Cleburne reports that the Yankees were felling trees all night, and consequently may occupy a position too strong to be taken by assault." Helm's Brigade would soon learn that Cleburne's fears were well founded.[42]

At 9:15 A.M., Breckinridge told Helm to advance within fifteen minutes, ordering him to stay aligned with Stovall's Brigade. The atmosphere belied the dangers the troops faced. Helm sat casually under a tree. Upon receiving Breckinridge's order, Jackman wrote: "The General got up and mounted his horse, laughing and talking as though he was going on parade." The brigade passed Union and Confederate corpses, Jackman noted, "lying thick over the ground," and "men and horses were lying so thick over the field, one could hardly walk for them." Despite the numerous dead, "the boys were lying in line of battle, and cracking jokes as usual."[43]

Helm and Breckinridge rode down the line, encouraging the men. Helm showed his personal connection with the troops and was seen "moving about quietly and infusing courage into the eager command." At 9:30 A.M., they marched forward with a yell, with Helm at the center of his brigade. Hill later reported that "the corps was in [a] single line without reserves, and if broken at one point was broken at all points." This inherent weakness while moving across rough terrain haunted Helm when Cleburne did not advance.[44]

Helm's infantry regiments were also extended in one long line. From left to right: the 2nd Kentucky, 9th Kentucky, 41st Alabama, 4th Kentucky, and finally, on the right flank, the 6th Kentucky, which included Helm's cousin Cofer. After marching seven hundred yards, Helm's Brigade halted at the edge of a clearing, in front of the Union works. Helm rode near the left wing, while Lewis, the next highest in rank, directed the troops on the right.[45]

Colonel Martin Stansel of the 41st Alabama later wrote that the Federals' two-foot high defenses were "concealed in a thick undergrowth." Lieutenant Colonel John C. Wickliffe of the 9th Kentucky remarked that the enemy position was "composed of fallen timber and rocks." They faced two Union brigades commanded by Colonel Benjamin F. Scribner and Brigadier General John H. King. Scribner noted: "I formed [the brigade] in two lines on the crest of a wooded slope. Between my front and the woods was a clear space, averaging 75 yards. This space was enfiladed by two guns of the Fourth Indiana Battery. Here we built temporary breastworks in front of both lines." When Helm appeared, the Union troops held their fire as the Confederates, two hundred yards away, adjusted their lines. Soon, Breckinridge reported, "the battle was opened by Helm's brigade with great fury."[46]

The Orphans yelled and charged. Lieutenant Young wrote that "three lines in solid phalanx, desperate and determined men, moved forward on the Federal stronghold to be met by a withering and blighting fire from the enemy behind their works." Helm struck the Union line where it bent from north to west. This angle, located near a stream on the Kelly farm, divided Helm's Brigade. The left side of his line, approximately six hundred men—the 2nd and 9th Kentucky, and four companies of the 41st Alabama—struck the earthworks. The right side of Helm's Brigade—the remaining companies of the 41st Alabama, and the 4th and 6th Kentucky—bypassed the works and pushed westward toward the LaFayette Road.[47]

Lieutenant Colonel Moss of the 2nd Kentucky hit "the enemy in a strong position and fortified with three lines of entrenchments." Here, Wickliffe added, they were "met with a murderous fire from the enemy behind their works." His superior, Colonel John Caldwell, was severely wounded in the arm, and Wickliffe took over the regiment. Private William Wallace Herr, who eventually married Emilie's sister Kitty Todd, recalled that the brigade "moved forward at a double quick, under a perfect storm of rifle shot and shell and canister," while Lieutenant George Mattingly noted that "the fire from the artillery and the small arms were something fearful." In their first charge, the left side of Helm's Brigade was shoved back. Colonel Oscar Moore of the 33rd Ohio Infantry Regiment reported that in this "very severe" fighting, "for awhile the result was doubtful, but finally the enemy was repulsed and driven back with great slaughter."[48]

Moss reported that "we charged their works, but receiving a very heavy enfilading fire from both artillery and musketry," fell back. Union Colonel Scribner wrote that the Rebels retreated "in haste and disorder, leaving the ground strewn with their dead and wounded." Although Helm's left was initially pushed back, they rallied and charged again. In the midst of the fighting, Helm raised his sword toward the Union works and yelled: "This is the road to Kentucky." Green recalled that "we were in range of the enemys [*sic*] small arms [and] the artilery [*sic*] was sending a regular hail of shot & shell at us. . . . A perfect shower of grape shot tore through our ranks."[49]

Already at a disadvantage from attacking earthworks, the rough terrain further hindered the Confederates. Green recalled that "the underbrus[h], the timber & formation of the ground prevented our batteries from giving as much assistance as usual." Cobb had tried to maneuver his guns into action, but the thick undergrowth stifled his advance. Furthermore, Cobb reported, his artillerymen were subjected to "a most galling fire" that enfiladed his line. He initially tried to deploy on Helm's left, behind the 2nd Kentucky, but the 4th Indiana Independent Battery struck the cannoneers before they could return fire. Hit hard, Cobb withdrew, and Helm attacked without artillery support.[50]

The fight was particularly confusing for the 41st Alabama. The left side of their line struck the Federal works while their right companies continued to move forward. While they were all "brought under one of the most murderous fusillades of the war," the 41st Alabama met a "galling fire from the front and . . . heavy enfilading fire." Their colonel wrote: "They seemed to waver." Helm saw his line split and told Colonel Stansel to command his four companies on the left while a major directed the remaining companies. Upon reaching the left side of his line, Stansel wrote: "I discovered that these four companies were desperately fighting the enemy in their fortifications, both to the front and on their left, and that many of them had already been killed and wounded."[51]

Although Helm's second assault gained more traction, it also failed. After the first repulse, the 2nd and 9th Kentucky fell back 75 yards, where they reorganized and charged again. Unfortunately, "the thickness of the undergrowth" made it difficult to remain together, and the second attack was piecemeal. Despite their disorganization, the Rebels got within forty yards of the Federal works and drove off the first line of defenders. Struck hard by enfilading fire, they fell back. According to historian Peter Cozzens, "desperate to escape the turbulence, wounded soldiers from the Ninth Kentucky crawled over the Federal breastworks and surrendered."[52]

Another disadvantage for Helm's men—in addition to attacking enemy works without artillery in an overgrown area—was that Cleburne's brigades to their left did not advance. Therefore, the unengaged Union troops on Helm's left fired into his line, creating a deadly crossfire. Herr wrote that the brigade "suffered from a severe enfilading fire as well as a perfect tornado of bullets from the front." Cleburne's early morning orders had been vague, and Cleburne's superior, the "bishop-general" Leonidas Polk, failed to send Cleburne forward at the right time. "On the left of our line the Confederate forces had not come up," Green lamented, "so the enemy to our left poured their fire into us as did those directly in our front." Helm's Brigade fell back a second time. Although the left regiments hoped to end the fruitless assault, Breckinridge's staff officers urged them forward "to relieve the pressure on their comrades" to the right, who were not facing the Union works. So Helm's left wing attacked for a third time.[53]

While Helm's left wing battered against the Federal works, the right side of the line pushed toward the road. Cofer reported that they struck Federals "concealed from view by a dense undergrowth, but [the enemy] readily yielded and fled before a vigorous charge." Moving toward the LaFayette Road, Helm's right wing captured two Union cannon. Near here, they also engaged the 15th Kentucky (U.S.), fought them hand-to-hand, and drove the Unionist Kentuckians back. Lewis soon realized that the left side of the brigade had disappeared. The thick undergrowth had prevented him from seeing Helm's Brigade split, and with no one supporting Lewis's left flank, Helm's right wing also suffered from enfilade fire. Breckinridge eventually pulled Lewis back two hundred yards to join the rest of the brigade before renewing the attack.[54]

While his right flank pressed toward the LaFayette Road, Helm's left struck the works for a third time. Again repulsed by a "terrible fire," the Orphans retreated for the final time. Wickliffe wrote: "Seeing the useless waste of life, I was compelled to order the regiment to fall back." Lewis believed that their "frightful loss show[ed] their constancy and bravery."[55]

Among the dead was Helm himself. Riding near the 2nd Kentucky, Lieutenant John Pirtle recalled that "we were about 150 yards from the enemy, in full view. It was foolhardy to set [*sic*] there on horseback, but Gen. Helm had no fear." Immediately before the third charge, Pirtle wrote, Helm called to him. "He had just said, 'John,' [when] I saw a twitching in his face and pallor. I called 'you are shot!' Before he could reply I dismounted, rushed to his horse, and he fell off into my arms." Helm had been struck in the right side. His staff swarmed around him. "Get an ambulance, quick, for God's sake," Helm told his aides. "Don't let me fall into [enemy] hands!" Pirtle and Herr carried Helm to the rear. Jackman recorded that "Gen'l Helm had received a mortal wound and had to be borne to the hospital on a litter."[56]

Breckinridge, who described Helm as "ever ready for action," was shaken by his subordinate's injury. He sent his son, a lieutenant serving as an aide, to tell Lewis that he now commanded the brigade. Cofer assumed command of Lewis's 6th Kentucky, and Lewis pulled the brigade back and awaited reinforcements. Moss recalled remaining there "under a very heavy fire." Cleburne's Confederates finally entered the fight, and the Orphan Brigade acted as their reserve. Although they were, Wickliffe reported, "suffering beyond endurance," the brigade supported other Confederates as they drove the Federals from the works. The Battle of Chickamauga—despite heavy losses in the Orphan Brigade—ended in Confederate victory.[57]

Helm was taken to a home owned by a widow named Reed, located near Reed's Bridge. Jackman wrote that this "hospital was more than a mile from the field, across the Chicamauga [*sic*]. The wounded, I found, scattered over a half acre of ground." After his clothes were cut off and his wound examined, Helm asked the surgeon, "Is there hope?" The doctor replied, "My dear General, there is no hope!" Helm was placed in a room with several other mortally wounded soldiers. One Kentuckian recalled that "the passage and yard were full of groaning and dying soldiers. Mrs. Reed was passing to and fro, rendering all the assistance in her power, and much distressed over our pitiable condition." Helm reputedly whispered "victory" and spoke no more. He died near midnight.[58]

Although the Battle of Chickamauga was a Confederate victory, Helm's Brigade suffered heavily. Of the approximately 1,400 men engaged, they lost 471 casualties, with 63 killed and 408 wounded. Those fighting against the breastworks suffered the heaviest losses. The 2nd Kentucky entered the fight with 282 men and had 146 casualties. According to Herr, "the Second Kentucky had about twenty-five commissioned officers on the morning of [September 20], and on the evening had only seven or eight fit for duty." The 9th Kentucky had 230 soldiers and 102 casualties. Of the 325 members of the split 41st Alabama, 27 were killed, 120 wounded, and 11 missing, or 158 casualties. In the first hour alone, the Orphans suffered 30 percent casualties, with multiple officers killed or wounded.[59]

Perhaps no one Kentuckian was mourned as widely as Helm. Diarist Kate Cumming learned that he was killed about a week after the battle. "We have many men here who knew General Helm personally," she wrote. "They deeply mourn his death, and say the country has lost one of its bravest—a true patriot and soldier." Kentucky Confederate Edward O. Guerrant simply wrote: "So the wail comes up with the shout of victory."[60]

Helm's corpse was taken to the home of Colonel W. H. Dabney in Atlanta. His remains lay there until September 23, when, after a funeral at St. Paul's Episcopal Church, he was placed in a tin box within a wooden coffin and buried with military honors at Atlanta's Citizens Graveyard. While some sources state that Emilie was in Selma, Alabama, with her sister, a telegram sent to her indicates she was instead in Griffin, Georgia, south of Atlanta. Sent September 22, it simply read: "Mrs. Genl. Helm is in Griffin. find [*sic*] her & send her up in train today the Genl is dead." Emilie reached Atlanta for the funeral. According to her daughter, she arrived "only in time for the last sad rites over her soldier husband."[61]

Condolences poured in. "Your husband commanded [the brigade] like a thorough soldier," Breckinridge wrote. "He loved them, they loved him, and he died at their head, a patriot and hero." Buckner told Emilie that "a sister cannot have a higher claim upon a brother than the wife of Hardin [has] upon me."[62]

The Lincolns also wanted news about Helm's death, and on September 24, the president contacted Rosecrans for information. While Lincoln undoubtedly heard about Helm's demise from several sources, E. M. Bruce wrote Lincoln on behalf of Emilie. He told the president that Helm was dead. "And although opposed, as he was, to your forces," Bruce wrote, "it will no doubt be a satisfaction to you to know that he fell at the head of his Brigade." Emilie was "crushed," he added, and asked Lincoln for a pass allowing her to return to Kentucky. Upon learning of Helm's death, Lincoln notified his wife, who was in New York City. Since the message traveled over relatively public telegraph wires, the president did not display the emotions he wrestled with in private. He simply mentioned Helm's death in a casual manner, halfway through the note. The Lincolns tried to keep their grief private, but several, like Justice David Davis, recorded the family's deep mourning.[63]

Now widowed, Emilie worked to return home. Failing to secure a pass from Grant, her family connections eventually prevailed. Emilie's father-in-law, former Kentucky governor John Helm, contacted Emilie's mother and asked Mrs. Todd to help with Emilie's return. On October 15, Lincoln allowed Mrs. Todd to travel south to retrieve her daughter. When Emilie reached Fort Monroe, however, she refused to take a Union loyalty oath. "I had just left the friends in arms of my husband and brothers, with tears in their eyes and hearts for me in my great bereavement, and they would have felt, if I had taken the oath, that I had deserted them and had not been true to the cause for which my husband had given up his life. My refusal was therefore not bravado." When Lincoln learned of her refusal to take the oath, he told the officers: "Send her to me."[64]

Emilie went to the White House, where Mary was heartbroken about the death of her son Willie, who died on February 12, 1862. Emilie later wrote that "we could only embrace each other in silence and tears." The deaths of multiple family members, including Hardin, Willie, Samuel, and Aleck overshadowed the visit. "Mr. Lincoln put his arms around me and we both wept," Emilie wrote. Mary "is doing everything to distract my mind and her own from our terrible grief," she later wrote, "but at times it overwhelms us; we can't get away from it, try as we will to be cheerful and accept fate."[65]

The visit naturally stirred controversy. Northern papers excoriated the Lincolns for hosting the Rebel widow, and Emilie also tangled with Union officials. Once, after a heated argument with her, Union Major General Daniel Sickles stormed up to Lincoln and spat: "You should not have that rebel in your house." "General Sickles, my wife and I are in the habit of choosing our own guests," Lincoln retorted. "We do not need from our friends either advice or assistance in the matter." Later, Lincoln's "eyes twinkled" as he said, "the child has a tongue like the rest of the Todds."[66]

Emilie planned to return to Kentucky and told Lincoln she "did not intend to embarrass him or make myself conspicuous in any way." Lincoln gave her a pass: "I have known you all your life, and I never knew you to do a mean thing." The pass protected her person and property, except slaves "of which I say nothing." Before she left, she and Lincoln hugged and cried, the weight of family divisions heavy on them.[67]

In October 1864, Emilie asked Lincoln for a pass to ship cotton from the South. "I have been a quiet citizen and request only the right which humanity and Justice always give to Widows and Orphans," she told Lincoln. "I also remind you that your *Minnie bullets* have made us what we are & I feel I have that additional claim upon you." The notion that Lincoln made Emilie a widow and, presumably, that Lincoln's guns caused the deaths of their Confederate brothers, ended the relationship between Emilie and Mary. The two never saw each other again.[68]

After the war, Emilie served as postmistress of Elizabethtown and was active in veterans' affairs. She eventually bought a home where her grandfather, Levi Todd, had established the pioneer settlement Todd's Station, near Lexington. Known as Helm Place, Emilie lived there until she died at age 93 on February 30, 1930. She is buried in the Lexington, Kentucky, cemetery.[69]

Helm was also eventually buried in the Bluegrass. On September 17, 1884, Helm's brother, John, his nephew, Helm Bruce, and his brother-in-law, Thomas G. Hayes, went to Atlanta to exhume Helm's remains. He had been buried for twenty-one years. According to the *New York Times,* roots from an oak tree had broken the coffin, which had rotted away. "Little was left of the body which was laid away so long ago. The skull was perfect, but the spine was gone, and there were no ribs. A few bones of the arms, legs and thighs were partially preserved. In the dust were found brass buttons from the General's uniform." Helm's remains were placed in a casket, and after a brief service, the casket went by train to Elizabethtown.[70]

Two days later, during an Orphan Brigade reunion, Helm was reinterred in the Helm family cemetery in Elizabethtown. Colonel Lewis, who succeeded Helm as commander of the brigade, marched the veterans to Emilie's home, where they received the casket and went to the cemetery in a long procession including civilians and Union and Confederate veterans. Several prominent Kentuckians, including Governor Proctor Knott, Buckner, and Lewis, spoke. More than 250 veterans and a crowd of thousands attended. As the band played "Home Sweet Home," Helm's casket was buried on family land. The beloved leader of the Orphans was finally home.[71]

Notes

1. Davis, who later became a U.S. senator from Illinois, is quoted in multiple sources, including William H. Townsend, *Lincoln and His Wife's Home Town* (Indianapolis, 1929), 336.

2. Lot D. Young of the Kentucky "Orphan Brigade" called Helm "one of the kindest-hearted and best men I ever knew." Young, *Reminiscences of a Soldier of the Orphan Brigade* (n.p., n.d.), 69. One postwar biographer commented that Helm "was an officer of rare ability and great promise," but "he perished at too early an age to fulfill the high expectations that had been formed for him . . . he fell while the laurels were still green upon his brow." "Sketch of General B. H. Helm," *The Land We Love* 3 (June 1867): 163. Historian Charles Elliott maintains that "assessing [Helm's] career remains problematic. His combat experiences . . . were rather minimal and show no particular military brilliance, but he commanded and fought well when he could." Elliott, "Brig. Gen. Benjamin Hardin Helm," in *Kentuckians in Gray: Confederate Generals and Field Officers of the Bluegrass State*, ed. Bruce S. Allardice and Lawrence Lee Hewitt (Lexington, KY, 2008), 143.

3. J. Winston Coleman Jr., *Historic Kentucky* (Lexington, KY, 1967), 16; *The Biographical Encyclopaedia of Kentucky of the Dead and Living Men of the Nineteenth Century* (Cincinnati, 1878), 438; Ed Porter Thompson, *History of the Orphan Brigade* (1868; repr., Dayton, OH, 1973), 380; "Circular Request for Information from U.S. Military Academy for Graduates Register," Emilie Todd Helm Papers, Box 1, Folder 1, Kentucky Historical Society Library, Frankfort (hereafter cited as Helm Papers, KHS); R. Gerald McMurtry, *Ben Hardin Helm* (Chicago, 1943), 2; John E. Kleber, ed., *The Kentucky Encyclopedia* (Lexington, KY, 1992), 403, 421; Elliott, "Benjamin Hardin Helm," 140; Maureen Helm Green, "Emilie," *Kentucky Ancestors* 44 (Autumn 2008): 4.

4. "Sketch of Helm," 163, 167; McMurtry, *Ben Hardin Helm*, 5–7; Thompson, *Orphan Brigade*, 380–81, 387; Kleber, *Kentucky Encyclopedia*, 421; William C. Davis, *The Orphan Brigade: The Kentucky Confederates Who Couldn't Go Home* (Garden City, NY, 1980), 34; "Circular Request," Helm Papers, KHS; Katherine Helm, *The True Story of Mary, Wife of Lincoln*, 3rd ed. (1938; Rutland, VT, 2001), 184; Elliott, "Benjamin Hardin Helm," 140; Patricia L. Faust, ed., *Historical Times Illustrated Encyclopedia of the Civil War* (New York, 1986), 356; Mark M. Boatner III, *The Civil War Dictionary*, rev. ed. (1959; New York, 1988), 393; Ezra J. Warner, *Generals in Gray: Lives of the Confederate Commanders* (Baton Rouge, LA, 1959), 132; Clement A. Evans, ed., *Confederate Military History*, 12 vols. (Atlanta, 1899), 9:242; Peter Cozzens, *This Terrible Sound: The Battle of Chickamauga* (1992; repr., Urbana, IL, 1996), 319; Stephen Berry, *House of Abraham: Lincoln and the Todds, A Family Divided By War* (New York, 2007), 49; Special Orders No. 135, Sept. 6, 1852, Box 1, Folder 1, Helm Papers, KHS.

5. *Biographical Encyclopaedia of Kentucky*, 438; McMurtry, *Ben Hardin Helm*, 8; Thompson, *Orphan Brigade*, 381; Kleber, *Kentucky Encyclopedia*, 421; "My Dear Lucinda," Oct. 25, 1855, Box 1, Folder 1, Helm Papers, KHS; Elliott, "Benjamin Hardin Helm," 140; Berry, *House of Abraham*, 49; Davis, *Orphan Brigade*, 34; "Circular Request," Helm Papers, KHS. For Cofer, see Thompson, *Orphan Brigade*, 423–28.

6. "Circular Request," Helm Papers, KHS; McMurtry, *Ben Hardin Helm*, 3, 10; Thompson, *Orphan Brigade*, 381; *Journal of the House of Representatives of the Commonwealth of Kentucky [1855–1856]* (Frankfort, 1856), 3, 4, 32, 43, 62, 77, 88, 94, 214, 292–93, 459; *Biographical Encyclopaedia of Kentucky*, 56, 438; Kleber, *Kentucky Encyclopedia*, 421; Lewis Collins, *History of Kentucky*, 2 vols. (Covington, KY, 1874), 2:307; Warner, *Generals in Gray*, 132; Jon L. Wakelyn, *Biographical Dictionary of the Confederacy* (Westport, CT, 1977), 225; Elliott, "Benjamin Hardin Helm," 140; Evans, *Confederate Military History*, 9:242; "Judge Horatio Washington Bruce," *Confederate Veteran* 11 (Feb. 1903): 79–80. For Judge H. W. Bruce, see H. Levin, comp., *The Lawyers and Lawmakers of Kentucky* (Chicago, 1897), 191–93, and *The Biographical Cyclopedia of the Commonwealth of Kentucky* (Chicago, 1896), 395.

7. Berry, *House of Abraham*, 48, 50; Green, "Emilie," 4–5; Helm, *Mary, Wife of Lincoln*, 120; Warner, *Generals in Gray*, 132; Coleman, *Historic Kentucky*, 195; McMurtry, *Ben Hardin Helm*, 11, 68; Lowell H. Harrison, *Lincoln of Kentucky* (Lexington, KY, 2000), 218; Elliott, "Benjamin Hardin Helm," 140; Evans, *Confederate Military History*, 9:242; "Mr. Lincoln and Ben Hardin Helm," *Confederate Veteran* 4, no. 3 (Mar. 1896): 72. Their three children were Katherine (born September 2, 1857), Elodie (born March 7, 1859), and Ben Hardin Helm Jr. (born May 16, 1862). Green, "Emilie," 6.

8. Helm to "My Dear Wife," June 18, 25, 1856; Helm to "My Dear Emma," June 20, July 4, 1856. These letters are in Box 1, Folder 1, Helm Papers, KHS.

9. "Circular Request," Helm Papers, KHS; McMurtry, *Ben Hardin Helm*, 1–2, 10, 12–14; Kleber, *Kentucky Encyclopedia*, 421; Warner, *Generals in Gray*, 132; *Biographical Encyclopaedia of Kentucky*, 438; Thompson, *Orphan Brigade*, 381; Helm, *Mary, Wife of Lincoln*, 127; Doris Kearns Goodwin, *Team of Rivals: The Political Genius of Abraham Lincoln* (New York, 2005), 350; Green, "Emilie," 6; Davis, *Orphan Brigade*, 34; Elliott, "Benjamin Hardin Helm," 141. The quote is from Harrison, *Lincoln of Kentucky*, 218.

10. McMurtry, *Ben Hardin Helm*, 9, 13, 15; "Circular Request," Helm Papers, KHS; Thompson, *Orphan Brigade*, 381, 382; Kleber, *Kentucky Encyclopedia*, 421; *Biographical Encyclopaedia of Kentucky*, 438; "Judge Horatio Washington Bruce," 79-80; "Sketch of Helm," *Land We Love*, 164; Magoffin [State Guard] Proclamation, Mar. 27, 1860, Box 1, Folder 1, Helm Papers, KHS; Helm, *Mary, Wife of Lincoln*, 128; Lowell H. Harrison, *The Civil War in Kentucky* (Lexington, KY, 1975), 5.

11. Harrison, *Lincoln of Kentucky*, 218; Cozzens, *This Terrible Sound*, 320. All quotes are from Helm, *Mary, Wife of Lincoln*, 184, 186, 187.

12. Helm, *Mary, Wife of Lincoln*, 186, 188.

13. Ibid., 185; William H. Townsend, *Lincoln and the Bluegrass: Slavery and Civil War in Kentucky* (Lexington, KY, 1955), 275; Glenn Tucker, *Chickamauga: Bloody Battle in the West* (1961; repr., Dayton, OH, 1992), 241; Townsend, *Lincoln and His Wife's Home Town*, 307; Berry, *House of Abraham*, 70. See also McMurtry, *Ben Hardin Helm*, 20.

14. McMurtry, *Ben Hardin Helm*, 22, 25–26; Berry, *House of Abraham*, 70–71, 52 (number of slaves); Tucker, *Chickamauga*, 241; Richard N. Current, ed., *Encyclopedia of the Confederacy*, 4 vols. (New York, 1993), 2:761; Helm, *Mary, Wife of Lincoln*, 128, 186–87; Goodwin, *Team of Rivals*, 351; Emilie Helm quoted in Green, "Emilie," 10; U.S. War Department, *The War of the Rebellion: A Compilation of the Official Records of the Union and Confederate Armies*, 128 vols. (Washington, DC, 1880–1901), ser. 1, vol. 4:415, 419 (hereafter cited as *OR*; all references are to series 1 unless otherwise indicated).

15. S. H. Buck, "First Kentucky Confederate Cavalry," *Confederate Veteran* 21, no. 9 (Sept. 1913): 449; Evans, *Confederate Military History*, 9:242; Warner, *Generals in Gray*, 132; Thompson, *Orphan Brigade*, 876.

16. Thompson, *Orphan Brigade*, 876; McMurtry, *Ben Hardin Helm*, 27; Davis, *Orphan Brigade*, 34; Helm to "My Dear Wife," Oct. 10, 1861, Box 1, Folder 2, Helm Papers, KHS. Helm's date of commission is noted in Davis, *Orphan Brigade*, 35; Evans, *Confederate Military History*, 9:243; Faust, *Historical Times Illustrated Encyclopedia*, 357; Boatner, *Civil War Dictionary*, 393; Warner, *Generals in Gray*, 132. He received his appointment in January 1862. War Department Order, Jan. 14, 1862, Box 1, Folder 2, Helm Papers, KHS.

17. Evans, *Confederate Military History*, 9:47; Thomas L. Connelly, *Army of the Heartland: The Army of Tennessee, 1861–1862* (Baton Rouge, LA, 1967), 66–67; *OR*, vol. 7:793.

18. *OR*, vol. 7:830–31, 838; Thompson, *Orphan Brigade*, 383, 881, 882; McMurtry, *Ben Hardin Helm*, 28; W. D. Rickett to Ben Hardin Helm, Feb. 11, 1862, Box 1, Folder 2, Helm Papers, KHS; Larry J. Daniel, *Shiloh: The Battle that Changed the Civil War* (New York, 1997), 90; *OR*, vol. 10, pt. 2:309, 338, 378.

19. Faust, *Historical Times Illustrated Encyclopedia*, 357; Daniel, *Shiloh*, 250; James Lee McDonough, *Shiloh: In Hell Before Night* (Knoxville, TN, 1977), 182, 192; Connelly, *Army of the Heartland*, 172; Elliott, "Benjamin Hardin Helm," 141; David H. Todd to his sister, Emilie Todd Helm, n.d., telling the death of their brother, Samuel Todd, Box 1, Folder 2, Helm Papers, KHS.

20. *OR*, vol. 52, pt. 2:302; Helm to "My Dear Wife," Apr. 20, 1862, Box 1, Folder 2, Helm Papers, KHS.

21. Helm to "My Dear Wife," Apr. 20, 1862, Box 1, Folder 2, Helm Papers, KHS; *OR*, vol. 10:642; McMurtry, *Ben Hardin Helm*, 30; Thompson, *Orphan Brigade*, 384, 883; Boatner, *Civil War Dictionary*, 393; Faust, *Historical Times Illustrated Encyclopedia*, 357; Kleber, *Kentucky Encyclopedia*, 421; Warner, *Generals in Gray*, 132. For Alexander Todd's order appointing him Helm's aide-de-camp, see War Department Order, May 26, 1862, Box 1, Folder 2, Helm Papers, KHS.

22. *OR*, vol. 10, pt. 2:550; Jack D. Welsh, *Medical Histories of Confederate Generals* (Kent, OH, 1995), 98; Davis, *Orphan Brigade*, 105, 112; John B. Pirtle, "The Defense of Vicksburg in 1862 and the Battle of Baton Rouge," *Confederate Veteran* 32, no. 7 (July 1924): 264; Evans, *Confederate Military History*, 9:243; Henry George, *History of the 3d, 7th, 8th, and 12th Kentucky, C.S.A.* (n.p., 1911), 34; Thompson, *Orphan Brigade*, 384; McMurtry, *Ben Hardin Helm*, 31; *OR*, vol. 15:1121; William C. Davis, *Breckinridge: Statesman, Soldier, Symbol* (Baton Rouge, LA, 1974), 318; Berry, *House of Abraham*, 124; John C. Breckinridge to Ben Hardin Helm, July 24, 1862, Box 1, Folder 2, Helm Papers, KHS.

23. Pirtle, "Defense of Vicksburg," 265; Davis, *Orphan Brigade*, 114–16; *OR*, vol. 15:39, 77; McMurtry, *Ben Hardin Helm*, 32; Gervis D. Grainger, *Four Years with the Boys in Gray* (Franklin, KY, 1909), 9. Breckinridge is quoted in Pirtle, "Defense of Vicksburg," 265 and Davis, *Orphan Brigade*, 115.

24. Pirtle, "Defense of Vicksburg," 265; Davis, *Orphan Brigade*, 116–17; Alcée Fortier, *A History of Louisiana*, 4 vols. (New York, 1904), 4:27–28; Davis, *Breckinridge*, 320; Elliott, "Benjamin Hardin Helm," 142; *OR*, vol. 15:77; John W. Green, *Johnny Green of the Orphan Brigade: The Journal of a Confederate Soldier*, ed. A. D. Kirwan (Lexington, KY, 1956), 46; Evans, *Confederate Military History*, 9:76; Thompson, *Orphan Brigade*, 124.

25. Helm to Emilie, Aug. 8, 1862, Box 1, Folder 2, Helm Papers, KHS. Mary Todd Lincoln quoted in Jean H. Baker, *Mary Todd Lincoln: A Biography* (New York, 1987), 223. Emilie Helm's comment is from Helm, *Mary, Wife of Lincoln*, 224. Rosecrans's report is from *OR*, vol. 17, pt. 2:181. For the Todd family's overall reaction to Alexander's death, see Berry, *House of Abraham*, 127–28. Alexander had attended Lincoln's inauguration, invited there by Abraham and Mary Lincoln. Green, "Emilie," 5.

26. Helm's request for leave of absence, Aug. 8, 1862, Box 1, Folder 2, Helm Papers, KHS; Samuel Jones to Helm, Oct. 15, 1862, Box 1, Folder 2, Helm Papers, KHS; Bragg to Samuel Cooper, *OR*, vol. 20, pt. 2:417. Helm's assignment to Chattanooga is noted in *OR*, vol. 20, pt. 2:508; Thompson, *Orphan Brigade*, 384; Welsh, *Medical Histories*, 98; Davis, *Orphan Brigade*, 163, 166; McMurtry, *Ben Hardin Helm*, 34, 35. Helm's assignment to Pollard, Alabama, is noted in "Sketch of Helm," 165.

27. Davis, *Orphan Brigade*, 161; *OR*, vol. 23, pt. 2:620, 622, 636; McMurtry, *Ben Hardin Helm*, 35, 36; Thompson, *Orphan Brigade*, 384; Berry, *House of*

Abraham, 132; David A. Powell, *The Chickamauga Campaign, Glory or the Grave: The Breakthrough, the Union Collapse, and the Defense of Horseshoe Ridge, September 20, 1863* (El Dorado Hills, CA, 2015), 88.

28. McMurtry, *Ben Hardin Helm,* 38; John S. Jackman, *Diary of a Confederate Soldier: John S. Jackman of the Orphan Brigade,* ed. William C. Davis (Columbia, SC, 1990), 72; *OR,* vol. 23, pt. 2:757; Davis, *Orphan Brigade,* 167; Cozzens, *This Terrible Sound,* 319; Green, *Johnny Green,* 72.

29. Helm to "My Dear Wife," Apr. 12, 1863, Helm Papers, KHS; *OR,* vol. 23, pt. 2:779, 780, 783, 787, 788, 790, 797, 846, 849; Jackman, *Diary of a Confederate Soldier,* 73; Evans, *Confederate Military History,* 9:243.

30. Davis, *Breckinridge,* 364, 365; Davis, *Orphan Brigade,* 172, 173; Green, *Johnny Green,* 78; *OR,* vol. 23, pt. 2:853; McMurtry, *Ben Hardin Helm,* 39, 40; *OR,* vol. 24, pt. 3:944, 945, 950.

31. Helm to "My Dear Wife," June 20, 1863, Box 1, Folder 2, Helm Papers, KHS.

32. McMurtry, *Ben Hardin Helm,* 40; Green, *Johnny Green,* 79, 80, 81–82; Davis, *Orphan Brigade,* 174, 175; *OR,* vol. 24, pt. 3:988, 992, 994, and pt. 2:654; Davis, *Breckinridge,* 366, 367; "Sketch of Helm," 166.

33. McMurtry, *Helm,* 41; Davis, *Breckinridge,* 367; "Sketch," *Land We Love,* 166; Davis, *Orphan Brigade,* 176, 177; Helm to "My Dear Wife," July 22, 1863, Box 1, Folder 2, Helm Papers, KHS; Green, *Johnny Green,* 84.

34. *OR,* vol. 24, pt. 3:1006, and vol. 30, pt. 4:557; Green, *Johnny Green,* 85.

35. Davis, *Breckinridge,* 368, 369; Boatner, *Civil War Dictionary,* 150; Davis, *Orphan Brigade,* 180; *OR,* vol. 30, pt. 2:197, 203, 207, 208, 214.

36. *OR,* vol. 30, pt. 2:202, 215; Davis, *Breckinridge,* 369; Davis, *Orphan Brigade,* 180; Cozzens, *This Terrible Sound,* 170; Kirk C. Jenkins, *The Battle Rages Higher: The Union's Fifteenth Kentucky Infantry* (Lexington, KY, 2003), 164.

37. *OR,* vol. 20, pt. 2:140, 198, 205, 211, 215; John Beatty, *The Citizen-Soldier: The Memoirs of a Civil War Volunteer* (1879; repr., Lincoln, NE, 1998), 332.

38. Fred Joyce, "Orphan Brigade at Chickamauga," *Southern Bivouac* 3, no. 1 (Sept. 1884): 30; Green, *Johnny Green,* 92, 93; Young, *Reminiscences,* 61–62; Jackman, *Diary of a Confederate Soldier,* 87; Daniel Harvey Hill, "Chickamauga—The Great Battle of the West," in *Battles and Leaders of the Civil War: Being for the Most Part Contributions by Union and Confederate Officers Based upon "The Century War Series,"* ed. Robert Underwood Johnson and Clarence Clough Buel, 4 vols. (1884—88; repr., New York, 1956), 3:650; *OR,* vol. 30, pt. 2:208; Jenkins, *Battle Rages Higher,* 168–69. Conflicting casualties are noted in *OR,* vol. 30, pt. 2:203 (fourteen casualties) and *OR,* vol. 30, pt. 2:198 (twenty-two casualties).

39. *OR,* vol. 30, pt. 2:198, 207, 210, 211, 215; Young, *Reminiscences,* 62; McMurtry, *Ben Hardin Helm,* 43; Davis, *Orphan Brigade,* 181; Joyce, "Orphan Brigade at Chickamauga," 30; Jackman, *Diary of a Confederate Soldier,* 87; Green, *Johnny*

Green, 93; Davis, *Breckinridge*, 360–70; George R. Mattingly, "Reminiscences of the Nelson Grays," transcript, Kentucky Historical Society Library, Frankfort, 14.

40. *OR*, vol. 30, pt. 2:141.

41. Ibid., 198, 202, 203, 207, 210, 211; Jackman, *Diary of a Confederate Soldier*, 87; Davis, *Breckinridge*, 371; Cozzens, *This Terrible Sound*, 320; Tucker, *Chickamauga*, 233; McMurtry, *Ben Hardin Helm*, 43; Evans, *Confederate Military History*, 9:176, 177; Joyce, "Orphan Brigade at Chickamauga," 31.

42. *OR*, vol. 30, pt. 2:198; Davis, *Breckinridge*, 373; Hill quoted in Craig L. Symonds, *Stonewall of the West: Patrick Cleburne and the Civil War* (Lawrence, KS, 1997), 147.

43. Cozzens, *This Terrible Sound*, 320; Jackman, *Diary of a Confederate Soldier*, 88. Jackman is also quoted in Davis, *Orphan Brigade*, 182.

44. Davis, *Orphan Brigade*, 181, 182; Joyce, "Orphan Brigade at Chickamauga," 31; *OR*, vol. 30, pt. 2:141–42, 198, 203; Hill, "Chickamauga," 3:655; McMurtry, *Ben Hardin Helm*, 43; Green, *Johnny Green*, 94; Cozzens, *This Terrible Sound*, 320.

45. Cozzens, *This Terrible Sound*, 320; Davis, *Orphan Brigade*, 182; *OR*, vol. 30, pt. 2:211, 287; Tucker, *Chickamauga*, 238.

46. Evans, *Confederate Military History*, 9:176; *OR*, vol. 30, pt. 2:199, 207, 213, and pt. 1:287, 310; Cozzens, *This Terrible Sound*, 320. The Union position was also described by Colonel Oscar Moore, 33rd Ohio Infantry Regiment, in *OR*, vol. 30, pt. 1:295.

47. Davis, *Orphan Brigade*, 183, 185; Cozzens, *This Terrible Sound*, 320, 321; Young, *Reminiscences*, 64; Tucker, *Chickamauga*, 238; Joyce, "Orphan Brigade at Chickamauga," 32; Davis, *Breckinridge*, 375; *OR*, vol. 30, pt. 2:199.

48. *OR*, vol. 30, pt. 2:208, 213; W. W. Herr, "Kentuckians at Chickamauga," *Confederate Veteran* 3, no. 10 (Oct. 1895): 295; Mattingly, "Reminiscences of the Nelson Grays," 14; *OR*, vol. 30, pt. 1:295. The Herr-Todd marriage is noted in Berry, *House of Abraham*, 146.

49. *OR*, vol. 30, pt. 2:208–9; *OR*, vol. 30, pt. 1:287. Helm is quoted in Elliott, "Benjamin Hardin Helm," 138; Green, *Johnny Green*, 94.

50. Green, *Johnny Green*, 94, 96; *OR*, vol. 30, pt. 2:215, 216; Cozzens, *This Terrible Sound*, 320.

51. *OR*, vol. 30, pt. 2:207; Herr, "Kentuckians at Chickamauga," 295.

52. *OR*, vol. 30, pt. 2:209, 213; Cozzens, *This Terrible Sound*, 321.

53. *OR*, vol. 30, pt. 2:199, 204, 213, 215; Herr, "Kentuckians at Chickamauga," 295; Davis, *Breckinridge*, 374; Symonds, *Stonewall of the West*, 147, 148; Davis, *Orphan Brigade*, 181; Tucker, *Chickamauga*, 239, 243; McMurtry, *Ben Hardin Helm*, 44; Green, *Johnny Green*, 95; Cozzens, *This Terrible Sound*, 321, 339.

54. *OR*, vol. 30, pt. 2:199, 203, 204, 211, 212, and pt. 1:204; Herr, "Kentuckians at Chickamauga," 295; Davis, *Orphan Brigade*, 183; Davis, *Breckinridge*, 373–74; Joyce, "Orphan Brigade at Chickamauga," 32; Tucker, *Chickamauga*, 239; Elliott, "Benjamin Hardin Helm," 138; Cozzens, *This Terrible Sound*, 324; Jenkins, *Battle Rages Higher*, 175, 178.

55. *OR*, vol. 30, pt. 2:204, 209, 214, and pt. 1:287, 291. The three failed charges are noted in Davis, *Breckinridge*, 374; Cozzens, *This Terrible Sound*, 321; Jackman, *Diary of a Confederate Soldier*, 88; Davis, *Orphan Brigade*, 185.

56. Elliott, "Benjamin Hardin Helm," 138; Davis, *Orphan Brigade*, 186; Cozzens, *This Terrible Sound*, 321; "Pirtle's Graphic Recital of the Particulars of Gen. Helm's Death," unidentified newspaper clipping, Box 10, Ben Hardin Helm Clippings File, Helm Papers, KHS. Jackman, *Diary of a Confederate Soldier*, 88; Powell, *The Chickamauga Campaign*, 100.

57. *OR*, vol. 30, pt. 2:142, 201, 203, 204, 205, 206, 209, 210, 213, 214, and pt. 4:173, 727; Cozzens, *This Terrible Sound*, 323; Davis, *Orphan Brigade*, 187; Davis, *Breckinridge*, 374; Hill, "Chickamauga," 3:655. Lewis was formally assigned to command the Orphan Brigade on October 4, 1863.

58. Welsh, *Medical Histories*, 98; Davis, *Orphan Brigade*, 186; Jackman, *Diary of a Confederate Soldier*, 89; Fred Joyce, "The Mother and Two Sons," *Southern Bivouac* 2, no. 7 (Mar. 1884): 314; Joyce, "Orphan Brigade at Chickamauga," 32. Helm and his doctor are quoted in Davis, *Orphan Brigade*, 191; Helm saying "victory" and dying at midnight is taken from Thompson, *Orphan Brigade*, 385.

59. Tucker, *Chickamauga*, 242; *OR*, vol. 30, pt. 2:199, 205, 208, 209, 214; Davis, *Orphan Brigade*, 190–91; Herr, "Kentuckians at Chickamauga," 295; Cozzens, *This Terrible Sound*, 325; Davis, *Breckinridge*, 374; Green, *Johnny Green*, 96.

60. Kate Cumming, *A Journal of Hospital Life in the Confederate Army of Tennessee, From the Battle of Shiloh to the End of the War* (Louisville, KY, n. d.), 94; Edward O. Guerrant, *Bluegrass Confederate: The Headquarters Diary of Edward O. Guerrant*, ed. William C. Davis and Meredith L. Swentor (Baton Rouge, LA, 1999), 331.

61. McMurtry, *Ben Hardin Helm*, 46, 51; Thompson, *Orphan Brigade*, 385; Collins, *History of Kentucky*, 1:246–47; *New York Times*, Sept. 15 and 18, 1884; Green, "Emilie," 8, 9; Elliott, "Benjamin Hardin Helm," 143; Kleber, *Kentucky Encyclopedia*, 421; Warner, *Generals in Gray*, 133; Telegram, Sept. 22, 1863, Box 1, Folder 2, Helm Papers, KHS; Helm, *Mary, Wife of Lincoln*, 220.

62. Breckinridge quoted in Thompson, *Orphan Brigade*, 386; Davis, *Orphan Brigade*, 191; Buckner to "My Dear Mrs. Helm," Nov. 21, 1863, Box 1, Folder 2, Helm Papers, KHS. The same box and folder contain condolence letters to Emilie Helm.

63. McMurtry, *Ben Hardin Helm*, 49, 50; E. M. Bruce to Lincoln, Oct. 6, 1863, Series 1, General Correspondence, 1833–1916, Abraham Lincoln Papers, Library of Congress, Washington, DC; *OR*, vol. 30, pt. 2:811; Baker, *Mary Todd Lincoln*, 223; Tucker, *Chickamauga*, 240; Helm, *Mary, Wife of Lincoln*, 216.

64. Goodwin, *Team of Rivals*, 590, 591; Helm, *Mary, Wife of Lincoln*, 219, 220–21; McMurtry, *Ben Hardin Helm*, 50, 51, 52, 54; Townsend, *Lincoln and His Wife's Home Town*, 336; Emilie Todd Helm, "President Lincoln and the Widow of General Helm," *Century Magazine* 52, no. 2 (June 1896): 318; Townsend, *Lincoln and the Bluegrass*, 313; Baker, *Mary Todd Lincoln*, 223.

65. Helm, "Lincoln and the Widow," 318; Harrison, *Lincoln of Kentucky*, 218. The quotes "we could only embrace" and "Mr. Lincoln put his arms around me" are from Green, "Emilie," 10, and the quote about Mary "doing everything to distract my mind" is from Helm, *Mary, Wife of Lincoln*, 223.

66. Sickles conversation quoted in David Herbert Donald, *Lincoln* (London, 1995), 475; Harrison, *Lincoln of Kentucky*, 219; Goodwin, *Team of Rivals*, 593; Helm, *Mary, Wife of Lincoln*, 231. Also see McMurtry, *Ben Hardin Helm*, 58–59.

67. Helm, "Lincoln and the Widow," 318; Helm, *Mary, Wife of Lincoln*, 232, 233; Lincoln's Pass for Emilie Todd Helm, Dec. 14, 1863, Lincoln Papers.

68. Emilie Todd Helm to Lincoln, Oct. 30, 1864, Lincoln Papers.

69. *New York Times*, Apr. 9, 1895; "Miscellany," *Southern Bivouac* 1, no. 7 (Mar. 1883): 314; McMurtry, *Ben Hardin Helm*, 70. Obituaries for Emilie Todd Helm can be found in the Benjamin Hardin Helm Biographical File, Kentucky Historical Society Library, Frankfort.

70. *New York Times*, Sept. 15 and 18, 1884.

71. Thompson, *Orphan Brigade*, 387; McMurtry, *Ben Hardin Helm*, 71; "Third Reunion of the Kentucky Brigade," *Southern Bivouac* 3, no. 3 (Nov. 1884): 116, 117; "General Ben Hardin Helm: His Reinterrment by the Orphan Brigade," unidentified newspaper clipping, Box 10, Ben Hardin Helm Clippings File, Helm Papers, KHS; Green, "Emilie," 12–13; Davis, *Orphan Brigade*, 267; Elliott, "Benjamin Hardin Helm," 143.

Major General Bushrod Rust Johnson. Library of Congress.

From Hoover's Gap to Chickamauga: Bushrod Rust Johnson's Best Three Months of the War

Michael R. Bradley

FIRING WAS BRISK AS BRIGADIER GENERAL BUSHROD RUST JOHNSON STOOD ON THE military crest of a hill watching skirmishers from one of his regiments engage the Union force stationed in the mouth of Hoover's Gap. One hundred Confederate soldiers from the 44th Tennessee Infantry Regiment had been sent forward to engage the enemy, men chosen because they were all armed with Enfield rifles. In June 1863, one of the problems still facing Johnson, and the rest of the Army of Tennessee, was a lack of modern weapons. Many of the men in Johnson's command still carried smooth-bore muskets. A messenger from the skirmishers made his way to the colonel commanding the regiment who rode over to Johnson's position. The men on the firing line were running out of ammunition, he reported, so Johnson sent a staff officer to the commander of the 23rd Tennessee Infantry Regiment to send out a relief party to take over the duties on the skirmish line.[1]

If one were to judge only from the obvious factors, Bushrod Rust Johnson should not have been on the battlefield at Hoover's Gap at all. He came from a Quaker background, and his family was from Ohio; as a young man he had espoused the cause of abolishing slavery, but the choices he made later in life had led him to be a professional soldier supporting the Confederate cause.

A degree of controversy had dogged Johnson most of his career. He had received his degree from West Point in time to see service in the war with Mexico but fate had assigned him to a rear area as a supply officer. He saw many classmates and acquaintances, whose combat experience gained the attention of their commanding officers, being promoted above him. In these circumstances, Johnson made a serious error of judgment: he used his position as a supply officer to secure space on a government transport to bring goods to the army camp for private resale. Faced with court-martial, Johnson resigned from the army and began looking for a way to earn a living. Teaching at a military school appealed to him, since such a job would draw on his West Point training and army experience, and military schools were quite popular at that time. While teaching at an academy in Georgetown, Kentucky, in 1847, Johnson met Mary E. Hatch, the daughter of a prosperous merchant. Five years later, in the spring of 1852, the pair were married. The marriage would last only six years until Mary died of a fever in Nashville, Tennessee, in the spring of 1858. The couple had one child, a son, Charles, who was learning disabled.[2]

Several schools with which Johnson was associated failed because of financial exigencies, poor administrative leadership, and outbreaks of diseases, but he persevered. When war came in 1861, he was teaching at the Western Military Academy in Nashville, a school slowly becoming successful. With his wife recently deceased, Johnson arranged for his son to live with relatives in the North, and then, in May 1861, he offered his sword to Tennessee as the state organized military forces that would be incorporated later into the Provisional Army of the Confederate States for service to the South. Now Johnson again would be a soldier, this time as a colonel in defense of his adopted homeland.[3]

When the war began, Johnson did well for himself. His experience as a training officer and engineer enabled him to make valuable contributions to the Confederate war effort and he was promoted brigadier general on January 24, 1862. He had the misfortune to be assigned to Fort Donelson, Tennessee, in February and was among those who surrendered when that position fell to Major General Ulysses S. Grant. The men of his command were shipped off to prison camps, but Johnson was left behind, awaiting transportation with other high-ranking officers. The general confusion amongst Union ranks in the face of the sudden and overwhelming victory afforded Johnson a chance to simply walk away from his captors—a chance he took, accompanied by one of his aides. While some viewed his escape as indicative of initiative and courage, some questioned whether he had violated his parole of honor, a criticism which no doubt fed on the circumstances under which he left the army during the Mexican War.[4]

Given command of a brigade as the Confederate forces assembled at Corinth, Mississippi, Johnson fought ably at Shiloh, Tennessee, until wounded by an exploding artillery shell. On recovering from his wound, Johnson received command of the brigade he would lead for the next two years. The all-Tennessee command consisted of the 17th, 23rd, 25th, and 44th infantry regiments, and for a time the Jefferson Artillery was attached to the brigade. For administrative reasons, other regiments were temporarily assigned to Johnson's Brigade on occasion. But the four Tennessee regiments formed the permanent core of his command. Johnson led these men in the thick of the battle at Perryville, Kentucky, but, as at Shiloh, he did not play a decisive role. At Murfreesboro, Tennessee, the same scenario played out, Johnson was competent, brave, and unremarkable. Always fate seemed to give the leading role in the battle to someone no better qualified for leadership but who found more chance to influence the outcome of events.[5]

During the months following the Murfreesboro Campaign, as the Army of Tennessee lay in winter quarters around Tullahoma, Johnson finally came into his own. The situation allowed time and opportunity for drill and training, and this was his forte. An aide to President Jefferson Davis made a tour of inspection of General Braxton Bragg's army and said of Johnson's Brigade: "On March 23 I saw Brig. Gen. Bushrod R. Johnson drill his brigade and witnessed a match or trial battalion drill. . . . The Tennesseeans' [*sic*] fine stature, manly bearing, steadiness of movement and rapidity and accuracy with which the battalion executed every maneuver at the double quick was unequaled."[6]

During these months, the Army of Tennessee was plagued by problems that Bragg tried to solve without success. The army needed reinforcements to make good the losses of Murfreesboro, but instead of increasing in size, the army shrank as the divisions of Major Generals John P. McCown and John C. Breckinridge were sent to other areas. The army needed more and better weapons. The artillery was armed with lightweight, short-range weapons, while a good portion of the infantry carried smooth-bores, but Richmond could not supply the needed ordnance. Supplies were a constant problem, despite the rail network that stretched to Chattanooga and on to Atlanta. By order of the Confederate commissary department, Bragg drew his supplies from the area west of his left flank, an area without a direct rail link to his position. Then there was the problem of morale. The general officers began taking sides, for and against Bragg, while the enlisted ranks knew only they had fought hard and retreated often. None of these problems had been solved when the Tullahoma Campaign began in late June.[7]

As spring gave way to summer, the infantry moved from winter quarters to front-line positions. Johnson's Brigade was part of the division of the newly promoted Major General Alexander Peter Stewart, who was posted in the village of Fairfield, not far from the community of Beech Grove at the mouth of Hoover's Gap. If there had been only one road to guard, the task assigned Stewart's Division would have been an easy one. However, Hoover's Gap, through which passed the Manchester Pike, was only one of a network of routes to be watched, so the men were spread thinly over a long front.

On June 24, about 1:00 P.M., couriers from the 3rd Consolidated Kentucky Cavalry reported to Stewart's headquarters that a Yankee column had

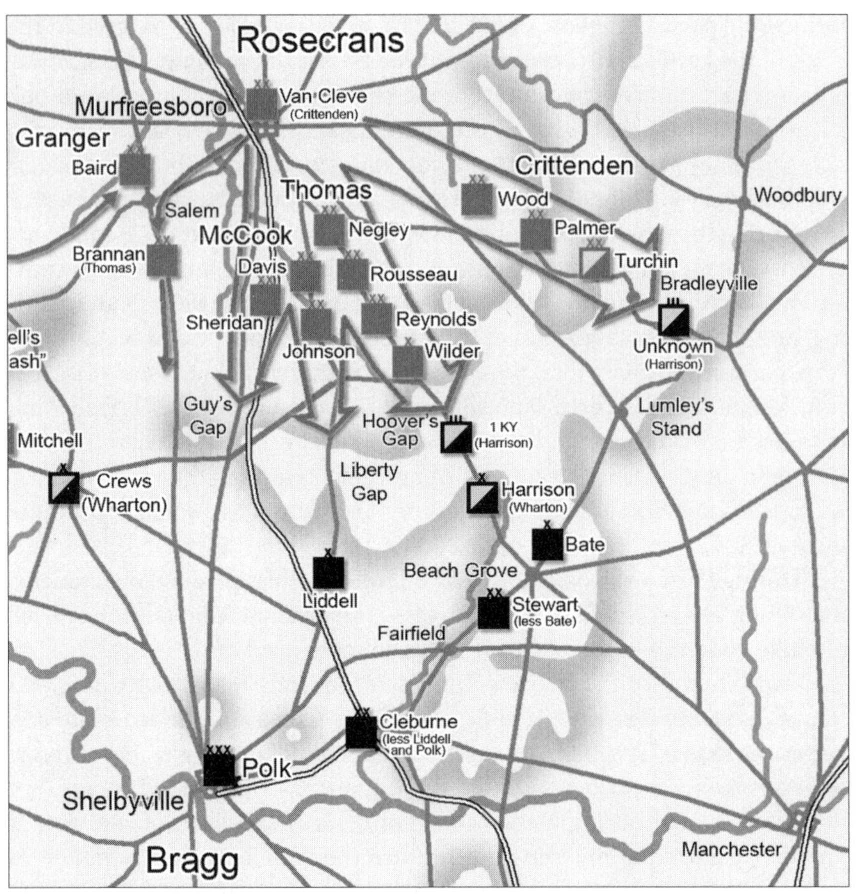

Union advance through Hoover's Gap. From *The Maps of Chickamauga* by David Powell and David Friedrichs (New York: Savas Beatie, 2009), 5. Used with permission.

penetrated Hoover's Gap, but they could not confirm which of several routes the U.S. troops had followed upon leaving the gap. In response, Stewart sent the brigade of Brigadier General William B. Bate to Hoover's Gap, and told Johnson to scout several other approaches leading from the gap to Fairfield. By this point, the battle was already decided. Hoover's Gap could easily be defended at many points within it, but once cleared of the southeastern mouth of the pass any defensive advantage evaporated. Not only did the Confederates need to counterattack, but Bate found himself confronting Colonel John T. Wilder's brigade of mounted infantry armed with Spencer repeating rifles followed by the rest of Major General George H. Thomas's 15th Corps. For the rest of the rainy, gloomy afternoon, Bate settled into a defensive posture and probed the Union position. During the night of

June 24–25, Johnson was ordered up to reinforce Bate. To spell Bate's weary troops, Johnson took over most of the front line. The darkness allowed only estimations of the position of the U.S. forces from the gleam of occasional campfires on the hills they presumably occupied. Johnson would spend part of the morning of the next day adjusting his lines.[8]

June 25 was spent in skirmishing and occasional artillery duels. Johnson was not anxious to provoke artillery exchanges because he was outgunned. Captain Eli Lilly's 18th Indiana Independent Battery, which included six three-inch rifles as well as four 12-pounder howitzers, provided U.S. artillery support, while Johnson could bring to bear mostly six-pound smooth-bores; only one section of the Eufaula (Alabama) Light Artillery consisted of rifled pieces. Also, only Company A of the 44th Tennessee was armed with rifles, and the rest of the regiment carried smooth-bore muskets. The ultimate factor in convincing Johnson to keep a low profile was that Thomas was massing his entire corps in Hoover's Gap with Major General Alexander M. McCook beginning to come up behind him with the 20th Corps. The men of the 23rd Tennessee were emotionally drained in this position. Several companies had been recruited from the area, and some men could literally see the smoke rising from the chimneys of their own homes.[9]

Rain continued to fall at intervals all day on June 25 and also when dawn broke the next day. The heavy rains prevented his men from resting at night, Johnson observed, as they had no tents on the field but lay exposed to the elements. Also, the skirmishers had continued to fire all night. By this time, Bragg knew his right flank was being turned by the Federal movement, and a decision had been reached to fall back to Tullahoma. About 10:00 A.M. on June 26, Thomas ordered Major General Lovell H. Rousseau to send forward the brigade of Regulars commanded by Major Sidney Coolidge against the Southern position. He intended to pin the defenders in place so they would be forced to face an overwhelming attack. A flanking move by Brigadier General John M. Brannan's division accompanied the frontal attack, aiming to cut off a Confederate retreat toward their base at Fairfield.[10]

The field conditions were such that the Regulars chose to advance in an unusual style: Coolidge formed his men in columns rather than lines, each two companies wide and four battalions deep. This compact formation allowed the soldiers to force their way across a field of head-high wheat whose stalks had become matted and tangled from the incessant rain. Johnson positioned men from the 15th and 37th Tennessee Infantry Regiments behind a stone wall to receive this attack, but he had also spotted Brannan's flanking movement so he did not wait for the attack to be pressed home before breaking contact.[11]

As is usual with Civil War battle reports, there was a different perspective from the attacking side. Captain John H. Otto, Company D, 21st

Wisconsin Infantry Regiment, reported close quarter fighting and bayonets used before "the enemy fled with precipitation towards Fairfield." Johnson reported one man killed and six wounded in this attack.[12]

Johnson conducted a textbook example of a withdrawal in the face of a superior enemy. He split his brigade into two sections and leapfrogged them backward. One section would take up a defensive position and hold it as long as possible without becoming involved in a general engagement, then withdraw through the position of the second section, only to take up yet another defensive position. So skillfully managed and persistent were the efforts of Johnson's men that it took five hours for two Union divisions to force Johnson back five miles to Fairfield. There the Northern force broke contact and returned to Hoover's Gap to take the road for Manchester. During this rearguard action, Johnson reported fifteen men wounded, only one being mortally injured, and his artillery lost one horse.[13]

The retrograde movement continued the following day as Johnson led his brigade back to Wartrace and then through Normandy to Tullahoma, a strongly fortified position where it seemed the Army of Tennessee would make a stand. Johnson held his position in the breastworks around Tullahoma until the night of June 30 when the order was given to fall back to the crossings of the Elk River. One of the defenders reported:

> We wer ordered to move further on the wright som 2 miles and thar we were in line of battle and thought the fight would come off thar the next day but alas what was the orders—I heard attension batallian in a vary low voice—it almost sounded like a deth bell everything was very still and in the distin the bugal softly blows—won could hardly hear the sound of a voice along the hole line but alas as they were already off we started—I new not whar—but soon found that we wer on a heavy march for the night. We went to Elk River that night.[14]

On July 1 Johnson's Brigade moved toward Decherd, crossing the Elk River on the Bethpage Bridge before resting. Late that afternoon, the unit recrossed the Elk, took up a defensive position on the west side of the stream, and remained there until dark. Johnson held this position until the morning of July 2 when he began to lead his men toward the mountains a few miles to his rear. A detachment from the brigade supported the cavalry in a rearguard action at Morris Ferry where the pursuit by Brigadier General John B. Turchin's Federal cavalry was checked. Johnson then continued to the top of the mountain beyond Cowan and paused at the village of University Station (present day Sewanee), the home of the University of the South.[15]

Johnson formed the rear guard of Lieutenant General William J. Hardee's Corps on July 3 and 4, moving to Battle Creek on July 5, and crossing the Tennessee River on July 6. From Hoover's Gap to Chattanooga, Johnson had lost three men killed, one officer and twenty-six men wounded, one officer and five men missing or captured.[16] Many of the regiments from Middle Tennessee reported additional serious losses from desertion as the Army of Tennessee left their homes in the hands of the enemy. The fact that Johnson reported only five men unaccounted for speaks highly of the morale of his brigade and provides a positive measure of the leadership Johnson gave his men.

The importance of the Tullahoma Campaign is generally overshadowed by the simultaneous events at Vicksburg and Gettysburg, yet, strategically, the Tullahoma Campaign was significant. Major General William Rosecrans's seizure of Middle Tennessee deprived the Confederates of an area with major food-producing and industrial capacity, along with large numbers of horses and mules. Moreover, the North now occupied an area which had enthusiastically supported secession and sent significant numbers of recruits into Confederate service.

During Bragg's retreat from Middle Tennessee, Johnson performed well, keeping the Yankees from pressing their numerical advantage, a task in which he was aided by the incessant rains that created bottomless bogs of mud and pools of water, hampering the movement of both armies. By August 1863, Johnson had added a patina to his record of competence and felt he deserved promotion to the rank of major general. There had been talk of promotion earlier, and Bragg had endorsed the idea by telling President Davis that in the year under his command Johnson had always been zealous in the performance of his duty and had received commendations after all the battles in which he had participated. The War Department bureaucrats in Richmond could find no division which needed a commander, so they took no action on Johnson. Following the Tullahoma Campaign, Johnson himself raised the question of promotion, noting that he put himself forward with reluctance since he had hoped to win a higher post through his actions. Again, Richmond discussed the issue at the cabinet level and still no vacancy existed for Johnson.[17]

Johnson was no doubt disappointed at this result, but he soldiered on. Stewart's Division, of which Johnson's Brigade was a part, was sent north of Chattanooga to guard bridges along a seventy-mile stretch of the East Tennessee & Georgia Railroad, the essential link between Chattanooga and Knoxville. This was an important position since it was thought Rosecrans's forces would move into the area to forge a link with Major General Ambrose E. Burnside's Union troops who were inching south from the Cumberland Gap toward Knoxville. Meanwhile, Bragg reorganized his army by sending

Hardee, one of his critics, to Mississippi to command there and replaced him with Lieutenant General Daniel Harvey Hill. Soon after this, Stewart's Division was transferred to a newly organized corps led by Major General Simon Bolivar Buckner with headquarters in Knoxville. As Rosecrans began to approach Chattanooga from the west and Burnside closed in on Knoxville, both Hill and Buckner were ordered to concentrate their forces at Chattanooga. Johnson led the vanguard of Buckner's corps down the Tennessee River valley from Knoxville to Chattanooga.[18]

Bragg felt the mountainous terrain west and northwest of Chattanooga favored his opponent, since Rosecrans could hide his movements behind the ridges. Bragg also discerned that the rough topography forced the enemy to divide into small, isolated units. This offered him the classic opportunity to defeat the enemy in detail by attacking each of the isolated units with his numerically superior concentrated force. The decision to abandon Chattanooga was a strategic withdrawal providing an excellent opportunity for a Confederate victory. A flow of reinforcements only enhanced the strategy. However, Bragg incorporated the new troops and reorganized his army while on the move, thus lessening its effectiveness. The creation of four infantry corps placed too many brigadiers and major generals under superior officers they didn't know and over troops they had never commanded. In the process of this shuffle, Johnson was given command of a division composed of his brigade and those of Brigadier Generals Evander McNair and John Gregg. When Lieutenant General James Longstreet arrived from Virginia, he came with a fifth infantry corps.[19] Even then, Bragg did not leave well enough alone and allow the command structure to settle into smooth operations. Instead, he divided the army into two wings and continued to shuffle units from corps to corps even on the battlefield at Chickamauga itself.

Before that engagement, Bragg tried several times to trap and destroy elements of the Union Army of the Cumberland in northern Georgia, but on each attempt, slow responses by subordinate officers frustrated the plan. As Rosecrans concentrated his army and began to move back toward Chattanooga, Bragg made one last attempt. This time, Johnson was to lead a movement across Chickamauga Creek at Reed's Bridge, swing to his left and move upstream, rolling up the left flank of the Union force. As the attack moved south, the Confederate forces on the east side of the stream would cross to the west side, reinforcing the attack. Johnson was ordered to begin this move by 6:00 A.M. on September 17, but he was on the road by 5:00. As Johnson moved through Catoosa Station on the way to his objective, three brigades of Longstreet's Corps arrived from Virginia, disembarked from the trains, and joined him. With the addition of the brigades of Brigadier Generals Henry L. Benning, Evander M. Law, and Jerome B. Robertson, Johnson now commanded what amounted to a corps in Bragg's revamped army. A

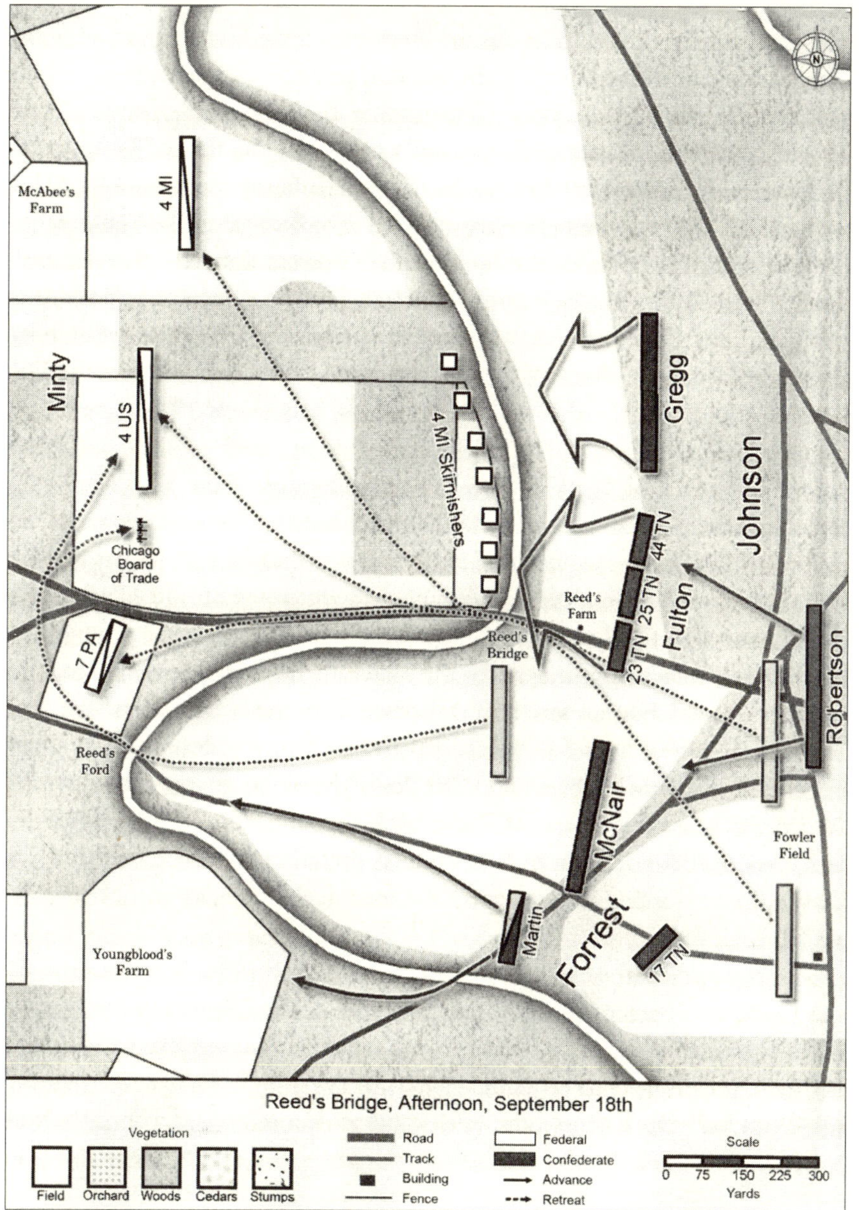

Reed's Bridge. *From Failure in the Saddle: Nathan Bedford Forrest, Joseph Wheeler, and the Confederate Cavalry in the Chickamauga Campaign* by David Powell (New York: Savas Beatie, 2010), 108. Used with permission.

brigade of Brigadier General Nathan Bedford Forrest's cavalry screened the column's advance.[20]

The original order Johnson received sent him in the direction of Leet's Tanyard, and he had covered three miles in that direction when fresh orders arrived from Bragg to advance on Reed's Bridge. By the time the column had reversed direction, it had added five miles to what would have been a seven-mile march. Memories must have flooded Johnson's mind as the ground passed under the feet of his men. He and Forrest had marched together to battle once before—at Fort Donelson on the day the Confederates had rolled back Grant's line and opened an escape route that never was taken. Now they marched again to roll up a flank.[21]

The Union commander at Reed's Bridge was Colonel Robert H. G. Minty, whose cavalry brigade was not disposed to give up the bridge without a fight. Johnson was engaged with Minty by about 11:00 A.M., but he found it necessary to deploy most of his men because Forrest had neglected to secure the bridge. Not until just after 3:00 P.M. did the crossing pass firmly into Confederate hands. Not long after this, Major General John Bell Hood arrived with part of his division, and as senior officer on the field, he assumed command of the force.[22]

Johnson had fought well and had followed orders. Unfortunately, he did not receive the credit he deserved. Unaware of the resistance Minty had put up at Reed's Bridge, Bragg had fumed that Johnson was not moving fast enough in getting across the creek and turning Rosecrans's left flank. In reality, Bragg had caused some of the delay by sending Johnson down the wrong road, thus stretching a march of seven miles into twelve.

With night fast falling, Johnson's men bivouacked where they stood, setting the stage for the opening shots of the second day of battle. Colonel Daniel McCook Jr.'s Union brigade had arrived near Reed's Bridge just as the tail of Johnson's column moved upstream, doing precisely what Bragg had ordered them to do. McCook took a few prisoners from the rear guard and, somehow, concluded that a single Confederate brigade was isolated in the woods in his front. Major General George H. Thomas, the ranking officer in the area, doubted this report, but he finally decided to send a brigade—not, to his disgust, McCook's—to check on the matter. On returning to his command, McCook found his men under attack from dismounted cavalry who had been ordered up by Forrest.[23]

Johnson was not part of this fight; he had moved upstream, and conflict awaited him there. He placed his men in line by 7:00 the following morning, but the hours passed with only minor action on their front. All the heavy fighting was happening to their right in the area they had held the day before. About 2:00 in the afternoon, the Federals attacked Johnson's front, and his men engaged in heavy fighting the rest of the day. Like the rest of

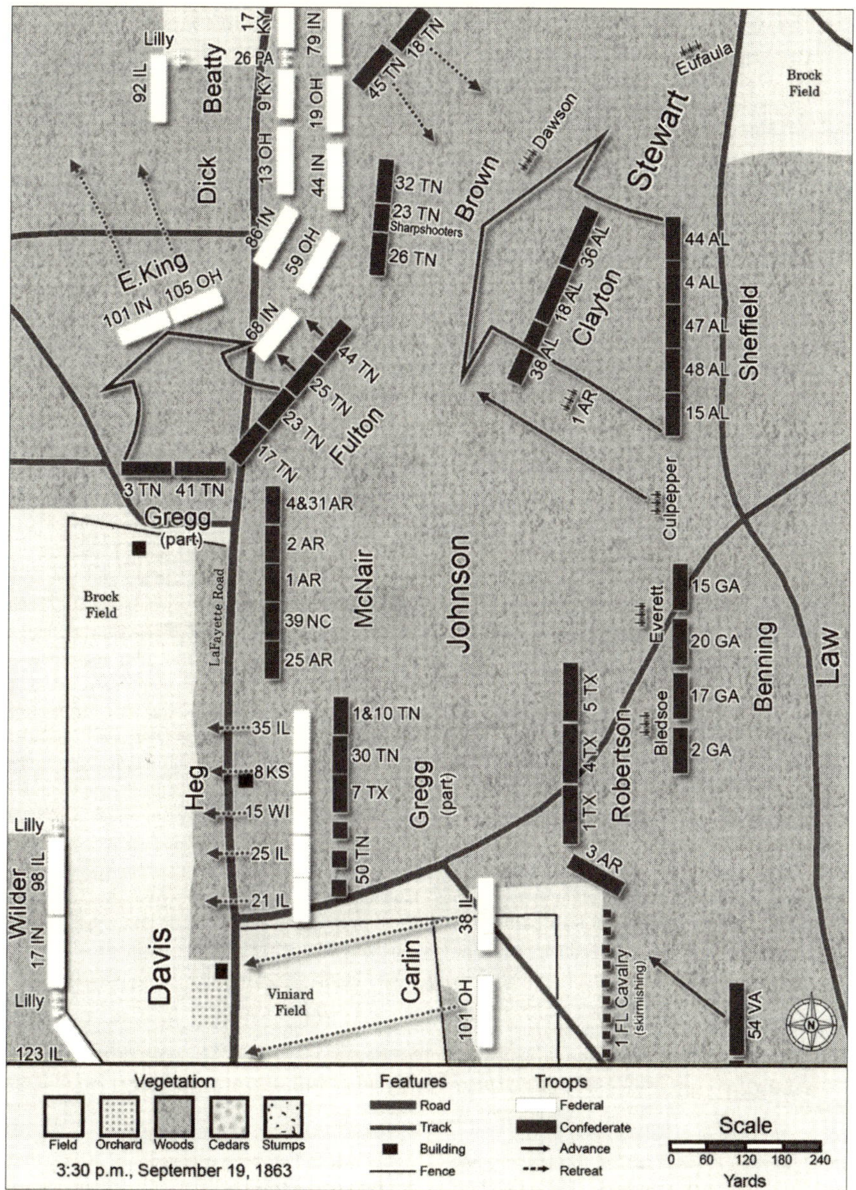

Battle of Chickamauga, 3:30 P.M., September 19, 1863. From *The Maps of Chickamauga* by David Powell and David Friedrichs (New York: Savas Beatie, 2009), 95. Used with permission.

the battle, this was a see-saw engagement with reinforcements tipping the balance several times. At one time Johnson had advanced well west of the LaFayette Road and captured a battery before being forced back east of the road and having the guns recaptured. During the afternoon of fighting, losses were some 50 dead and 250 wounded.[24] There was little glory to be gained from such fighting as Johnson had done this day; neither was much skill required of a commanding officer. The battle had been an enlisted man's fight, conducted in dense woods where targets suddenly appeared in the smoky shadows and enemies came charging out of the gloom. Still, Johnson had stood the test and had nothing of which he needed to be ashamed.

That night, Bragg again reorganized his army. Johnson remained under Hood's command but became part of a "wing" comprising multiple corps commanded by Longstreet. Somehow, amidst the confusion and in the darkness, the army was shuffled into place to await the dawn. The battle orders called for an attack en echelon from right to left, beginning at daylight.

Longstreet spent time and effort in preparing his attack. Only a few weeks before this day in Georgia he had made another attack in Pennsylvania, one with which he was not pleased. Although postwar critics often charged Longstreet "with being hesitant to attack because he was dedicated to defensive tactics," it should be noted that Longstreet made two of the most successful assaults of the entire war: the crushing flank attack at Second Manassas and the line-busting attack at Chickamauga. For the attack he was about to launch, Longstreet had crammed eight brigades into just over seventy acres of woodland. His main line lay six hundred yards east of the LaFayette Road, the front of the Union position, with skirmishers three hundred yards in advance of his main line. The attackers were formed in a column with a front two brigades wide, the leading division under the command of Johnson, a position of trust and responsibility. The task of leading such an attack would not have been given to a sub-par officer: clearly, Johnson was rising in esteem in the eyes of his peers and superiors. Longstreet may well have preferred one of his Army of Northern Virginia units to lead the attack but the tangled woods, the confusion in the battle lines, and the press of time made a rearrangement of the formation impossible. And, Johnson had done well so far.

Johnson had placed his men with McNair's Brigade on the right and his own brigade, led by Colonel John S. Fulton, on the left. The second line contained Gregg's Brigade. Two batteries of artillery—Lieutenant William S. Everett's Company E, 9th Georgia Artillery Battalion, and Lieutenant R. L. Wood's Bledsoe's Missouri Battery—were in line to move forward with the assault column. Behind Johnson, Longstreet had placed Hood's Division and a small division under Brigadier General Joseph B. Kershaw. In all, Longstreet had disposed eleven thousand men for the attack, with Stewart's, Major General Thomas C. Hindman's, and Brigadier General William Preston's divi-

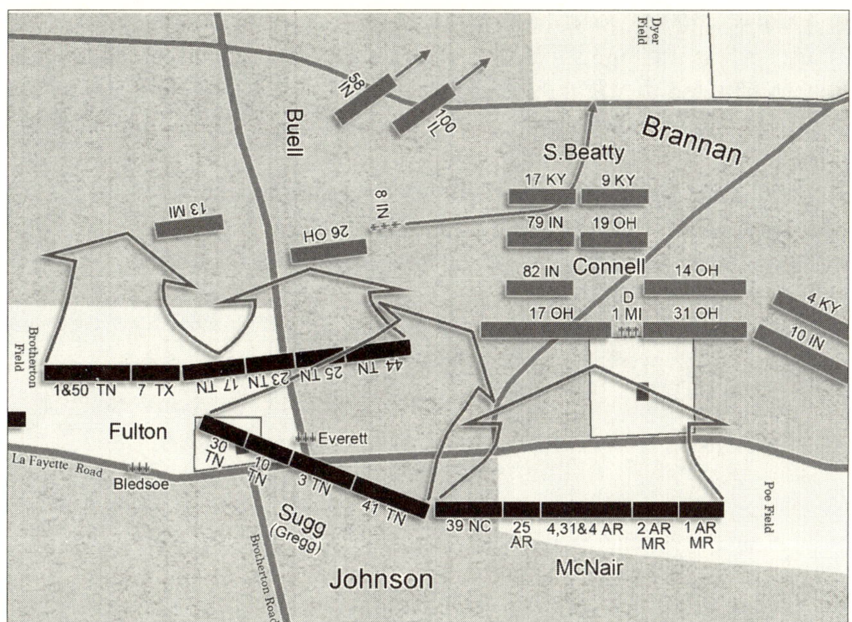

Battle of Chickamauga, midday, September 20, 1863. From *The Maps of Chickamauga* by David Powell and David Friedrichs (New York: Savas Beatie, 2009), 169. Used with permission.

sions ready to move forward on his flanks. A total of twenty-three thousand men were poised to move against the U.S. line, twice as many as had been launched in Pickett's Charge at Gettysburg. Johnson would be leading the way, but the attack would be guided by Tom Brotherton, a Confederate private whose family owned the 700-acre farm that would be the focal point of the assault.[25]

Across the way, a degree of confusion existed in the Union lines. Directly in front of Johnson, Union Brigadier General Thomas J. Wood had just received an order from Rosecrans to shift his division to its left to support the troops there. This was going to present Johnson with the incredible opportunity to attack into a 400 to 500-yard gap in the enemy's line.[26]

Just after 11:00 A.M., Johnson received the order to advance. Breaking into the cleared ground along the LaFayette Road, his troops were met by skirmish fire and artillery fire from a battery south of the Brotherton House. But no fire came from directly ahead. One of Johnson's regiments, the 17th Tennessee, overran the troublesome battery and the rest of his division stormed ahead, sweeping up Yankee skirmishers and wounded men from yesterday's fighting and running past four Brotherton family cows who continued placidly chewing their cuds in the midst of the gunfire. In only a few minutes, Johnson had led his men at a run past the Brotherton House, across the family's field, and had reached the road that led to what now constituted the right flank of the U.S. position and to the home of the Widow Glenn where Rosecrans had his headquarters. In making this move, Johnson caught up with the rear of the column Wood was leading to its new position and quickly wrecked it. The artillery accompanying Johnson skillfully deployed in the cleared fields and began to shell the retreating Union troops on either side of the Confederate advance.[27]

At this point Johnson paused momentarily to allow his second line, Gregg's Brigade, to catch up and to reinforce his front line. Moving west across the road that led south to the Glenn House, Johnson faced cleared land which sloped gradually to the west. These fields were covered with retreating soldiers in blue. Johnson later wrote:

> The scene now presented was unspeakably grand. The resolute and impetuous charge, the rush of our heavy columns sweeping out from the shadow and gloom of the forest into the open fields flooded with sunlight, the glitter of arms, the onward dash of artillery and mounted men, the retreat of the foe, the shouts of the hosts of our army, the dust, the smoke, the noise of fire-arms—of whistling balls and grape-shot and of bursting shell—made up a battle scene of unsurpassed grandeur.[28]

Moving on again after adjusting his lines, Johnson was approached by Major General Hood. Looking over the situation, Hood gave Johnson the informal order to "go ahead, and keep ahead of everything." Only a few minutes later, Hood would suffer a wound that would lead to the amputation of his right leg. Johnson, however, did precisely what he was ordered to do. Within a few minutes his advance overran another U.S. artillery position, and nine more cannon were sent to the rear under guard. Only a few hundred feet away McNair's Brigade was taking two other batteries. In under an hour, Johnson's division had split the Army of the Cumberland in two, captured three batteries in three separate locations, and had placed their own artillery in position to pummel the Union right wing's line of retreat. It was time to pause and regroup.[29]

About 1:30 P.M., Johnson met Brigadier General Kershaw, who was accompanied by a member of Hood's staff. The three men consulted and decided that Kershaw would command the effort to break the developing Federal defense on Snodgrass Hill. Johnson agreed to this arrangement even though by the date of commission he outranked Kershaw. Major General Hindman also made an appearance and gave Johnson command of his men since he had been ill as well as wounded by a shell fragment.[30]

In subsequent attacks on the U.S. position held by Thomas on Snodgrass Hill, Kershaw would assault in the area around the Snodgrass cabin, using frontal attacks up the hill, while Johnson tried to turn the Union right flank further to the west. Bringing up reinforcements, positioning artillery, and getting units into battle formation expended almost two hours. The fight for Snodgrass Hill began about 3:30 P.M. and continued until dusk. The strength of their position, the arrival of reinforcements, and the Yankees' determined fighting doomed the Confederate attacks. At dusk Johnson and his weary men fell back some 250 yards and took what rest they could. The following morning Snodgrass Hill was vacant of defenders. This was Johnson's best day of the war, coming at the end of his best three months of the conflict. Twenty-five years later, one of Johnson's opponents at Chickamauga, Brigadier General Turchin, would say that Johnson was "one of the best, if not the best, of Bragg's army."[31]

Such a victory, especially such a long-awaited one as Chickamauga, would have generated a season of congratulations and the distribution of rewards in any normal army. So based on his performance during the summer of 1863, Johnson had good reason to expect promotion to major general. But the Army of Tennessee was not such an army. The acrimony between Bragg and his officer corps, simmering since the Kentucky Campaign the previous fall, again broke into the open with renewed vigor. Johnson had remained neutral during the imbroglio preceding the Tullahoma Campaign, but now he openly joined the Bragg critics, a move that would haunt him once Bragg became military adviser to President Davis.

In November 1863, Johnson was sent to be part of Longstreet's Knoxville Campaign. The ad hoc division he had led at Chickamauga was broken up in yet another reorganization of the army, and Johnson was left to command a much reduced brigade. Even so, almost a third of these men were detached from Johnson when he went to Knoxville. In an engagement at Bean's Station, his brigade sustained several dozen casualties.[32] And during this dreary winter, his hopes of promotion withered but did not die.

In early May 1864, the weak brigade Johnson commanded became part of the reinforcements sent to the Richmond area as the Confederacy scraped the bottom of the manpower barrel trying to prolong the war until the U.S. presidential election. Assigned to the area south of the James River, Johnson's command formed part of the small force pieced together in mid-June to contain the Federal breakthrough that had penetrated General Pierre G. T. Beauregard's fortifications surrounding Petersburg. The fighting Johnson did that day was later characterized as "almost flawless."[33]

From that time, until the end of the war, Johnson was a key player in the defense of Petersburg. Rewarded with a commission as major general and a division for his fight to save the city, his command initially comprised the four brigades of Matt W. Ransom, Stephen Elliott Jr., Henry A. Wise, and Alfred H. Colquitt. His division later found itself the focus of the Battle of the Crater when a mine under a part of the line held by Elliott was exploded, and the Federals delivered a massive attack against the gap left in the Confederate line. Johnson's Division stood firm and held the position until reinforcements arrived and restored Southern control.[34]

Johnson's stand received no praise at the time, nor has it been celebrated by writers to the extent that the counterattack by Brigadier General William Mahone has been. He is often pictured as the Confederate hero of the day, since it was Major General Richard Anderson's Division— temporarily under Mahone—that sealed the final gap in the Southern lines. Yet without Johnson's brave defense, the day would have been lost; indeed, the Army of Northern Virginia might well have met its demise at the Battle of the Crater. Following the fighting at the Crater, Johnson's Division continued to do good service, manning the front lines so long that by the winter of 1864–65, incidents of scurvy were being reported in the command.

Despite his effective and loyal service, Johnson became a victim of circumstances as the war was ending. When the lines before Petersburg finally broke on April 2, Johnson's command became part of the column struggling its way west over muddy roads in what proved to be an impossible attempt to escape. On the morning of April 6, 1865, as the Confederate column approached the valley of Little Sailor's Creek, Johnson's Division was in Lieutenant General Richard Anderson's Corps, the second of four corps in the column. A gap developed between Anderson and the lead corps commanded by Longstreet, and around 1:00 P.M. Federal cavalry penetrated this gap and seized the road, halting the column. To the rear of Anderson, Lieutenant General Richard Ewell's ad hoc corps pressed forward into the valley, but the wagon train following Ewell took a road to the north to avoid the traffic jam. Major General John B. Gordon's corps followed the wagons, inadvertently leaving open the road to Ewell's rear. Union infantry took advantage of this open route and attacked. Caught between U.S. forces to their front and in their rear, with both flanks rapidly being surrounded, the Confederate defense crumbled. Some units fought well but some six thousand men were captured.[35]

On the morning of April 7, Johnson reported to General Robert E. Lee and was in the process of recounting the destruction of his division when Brigadier General Wise came marching up the road at the head of his brigade, the largest unit Johnson had taken into the fight at Little Sailor's Creek. An ensuing conversation between Lee and Wise seems to have convinced Lee that Johnson had not provided proper leadership during the battle and had, perhaps, abandoned his men. Wise was given command of the remnants of the division, and the next day Johnson was dismissed from the army.[36]

Other generals lost as heavily as Johnson during the final retreat and many behaved no better, but Johnson was not one of the inner circle of the Virginia army—a man with a Quaker abolitionist background, a native of Ohio, a man about whom "gentlemen" might raise questions concerning the probity of some of his acts. Perhaps this made it easy for Johnson to be underpraised, overlooked for promotion, and made a scapegoat for disaster.

Johnson made his way back to Nashville along with other Tennesseans who had served in Lee's army, among them some of his former students. While his home town, Nashville, had escaped most of the physical devastation of war, the economy of the state, and of the South, was in ruins. Occupation forces had used the buildings of Western Military Academy as barracks and hospitals, rendering them unfit for use as a school, even had pupils been available. With men he had known before the war, Johnson set up a real estate firm known as Anderson, Johnson, and Smith.[37]

The shaky economic climate exacerbated the volatile politics of the state, which pitted native unionists, freedmen, and carpetbaggers against former Confederates. The Ku Klux Klan was one manifestation of this unrest, and in 1868, the approach of state and national elections threatened to bring Tennessee to a state of open warfare. Johnson, along with other former Confederate generals such as Benjamin F. Cheatham, John Calvin Brown, and George F. Maney tried to exert a calming influence to prevent violence.[38]

In 1869, the new governor of Tennessee, DeWitt Clinton Senter, allowed former Confederates to vote and reconstruction ended in the state. However, the economy did not rebound. Johnson's attempts to establish himself in business failed, and in 1875, the assets of the school in which Johnson had labored long and hard were sold. Its buildings became the Peabody Normal School, today known as Peabody College of Vanderbilt University. The only asset Johnson had left was the farm he owned in Brighton, Illinois, so he went north.[39]

Johnson slowly made friends among those who had been his enemies, but he was not a good farmer and he was not successful in finding good tenants. After five years of genteel poverty, Johnson died quietly on September 12, 1880, and was buried in Miles Station, near Brighton. In 1975, following months of work by Mr. Noble Wyatt and others, the body of Bushrod Rust Johnson was removed from his neglected burial place and reinterred beside his wife in the Old City Cemetery in Nashville.[40]

During the Civil War, Bushrod Johnson served well and he served long. His service was always marked by competence and devotion to the Confederate cause. But his best days were in the summer of 1863. Never again would Johnson reap the rewards of victory, or rise to the level of personal performance that he exhibited from Hoover's Gap to Chickamauga.

Writing about the Civil War has a tendency to focus on the "big names," the best known leaders whose actions are deemed to have shaped the events of the war in decisive ways. The truth is, the course of the war was determined by many men like Bushrod Rust Johnson, men who had above average abilities and unremarkable careers, yet who occasionally showed flashes of talent which dramatically affected the outcome of specific events. For that reason, Johnson, and his best days, deserve to be remembered.

Notes

1. U.S. War Department. *The War of the Rebellion: A Compilation of the Official Records of the Union and Confederate Armies,* 128 vols. (Washington, DC, 1880–1901), ser. 1, vol. 23, pt. 2:601-10 (hereafter cited as *OR*; all references are to series 1 unless otherwise indicated).
2. Charles Cummings, *Yankee Quaker, Confederate General: The Curious Career of Bushrod Rust Johnson* (Rutherford, NJ, 1971), 137.
3. Ezra J. Warner, *Generals in Gray: Lives of the Confederate Commanders* (Baton Rouge, LA, 1959), 146–47.
4. Benjamin F. Cooling, *Forts Henry and Donelson: The Key to the Confederate Heartland* (Knoxville, TN, 1987), 215–16.
5. Cummings, *Yankee Quaker, Confederate General,* 214-45.
6. *OR*, vol. 23, pt. 2:757.
7. Michael R. Bradley, *Tullahoma: The 1863 Campaign for Control of Middle Tennessee* (Shippensburg, PA, 2000), 30–31.
8. Ibid., 64–67.
9. Michael R. Bradley, "Tullahoma: The Wrongly Forgotten Campaign," *Blue & Gray* 27, no. 1 (2010): 43; *OR*, vol. 23, pt. 1:601–3.
10. Bradley, "Tullahoma," 43.
11. Ibid., 43.
12. Christopher L. Kolakowski, *The Stones River and Tullahoma Campaigns* (Charleston, SC, 2011), 123; *OR*, vol. 23, pt. 1:605; Bradley, *Tullahoma,* 80.
13. *OR*, vol. 23, pt.1:607.
14. Benjamin M. Seaton, *The Bugle Softly Blows: The Confederate Diary of Benjamin M. Seaton,* ed. Harold B. Simpson (Waco, TX, 1965), 35.
15. *OR*, vol. 23, pt. 1:608–9.
16. Ibid., 610.
17. Cummings, *Yankee Quaker, Confederate General,* 245–47.
18. *OR*, vol. 31, pt. 4:620.

19. Cummings, *Yankee Quaker, Confederate General,* 250.

20. Glenn Tucker, *Chickamauga: Bloody Battle in the West* (Indianapolis, 1961), 112–13.

21. Cummings, *Yankee Quaker, Confederate General,* 252–53; Tucker, *Chickamauga,* 112–13.

22. David A. Powell, *Failure in the Saddle: Nathan Bedford Forrest, Joe Wheeler, and the Confederate Cavalry in the Chickamauga Campaign* (New York, 2010), 108, 110.

23. Peter Cozzens, *This Terrible Sound: The Battle of Chickamauga* (1992; repr., Urbana, IL, 1996), 123–25.

24. Cummings, *Yankee Quaker, Confederate General,* 256–57.

25. Tucker, *Chickamauga,* 260–61; Cummings, *Yankee Quaker, Confederate General,* 259; *OR,* vol. 36, pt. 3:857; David A. Powell, *The Chickamauga Campaign, Glory or the Grave: The Breakthrough, the Union Collapse, and the Defense of Horseshoe Ridge, September 20, 1863* (El Dorado Hills, CA, 2015), 108–9.

26. Tucker, *Chickamauga,* 264; Cozzens, *This Terrible Sound,* 369.

27. Tucker, *Chickamauga,* 265.

28. John T. Goodrich, "Gregg's Brigade in the Battle of Chickamauga," *Confederate Veteran* 22, no. 6 (June 1914): 265; *OR,* vol. 30, pt. 2:457–58.

29. Tucker, *Chickamauga,* 272–73.

30. *OR,* vol. 30, pt. 2:563.

31. Ibid., 451-70; John Basil Turchin, *Chickamauga* (1888; repr., Charleston, SC, 2010), 209.

32. *OR,* vol. 31, pt. 1:536.

33. Douglas S. Freeman, *R. E. Lee: A Biography,* 4 vols. (New York, 1934), 3:422.

34. Ibid., 467-78.

35. Burke Davis, *To Appomattox: Nine April Days, 1865* (New York, 1959), 245–47.

36. Ibid., 281; Freeman, *R. E. Lee,* 4:96–97; Henry A. Wise, "The Career of Wise's Brigade," *Southern Historical Society Papers* 25 (1897):19.

37. Cummings, *Yankee Quaker, Confederate General,* 341–42.

38. *Messages of the Governors of Tennessee,* ed. Robert H. White, vol. 5, *1857–1869* (Nashville, 1959), 618–19.

39. Cummings, *Yankee Quaker, Confederate General,* 362.

40. R. D. Fletcher, "Burial Place of Gen. B. R. Johnson," *Confederate Veteran* 15, no. 12 (Dec. 1907): 551; Cummings, *Yankee Quaker, Confederate General,* 425.

Brigadier General Abraham Buford. Courtesy of the National Archives and Records Service.

"Hellraising" Abraham Buford: Nathan Bedford Forrest's Dependable Lieutenant

Brian S. Wills

Riding with Nathan Bedford Forrest during the American Civil War presented its share of challenges. Few of the officers who served under Forrest rose to independent prominence, but most adapted to the rugged backwoodsman's methods and performed admirably in the adverse conditions associated with long-distance raiding and other mounted operations. Although he did not resemble physically the popular image of a dashing cavalier, Kentuckian Abraham Buford proved himself to be among the most dependable of Forrest's lieutenants and exhibited a fortitude and command capacity that matched his esteemed chief. A contemporary described him simply as "a man of great courage and soldiery genius."[1]

Born on January 18, 1820 in Woodford, Kentucky, Abraham Buford attended Centre College, in 1835–36. He entered the U.S. Military Academy at West Point in 1837 just a few months past his seventeenth birthday. Adjustment to the new environment for the plebe from Kentucky proved challenging. His overall rank in the Fourth Class was fifty-ninth, and he managed to accumulate 140 demerits. Buford's Third Class standing improved only one place to fifty-eight and contained 124 blemishes on his account. His best year at West Point was his Second Class one, where respectable postings in natural philosophy (41), chemistry (51), and drawing (43) allowed him to move into the forty-sixth slot in the class, although 68 demerits marred the record. His final year saw Buford slip to fifty-first among his classmates, with 63 demerits. A ranking of twenth-eighth in infantry tactics demonstrated an aptitude in that area of his studies that he was unable to duplicate in engineering (49), ethics (47), artillery (46), or mineralogy and geology (47).[2]

Buford had remained anchored in the lower portion of his class, but this was nevertheless sufficient to allow for graduation in the class of 1841 from the institution and for him to secure the brevet rank of second lieutenant in the 1st Dragoons. From that time until 1846, he served on the frontier at various posts. While stationed at Fort Gibson, on the Arkansas River in Indian Territory, Buford received promotion to second lieutenant, dating from April 12, 1842.[3]

During this period, Buford enjoyed the opportunities his duties allowed for him to hone and display his skills in horsemanship and hunting. By one account of an expedition, he proved to be "the most successful" at the sport, "having bagged 92 buffalo, 4 deer, 2 elk, besides small game."[4] Letters from the Fort Gibson years also suggest a turbulent period for the Kentuckian. Buford clashed with fellow officer and post commander, Captain Enoch Steen, and experienced less than cordial relations with other colleagues. In December 1844, Lieutenant Robert H. Chilton observed in a letter: "Steene hates Buford as he hates the devil."[5] Subsequently, Chilton found little ground for supporting either man in a dispute that threatened to end in charges being preferred from one party or the other. "From all I can learn they will both fare badly if an investigation does take place," Chilton insisted. But, he saved his strongest expressions of disdain for Buford, insisting that he could "bearly [*sic*] treat the fellow with common civility such a contempt have I for the man and his conduct."[6]

Chilton's anger toward Buford may not simply have been reflective of a clash of personalities. Buford had won the heart of Amanda Harris, sister of fellow West Pointer Arnold Harris. Chilton bristled at what he considered his comrade's reprehensible behavior, particularly with regard to Buford's apparently inappropriate comments about the nature of the engaged couple's intimate relationship. Although it is unclear exactly when Abraham and Amanda formalized their marriage or the degree to which any actual improprieties on Buford's part existed, Chilton remained sensitive, observing in February 1845: "Buford much to my regret has transfer'd . . . and the Company is now saddled with a married man. He looks quite the married man, though a little shy yet in consequence of the many filthy expressions he used relative to his wife while engaged to her, but as the matter is now settled 'tis best that these things should not come up in judgement against him."[7]

In the midst of the turmoil, Buford prepared to leave the post on furlough. As part of his arrangements, the Kentuckian offered a comrade his "fine saddle horse to keep and use as one of your own until I rejoin the Regt. he is a Thorough bred horse. And I think you will find him the finest saddle horse you ever backed. . . . He is a horse I value highly and would not sell under any circumstances as so long as I am a Drgn." The disagreement with his commander remained on his mind as well. "I intend prosecuting the charges

I have preferred against Capt Steen at all hazzard," the sensitive subordinate maintained. Buford continued: "It is the most willful and malicious attempt to injure I ever heard."[8]

Personal misfortune escalated for Buford when he left the territory. The tragic premature birth of a child and the disposal of the infant's remains led to charges against him. "Buford has been tried & acquitted," Chilton explained. "The baby which was afterwards recover'd on the river, was not entirely formed." But Chilton worried most that the Kentuckian would return to the post: "Will he come back God forbid."[9]

Antagonistic feelings toward Buford had not cooled by October, when Lieutenant Henry S. Turner wrote his friend, Lieutenant Abraham R. Johnston: "As for Buford, he must be an unprincipled worsted: and I am only surprised that he has had the face to return to the Regt. . . . Kentucky has been unfortunately represented among us." For this comrade, Buford remained "the slayer of his own child," but, indeed, "better things could hardly have been expected however of a man who would marry his own Misstress[*sic*]. The presumption is she urged him to commit the act."[10]

Despite the intensity of Buford's personal and professional travails, they quickly became lost in an international incident that threatened war between the United States and Mexico in 1846. A border clash in the disputed region between the Nueces River and Rio Grande led to a call by President James K. Polk for war with Mexico. Buford's service with the 1st Dragoons in the war with Mexico led to a commission as first lieutenant on December 6, 1846. The following February he saw action at Buena Vista that garnered him a brevet for gallantry.

Happier events awaited Buford's return from the war. The birth of a son, William A. Buford, on Christmas Eve in 1848 highlighted the Kentuckian's reappearance at Fort Gibson. Yet, service on the frontier frustrated Buford. Activities among some of the Native Americans in the region spurred various searches and punitive expeditions that produced few results. In 1849, after an Apache raid, Buford led a twenty-man patrol in pursuit. Apparently, his zeal overcame the necessity for adequate preparation, and the band of dragoons found themselves short of rations, men, and guides. The whole exercise exasperated Buford and enflamed his feelings toward the Indians. He considered "any treaty with them as worthless." They should be "taught . . . a lesson to respect the rights of another nation."[11]

Buford continued pursuing the routine duties of a frontier army officer as U.S. forces sought to gain control of U.S. territory. In the late summer of 1851, he led his command to the site designated for Fort Fillmore to oversee construction activities and await the arrival of infantry that would solidify the U.S. presence. They arrived on September 15, establishing the fort formally eight days later.

After a brief lull, brought on by agreements between U.S. officials and Mescalero Apaches, another raid shattered the quiet in December 1851. Commanding Company H, 1st Dragoons, Buford mustered his men and set off in pursuit. But again he confronted difficulties that rendered positive results in his operations unlikely. "They could travel night and day, and I could follow only by daylight," Buford explained in a report. "I had only 20 men in the saddle with me . . . raw recruits that I have never had an opportunity to drill or instruct in the least consequence." The harried officer understood he would not be able to pursue his opponents with vigor. "With such a command as this I knew it would be folly in the extreme to enter the mountains with the view of carrying on war against the Indians."[12]

Despite the limitations for success that came with service in the saddle, a celebration of life never seemed far from the robust Kentuckian's experiences. In July 1852, Richard Ewell recounted for his brother Ben the exciting times the men had shared when they first came to New Mexico:

> Last night Capt. Buford 1. Drg. staid with me, on his way to the states. He came out with me in 50. without much money, but several fine blooded horses & great skill in cards. He won on one horse race $1800. & by judicious sales of his horses & good luck at cards goes home with 2 yrs pay due & about $8000 in cash. He is on recruiting service. He is a Kentuckian & his Father was one of the most successful racers & stock raisers of his day, the owner of the celebrated Medoc, whose Offspring probably won $20 000 for the old man. One of them was the gainer of the race I mentioned above.

Buford might have impressed his comrade with his prowess at the card table and the race track, but Ewell seemed less taken by other attributes: "Buford as you may suppose is hardly calculated to shine in any ball room except a Mexico fandango, where he seems in his element." Nevertheless, the soldier had established a reputation. "Here," Ewell explained, "the natives call him, Hellraising Buford."[13]

In this period, Buford moved from post to post before accepting assignment to the school of cavalry instruction at Carlisle Barracks, Pennsylvania, in 1852. Promotion to captain came on June 15, 1853, but in October 1854, he resigned his commission to settle near Versailles in Kentucky with his family. Buford named the 267-acre estate he purchased for $21,296, Bosque Bonita ("Beautiful Woods") and began to raise cattle and thoroughbred racing horses on the sprawling grounds.[14]

Buford quickly established himself as a figure of renown in equine circles and seemed to thrive in the civilian world. In December 1860, a relative noted that she enjoyed "eggnog and oysters" at the Buford home for Christmas. Years later, Buford's obituary described a man of property and social significance: "He owned a magnificent stock farm in Woodford County, Ky., called Bosque Bonita, which was the most princely residence of the blue grass region, and there he used to entertain annually all the prominent politicians and sporting men of the country."[15]

In the prime of adulthood, Buford presented a formidable physical presence. "He weighed something over three hundred pounds," an associate remembered, "of powerful frame, a round ruddy face covered with a short, stubby red beard." Buford also exhibited fascinating contradictions. "With all the weight," the friend explained, "he was the most graceful dancer I ever saw swing a lady on the light and fantastic." Another contemporary remembered simply, "He was a big man on a big horse."[16]

In the midst of the broiling political tensions of the times, Buford sought to maintain a status quo with regard to lifestyle at least. He continued to raise and race horses. In an age where a sense of honor held strong sway, his horse, Revenue, reflected well on his owner and the bank account, winning a "$1000 Thoroughbred stallion prize" at the 1858 St. Louis Fair and achieving a status as "the premier sire of 1860."[17]

As a local citizen with a military education and experience in the field leading troops, Buford also attracted the notice of his neighbors for other reasons as well. His cousin, Martha Jones, noted that her illustrious relative served as "Marshal" for militia companies that gathered under the watchful eye of the governor and his retinue at the end of May 1860.[18]

As the election of 1860 and the pending elevation of Republican Abraham Lincoln to the presidency sent shock waves through the Deep South and spurred the secession of several states, Buford took a stance that reflected the position of many other citizens in the Commonwealth of Kentucky. He favored state's rights but held against secession as a remedy for the South's ills.[19]

In August 1861, months after hostilities had commenced between the Confederacy and the United States, Buford told his brother-in-law: "We are expecting trouble daily in Kentucky, the immediate cause being the violation of our neutrality by the Northern Government." Buford focused his greatest disapproval on William "Bull" Nelson, a naval commander given a role as a brigadier general with recruitment responsibilities in the state. Labeling the Union officer "a salt-water general" and "as d—d a Black Republican as is to be found anywhere in the country," Buford thought that officer's activities reprehensible. "I saw the order before I left Washington authorizing Nelson to organize these troops," Buford explained, intimating that Secretary of War Simon Cameron had offered him a post as well, "with the promise of promotion to the position of brigadier-general so soon as a brigade was organized." He "positively declined" this offer, he said, thus placing himself among a "majority of Union men in Kentucky [who] are bitterly opposed to this Nelson movement, and are now doing all in their power to remove him and his troops from the State." Rejecting the report that he had accepted a generalship from President Lincoln as "false, and without the slightest foundation," Buford maintained, "I have battled long and ardently as well as honestly for the Union." For him the motive was "love of country," but Buford felt the repercussions of these convictions. "I have compromised myself so far on the side of the Union that it will take me some time to get all right."[20]

Buford's moment of decision did not come in 1861, even when Southern troops under the Episcopal bishop and Confederate Major General Leonidas Polk moved into the state near Columbus in September. But there was no question of his Southern sympathies. "If my services are acceptable to Jeff Davis, and he is willing to trust a man who has fought as long and honestly as I have for the neutrality of his native State," he would serve. Buford continued to bide his time and focused his attentions on maintaining as much of the routine he had established prior to the whirlwind of events that now enveloped his world. "I have plenty of good old whiskey and bacon," he told his brother-in-law. "My race horses are doing well, and if [General] Nelson don't interrupt our sport this fall . . . we will have a good time during the race week at Lexington and Louisville."[21]

That illusion of tranquility ended for Buford during the summer of 1862 when Confederate troops under General Braxton Bragg and Major General Edmund Kirby Smith moved into his home state. The Kentuckian could no longer defer the call to service from the South. Receiving a commission as brigadier general to rank from September 2, 1862, he initially commanded a brigade of three Kentucky regiments under Major General William W. Loring.

Subsequent duty placed Buford and his men on patrol in central Kentucky as part of a force meant to neutralize "Home Guard" units that supported the Union. Fellow Kentuckian Edward O. Guerrant encountered these men "on the road to Harrodsburg," and noted the general's appearance in his diary: "Buford [is] a large red faced-red headed looking man,—clothing singular." Guerrant left no additional observation to clarify the nature of the officer's uniform, but it was clear that Buford and some one thousand cavalry were moving through the region.[22]

While under Loring, Buford continued to indulge in his penchant for diversion. A member of the 27th Alabama Infantry Regiment recorded that on one occasion the local citizenry gathered to watch a review when "General Buford being somewhat of a ladies man got up a sham battle for their entertainment." The festivities proved less pleasurable for the participants than their observers. "It was a hot day and we double-quicked, yelled, and charged the Pointe Coupee battery all afternoon, until we were ready to drop from exhaustion," the fellow noted. "It was fun for the General and spectators, but we didn't enjoy it 'a little bit.'"[23]

By the end of 1862, Buford joined Bragg's forces in the vicinity of Murfreesboro, Tennessee. In conjunction with cavalry under Brigadier General John A. Wharton on the Confederate left, Buford had responsibility for protecting the railroad as Bragg's command grappled with the mounted forces of Major General William S. Rosecrans. In the heavy fighting that spanned the new year of 1863 in the vicinity of Stones River, near Murfreesboro, Tennessee, Buford's cavalry suffered only minimal casualties.[24]

In January 1863, Buford illustrated once more his impassioned nature and desire for justice when he preferred charges against Colonel John R. Butler of the 3rd Kentucky Cavalry Regiment for, what one historian termed, "misbehavior before the enemy." Although it was unclear from Buford's post-action report what the nature of the dereliction might be, the officer pointedly omitted Butler in noting "the good conduct and military bearing of most of the officers and men of my command." Reminiscent of his fiery relations with Captain Steen before the Civil War, such responses remained a part of Buford's character for the remainder of his life as well. In later years, this characterization appeared to some as a broader trait; for instance, a writer in the *New York Times* observed that: "The Buford family has always been looked upon as quick-tempered."[25]

In any case, shortly after the Butler incident, Brigadier General Buford transferred to Port Hudson, Louisiana, below Vicksburg on the Mississippi River. Returns for the command placed his numbers at 230 officers and 2,565 men from units that hailed from Alabama, Kentucky, and Louisiana under his charge. But the Kentuckian soon expressed a desire for reassignment from this remote posting. "Buford wishes to take the field under your command," Port Hudson commander Major General Franklin Gardner informed Lieutenant General John C. Pemberton at Jackson, Mississippi. Orders went out promptly to reassign the Kentuckian accordingly.[26]

During the Vicksburg Campaign, Buford commanded a brigade in Loring's Division. At Champion Hill this consisted of four Alabama regiments, two from Kentucky and one each from Arkansas and Louisiana, along with Companies A and C, Pointe Coupee Louisiana Artillery. Pushing his men forward under what he termed "a scorching sun" in his after-action report, Buford reached a critical point in the crumbling Confederate line. No longer in a position to embrace the offensive, the Kentuckian was able to facilitate a retreat. One scholar noted simply that "Buford would play a key role in making the departure possible." Buford received commendation from his commander for his performance at Champion Hill, where his command endured losses of eleven killed and forty-nine wounded. A contemporary

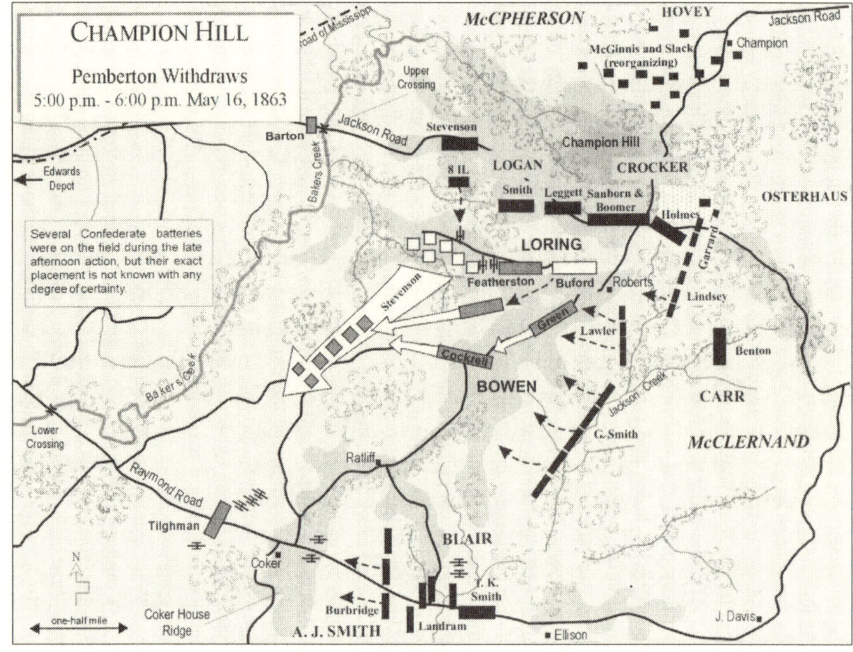

Battle of Champion Hill. Reproduced by permission from Timothy B. Smith, *Champion Hill: Decisive Battle for Vicksburg* (New York: Savas Beatie, 2004), 333.

noted simply in his journal: "Buford's Ky. brigade had a pretty lively fight on the extreme right of the army."[27]

In the aftermath of the heavy fighting that summer, Buford determined to keep his men sharp. One soldier recalled that while bivouacked in Mississippi, "we had a splendid drill ground and our education in that line was not neglected, as we drilled more during our stay here than in all our two years service." The commander sought additional ways in which to instill an edge for his troops. "General Buford instituted competitive drills between the different regiments of his brigade, which aroused such a spirit of emulation that we became very proficient in Hardee's tactics."[28]

In the spring of 1864, Buford became connected with Major General Nathan Bedford Forrest's command. The Confederate cavalryman had fought a bitter running battle in February with Union Brigadier General William Sooy Smith near Okolona, Mississippi, which had cost him heavily in men, including the death of his youngest brother, Colonel Jeffrey E. Forrest. Returning to the field for new operations was an imperative that required replacing the losses in officers, troopers, and mounts. Buford's addition, along with three short-handed and indifferently mounted regiments of Kentuckians, did not build Forrest's force appreciably in numbers, but they provided the nucleus of men who would serve the Confederate cavalry chieftain well for the remainder of the war.[29]

Assuming his post on March 8, Buford took charge of a division that consisted of Colonel Albert P. Thompson's and Colonel Tyree H. Bell's brigades, totaling 2,800 men ostensibly fit for duty. But the Kentuckian understood the condition of his command, characterized by artillerist Captain John Morton as "mere fragments" of units that suffered from inadequate uniforms and equipage, as well as a limited number of mounts. He lobbied his new chief vigorously for the opportunity to remedy the shortages.[30]

As their relationship developed, Forrest's new division commander became a mainstay for him. Forrest, nicknamed "The Wizard of the Saddle," trusted Buford for independent missions, allowing the command to extend its reach and enhance its psychological impact on their opponents. The convivial and popular subordinate's presence also rendered camp life more palatable for everyone. One contemporary indicated that "generally," Buford's "chief commissary kept a supply of good Nelson County Bourbon, which he always set before us" when the occasion arose to visit his headquarters.[31]

Another incident illustrated the ways in which one regiment foiled their commander's attempt at a lesson in discipline. To Buford's dismay, when he arrived for an inspection, the men had so thoroughly policed the grounds that the general could find nothing to criticize. However, the next camp was less prepared for the visitor, and the men proved less fortunate. A member of the first regiment gloated with unalloyed satisfaction at the second regiment's fate. "The General ordered the Colonel to drill them under his supervision until they could hardly stand."[32]

Buford's most notable service under Forrest came in 1864, which opened with a campaign swing through the western portions of Tennessee and Kentucky. On March 25, Buford led his command into Paducah, drawing fire from the Union garrison defending nearby Fort Anderson, along with two support gunboats from the river. His command suffered its heaviest losses when Colonel Albert P. Thompson, who lived in Paducah, led an ill-advised mounted charge from some sheltering buildings across the open ground between the fort and river. Union artillery fire blasted Thompson from his horse and emptied other saddles. Forrest's troops had to content themselves with rifling the town for such spoils they could find and in engaging the Union forces in a long-range duel. In the aftermath of the fighting, in view of its losses and the generally weakened condition of the division, as well as the proximity of the men to their homes during the campaign, Forrest allowed many of the Kentuckians to scatter to obtain remounts and recruits. This activity allowed Buford to miss the Confederate assault on Fort Pillow and the resulting notoriety associated with it.[33]

In the course of the raid into the western regions of Kentucky and Tennessee, word began spreading (erroneously) that Forrest had perished. Farther to the east, Guerrant took the news with mixed reactions. "There is also a distressing rumor of the death of Genl. Forrest, the hero of West. Tenn. & K'y. We hope & believe it is untrue." But, Guerrant also saw a reason to be encouraged even if the worst had transpired: "Genl. Buford is said to be in West'n Ky, & proclaim his ability & intention to hold it. One good Abe!"[34]

Forrest was not dead, but Buford enjoyed a measure of satisfaction when reports reached him that the Federals in Paducah had bragged in newspaper accounts of successfully hiding a number of horses in an abandoned mill when the Confederates first struck. Spurred by this intelligence, Buford boldly returned to the river town on the afternoon of April 14 and claimed the prized animals he had missed previously while pinning the Union defenders in their works. This operation not only demonstrated the grit and determination that typically motivated Buford, but his ability to act independently. It also underscored the degree to which the Confederate cavalry now needed to go to replenish their lost or broken-down horses.[35]

In June, Buford delivered his most effective service under Forrest at Brice's Cross Roads. The Confederates faced a formidable Federal combined force: eight thousand infantry and cavalry under Major General Samuel D. Sturgis advancing from Memphis across upper Mississippi. Forrest had hastened back from an abortive raid and scrambled to determine the precise course of the Union line of march. At a council of war held on June 9, Buford suggested that the nature of the advance would allow the Southerners to defeat the Federal cavalry before their infantry comrades could reach them in support, and Forrest adopted the formula.[36]

In the early morning hours of June 10, Forrest met with Buford at Booneville and instructed him to wait for Colonel Bell's arrival before moving forward. Buford allowed Bell's men to draw rations and left Booneville at approximately 7:30 A.M. while Forrest pressed ahead for Brice's Cross Roads. When word of fighting there reached him, Buford knew his chief needed him on the field. He paused to send out a flanking force under Colonel Clark S. Barteau at Old Carrollville and then rode the length of his command, exhorting the men to pick up the pace.

Buford arrived at the battlefield about 1 P.M., with Captain John Morton and the Confederate artillery in tow. According to Morton, Forrest asked Buford, "What do you think of the situation of the two armies, general?" Assessing the circumstances as he understood them, the Kentuckian responded in a fashion that could only please his fiery commander: "Our troops are nearly all up; the artillery will soon reach us; the enemy is scattered; the only thing for us to do is to fight, and fight d—n quick!" Although Bell's men were yet to arrive, Forrest ordered the artillery into action immediately, to "develop the position of the enemy's batteries and his lines."[37]

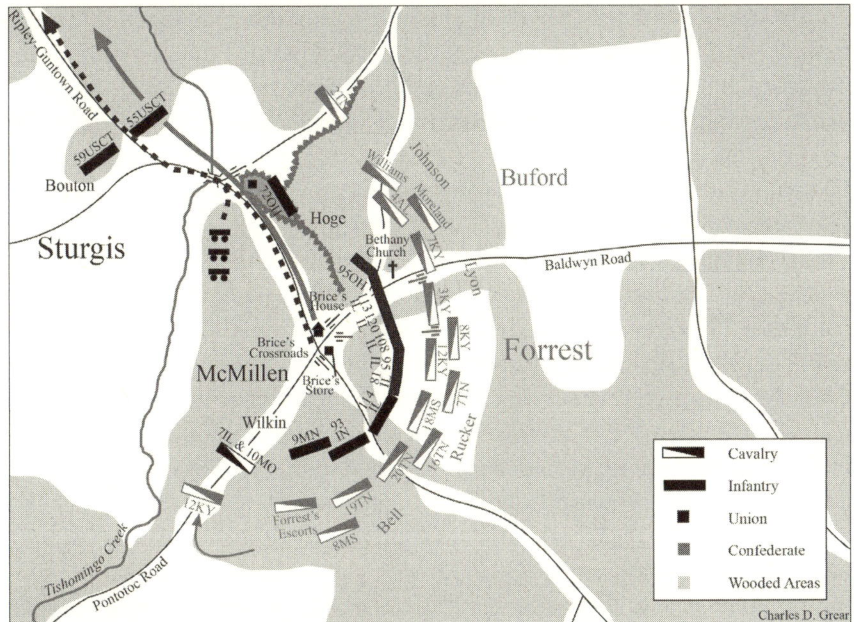

Battle of Brice's Cross Roads—afternoon assault on Union infantry. Reproduced by permission from Stewart Bennett, *The Battle of Brice's Crossroads* (Charleston, SC: History Press, 2012), 99.

In the course of the engagement and knowing the precarious nature of the fighting that remained, Buford used deception to strengthen his hand. Late in the day, as the winded Union foot soldiers replaced their mounted comrades, Buford drew upon his infantryman's service by barking out orders that normally applied only to infantry units. Employing a "stentorian" voice that carried across the lines, the Kentuckian commanded: "Fix bayonets." A young participant recalled years later that the general understood his tactic well, "talking" as he was "for the benefit of the Yankees." As the Confederates surged forward, the subterfuge provided at least a psychological nudge to the wavering bluecoat defenders, who could not be sure of the nature of the force they were actually facing amidst the blackjack thickets that covered much of the battlefield.[38]

Success seemed to have swung toward the Confederates, but as he rode forward to the Brice House at the critical crossroads, Buford thought the artillery pieces on his front were exposed and required more adequate protection in their position. When Buford told Forrest about the situation, he received the distinctive reply, "Support h—l, let it support itself; all the d—n Yankees in the country can't take it."[39]

As the Union forces gave way under the pressure, Buford joined in the pursuit. In the process, he demonstrated an endurance that surpassed his commander's when he followed the broken blue-coated formations back toward Memphis, even after the redoubtable Forrest had collapsed from the saddle in exhaustion. A participant recalled that "mounted on a Kentucky thoroughbred, one of his own rearing, he hung on to that flying column, and every chance he got would rush down on them."

In the darkness of the night, two Federal stragglers stumbled into the midst of the Southern pursuers and inquired whose command they had encountered. "My command, A. Buford," came the reply, and the two Federals scampered off. After this incident, Buford insisted upon greater vigilance from his tired men and berated them for being "a lot of d—n sandlappers riding along half asleep." Some of the men tried to offer the sheepish defense of darkness preventing proper identification, but Buford was having none of it. "See h—l," he responded vigorously, "smell 'em."

Near the end of the grueling pursuit from Brice's Cross Roads, Buford began finally to show signs of wear from the exertions he and the remaining Confederates were experiencing. "Call in your skirmishers, take some of them down the road, and put out a picket," he directed. "We will stay right here till morning." Then as a telling aside he noted sharply, "Every d—n man with me is sound asleep."[40]

Sturgis's effort had ended in a spectacular defeat, but new Federal advances followed. When a Union expedition set out once more from Memphis under Major General Andrew Jackson Smith, Forrest and newly promoted Lieutenant General Stephen D. Lee determined to block the way and defeat the invading force. Forrest dispatched Buford with orders for him "to develop the enemy's strength," but he was not to bring on a general engagement before his commander was ready or allow himself to suffer any unexpected setback in the process. Forrest understood Buford would be sufficiently aggressive, without assuming undue risks. Smith was pushing the Confederates before him, but then turned suddenly eastward, compelling Forrest to adjust accordingly.[41]

By July 14, Smith was a few miles west of Tupelo at Harrisburg, dug in and awaiting whatever Forrest and Lee might send against him. Buford thought the notion of a frontal assault a foolish proposition and predicted "we are going to be badly whipped." Forrest had been suffering from various ailments and from irritation at his inability to inflict much damage on Smith's column as it marched. His response suggested less judiciousness than the situation required. "You don't know what you are talking about," Forrest blurted, "we'll whip 'em in five minutes." But Buford had reckoned more realistically with this opponent and the defensive position the Federals held to be swept up by a show of intrepidity. "I hope you may be right," he noted quietly, "but I don't believe it."[42]

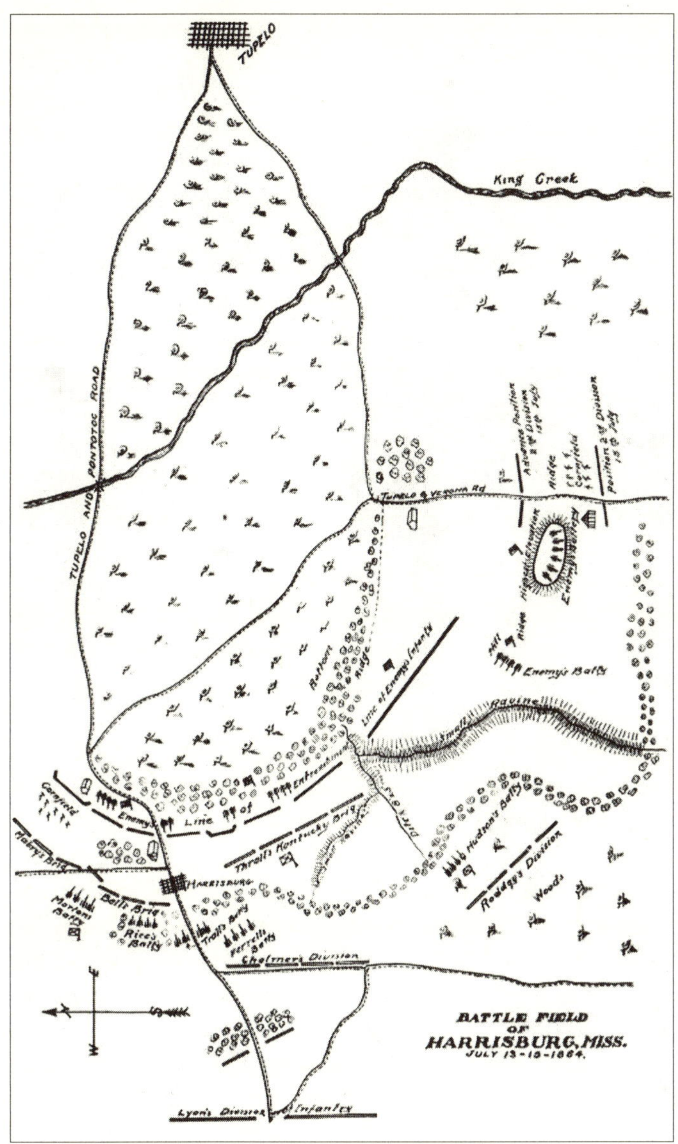

Battle of Harrisburg (or Tupelo). Library of Congress.

At Harrisburg, Buford's 3,200-man division occupied the Confederate left. A misreading of intelligence regarding Union intentions prompted Forrest to unleash an assault piecemeal that became bogged down in a confusion of orders and the brutal Union fire that opened on them. Despite their commander's reservations, Buford's men surged forward. Major General Smith noted the way in which order rapidly broke down among his attacking opponents, with men engaged in what amounted to "a foot race to see who should reach us first." Blazing Federal artillery and musket fire dissolved the attacking ranks, repeating the process every time the Confederates rallied, reformed, and came on again. Forrest did what he could through the starch of his personality, but stiffening of resolve was not going to salvage the poorly coordinated and disorganized offensive. Buford's command alone lost 153 killed and 798 wounded in the fighting.[43]

The heavy casualties impacted the Kentuckian's mood so severely that when Forrest inquired of his men, the "much grieved" subordinate could only say, "I have no command. They are all killed." Despite his successful defense at Harrisburg, Smith's subsequent retreat to Memphis ended the immediate Union threat. However, Buford remained committed to thwarting similar thrusts into the heart of Mississippi, including another by Smith in August.[44]

In the meantime, tempers flared among Forrest's officers as the heat of summer at last subsided. Forrest had clashed over a relatively trivial matter earlier in the year with Brigadier General James R. Chalmers, first relieving and then restoring him to command. Both men served well together after this, but in the fall, Chalmers had a similar confrontation with Buford in which he brought charges for insubordinate conduct when the Kentuckian denounced his fellow general heatedly and publicly over accusations that Buford had retained some of the runaway slaves his men had captured for their own use.[45]

Whatever prejudice to the cause either man felt the other had exhibited, both quickly had more than enough reason from the Federals to set internecine squabbling aside. The Union operations in Mississippi in the summer of 1864 had achieved a larger strategic effect by preventing Forrest and his men from threatening the supply lines sustaining Major General William T. Sherman's push toward Atlanta. Atlanta was in Union hands before Forrest could turn to the task of disruption, a task others had expected earlier. Even when he finally pounced on the Federal supply lines, these efforts remained largely confined to northern Alabama and the lower portion of Middle Tennessee, but at the end of October Forrest set his sights on Johnsonville's substantial Union supply depot on the banks of the Tennessee River.

Buford led the vanguard of the expedition, reaching the Tennessee River near Fort Heiman on October 24, and ordered his artillery into positions to command the waterway. With these dispositions complete, before long Buford noted the approach of four vessels heading northward, or downstream, from Johnsonville, but the cavalry commander allowed the empty boats to pass unmolested. "I want a loaded boat, a richer prize," he explained. "Just wait until one comes up the river, then you may take her if you can."[46]

The opportunity came on October 29. The steamer *Mazeppa* approached, with a barge in tow. Once the shelling started, the vessel quickly headed onto the opposite bank and the crew abandoned her. An enterprising horseman swam across the river and attached a line with which the Confederates secured their prize. Filled with articles of clothing and supplies, the *Mazeppa* contained an additional boon for the Kentucky general who preferred his amenities when he could have them. "Plenty of meat, boys, plenty of hardtack, plenty of shoes and clothes for the boys," Buford was supposed to have observed, "but just enough brandy for the General."[47]

The Confederates would have other successes, capturing another steamboat and a gunboat that they tried to use themselves, but the career of Forrest's men on water proved short-lived. Most importantly, effective placement of artillery across the Tennessee from the depot and Johnsonville defenses allowed the Confederates to wreak considerable damage to the supplies and other assets gathered there. Forrest set the amount of property destroyed at almost $7 million, including gunboats, transports, barges, and warehouse and dock facilities. During the barrage battering the Union depot and defenses, Buford joined with a jubilant Forrest to serve as a crew member on one of the artillery pieces.[48]

From Johnsonville, the Confederate raiders joined General John Bell Hood's Army of Tennessee as it marched toward Nashville. During that difficult campaign, Buford attempted to threaten Major General John M. Schofield's command before it could unite with Major General George H. Thomas in the Tennessee capital. The rigorous work cost Buford at least one mount to hostile fire, and lack of ammunition prevented him from assisting effectively against Union forces near Spring Hill and Franklin. The missed opportunity for a decisive blow at Spring Hill and the subsequent mauling of Hood's infantry at Franklin (including the loss of fourteen general officers) crippled the army for the balance of the campaign.

While Hood remained ensconced with his main force outside the defenses of Nashville, he detached Forrest to disrupt and disable the Nashville & Chattanooga Railroad. On December 2, Forrest detailed Buford's division "for the purpose of destroying stockades and block-houses" on the rail line, and over the next several days, the Kentuckian bent to his work with gusto. Capturing a number of the Union structures meant to protect the railroad, Buford and his men took some 350 Federal prisoners and inflicted as much damage as possible under the circumstances of a swift-moving campaign.[49]

Once, however, Buford's failure to disable the rail line allowed reinforcements to reach one of the endangered blockhouses. A seething Forrest ordered his lieutenant to assault the work anyway. "Stop the port-holes with rails and burn it," he insisted. Buford balked at such a suicidal approach, but he did succeed in securing the surrender of the garrison with the help of Captain Morton's artillery pieces instead of having to make a costly direct assault.[50]

A few days later, at Murfreesboro, the Kentuckian helped Forrest prevent a serious disaster when infantry assigned to his expedition broke and fled from a Union attack outside the formidable Fortress Rosecrans. Buford's demonstration on the opposite end of the town, carried out under his own initiative, caused the Federals to pull back sufficiently to allow Forrest to regain control and extract his main force from danger.[51]

Thomas's rout of Hood's forces outside Nashville on December 15–16 compelled Forrest to break off his operations around Murfreesboro. He ordered Buford to move to the assistance of the Army of Tennessee as it retreated. The Kentuckian and his men joined the already-pressed Southern rear guard near Franklin. Buford's horsemen undertook the difficult duty with the dedication that characterized their general's usual approach to the tasks assigned to him. During the ensuing fight on December 17, Buford came perilously close to being killed or seriously hurt. Only timely intervention prevented it when a Confederate comrade used an empty gun to parry a saber blow aimed at Buford's head. Then the strapping cavalry commander delivered himself by taking hold of his antagonist so firmly that the man claimed later that he would have preferred to have been "hugged by a bear." The bluecoat ended the engagement as a prisoner after being unhorsed himself. A participant recalled later that in the aftermath of the fight, Buford showed the effects of the combat. "His head was tied up," James McNeilly explained, adding from his perspective as a clergyman that Buford "was in a bad humor, even profane temper."[52]

In a subsequent rearguard action at Richland's Creek on Christmas Eve, however, Buford was even less fortunate, suffering a severe leg wound that forced him to relinquish command in the field. He had recovered from his injury sufficiently to accept an assignment in Alabama during the closing days of the conflict. But the effects of his rough-handling during the retreat from Tennessee lingered into the new year and had at least one unintended social consequence. While attending the February 8, 1865, wedding of his comrade, Stephen D. Lee, Buford's formidable stamina gave way and he fainted at the reception.[53]

Shortly after this incident, Buford returned to duty in Alabama under now Lieutenant General Nathan Bedford Forrest, but was unable to assist in preventing the fall of Selma to an overwhelming Union force under Major General James Harrison Wilson in April. Wilson's command proceeded to capture Montgomery and then moved on to Columbus, Georgia, where Buford experienced a final brush with death as he got separated from his command while conducting a reconnaissance. Riding back toward what he thought was the safety of his camp, he confronted a Union soldier who demanded his surrender. Spurring his horse and firing at his antagonist as he passed, Buford escaped, but the moment remained embedded in his mind and led to an alarming postwar encounter that he deemed even more frightening. In that instance, Buford found himself alone in a Springfield, Illinois, hotel lobby when a group of Union soldiers noted his presence and appeared increasingly agitated. When one of the men approached, after confirming his name on the registry, Buford expected the worst. Instead, the man offered his hand, explained that he was the soldier who had tried to stop him in Georgia and felt fortunate to have only sustained a wound in the arm. "I never was so glad to shake a hand in my life," the former Confederate recalled. "The other soldiers crowded around. It seems they were only excited because a late enemy was there. Before I left we all drank to the success of our common country"[54]

By May, with the surrender of Forrest's command at Gainesville, Alabama, Brigadier General Buford was prepared to lay down his arms and resume his civilian life. Brigadier General William Whipple, George H. Thomas's chief of staff, informed the commander of the Memphis garrison that the Confederate could not enter his home state unless he first took an oath of allegiance to the United States, "thereby divesting himself of the character of an officer in the rebel Army." While staying at the Gayoso House Hotel in Memphis as he awaited river transportation northward, Buford underscored the connection that remained between himself and his men when he provided a new suit and funds for a destitute former subordinate who was also trying to make his way home.[55]

With the war over, Abraham Buford enjoyed renewed prominence as a horse-breeder and racer in his native state. In 1866, he became part of an association composed of "thorough horsemen" striving to "improve the stock of Kentucky." Buford's passion remained developing animals that could dominate the racecourse and sire future winners, but he never seemed far removed from serious reverses. An account from just after his death noted: "He was always the victim of misfortune. In 1866 his stable, containing 26 horses, was burned and he lost $18,000." One of his most promising entries, the speedster Crossland, bore the name of fellow Kentuckian, Edward Crossland, who had also served with Forrest. However, the animal suffered a tragic ending. While engaged in a four-mile race, the horse pulled up and witnesses heard Buford exclaim that the steed had broken its leg. Nothing could be done to save the animal, and he had to be put down on the track.[56]

Buford's sense of honor remained a primary feature of his character, in addition to his passion for raising and racing horses. During the 1870 season, he found himself embroiled in a contretemps when a fellow turfman from Rhode Island questioned his veracity over a recent competition. "The General turned to him and told him to be careful what he was saying and remember to whom he was talking," a witness explained. But the fellow insisted, in the strongest terms, that Buford's account was wrong. "Thereupon

Gen. Buford knocked him down, pulled his coat over his head and stamped him," until others could pull the Kentuckian away. "The difficulty created the usual amount of excitement for awhile," the man noted, adding that no one seemed to regret the public display more than Buford, although the situation "left him no alternative."[57]

Post-war legal wrangling brought the Kentuckian to the bar more than once, and these contests frequently included wartime colleagues and adversaries in a new style of combat. In 1871, Buford engaged John C. Breckinridge, the former U.S. vice president and Confederate major general and secretary of war, to represent him in a civil suit. The comrades and fellow students at Centre College in Kentucky found themselves on opposite sides in the following year, when Breckinridge represented Lieutenant Colonel George Armstrong Custer in a legal action against Buford for an alleged failure to make restitution for the sale of an unsound animal.[58]

Personal tragedy befell Abraham Buford during 1872 as well. On November 2, his young son William died. The twenty-three-year-old was the couple's only child, and although the void in the Buford household was monumental, the "veteran turfman" had his racehorses and stock animals to blunt his deep sense of loss.[59]

The track provided a welcome diversion for the noted horseman. His horses continued to garner wins, although even the best of these was not immune to misfortune. In July 1878, at races in St. Louis, Missouri, Buford's champion McWhirter suffered a tragic experience that one newspaperman described as "the saddest and most heart-rending scene on any race-track in the world." The chestnut, worth $3,000, injured both forelegs as he made the valiant effort to finish the race. A botched effort to end the animal's agony only prolonged it and added to the distress for the owner who "had [already] determined to take him off the track" at the conclusion of the race.[60]

Buford enjoyed a brief moment of political success when he won a term in the Kentucky legislature in 1879. But numerous personal setbacks continued to beset him. On February 3 of that year, his wife Amanda died. A month later, his brother, Colonel Thomas Buford, shot and killed Judge Thomas M. Elliott of the Court of Appeals in Frankfort, Kentucky, for the role he perceived the jurist to have played in defrauding him and his sister of their property. Found guilty of first degree murder in July, Thomas was acquitted in a new trial on the grounds of insanity. Throughout the ordeal, Buford had been his brother's chief supporter and as such spent enormous personal sums of money. According to one source, "Abe, who was already in financial straits, became bankrupt through assisting the assassin in his defense." Another notice in a Memphis newspaper placed the effects of his strained finances in a different context: "General Buford was at one time an energetic better, but his circumstances at this time do not justify him in indulging in such uncertain business freely."[61]

As he contemplated his future, the former soldier sought a new form of refuge. Long considering his interests in the track as incompatible with church membership, Buford struggled to reconcile these matters in his own mind. In a lecture entitled "Church and Turf," he attempted to do so publicly, noting the devotion of his parents and his desire to embrace Christianity. The old soldier's most fervent argument was that the nation required the best in horseflesh for military purposes and that developing the best in the breed served that cause. Drawing upon his own experience and having established the improvements in the animals through the ages, he remarked: "What sort of a race would I have made during the war when chasing Sturgis back into Memphis mounted on one of Noah's mustang ponies? Or what would have become of me when Wilson was chasing me across the bridge near Columbus, Georgia on which the Yankee picket seized the bridle of my horse and struck me over the head with his sabre, mounted on one of Noah's horses? I would, indeed have been a lost child." In the wake of subsequent criticism for his stance, Buford noted simply that he had not expected so vehement a response and insisted that his motives for the original lecture were pure, drawing upon the image of the prophet Elijah's entrance into Heaven. "My earthly career is drawing more rapidly to a close, and my great aim now is to win the race for eternal life; and . . . if I can pass through the pearly gates of heaven in a chariot drawn by Enquirer and McWhirter, I would shout with great joy."[62]

Buford took his message to other audiences as well. Delivering his lecture on "Church and Turf" in Chicago, he paused during his visit to speak with a newspaperman who recorded the essence of "a long and pleasant interview" with the "well-known Confederate and daring General." Buford recalled that his wife "had often begged him to join the church" and observed that he "wished" he had done so "before she died."[63]

Despite his desire for a measure of peace in his life, the many tragedies, exacerbated by severe bouts of depression, weighed heavily on Buford. Even so, he made every effort to remain involved in community affairs, including writing for turf magazines and attending fairs, races, and other events. On one such occasion, Buford related an adventurous experience during his service on the plains prior to the war. The incident involved an 1842 chase for a "great white horse" that the Kentuckian had hoped to corral. Although well-mounted and determined, he failed in the effort and his comrades taunted: "Why, Medoc (which was my nickname among the officers) I thought you were going to capture the 'white horse,' mounted on your thoroughbred from the blue-grass region?" Buford explained that his horse, Cid, carrying a rider, "was too heavily handicapped, although my avoirdupois was not near so great as it is to-day." A short time later, while in Lexington, Kentucky, Buford also displayed his sense of humor when a local lad offered to hold his overcoat for a quarter. "My boy," the old warrior remarked, "you should not commence this extortion so soon in life."[64]

The death of his wife and his brother's travails left him grief-stricken and financially vulnerable. The loss of his home in April to these monetary difficulties further devastated the proud Kentuckian. The following month he was forced to sell off his prized racehorses; one of these thoroughbreds—Enquirer—went to a former comrade, William H. "Red" Jackson, who had also ridden with Forrest, but this was of little solace.[65]

In June 1884, Buford traveled to Danville, Indiana, where he stayed with his nephew, Benjamin T. Buford. "[G]reat joviality" had always marked earlier visits, but on this occasion his demeanor was decidedly darker, and "he was despondent, and he appeared gloomy and distressed." Buford's mood worsened when a newspaper account revisited the fate of his brother, who had just been returned to Anchorage Insane Hospital in a state of extreme duress.

Under these difficult circumstances, Buford excused himself from breakfast and "retired to his room." Writing his thoughts on two scraps of paper, he drew a pistol and pulled the trigger, dying by his own hand on June 9, 1884. In both notes, Buford exposed his state of mind, although he instructed his nephew not to be "affrighted" by what was about to happen. "I have no home to go to, and prefer death to any further struggle with life," he explained. "My cross is too heavy; I can't keep it out of the dust. . . . My troubles and those of my unfortunate brother Tom have driven me mad."

In another message found with his body, Buford expressed his wish to be interred in Lexington Cemetery, in Lexington, Kentucky, alongside his wife and son. At the same time, he observed that his "financial troubles have driven me to despair" and lamented having "lost my only chance to retrieve my unfortunate brother and self." The "future" had become too "dark for me to struggle against any further." Buford closed with a wish for peace and "may God have mercy on my troubled soul." The man who had overcome so many obstacles in warfare and whose thoroughbreds so often surged to success on the track or sired future champions had reached the end of his own life's race.[66]

In the war that marked the heart of his adult years, Abraham Buford performed extensive service to both the United and the Confederate States. As both a soldier and a citizen he essentially seemed to fit the profile of the "character of Kentucky troops" that John Hunt Morgan's kinsman Basil W. Duke had drawn:

> Give them officers that they love, respect, and rely on, and any thing can be accomplished with them. While almost irrepressibly fond of whisky, and incorrigible, when not on active service . . . they, nevertheless, stick to work at the time when it is necessary, and answer to the roll-call in an emergency unfailingly, no matter

> what may be the prospect before them. . . . They can not endure harsh and insulting language, or any thing that is humiliating. In this respect they show the traits which characterize all of their Southern brethren.[67]

As a commander of both infantry and cavalry, Buford developed a sense of discipline for himself and his men that helped produce positive results in the field. His performance as an officer under Nathan Bedford Forrest was especially significant. During 1864, Buford contributed to Forrest's campaigns in ways that others could not match in the degree of determination and effectiveness. The writer of a sketch of the officer just prior to Buford's death related to readers the relationship between the Confederates: "General Forrest placed great reliance upon his military skill and his invariably admirable conduct in the face of the enemy. He had all the instincts and sagacity of a great soldier." A modern historian noted simply that Buford was one of the rare West Pointers that Forrest came to respect and trust.[68]

Although the colorful persona of "The Wizard of the Saddle" often overshadowed the exploits of his subordinates, Buford had been the one Forrest could count upon in the direst of circumstances. But, as one of Buford's troopers ultimately concluded, "the grand old man who contributed so much to the fame of Forrest's command," received "so little consideration" for his accomplishments.[69]

Even so, Abraham Buford was content with the verdict of his men and the commander he had served and a wartime record that established him as one of Forrest's most capable lieutenants.

Notes

1. Bennett H. Young, quoted in Henry George, *History of the 3d, 7th, 8th, and 12th Kentucky, C.S.A.* (1911; repr., Melber, KY, 1987), vii.
2. Ezra J. Warner, *Generals in Gray: Lives of the Confederate Commanders* (Baton Rouge, LA, 1959), 39; "General A. Buford," *Memphis Public Ledger*, Oct. 27, 1882; *Official Register of the Officers and Cadets of the U.S. Military Academy, West Point, New York* (n.p., 1838), 17, 23 and (n.p., 1841), 10, 20; *Register of the Officers and Cadets of the U.S. Military Academy, West Point, New York* (n.p., 1839), 13, 24 and (n.p., 1840), 12, 23.
3. Richard S. Ewell, *Letters of General Richard S. Ewell: Stonewall's Successor*, ed. Donald C. Pfanz (Knoxville, TN, 2012), 111. Originally established on April 20, 1824, Fort Gibson had been closed in 1836, but reopened in January 1837 and remained occupied until June 1857. Robert W. Frazer, *Forts of the West: Military Forts and Presidios and Posts Commonly Called Forts West of the Mississippi River to 1898* (Norman, OK, 1972), 120–21; "General A. Buford."

4. "General A. Buford."

5. R. H. Chilton to Dr. Jno, Dec. 23, 1844, Robert H. Chilton Collection, Library of the Museum of the Confederacy, Richmond, VA (hereafter cited as Chilton Collection, LMC).

6. R. H. Chilton to Dr. Jno, Feb. 1, 1845, Chilton Collection, LMC.

7. Ibid. Although Chilton's and Henry S. Turner's letters indicate the couple to have been married before February 1845, other sources list December 15, 1845 as the date for their wedding based upon Amanda's tombstone. See "General A. Buford"; Marshall D. Krolick, "Brig. Gen. Abraham H. Buford," in *Kentuckians in Gray: Confederate Generals and Field Officers of the Bluegrass State*, ed. Bruce S. Allardice and Lawrence Lee Hewitt (Lexington, KY, 2008), 50.

8. Buford to "Dear Johnson," Apr. 10, [18]45, Chilton Collection, LMC.

9. R. H. Chilton to Dr Jno, July 13 [1845], Chilton Collection, LMC.

10. Turner to "My dear John," Oct. 30, 1845, Chilton Collection, LMC.

11. Quoted in William S. Kiser, *Dragoons in Apacheland: Conquest and Resistance in Southern New Mexico, 1846–1861* (Norman, OK, 2012), 66.

12. Kiser, *Dragoons in Apacheland*, 104, 238; Frazer, *Forts of the West*, 99.

13. R. S. Ewell to "Dear Ben," July 21, 1852, in Ewell, *Letters of General Richard S. Ewell*, 109.

14. Lowell H. Harrison, "Kentucky-born Generals in the Civil War," *Register of the Kentucky Historical Society* 64 (Apr. 1966): 134; Krolick, "Brig. Gen. Abraham H. Buford," 50.

15. Martha McDowell Buford Jones, *Peach Leather and Rebel Gray: Bluegrass Life and the War, 1860–1865. Farm and Social life, Famous Horses, Tragedies of War. Diary and Letters of a Confederate Wife*, eds. Mary E. Wharton and Ellen F. Williams (Lexington, KY, 1986), 17; "Suicide of Abe Buford," *New York Times*, June 10, 1884.

16. Mercer Otey, "The Story of Our Great War," *Confederate Veteran* 9, no. 3 (Mar. 1901): 110; James H. McNeilly, "With the Rear Guard," *Confederate Veteran* 26, no. 8 (Aug. 1918): 338.

17. Jones, *Peach Leather and Rebel Gray*, 20, 26, 85.

18. Ibid., 10–11.

19. Krolick's argument that "Buford became an ardent advocate of states' [*sic*] rights, but counseled against secession" fit the Kentuckian's course at the opening of the Civil War. Krolick, "Brig. Gen. Abraham H. Buford," 51. In his postwar memoir, George maintained that Buford acted unequivocally: "When it became evident that war between the North and South could not be averted, Captain Buford without hesitation cast his lot with the South." George, *History of the 3d, 7th, 8th, and 12th Kentucky, C.S.A.*, 148.

20. U.S. War Department, *The War of the Rebellion: A Compilation of the Official Records of the Union and Confederate Armies,* 128 vols. (Washington, DC, 1880–1901), ser. 2, vol. 2:1523 (hereafter cited as *OR;* all references are to series 1 unless otherwise indicated).

21. Ibid., 1523–24.

22. *OR,* vol. 16, pt. 2:867; Edward O. Guerrant, *Bluegrass Confederate: The Headquarters Diary of Edward O. Guerrant,* ed. William C. Davis and Meredith L. Swentor (Baton Rouge, LA, 1999), 154–55.

23. J. P. Cannon, *Bloody Banners and Barefoot Boys: A History of the 27th Regiment Alabama Infantry CSA: The Civil War Memoirs and Diary Entries of J. P. Cannon M.D.,* ed. Noel Crowson and John V. Brogden (Shippensburg, PA, 1997), 36.

24. *OR,* vol. 20, pt. 1:663–64.

25. Krolick maintained that this incident may have played a role in Bragg's decision to transfer Butler's regiment and reassign Buford to Mississippi under Lieutenant General John C. Pemberton to ease the tensions and bring a close to the matter. Krolick, "Brig. Gen. Abraham H. Buford," 51–52; *OR,* vol. 20, pt. 1:971; "Gen. Abe Buford of Kentucky," *New York Times,* Feb. 10, 1882.

26. *OR,* vol. 15:273–74; 1032, 1033, 1037.

27. Timothy B. Smith, *Champion Hill: Decisive Battle for Vicksburg* (New York, 2004), 305, 412–13; *OR,* vol. 24, pt. 2:86, 88, 89; John S. Jackman, *Diary of a Confederate Soldier: John S. Jackman of the Orphan Brigade,* ed. William C. Davis (Columbia, SC, 1990), 79.

28. Cannon, *Bloody Banners and Barefoot Boys,* 49.

29. Forrest set his casualties in the three days of fighting at 27 killed, 97 wounded, and 20 missing. *OR,* vol. 32, pt. 1:354–55; John Allan Wyeth, *Life of General Nathan Bedford Forrest* (New York, 1899), 296–323. Information on Buford in his career with Forrest is drawn widely from Brian S. Wills, *A Battle from the Start: The Life of Nathan Bedford Forrest* (New York, 1992), 169–300 passim, and Robert Selph Henry, *"First with the Most" Forrest* (Indianapolis, 1944), 235–442 passim.

30. John Watson Morton, *The Artillery of Nathan Bedford Forrest's Cavalry* (Nashville, 1909), 160; Thomas Jordan and J. P. Pryor, *The Campaigns of Lieut.-Gen. N. B. Forrest, and of Forrest's Cavalry, with Portraits, Maps, and Illustrations* (New Orleans, 1868), 403–4, 406.

31. Otey, "Story of Our Great War," 110.

32. Cannon, *Bloody Banners and Barefoot Boys,* 44–45, 133.

33. Jordan and Pryor, *Campaigns of Lieut.-Gen. N. B. Forrest,* 415.

34. Guerrant, *Bluegrass Confederate,* 415–16.

35. Jordan and Pryor, *Campaigns of Lieut.-Gen. N.B. Forrest,* 417.

36. Nathaniel Cheairs Hughes Jr., et al., *Brigadier General Tyree H. Bell, C.S.A.: Forrest's Fighting Lieutenant* (Knoxville, TN, 2004), 141.

37. Wyeth, *Life of General Nathan Bedford Forrest*, 416; Buford quoted in John Watson Morton, "Battle of Tishomingo Creek or Brice's Cross-Roads," *Southern Bivouac* 1, nos. 9–10 (May-June 1883), 369. Morton placed the account at the Brice House after the Confederates had broken the Union line.

38. Henry Ewell Hord, "Brice's X Roads from a Private's View," *Confederate Veteran* 12, no. 11 (Nov. 1904): 529–30.

39. Morton, "Battle of Tishomingo Creek," 371. Wyeth quoted Forrest differently: "Buford, all the Yankees in front of us cannot get to Morton's guns." Wyeth, *Life of General Nathan Bedford Forrest*, 416.

40. Previous paragraphs based upon Henry Ewell Hord, "Pursuit of Gen. Sturgis," *Confederate Veteran* 13, no. 1 (Jan. 1905): 18.

41. Buford report, July 22, 1864, *OR*, vol. 39, pt. 1:329. For a fuller assessment of the campaign and Buford's role in it, see also Thomas E. Parson, *Work for Giants: The Campaign and Battle of Tupelo/Harrisburg, Mississippi, June-July 1864* (Kent, OH), 2014.

42. General [James R.] Chalmers, "Forrest and His Campaigns," *Southern Historical Society Papers* 7 (1879): 476–77.

43. *OR*, vol. 39, pt. 1:252, 331–37.

44. James Dinkins, *1861 to 1865, by an Old Johnnie: Personal Recollections and Experiences in the Confederate Army* (Cincinnati, 1897), 169.

45. Wills, *Battle from the Start*, 169–71; Andrew Ward, *River Run Red: The Fort Pillow Massacre in the American Civil War* (New York, 2005), 353, 487n16.

46. R. R. Hancock, *Hancock's Diary: or a History of the Second Tennessee Confederate Cavalry, with Sketches of First and Seventh Battalions; also Portraits and Biographical Sketches* (Nashville, 1887), 495.

47. Ibid., 496.

48. *OR*, vol. 39, pt. 1:871.

49. Ibid., vol. 45, pt. 1:754–55.

50. Hancock, *Hancock's Diary*, 523–24.

51. *OR*, vol. 45, pt. 1:613, 755–56.

52. Hancock, *Hancock's Diary*, 534; Dinkins, *1861 to 1864*, 251. Captain H. A. Tyler enlarged the number of opponents to three: the first Buford shot, a second he struck with the handgrip of his pistol, and the third he "grabbed by the hair" and toppled from horseback. Tyler, "Forrest Covers Hood's Retreat," *Confederate Veteran* 12, no. 9 (Sept. 1904), 436; McNeilly, "With the Rear Guard," 338.

53. *OR*, vol. 45, pt. 1:567, 593, 757–58; Herman Hattaway, *General Stephen D. Lee* (Jackson, MS, 1976), 150–51.

54. "Why Buford was Scared," *Point Pleasant (WV) Weekly Register*, July 16, 1884.

55. *OR*, ser. 2, vol. 8:588; Henry Hord, "Scouting About Memphis," *Confederate Veteran* 20, no. 5 (May 1912), 208.

56. "Horses in Kentucky," *Nashville Daily Union and American*, Mar. 28, 1866; "Gen. Abe Buford's Suicide," *Stanford (KY) Semi-Weekly Interior Journal*, June 13, 1884; Otey, "Story of Our Great War," 110.

57. "From Saratoga. The Buford-Babcock Difficulty," *Nashville Daily Union and American*, July 31, 1870.

58. William C. Davis, *Breckinridge: Statesman, Soldier, Symbol* (Baton Rouge, LA, 1974), 599.

59. "Gen. Abe Buford of Kentucky."

60. "M'Whirter's Death," *Opelousas (LA) Courier*, July 6, 1878.

61. "Suicide of Abe Buford," *Memphis Daily Appeal*, July 10, 1881.

62. A. Buford, *Church and Turf. Lecture by Gen'l. A. Buford. Delivered in Campbell-Street Church, Louisville, Ky., April 30th, 1882* (Louisville, KY, 1882), 4–5, 7, 12–13.

63. P. K. M., "Another Letter from Our Summer Wanderer," *Pascagoula (MS) Democrat-Sun*, Aug. 4, 1882.

64. "Horses and Wolves," *Barbour County Index* (Medicine Lodge, KS), June 29, 1882; *Dodge City (KS) Times*, Sept, 28, 1882; *Maysville (KY) Daily Evening Bulletin*, Sept. 19, 1882.

65. Krolick, "Brig. Gen. Abraham H. Buford," 54–44; Hughes, *Brigadier General Tyree H. Bell*, 284.

66. "Suicide of Abe Buford." According to this *New York Times* article, "the General was found dead, with a bullet through his heart, a centre shot. Death was instantaneous." However, the *Stanford (KY) Semi-Weekly Interior Journal* article "Gen. Abe Buford's Suicide," disputed the location of the fatal wound, quoting from a Louisville newspaper account: "Yesterday morning, the report of a pistol was heard in his room, and when the door was opened he was found dead in his chair with his feet on a trunk. He had shot himself through the head." See also "Death of Col. Thomas Buford," *New York Times*, Feb. 14, 1885.

67. Basil W. Duke, *A History of Morgan's Cavalry* (Cincinnati, 1867), 208–9.

68. "General A. Buford," Parsons, *Work for Giants*, 147.

69. Hunter B. Williams, "Military Operations in the Jackson Purchase Area of Kentucky, 1862–1865, Part II," *Register of the Kentucky Historical Society* 63 (July 1965): 251.

Brigadier General Gideon J. Pillow. Courtesy of Lawrence Lee Hewitt.

Unwept, Unhonored, and Unsung: Gideon J. Pillow

Nathaniel Cheairs Hughes Jr.

Gideon Johnson Pillow looked to Andrew Jackson as his mentor and his model. So did his family. The Pillows of Maury and Giles Counties in Tennessee, powerful politically and wealthy landowners, were known to be ferocious Indian fighters and loyal Jackson lieutenants in Tennessee's turbulent early years. They had followed Jackson against the Creeks at Horseshoe Bend, and his uncle Colonel William Pillow, commander of the 2nd Tennessee Militia Regiment, had stood with him against the British at New Orleans.[1]

The son of Gideon Pillow and Annie Payne, Gideon Johnson Pillow Jr. was born in Maury County, Tennessee, June 8, 1806, and received his early schooling at Wurttenburg Academy in Pulaski, Tennessee, before entering Woodward Academy in nearby Columbia. He proved an able student, especially in Greek and Latin, and went on to the University of Nashville in 1823, where he continued to excel. Jackson would invite the young student to the Hermitage on Friday nights to spend the weekends, and they would talk.[2]

Pillow began reading law following graduation, and during this time in Nashville, he cultivated the friendship and won the confidence of Governor William Carroll (father of future Confederate Brigadier General William Henry Carroll). Pennsylvanian, merchant-soldier-politician, trusted follower of Andrew Jackson, and passionate Democrat, Carroll succeeded Jackson as major general of Tennessee's militia and would become Pillow's second model. In 1830, Pillow and Carroll went to Georgia at President Jackson's insistence to negotiate with the Cherokees; Pillow acted as secretary of the mission. Upon his return to Tennessee, Pillow opened his law office in Columbia. He proved quite good, a hard worker with a quick mind and a compelling speaking voice. He gained wide attention for winning the Grant A. Johnson case, and observers remarked that Felix Grundy,

Tennessee's undisputed champion as a criminal lawyer, had a challenger. Pillow would make a fortune handling both civil and criminal cases. Charming and capable, yet cocky, pretentious, quick tempered, and sensitive to slight and criticism, he held grudges and made enemies, a long list of whom included Andrew Johnson, Winfield Scott, and Andrew Jackson Donelson, the president's right-hand man and nephew. Blessed with boundless energy, affable, capable, inquisitive, and articulate, the young attorney fortunately made friends more easily than foes.

Quietly in 1830, at the behest of Governor Carroll, young Pillow began revising the *Digest and Revision of the Statute Laws of Tennessee*. The governor rewarded him further in 1831 when he appointed him as attorney general for the Ninth Solicitorial District. Two years later Pillow, now Major General Carroll's aide-de-camp with the rank of colonel in the Tennessee militia, would be named adjutant general of the state with the rank of brigadier general. The twenty-seven-year-old Pillow held this position for four years and would retain the title "General" for life. He grew convinced he could lead the soldiers of Tennessee in war. Intelligent men with common sense and leadership ability, Pillow thought, could succeed at arms despite a lack of formal military education or training. Andrew Jackson and William Carroll had proven this to his satisfaction.[3]

Pillow made a close friend of lawyer-politician James K. Polk of Columbia and supported him strongly in the Tennessee political wars of the 1830s. Indeed, Polk became indebted to Pillow when the latter defended his younger brother, who shot and killed attorney Robert H. Hayes on the street in Columbia. Polk and Pillow proved an effective team as the Democrats won control of both houses of the legislature as well as the governor's chair. Supporters approached Pillow about running for Congress, but he demurred, being fully involved with his plantation Clifton Place, just west of Columbia.

Pillow loved farming and was a fine farm manager, and under him Clifton became quite profitable. Pillow raised his sights, buying more slaves and more land, particularly in eastern Arkansas and northern Mississippi. He diversified, experimented, read agricultural periodicals avidly, and corresponded with agriculturalists like J. D. B. DeBow and Felix Kirk Zollicoffer. He experimented with different types of fertilizers to renew "the power of the soil." He toured the state urging Tennesseans to abandon their dependence upon cotton production, advocating corn, wheat, oats, and grass as staple products, as well as livestock. He championed labor-saving machinery, water power, railroads, and river improvements. Electricity intrigued him. Indeed, Pillow was enraptured with inventions of all sorts and advocated development of natural resources for the benefit of industry. "Push forward with energy and courage," he preached. As for himself, he produced pork and wool in significant quantity and won an important U.S. Navy hemp contract. He introduced a steam engine to manufacture twine, rope, and bagging. His dairy at Clifton was a marvel.[4]

Pillow never stood for electoral office and never held an office—oddly, to laymen of his day and to some later historians, especially as he exuded ambition. However, in 1844, Pillow's emphasis changed. Tennessee sent a delegation to the national convention of the Democratic Party with Pillow as its chairman, a surprising choice considering the political experience and reputation of the others. Polk wanted to be nominated as vice president, and Pillow made that his objective and the goal of the Tennessee delegation. Despite a badly divided group that included Andrew Johnson—and the fact that Polk did not attend—Pillow pushed Polk's cause splendidly at the convention. Rallying the influential, including delegates from the midwest and New England, he lifted their aims, in effect selling Polk to them as the compromise Democratic candidate for president. Dark horse Polk went on to win the nomination on the ninth ballot and, to the shock of the politically attuned, carried the election that fall against Whig Henry Clay with a plurality.

As his reward, Polk appointed Pillow to the rank of brigadier general and assigned him to command the Tennessee brigade headed to Texas. Literally with the luck of the draw, Pillow ranked second in seniority among the six new brigadiers appointed from civilian life and collecting in May 1846 on the banks of the Rio Grande. Pillow's brigade included as regimental commanders staunch Whigs William B. Campbell and William Haskell. Illness took a heavy toll on the brigade in Mexico—over half of the men ended up on the sick rolls—and in October 1846 Pillow himself fell victim to typhoid and "bloody dysantary."[5]

The following spring Polk promoted Pillow to major general of volunteers just in time for him to participate conspicuously in the siege of Vera Cruz and the fighting at Cerro Gordo, Contreras, and Chapultepec, all under Winfield Scott, who had succeeded Zachary Taylor as commander of American forces in Mexico. As division commander, Pillow fought well at Vera Cruz, then amateurishly at Cerro Gordo, winning a painful wound for his trouble. At Contreras, however, he played an important role competently and boldly, and at Chapultepec he was wounded again by a grapeshot that broke his ankle and tore apart the tendons of the top of the foot. He would not be denied, however, and had his men carry him up the hill on a blanket into the academy where he saw the American flag raised over the walls of the fortress.[6]

What remained for Pillow in Mexico was physical suffering, open discord with Scott, and court-martial. Ultimately Scott was removed from command, shocking the army and infuriating the professional officer corps.

Other dangers appeared. Senator John C. Calhoun recommended convening a Southern convention to deal with federal regulation of slavery in the territory acquired from Mexico. With talk of disunion and a confederacy among Southern states being bruited about, many responsible Southern leaders worried that such a move was dangerous. Representatives (only Democrats, however) of nine Southern states met in Nashville on June 2, 1850, with Pillow as chairman of the Tennessee delegation. Pillow worked for conciliation and compromise throughout and took direct steps to soften the stance of Robert B. Rhett and other radicals. The Tennessee delegation at Nashville stood for moderation, for flexibility and acquiescence in the decisions of Congress. Thus Pillow represented union, patriotism, and as a good Jacksonian, he fought all attempts to promote the idea of secession.[7]

Politics dominated Pillow's life during the 1850s. He had good relations with his Mexican War comrade Franklin Pierce and did what he could to support the administration, who rewarded the Pillow family by naming his brother-in-law Aaron V. Brown as postmaster general. Pillow wanted a seat in the Senate, but Andrew Johnson wanted one also, so the two continued their battles. Johnson won, being joined by Simon Bolivar Buckner—Kentuckian, West Pointer, and former officer in the regular army—who attacked Pillow in articles in the *Nashville Republican Banner*; these pieces were "masterpieces of gibes, ridicule, irony, and sarcasm," according to Democrats, and defended Scott at Pillow's expense. Nashville observers expected a duel. Pillow bided his time. And his time would come, five years later, with disastrous consequences.[8]

In 1852 Pillow threw his candidacy for vice president behind presidential aspirant Stephen A. Douglas. But Cave Johnson persuaded Tennesseans to put forward the name of Governor William Trousdale, thus effectively extinguishing Pillow's ambitions. Rumor had it Pillow wanted to unite with Douglas "and create strife in Tennessee." Indeed, strife came. Pillow, disappointed, backed away from Douglas and began laying the groundwork for a ticket of Franklin Pierce and Gideon J. Pillow. Bitter disappointment awaited. Pillow's New England friend and supporter Caleb Cushing allied with New Hampshire's Edmund Burke in support of William R. King of Alabama for the vice presidential nomination. As Pierce went up, Pillow went down, and King emerged as the Democracy's candidate. Passionate Democrat to the end, Pillow worked hard for Pierce's election in Tennessee and took great pride in his victory. Pierce's success, of course, meant the end of Winfield Scott politically, a cause for rejoicing, at least for the Democracy.[9]

As the 1850s progressed, Pillow had involved himself more deeply in a wide range of private affairs. In Arkansas, he became a feature at Democratic rallies, an associate of the state's principal politicians; he even intervened in a duel between a Whig stalwart and a young Democratic aspirant,

Thomas C. Hindman. Pillow, after returning home from Mexico, had invested steadily in Arkansas and came to own a small empire in the eastern portion of the state, primarily five plantations in Phillips County—he owned 6,788 acres there in 1859—with smaller tracts in two other counties. In his study of the slaveholding elite, historian William K. Scarborough finds that Pillow in 1860 ranked third among the slaveholders of Tennessee and was the sixth largest slaveholder in Arkansas. He kept buying slaves and land and prospered, raising needed capital in Philadelphia and New England. One endorser spoke of Pillow's "untarnished name financially," and continued by saying that "he is one of those men that in general estimation never touches anything without turning it to gold."[10]

In 1857 Pillow gained a friend and political ally—Isham G. Harris, who came to the governor's chair of Tennessee. By 1860, however, sectional differences had hardened. Even Tennessee's Democracy reflected the general division and disaffection, as did Pillow himself, and in the Democrats' state convention of 1860, as he had in 1852, he threw his candidacy for vice president behind Douglas's. All came to naught, however, when the Tennessee Democracy exploded in its nominating convention of January 1860. The slavery planks in the state platform, which Pillow helped construct, accommodated Douglas's position on popular sovereignty. The platform blasted the Republican Party for its hostility to slavery and proposed a return to the middle ground of the Nashville Convention. Pillow continued to oppose Andrew Johnson, and he spoke against John Bell. He joined Governor Harris and the mainline Democrats in backing Kentuckian John C. Breckinridge, James Buchanan's vice president. It was futile to argue; no one was listening.[11]

When Abraham Lincoln was elected president November 6, 1860, Pillow wrote a long letter to the editor of the *Nashville Patriot*. He had changed his stripes. The election, Pillow stated, had placed the government of the United States "in the hands of the enemies of the South." That winter, abandoning unionism and his Jacksonian heritage, he worked hard to unify public opinion behind Governor Harris and the idea of secession. As Tennessee's best known soldier, Pillow threw his energy and money behind developing the state's army, the Provisional Army of Tennessee. He would lead it with the full support of Harris. Pillow also sought to enlist the services of former Whigs, particularly Campbell, once governor and one of Pillow's regimental commanders in Mexico. Campbell hesitated, then declined in mid-May.

Once an army bill was passed, Tennessee began to mobilize in earnest. To arm them, Pillow organized a force to seize the government munitions at Fort Smith, Arkansas, but the Unionists were too quick for him and Arkansas Governor Henry M. Rector, and the weapons were whisked away to the Federal arsenal in St. Louis. Representing Tennessee, Pillow journeyed to Kentucky and conferred with Governor Beriah Magoffin and the state's military leaders about common defensive arrangements. Pillow lieutenants John C. Burch and Nathan Bedford Forrest also worked in Kentucky, buying horses and equipment and gathering intelligence.

Pillow came back to Tennessee and established headquarters of the Provisional Army of Tennessee in Memphis, running up a Confederate flag. Upstream at Randolph, Tennessee, on the east bank of the Mississippi River, Pillow began to gather his troops and construct Fort Randolph. Soon Pillow's young friend Patrick Cleburne appeared leading an Arkansas regiment.

Harris had named Pillow commander of the Provisional Army on May 9, 1861, with a subordinate major general and five brigadiers. Funding of the army as well as arms, ordnance, and supplies, however, came from Nashville and the state military board. This arrangement did not work, and Pillow began to dig, then dig more deeply, into his personal credit line. Extending his authority, Pillow blockaded the Mississippi, seized steamers headed for Cincinnati and Pittsburgh, and ordered their cargoes sold.

Troops poured into Memphis by the thousands, but Pillow found arming them almost impossible. Nevertheless, he tried and excelled at this massive organizational job, taking full responsibility. By the end of May 1861, Tennessee had twenty-one regiments organized under his command. From the first, Pillow eyed the Mississippi as the enemy's paramount objective and spread his resources and manpower accordingly. Pillow's grand strategy evaporated when Tennessee joined the Confederacy at the end of June. Pillow himself was accepted by the Confederate War Department but only as a brigadier, and his military empire in Tennessee collapsed, passing to the command of Major General (and Episcopalian bishop) Leonidas Polk. This action by President Jefferson Davis humiliated Pillow. His eyes turned west.

Pillow had no time for Bishop Polk, who had influence with Governor Harris and even greater influence with the president. Pillow disagreed with both Polk and Davis about East Tennessee and resisted the transfer of manpower east from the Mississippi. He wanted to open a second front in Missouri, and Harris had agreed initially—that is, until the idea of sending troops to East Tennessee developed. The Battle of Mill Springs in January 1862 put an end to the scheme of moving the troops to East Tennessee.

On July 28 Pillow crossed the Mississippi, occupied New Madrid, Missouri, and prepared to set out north for St. Louis. He planned to join and cooperate with other Confederate leaders strung out along the southern border of Missouri. It all collapsed, however, when Arkansas politicians objected to their state troops being absorbed into Jefferson Davis's army rather than operating within the state. Coordination and cooperation broke down, and Polk, who had been surprised by this Missouri enterprise anyway, restrained his subordinate. Pillow struck back, ignoring Polk's order and transferring

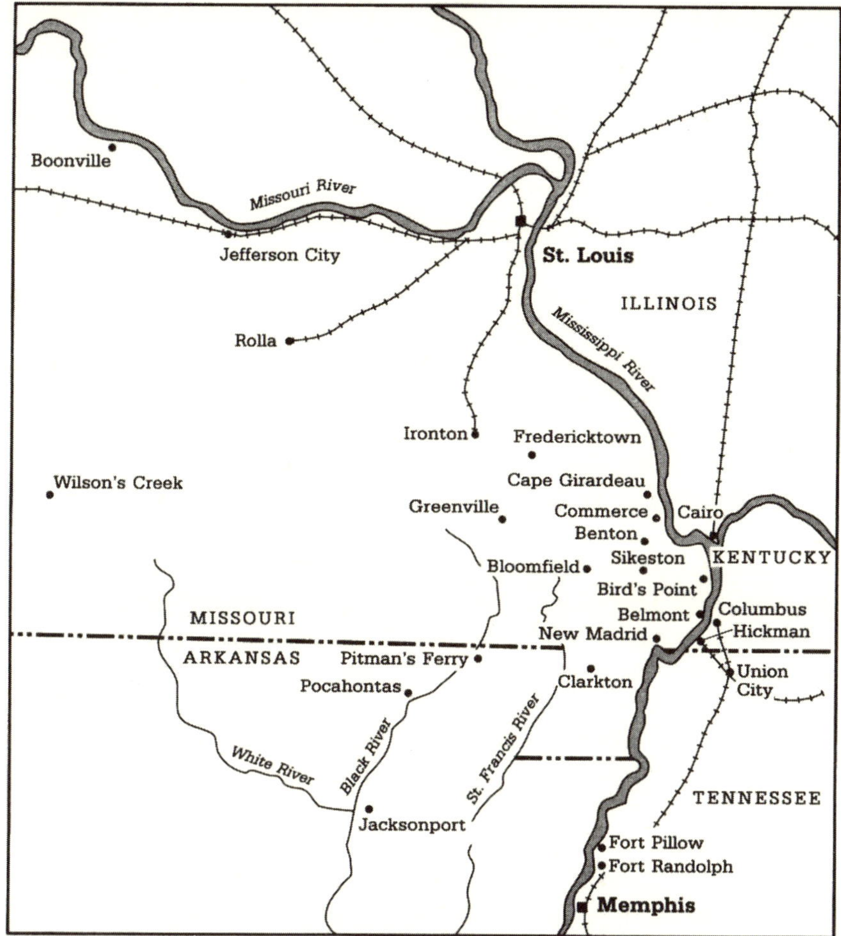

Upper Mississippi Valley, April–December 1861. From Nathaniel C. Hughes Jr. and Roy P. Stonesifer Jr., *The Life and Wars of Gideon J. Pillow* (1993; reprint, Knoxville: Univ. of Tennessee Press, 2011), 178. Used with permission.

his troops back to Tennessee, and then, violating the state's neutrality, he marched north over the Kentucky line and seized Columbus on September 4.

Pillow remained there, as second-in-command to Polk and commander of the 1st Division, Department of the West, a paper-thin defensive chain of Confederates stretching from the Cumberland Gap across the Mississippi to Indian Territory. Polk did make the logical but (as it turned out) mistaken assignment. He put Pillow in charge of the fortress and troops at Columbus. Pillow convinced Polk to order up the troops assembling in camps of instruction at Union City, Tennessee, to confront a Union reinforced regiment across the Mississippi at a river landing called Belmont. It worked. The

Federals withdrew up river. Columbus appeared secure when General Albert Sidney Johnston arrived a few days later and superseded Polk in command of the department.

On November 7, 1861, however, a full brigade of Federal infantry accompanied by cavalry and artillery supported by gunboats and transports reappeared. Johnston had ordered Pillow to move east to Clarksville, Tennessee, with his division, and that very morning they began their cross-country march, only to be turned about and countermarched to Columbus to deal with Brigadier General Ulysses S. Grant's amphibious force disembarking on the west bank of the Mississippi above Belmont.

Pillow crossed his force over the river and took a defensive position blocking Grant's approach to the Belmont encampment with five infantry regiments and one field battery. The Federals occupied a concealed position in the woods while Pillow deployed most of his infantry, leaving them easy, exposed targets in a cornfield. Casualties mounted more quickly for the unprotected Rebels, and Pillow, conspicuously mounted in the open with his staff surrounding him in their colorful uniforms, grew impatient awaiting reinforcements. As his men began to run out of ammunition, he turned to a British expedient and ordered a bayonet charge into the woods to their front. Coordination and cohesion were lost. The green troops broke apart, and the remainder of the Confederates displaced to the rear. Pillow's Confederates, under heavy fire, retreated in confusion to the tent camp. However, fresh

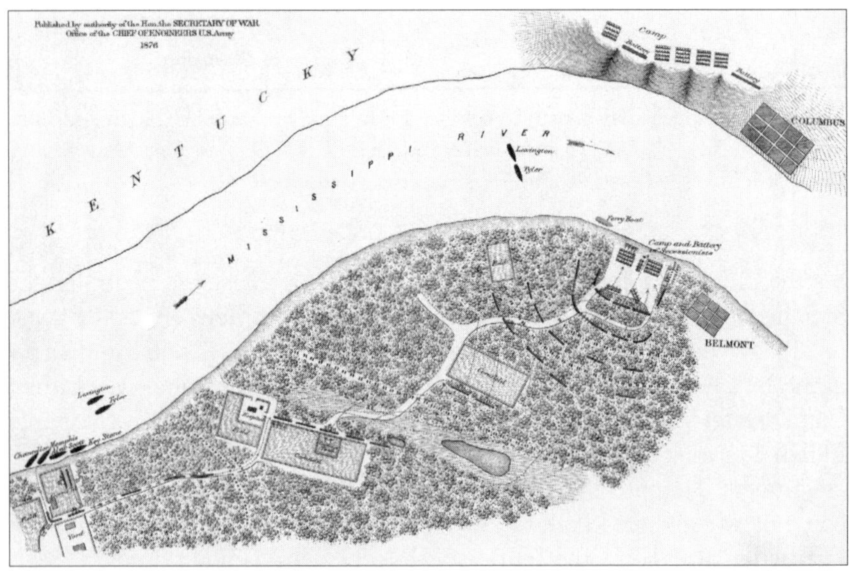

Battle of Belmont. Library of Congress.

troops from Columbus quickly reinforced them, disembarking on the west bank and taking over the fight against the enemy.

These fresh Confederates tipped the balance. As they began to be overwhelmed, Grant's men came to their senses and formed on the defensive, soon falling back in columns toward their boats. As more Confederate troops came ashore and the remnants of Pillow's original command who had taken cover under the river bank began ambushing them, the Union casualties mounted quickly. The Battle of Belmont ended with the Confederates holding the battlefield and Grant's steamers sailing upriver toward their base at Cairo, Illinois.

Both sides claimed victory, and the Confederates returned to their commanding, impregnable position on the bluffs at Columbus. There they would remain until Grant struck Johnston's line again, this time at Forts Henry and Donelson, but with far greater force. While Grant concentrated his forces for this expedition, Pillow and Polk continued to quarrel into the winter, when Pillow dramatically and in high dudgeon, resigned from the army, left the thousands of Tennesseans at Columbus, the army he had built with such high hopes, and returned home to Clifton Place.[12]

Pillow waited at Clifton throughout the month of January 1862 for an opportunity to return to the army without the loss of face. It is unclear what prompted his return—perhaps Sidney Johnston sent for him; perhaps it was the demoralizing defeat and consequent death of Brigadier General Felix Kirk Zollicoffer at Mill Springs, Kentucky, on January 19, 1862. At any rate, Johnston, shaken by Grant's success at Fort Henry, welcomed Pillow, his most experienced general officer, at Bowling Green, Kentucky, and immediately sent him to Clarksville, Tennessee, to gather troops and take a defensive position, thus providing a tenuous link between Johnston's two remaining wings at Columbus and Bowling Green. But at Clarksville, Pillow encountered his old nemesis Brigadier General Simon Bolivar Buckner, along with Brigadier General John B. Floyd, formerly Buchanan's secretary of war. Floyd, senior in rank but short on field experience, quickly found himself disagreeing with Pillow who wished to move up and occupy Fort Donelson rather than remain at Clarksville. Pillow, believing that he knew best, solicited Johnston's permission and moved up troops as soon as they arrived. Unfortunately, he was proved wrong.

Although he did good work fortifying Donelson and organizing its defense, Pillow did not coordinate with other commanders. Without his knowledge, Buckner and Floyd held a meeting in Clarksville and agreed that Fort Donelson should be vacated, undercutting Pillow's frenzied work. Pillow balked and suspended Floyd's order. Then came the Union attack, with Floyd coming up in person to the rescue. As fighting began in earnest, Grant's strong attacks were repulsed, and an elated Pillow, who fought well,

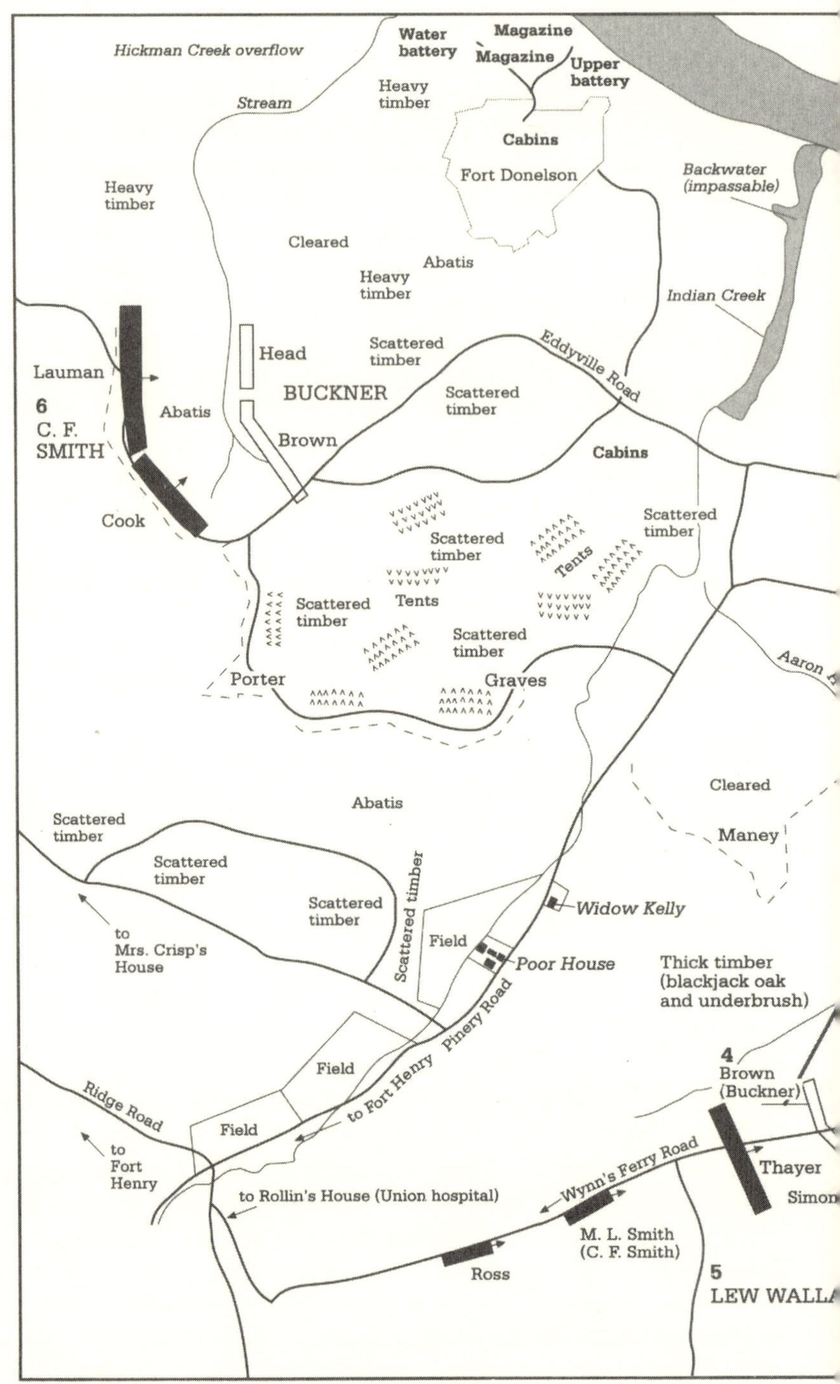

Battle of Fort Donelson, February 15, 1862. From Nathaniel C. Hughes Jr. and Roy P. Stonesifer Jr., *The Life and Wars of Gideon J. Pillow* (1993; reprint, Knoxville: Univ. of Tennessee Press, 2011), 218–19. Used with permission

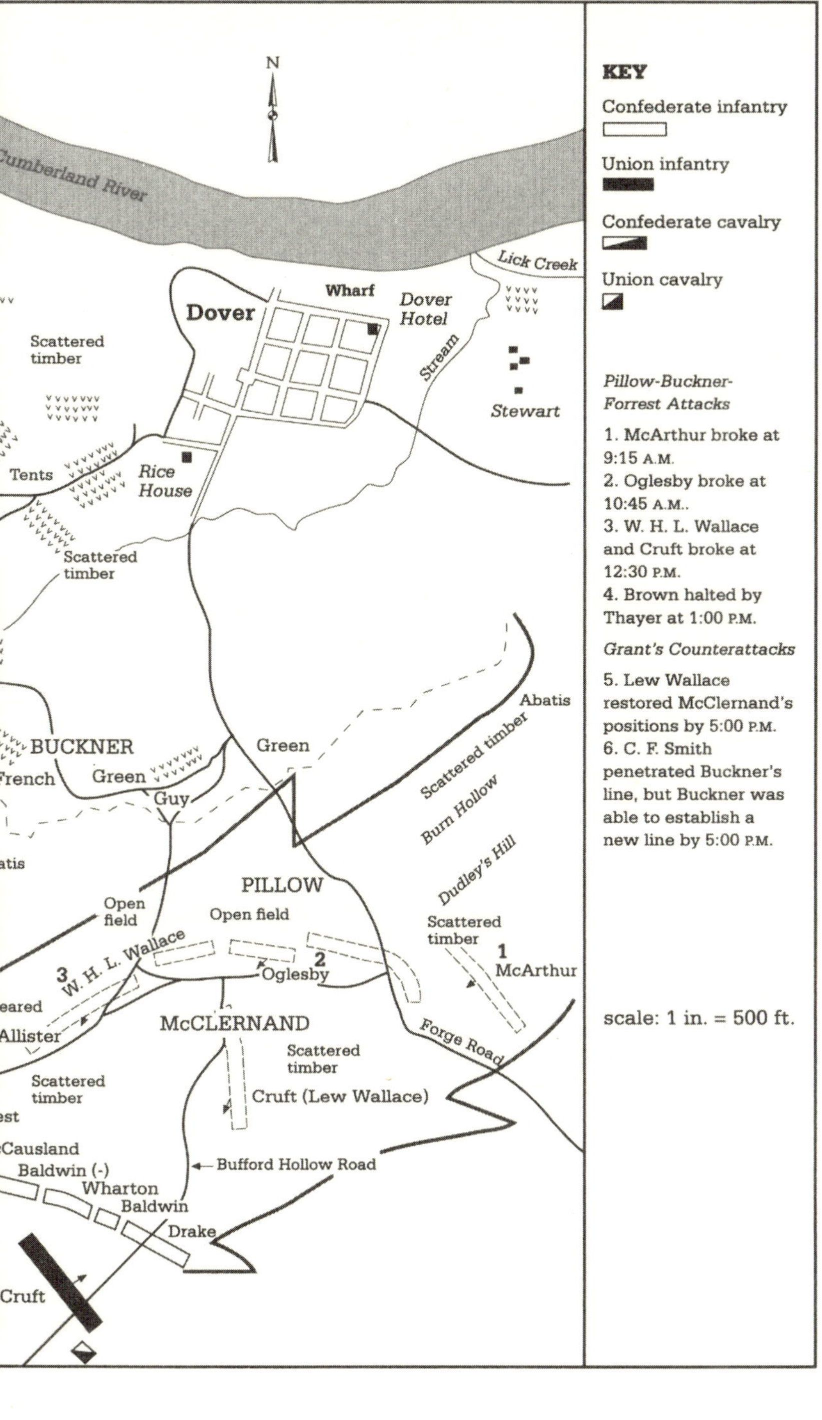
N
Cumberland River
Lick Creek
Wharf
Dover
Dover Hotel
Stream
Stewart
Scattered timber
Tents
Rice House
Scattered timber
Abatis
BUCKNER
French
Green
Green
Guy
Scattered timber
Burn Hollow
Dudley's Hill
atis
PILLOW
Open field
Open field
Scattered timber
3
W. H. L. Wallace
2
Oglesby
1
McArthur
eared
Allister
McCLERNAND
Forge Road
Scattered timber
Scattered timber
Cruft (Lew Wallace)
est
:Causland
Baldwin (-)
Wharton
Baldwin
Bufford Hollow Road
Drake
Cruft
KEY
Confederate infantry
Union infantry
Confederate cavalry
Union cavalry
Pillow-Buckner-Forrest Attacks
1. McArthur broke at 9:15 A.M.
2. Oglesby broke at 10:45 A.M..
3. W. H. L. Wallace and Cruft broke at 12:30 P.M.
4. Brown halted by Thayer at 1:00 P.M.
Grant's Counterattacks
5. Lew Wallace restored McClernand's positions by 5:00 P.M.
6. C. F. Smith penetrated Buckner's line, but Buckner was able to establish a new line by 5:00 P.M.
scale: 1 in. = 500 ft.

reported the state of affairs to Johnston. Partially surrounded in Fort Donelson that night of February 13, Floyd, Pillow, and Buckner conferred and decided to break out. Their attack the following day was botched, but the Confederates turned their attention to the Union gunboats and managed to drive them downstream to the joy of the frozen Rebels remaining in their trenches.

On the evening of February 14, the Confederate leaders met again, and Pillow argued that the attack should be renewed. Again the Confederates attacked. Pillow massed his troops well, and the Union flank gave way, but Pillow and Buckner quarreled on the field. Pillow took command of Buckner's troops, attacked on a broad front and succeeded in opening the passage for infantry to Nashville. The attack lost momentum, however, and before the exhausted Confederates could reform, a fresh Union brigade came up and stabilized the broken Federal line. Pillow, outrageously exceeding his authority and to the amazement of Buckner and Floyd, now ordered the small Rebel army back to their works. Buckner had had enough and convinced Floyd that they could not cut their way out and that their position was hopeless. Pillow argued to the contrary, but Floyd agreed with Buckner. "We will have to capitulate," he said. Pillow acquiesced, although he refused to surrender. "Nor will I," echoed Floyd. So Pillow took his staff and rode off to Clarksville and there embarked upon a steamboat for Nashville. Floyd went too, taking all the Virginia troops with him.[13]

Pillow found chaos in Nashville. The surrender at Fort Donelson had transformed "almost unbounded confidence on Sunday to perfect tumult." The streets, awash from heavy sleet and rain, were filled with a "complete jam of citizens and soldiers." The city fathers feared the army would desert them, abandoning Nashville to her fate. To calm the good citizens, Pillow spoke to a large crowd on the Public Square, assuring people that Albert Sidney Johnston's army would fight for Nashville. "The Federals will be with you only for a time and I pledge to you my honor that this war will not end until they are driven across the Ohio river. The officers who will come among you are gentleman, and, of course, will behave as such toward you." Floyd took Pillow's place, and while Floyd spoke, Pillow slipped away from the crowd and made his way to the depot where a train waited to take him to Columbia.[14]

Pillow ruined his name at Fort Donelson. His fellow officers imprisoned at Fort Warren, Massachusetts, tried him in absentia for deserting his troops. They labeled him a coward, and this charge was picked up in newspaper columns, not only in Tennessee but across the Confederacy. Tennesseans turned their backs on him. "Fort Donelson was surrendered . . . after a hard fight and a brilliant victory on Saturday, February 15, 1862, by a cowardly general, to wit, Gen. Pillow, who deserted us Saturday night."

Colonel Edward C. Cook of the 32nd Tennessee Infantry Regiment, who had fought beside Pillow elaborated: "His course is ruined," wrote Cook, and inspired by Tennyson's "Lay of the Last Minstrel," he continued, "and he will go down unwept, unhonored and unsung." One of the Fort Donelson prisoners, Major Nathaniel F. Cheairs of the 3rd Tennessee Infantry Regiment, wrote from prison in Massachusetts: "I would not exchange conditions with him, if I knew I had to remain here for 50 years."[15]

Pillow damaged himself with Davis and the War Department by resorting to the type of behavior that had discredited him in Mexico. He gave the *Memphis Daily Appeal* his official Fort Donelson report before submitting it to General Johnston and before sending it to the War Department. This military sin resulted in Johnston, acting on Davis's orders, relieving Pillow from command of his division as "preliminary to an investigation." He and his family abandoned Clifton and established themselves at Oxford, Mississippi. Meanwhile, across the Mississippi, Union Major General Samuel R. Curtis confiscated Pillow's Mound Plantation, burned the cotton, and took control of over four hundred of his slaves.[16]

That summer while the War Department reviewed his situation, Pillow went to Tupelo, headquarters of the Army of the Mississippi. There he visited old army friends and impressed General Braxton Bragg, the army's new commander, enough that Bragg requested the War Department assign Pillow to his army. But the bureaucratic wheels turned slowly, and when the army headed north to Chattanooga in late July it moved without Gideon J. Pillow.

Exasperated, Pillow continued jousting with Secretary of War George W. Randolph, but found no relief. Indeed, Randolph interpreted one of Pillow's argumentative letters as an offer of resignation, which he accepted on October 21, 1862. Pillow went to Richmond and appealed Randolph's action to the president who promised him, according to Pillow, that he "would do me justice." Which he did, having Pillow's "resignation" rescinded and ordering him to report to Bragg in Murfreesboro.[17]

Arriving January 2, 1863, in the very midst of a sizeable battle at Murfreesboro, Pillow was given a veteran brigade of Tennesseans (formerly John Calvin Brown's) commanded by Colonel Joseph B. Palmer in Breckinridge's Division. The decision to give the brigade to Pillow was not popular, but Palmer, ever the good soldier, remained with the brigade, leading his old regiment, the 18th Tennessee Infantry. Pillow rode up to his new command as it formed to attack at 4 P.M. Quickly he had skirmishers advance against four Federal brigades backed up by three more waiting in reserve on high ground just west of Stones River. Brigadier General Roger Hanson and Pillow commanded the front line of Breckinridge's Division. Pillow's Brigade numbered 1,700, the division 4,500.

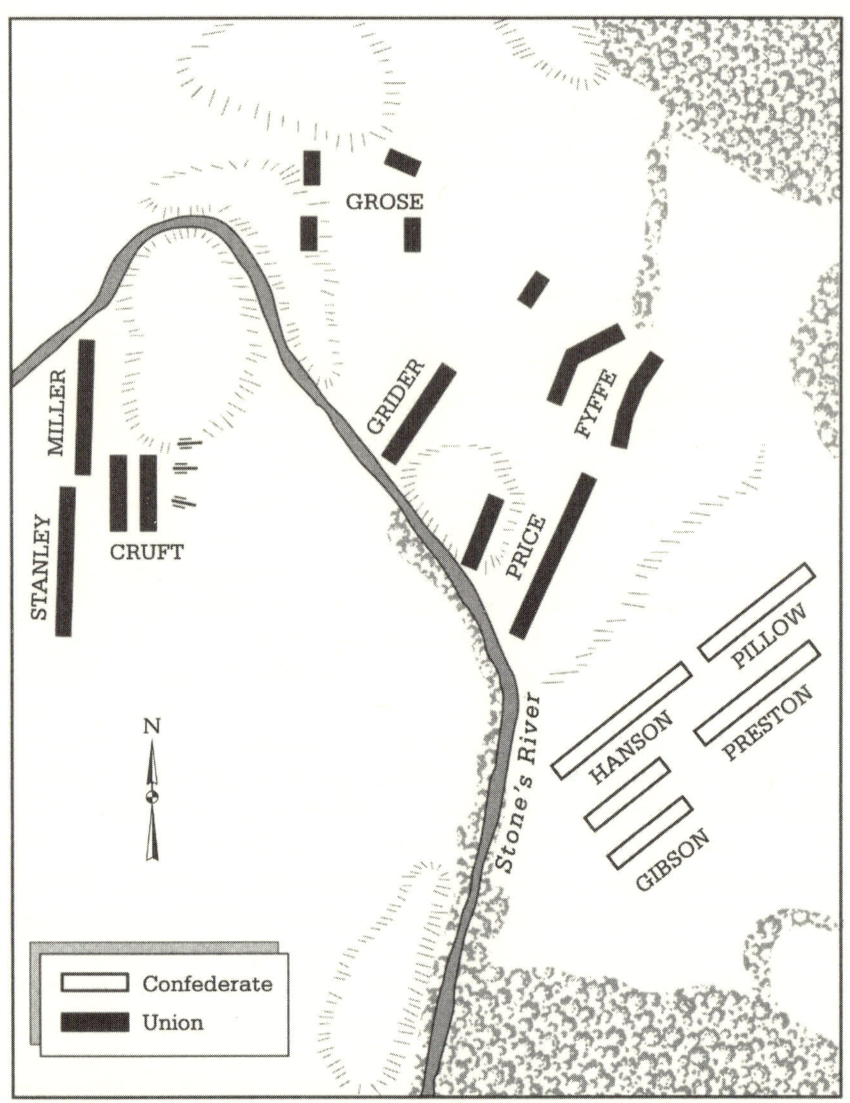

Battle of Murfreesboro, January 2, 1863. From Nathaniel C. Hughes Jr. and Roy P. Stonesifer Jr., *The Life and Wars of Gideon J. Pillow* (1993; reprint, Knoxville: Univ. of Tennessee Press, 2011), 252. Used with permission.

The Confederates stepped off smartly with fixed bayonets, scattering enemy skirmishers as they advanced cheering. It seemed like a glorious parade until Hanson's and Pillow's troops reached the middle of the field and were blasted by the fire from massed Federal artillery made up of fifty-eight guns. The Rebel infantry tended to overlap, and its front line soon began to be jammed against the river. The Federal reserve now joined in the fire against the advancing Confederates. Hanson went down fatally wounded. As fire hit the attackers from the right flank, they broke and ran, abandoning the river bank they had so dearly won. Breckinridge's casualties numbered 1,300; Pillow lost 425, a quarter of his command. Palmer's regiment lost nine color-bearers.[18]

Brigadier General Brown arrived ten days later and wanted his brigade back. So Pillow went to the commanding general's tent and asked for a "respectable division or brigade," suggesting that he "could do much to bring back those improperly absent." These were welcome words for Bragg. Just days before, Adjutant and Inspector General Samuel Cooper had issued a circular encouraging armies to attempt "field recruitment" of conscripts. The conscript bureau, directed from Richmond, had produced only a trickle of men, and Bragg saw an opportunity. The two men talked and fed each other's excitement. Pillow, who had recruited and outfitted an army in 1861, assured an attentive Bragg that with proper backing he could fill up the empty holes in the Army of Tennessee. Thus the Volunteer and Conscript Bureau of the Army of Tennessee, under Gideon J. Pillow, came into being.[19]

Bragg generously provided manpower, shifting three field officers and two companies of cavalry from each corps, a captain and six lieutenants from each regiment, and sufficient surgeons to examine recruits and conscripts; officers who had been displaced by the consolidation of regiments were also assigned. Forrest, unofficially, joined Pillow. Out they went, striking first at Bedford County, Tennessee, a hotbed of resistance to the conscript law; Pillow believed he would find 1,500 men in Bedford, either deserters or men subject to conscription, and he did. Pillow and his force proved highly effective, and as might have been expected, stretched their authority to the limit and beyond. Pillow worked hard, and troops began to pour into Tullahoma, headquarters of the Army of Tennessee. A delighted Bragg wired Davis that he could now put an army of forty thousand in the field. "You must give me credit for being the first to find a place fit for him [Pillow], and a place that he so exactly fits." Of course, Pillow eventually extended his empire from Asheville, North Carolina, to East Texas, with two dozen rendezvous for conscripts in Alabama alone. He found and forwarded hundreds of army weapons, replaced able soldiers with slaves as teamsters, and brought in intelligence gathered along the way.[20]

In the process, however, Pillow's success was his own undoing. An aggrieved Bureau of Conscription in Richmond obstructed his press gangs; the War Department sniped at him; Bragg was transferred to Richmond; and Pillow now looked to General Joseph E. Johnston as his immediate superior. Johnston gave him great latitude. For that matter, Lieutenant General Leonidas Polk, Pillow's archenemy of Columbus days, pushed for Pillow to be placed in charge of conscription for the Confederacy. "He deserves to be promoted to major general," Polk suggested. Instead the War Department relieved Pillow of command, and the Richmond conscript bureau absorbed his troops. Combat veteran and fellow Tennessean Major General Frank Cheatham observed, "although he has not been on duty in the field for the past twelve months, I consider that he [Pillow] has done more for the Army of Tennessee during that time than any one officer."[21]

When Johnston replaced Bragg as commander of the shaken Army of Tennessee—it had just been driven from Chattanooga weeks after a decisive victory at Chickamauga—at Dalton, Georgia, in December 1863, Pillow quickly came forth with another idea. He suggested that Johnston let him become the link between Johnston's department in Georgia and Polk's department in Mississippi. Stationing himself in Tuscumbia, Alabama, Pillow suggested he might protect Polk's right flank and Johnston's left, all the while serving as a shield before the vulnerable Alabama iron and coal complex and the scattered government facilities at Talladega, Tuscaloosa, and Selma. All he required would be two brigades of cavalry. And, he added modestly, "I would yield an implicit obedience to the commands of both."[22]

Polk agreed enthusiastically while Johnston recommended Pillow's plan in a letter to Cooper. Davis discerned hope for the Deep South at a modest cost in manpower. As the core of Pillow's command, Davis promised Colonel Robert V. Richardson's brigade, four loosely organized, under-strength, partially armed regiments from West Tennessee. As for the second brigade (in what Pillow hoped would become a cavalry division), Davis allowed him to have such companies as he had raised for conscript service, at least those "that may not be needed by Colonel [John S.] Preston, head of the Conscription Bureau."[23]

While Pillow carved out a command for himself by lobbying Richmond, a thousand miles away in Phillips County, Arkansas, the U.S. Treasury Department sponsored a meeting of loyal citizens in Helena, "gentlemen from various northern states," to deal with leasing abandoned plantations gathered at Mound Plantation, a former Freedmen's Bureau home. They would stake out land in sections, employing the freedmen to farm them. Pillow's Swan Lake Plantation (650 acres), located five miles south of Helena, was leased to George W. Perry of Wisconsin and Washington Warwick of Iowa, employing one freedman for each twelve acres, setting aside one acre for the employee's benefit.[24]

Of course, Pillow had dismissed thoughts of recovering his Arkansas lands in the immediate future. He focused on his defensive mission in the Northern District of Alabama, which existed only on paper, because he had no troops. Armed with orders from the secretary of war, he summoned all the conscript companies he could locate, informing them and the citizens of Alabama that he was forming a cavalry division. He placed advertisements in newspapers urging men to recruit companies and join him. He sent for conscription support units he had organized in 1863 in Florida and Mississippi. He beckoned the cadets at the University of Alabama (all under eighteen).

The effort met resistance at every turn. General Pierre G. T. Beauregard would not part with his Florida cavalry; Polk held back a squadron of cavalry Pillow coveted. Opposition rose to his use of the cadets at the university. One father wrote Pillow to excuse his fifteen-year-old son. How could he be an effective soldier? He "hasn't worked a day in his life," the father explained.[25] Four regiments (Richardson's brigade) that Pillow counted on had been incorporated into Forrest's command in West Tennessee by Polk. Polk compensated by sending Pillow the misbegotten brigade of Brigadier General James H. Clanton—sixteen ragged companies which had mutinied six months earlier and an "unarmed" regiment.[26]

In late April 1864, Major General Stephen D. Lee assumed command of the cavalry in Polk's department and thus became Pillow's commanding officer. Surprisingly, Pillow worked well with the thirty-year-old Lee, and Lee did his best to provide troops for him. Lee, however, could not pry troops loose from Forrest's command, so he ordered Pillow to station his four regiments so he might block any sudden Federal thrust through north Alabama toward Selma, a critical munitions and supply center. As the situation grew more serious in May 1864, Lee sent Pillow to Selma to inspect the city's defenses, as well as those of nearby Montgomery, and to take charge of the troops in the area. Pillow found the Selma defenses totally inadequate: 1,500 men to man an "unfavorably located" defense line two-and-a-half miles long. Lee responded promptly and sent the regiments of Colonels Charles G. Armistead and Charles P. Ball to help and stationed Brigadier General James R. Chalmers's division at Montevallo, Alabama, as a blocking force.[27]

Lee now moved Pillow in position to defend the Alabama iron and coal complex at Blue Mountain near the Georgia line. Joining him at Blue Mountain were Clanton's Brigade, and from Montevallo the cavalry brigade of Colonel James J. Neely, formerly a lieutenant of Forrest. Chalmers asked for Pillow to send Neely back because of a threat in Mississippi, but Neely felt obligated to follow orders already received to continue on and rendezvous with Pillow at Blue Mountain. Pillow also attempted to retrieve four West Tennessee regiments from Forrest under Brigadier General Tyree Bell, but Pillow's friend, Forrest, declined, suggesting instead that Pillow be sent to him to assume command of Chalmers's division.[28]

The Confederate War Department had other ideas. They intended Pillow to relieve the pressure being applied on Johnston's army in north Georgia by Union Major General William T. Sherman by trying to "interrupt the enemy's line of communications," an old idea, but promising. Sherman anticipated the move, however, creating the District of Etowah under Brigadier General James B. Steedman on June 10, 1864, with the specific mission of protecting the Federal supply line from Chattanooga to the front.[29]

No matter. An excited Pillow decided he would attempt the raid. He had two brigades at his disposal: Neely's and Armistead's. Neely was young but experienced, a good fighter whom Forrest trusted. The brigade itself was a grab-bag affair consisting of "the debris of Richardson's Brigade and a mix of partisan and small irregular organizations and commands" raised behind the lines in West Tennessee. In the meantime, the move east from Mississippi to eastern Alabama had worn out Neely's men and horses, and many of his troopers were sick from eating spoiled corn along the way. Although Pillow gave Neely's men nearly a week to rest, steady rain continued, as it had through June. Neely's recovering Tennesseans began to bait Armistead's men with insulting imitations of the birdcall of the Alabama yellow-hammer. Quarrels broke out between the units, but that was a good sign, signaling that is was time to move on.[30]

The objective was LaFayette, Georgia, a small but prosperous north Georgia town halfway between Chattanooga and Summerville. Pillow alerted his command on June 18, having Neely prepare four days' cooked rations and issue forty rounds of ammunition per man. To keep the column lean, Pillow had Neely choose six hundred troopers and send these men, his wagons, and disabled horses to the rear. He issued similar orders to Colonel Armistead. Armistead's brigade would lead, Neely's Tennesseans, a mini-division of 1,200, following. From Blue Mountain, they rode east to the swollen Coosa River and a difficult crossing. Neely tried at several places and finally had to march his brigade to Gadsden, Alabama, where it took all night, June 21–22, to ferry horses and men over.

Every stream imposed a halt, and every halt consumed more rations. Pillow worried that they might run out of food. Pillow knew that by the time he reached Blue Pond, Alabama, just to conserve rations he would have to send back not only his train but a number of men, so he continued to cull his numbers, retaining only the best mounted and most effective men. Anticipating difficulty at LaFayette, he wired Lee to make a diversion upon Rome, Georgia.

On June 22 Pillow reached Blue Pond, where the column camped and waited. The repeated river crossings had been slow and cost them at least a day. The fiery Neely chafed at the delay and sniped at Pillow. Pillow, always impatient, always eager for the offensive, sent back all vehicles except two ambulances, and again he inspected the command, weeding out suspicious horses and "invalids," sending them back to Blue Mountain with the wagons. Fortunately, a wheat field was discovered nearby, so Pillow had

Northern Alabama and Georgia, spring 1864. From Nathaniel C. Hughes Jr. and Roy P. Stonesifer Jr., *The Life and Wars of Gideon J. Pillow* (1993; reprint, Knoxville: Univ. of Tennessee Press, 2011), 282. Used with permission.

each man ride among the shocks of wheat and get "a bundle or two" for his mounts.

Pillow left Blue Pond, his column reduced to a strike force of one thousand troopers, but almost immediately encountered yet another water obstacle—Little River, a tributary of the Coosa River. Even without the wagons, he found he had to ferry the two brigades across. Hours passed. Once across Little River, however, Pillow made excellent time, moving east to Gaylesville, Alabama, then turning north to Alpine, Georgia, then east to Summerville. The column arrived there about nightfall on June 23, dead weary.[31]

The objective of this march is unclear. Joseph E. Johnston never designated it, and neither had Lee nor Pillow. Speculation figured it as either one of the large wooden trestles between Bridgeport, Alabama, and Chattanooga or the vital bridge across the Tennessee River at Bridgeport. Pillow's route, on the other hand, suggests the goal of breaking the railroad or destroying a bridge or tunnel between Ringgold and Dalton.[32]

Soon after arriving at Summerville, scouts brought word of a garrison of four hundred Federals at LaFayette, now twenty miles north—a tempting prize, if they could be surprised and overpowered. Yet, if bypassed, they posed a danger to the Confederate flank and rear, and so Pillow decided to engage LaFayette immediately. Remounting his tired troopers, they set out into the night. Pillow ordered strict silence as they approached the town. With Armistead again in the lead, Pillow's force closed on LaFayette. Seven miles out the road split, and Pillow ordered Armistead left, to the west; Pillow, supervising Neely and the Tennesseans, took the right fork. The plan, the hope, was that both columns would strike the sleeping LaFayette garrison simultaneously at dawn—Armistead from the west and north, charging in on the Bluebird Gap road and swinging north to sever the Chattanooga road, Neely from the south on the Summerville road. The signal for attack, if one were designated, would be Neely's opening volleys, since he seemed to have the more direct route and should strike the enemy first.[33]

Unfortunately for Pillow and his cavalry division, two unlikely things occurred to sabotage Pillow's first independent field command in battle. First, a Yankee soldier, a member of the LaFayette garrison, happened to be out fishing that night south of town. He heard enemy cavalry coming and ducked under a bridge. The Confederates chanced to halt there too, within the Yankee's hearing. Pillow apparently chose that moment to give instructions to his columns. The Rebels moved off with a thick clatter, with the Federal private still under the bridge trying to count their horses. When they had passed overhead, he sprang out and took a shortcut through fields to LaFayette, running, walking; running, walking. He dashed into the hotel and alerted Colonel Louis D. Watkins, the Union commander.[34]

In yet another untimely circumstance for Pillow and his men, Watkins, as well as many of his officers, happened to be up and dressed before dawn. It seems that not long before, the vigilant commandant of Nashville had raided the gambling houses there and confiscated vast heaps of poker chips. An alert officer in Watkins's command, however, was at headquarters in Nashville at the time and made off with a supply himself, which he brought down to LaFayette. Some old Southern farmers in the area heard about the poker chips and knew about Yankee hard money, so a game of draw developed, the farmers putting up five-pound packages of "fine smoking tobacco," "just as good as gold." The breathless fisherman-trooper had rushed in just as this game between the Federal officers and the locals was breaking up.[35]

LaFayette was a typical Southern county seat, laid off in a square, with the two-story brick courthouse, finished in white stucco, in the center; the jail, which faced it, was also brick. LaFayette had been occupied on June 19 by four hundred Federals, detachments from the 4th, 6th, and 7th Kentucky cavalry regiments of the brigade of Colonel Watkins. He had been ordered to LaFayette to scout west of the town to the Alabama line, a "vicinity infested by guerrillas." Watkins's troops were quartered in frame houses on or near the square, with a large number of the 7th Kentucky's troopers camped at a seminary about a quarter of a mile north of town on the Chattanooga road within easy supporting distance.[36]

About 3:00 A.M. Colonel Armistead approached LaFayette from the west along the Bluebird Gap road. He had made good time, except that Major Thomas H. Lewis's Alabama Cavalry Battalion, to the rear somewhere, had been left behind when a bridge collapsed. Armistead was unsure of the distance remaining, so he cautiously dismounted about half his men, sending ahead a small detachment to capture the enemy pickets. He placed the dismounted Confederates—primarily the 8th Alabama Cavalry Regiment under Colonel Ball—in position. Ball's objective was to reach the Chattanooga road leading north from town. Behind Ball's men, Armistead formed the mounted troops into columns and prepared to dash directly into LaFayette. It was almost dawn when Armistead heard firing far ahead from the picket line. This surprised him; the distance to town was much greater than anticipated. The heavy fog covering the ground gave everything an eerie feeling and limited vision.[37]

Ball's dismounted men rushed forward at the double-quick, but distance itself almost defeated them for they reached the back streets of the town exhausted. Then Armistead's mounted troops came thundering down the Bluebird Gap road. They swung north, bypassing Ball's weary troops, to a point almost on the Chattanooga road where they encountered light resistance that was broken after a sharp fight. More Federals, led by Colonel Watkins himself, then galloped out from town to confront Armistead, who mistook them for friendly forces and found himself a prisoner. But he was able to escape and rejoined Ball and Lewis, who had come up at last with his Alabama battalion. Together they drove Watkins back into town, pursuing him to the square. Once in town, however, they were jolted by terrible volleys from the jail, the courthouse, and frame buildings on and near the square. Major Lewis was killed, and a number of officers wounded, including Armistead. The brigade recoiled and withdrew from the square. Command of it passed to Ball.[38]

Meanwhile, Neely advanced from the south. Pillow had kept Neely under close rein during the approach, which annoyed the freewheeling cavalryman. Even the officer in charge of Neely's advance guard of forty men of the 15th Tennessee Cavalry Regiment "received his orders from the brigadier-general commanding." Close to the picket line, Pillow had Neely halt the brigade. Pillow proceeded to conduct his own reconnaissance in fog so thick one could scarcely see forty yards ahead. "After some delay of a half hour, I suppose,"[39] Pillow returned and directed Neely to move off the Summerville road through some fields to the west and attack the town. Pillow and the advance guard would remain on the road and engage the pickets guarding it once he heard the sound of Neely's attack.

As Neely entered the field, he heard the sound of Armistead's struggle with the enemy north of town. At the same time, the pickets Pillow was to have attacked opened fire; surprise was gone. Neely tore down the fences of the field and pushed forward a line of skirmishers, followed closely by Colonel Francis M. Stewart and the 15th Tennessee Cavalry. They advanced past light resistance from Yankee sharpshooters in outlying houses and gained the "houses in the suburbs of the town."[40] Neely deployed Colonel Raleigh R. White's 14th Tennessee Cavalry Regiment to Stewart's left and the advance moved on, with the 12th Tennessee Cavalry Regiment held in reserve. Neely's brigade continued to move ahead, although his line swung farther and farther to the left, "driving the enemy from the houses back toward the center of the town." In effect, as Neely swung left, he crossed the front of Armistead's brigade, which had been repulsed and fallen back. Thus, as Pillow's total force prepared to assault the town, Neely's line ran "nearly parallel with the west side of the square." Most of Armistead's brigade were behind and to Neely's left.

Pillow ordered Neely to direct the assault on the courthouse, and the latter sent a staff officer to bring up Ball's brigade, but the Alabama troops were confused. Command had changed, and the lieutenant colonel of Ball's 8th Alabama Cavalry had been wounded. Ball was off reconnoitering, Neely's staff officer learned, so he himself ordered the Alabama regiments forward. They refused to budge without an order from Ball, however, so Neely had to send for Pillow, who intervened with one of his staff and got Ball's units moving. All this caused further delay. Finally, Ball appeared, and the two brigades moved forward together into the center of town. They seized a number of houses and buildings on the side streets, but the effort was piecemeal, and many of Ball's brigade hung back.

The firing of weapons from the courthouse was intense. The bluecoats had barricaded the doors and blocked the windows with sacks of corn. Again the Federals had been lucky: a big shipment of grain had arrived on June 23 and been placed in the courthouse, making it easy to fortify. Colonel Watkins, some two hundred cavalrymen, a number of their best horses, and a company of captured Confederates were jammed inside that sturdy brick building. If Pillow had had even one field piece, he could have bagged the lot.[41]

At this point in the fight, about 7:00 A.M., Pillow sent a flag of truce to Watkins: "Sir: To prevent an unnecessary shedding of blood I demand of you an immediate surrender of this post and your forces. I have the force to take the place and am determined to do it. If necessary I will resort to the torch as well as to shot and shell to drive you from your present position. An immediate answer is required." Watkins refused Pillow's demand out of hand, and the "fight resumed with great fury."[42]

The Rebels launched three attacks against the square, capturing individual buildings, even the bottom floor of the jail. Ball, showing great courage, managed to reach the door of the courthouse accompanied by a first sergeant and a single private, but they found they could not force the door. Although the Confederates had made little headway breaking into the courthouse, Watkins and his men, with no water and dwindling ammunition, were surrounded. "Thousands of bullets . . . pitted and marked the stucco, until, looked at from a little distance, each of the walls suggested a human face badly marked by recent smallpox."[43]

Pillow would contend in his afteraction report that at this time, considering his losses and the strength of the enemy position, he decided to abandon the attack. Without artillery to reduce the courthouse, continued attack would have been futile. He had sent almost one hundred prisoners back toward Summerville, as well as a number of horses, and Neely had the flag of the 3rd Kentucky (US) Cavalry Regiment as a trophy.

However, accounts of the battle conflict. It appears Pillow had decided to burn the courthouse and was preparing for this when, suddenly, down the Chattanooga road crashed the 4th Kentucky (U.S.) Mounted Infantry Regiment led by Colonel John T. Crofton and Lieutenant Colonel Robert M. Kelly, armed with Spencer carbines and Ballad breech-loaders. They struck hard and on a broad front, surprising and routing Pillow's Confederates. "We left that place much quicker than we went there," reported Private Charles G. Joy, Company C, 14th Tennessee Cavalry. "How many Yankees there were I never knew, but they stampeded us." Confederates lucky enough to have their horses at hand fled down the Summerville road, across fields, "through an old tankard, our horses jumping the vats."[44]

Rebel Private John Johnston, while trying to locate and save a wounded comrade, got separated from his regiment. He wandered off onto an "old deserted-looking road." There, to his surprise, he discovered Pillow and his staff. He asked Pillow where the 14th Tennessee Cavalry was, and Pillow replied, "We do not know. We are lost ourselves." Johnston rode on, leaving Pillow and his staff "standing in the middle of the road. It struck me as something very remarkable that the commander of a division of cavalry on so important an occasion should have been thus lost in the woods."[45]

The Alabama troops were not so lucky. Many of their horses were being held a good distance away. When they hurried back for their mounts, they found Pillow had ordered them moved. Then a large number of horses stampeded, and the men panicked. Ball attempted to rally his troops, but it was useless; his brigade disintegrated. Fortunately, the Federal pursuit lacked sufficient force. Neely had the 14th Tennessee Cavalry form a rear guard, and they were able to protect the fleeing Alabama troops, who passed through their lines to safety.[46]

The retreat south through Summerville to Blue Pond hardly could be described as orderly. Perhaps the Tennessee regiments and some of the Alabama troops maintained march integrity, but not many. The frightened Confederates—officers and men—fled directly to Talladega and spread word of disaster. A furious Pillow would later denounce them and their "most exaggerated and false reports," promising these miscreants a speedy court-martial. It could not be denied, however, that Pillow's men had abandoned many wounded, and many prisoners who had left LaFayette under guard had escaped and returned there. "Pillow ran fifty miles the day of the fight, and was still going towards Blue Mountain," one asserted.[47]

The Battle of LaFayette cost Pillow twenty-four men killed, fifty-three wounded, and seventy-seven captured; the Federals lost four men killed, seven wounded, and sixty-four captured. Most Confederate losses came in the Alabama brigade (Ball's 8th Alabama Cavalry Regiment and Armistead's 12th Mississippi Cavalry Regiment).[48] It was a disheartening defeat. Pillow blamed Armistead for attacking prematurely and carped at Lee for not having provided him with artillery. "Before leaving I made known my extreme reluctance to move without this arm of the service," Pillow elaborated. "These remarks are not made in complaint, but as an explanation of my failure to accomplish all that was expected."[49]

The Confederate flight continued to the Coosa River, which they recrossed on June 27. Finally feeling safe from pursuit, Pillow rested his command. As he sat by the river, he felt compelled to tell Private Johnston, who was seated beside him, why the attack had been made and why it had failed. "The soldiers all liked Gen. Pillow personally," Johnston believed, "although they did not have any great confidence in his military ability. . . . He was always pleasant and approachable and indeed seemed to be fond of talking to the private soldiers, and he was withal a gallant, old fellow, but had a good deal of egotism of an inoffensive sort. He loved to talk of himself and the great things he would do or had done, but was not arrogant or unkind to other people."[50]

Pillow's LaFayette raid had accomplished nothing: no bridges destroyed, no tunnels blown, no railroads cut. It wore out two Confederate cavalry brigades badly needed elsewhere. It also seems to have broken the spirit of Armistead's inexperienced and largely conscript brigade, which would bolt again in their next fight. Plus, it alerted Sherman. "You cannot be too vigilant," he wired Steedman.[51]

Fundamentally, Pillow had lost sight of his mission. A quick showy victory enticed him to engage at LaFayette, and to engage prematurely. Then he rationalized his decision, blaming it on his reluctance to leave a dangerous enemy on his flank. Thus his lean, mobile column got itself entangled in confused street fighting, ultimately destroying its offensive capability and opportunity. The march itself, at least from Blue Mountain to Summerville, despite the problem of high water, appears to have been sloppily handled, particularly the river crossings and the logistics. Pillow seemed preoccupied with his wagon train, a rock tied around the neck of the column until it crossed Little River.

The decision at Summerville to race weary troops through the night to attack LaFayette can, in fact, be justified. Most bold commanders, wary of the loss of surprise, would have agreed, although prudence might have suggested reducing the distance traveled on June 23. The attack itself on the town displayed poor coordination and terrible command control. Pillow attached himself to Neely's brigade, leaving the much less experienced Armistead the more difficult task of maneuver and the most complex approach. No attempt to capture the pickets seems to have been made, unlike the efforts south and west of town. These pickets fled and reached Crofton, who was camped ten miles north at Rock Spring Church, and who brought back reinforcements and counterattacked fast. Which threw the ill-prepared Rebels off balance and drove them from their positions.

Up to the assault phase, Pillow had kept Neely under tight control, but then, instead of leading Neely's brigade into town, he held it inactive while the balance of his force indulged in small unit action and reconnaissance, losing time, perspective, and control. Once the attack commenced, Pillow should have provided strong security, particularly on the north side of town, interdicting the battlefield against interference from Chattanooga. He never should have moved the Alabama mounts without notifying the proper subordinates. In the reports and accounts of the battle, Pillow's lack of effective personal battlefield leadership is glaring.

He had been given an unusual opportunity with this north Georgia raid of June 1864. If he had been able to snap Sherman's line of communications, even for a few days, or if he had won a smart little victory at LaFayette, so much might have been redeemed. It was, after all, the only action where he independently commanded a substantial body of Confederate troops throughout.[52]

Scattered assignments and reassignments carried Pillow through the last six months of 1864. Lee took Neely's brigade from him and reassigned it to Forrest despite Pillow's plea to let him try again. But with the arrival of Major General Lovell H. Rousseau and a host of Yankee cavalry, Pillow disregarded the reassignment. He attempted to pursue Rousseau, but failed to collar him because he misjudged his objective and displayed virtually no control over Clanton, Pillow's subordinate whose troops lay in Rousseau's path. Rousseau, losing less than fifty men, had broken the railroad between Montgomery and Opelika, destroyed a vast amount of supplies, and demonstrated the flimsiness of Pillow's shield protecting the heart of Alabama. Pillow lamely reported his feeble defensive attempt to Lee, all the while preoccupied with presenting a written excuse why his oldest son George, a member of Lee's staff, had lost a confidential dispatch on the streets of Demopolis.[53]

The War Department relieved Pillow after the Rousseau fiasco, and he spent the balance of the summer of 1864 inactive in Montgomery while the Army of Tennessee fought for its life at Atlanta. Finally, he petitioned his enemy Rousseau, now commanding the Tennessee District, to ask if he might come to Clifton to bring out his family, accompanied by an escort of twenty-five men to protect against bushwhackers. Receiving no answer to this incredible request, he turned next to Sherman who was preparing to leave Atlanta on his march to the sea. Again, he received no response.[54]

When Pillow learned General John Bell Hood was crossing the Tennessee River at Florence, Alabama, to invade Tennessee he volunteered to accompany the army and organize the Tennessee state reserves. Hood welcomed him and asked him to resume recruiting duty, and Pillow set to work, causing a citizen of Maury County to comment on December 16 that Pillow aimed to take every man, even those who had previously provided substitutes. Men vacated the county in droves.[55]

Pillow missed the Battles of Franklin (November 30) and Nashville (December 15–16) as he was busy chasing conscripts and deserters. After these disasters, as the Army of Tennessee retreated south through the bitter cold, Pillow accompanied them. After crossing the Tennessee River, he made his way south to Macon, Georgia. There he remained until February 1865 before returning to Clifton where an unexpected letter from Cooper found him. In it Cooper announced that Pillow had been appointed Commissary General of Prisoners, effective immediately. Pillow preferred to return to the conscript service and told Cooper that he and General Beauregard had so agreed. "Which does the President prefer I should do," he asked. Davis preferred he assume responsibility for the prisoners, so Pillow headed south again and established his headquarters at Macon.[56]

With the war nearing its end, the situation had changed. Prisoners were being rapidly paroled for exchange, and Pillow, seeing an opportunity, set about reaching some form of an agreement with Federal authorities. He first attempted to ship the Andersonville prisoners to Union authorities in Jacksonville, Florida, and planned to deliver prisoners at the rate of eight hundred a day thereafter. Pillow also ordered that former slaves captured in battle in Florida be sent to Andersonville as laborers. Initially successful, Pillow increased his efforts with Union General Eliakim P. Scammon in Jacksonville, and in March 1865 Pillow went so far as to propose a cartel to select "healthy prison locations, to issue rations in kind and clothing corresponding as nearly as practicable with the uniform." Scammon reacted positively, but his command chain denied further steps along this line. Federal prisoners en route to Jacksonville had to turn around and return to Andersonville.[57]

When Grant's famous raider, Brigadier General James H. Wilson, began closing in on Macon, Pillow fled the city, joining General Beauregard and Governor Thomas H. Watts of Alabama as they prepared to head west in seven wagons. Illinois cavalry, however, intercepted them at Union Springs, about thirty-five miles southeast of Montgomery and took them into the state capital. Pillow surrendered there and was granted permission to return to Clifton Place. Accompanied by one daughter and a few servants, he arrived home May 20, 1865.[58]

Pillow had more battles to fight, however. He regained control of Clifton by driving off the man who had leased it from the U.S. Treasury Department in 1864. He took the loyalty oath in Phillips County, Arkansas, and received his pardon from President Andrew Johnson in August. The following month, through the good offices of the head of the Freedmen's Bureau, Major General Oliver O. Howard, Pillow regained ownership of his property, which had been held as "abandoned or confiscable," as well as rents on these lands. He helped organize a widespread group of Southern planters in New York City, complimented Johnson publically, and set about raising capital. Pillow came home with $150,000. "There seems to be no prominent man in the Southern States," the *New York Times* commented, "who is doing more for the solution of the industrial problem. . . . The whole country will profit by hearing from time to time the industrial reports of General Pillow."[59]

Clouds that never really disappeared began gathering in the spring of 1866. A wide range of lawsuits were brought against Pillow, even one for $2,200 from his friend and former law partner Isham G. Harris, another for $125,000 by Riddle, Coleman & Company of Pittsburgh and Wisconsin, another for thirty thousand barrels of Pittsburgh coal and eleven coal barges. These suits and claims, plus one from the Manchester & Alabama Railroad for $50,000, were in addition to the amounts he needed to repay personal loans from brother Jerome ($42,000) and ward Cynthia Pillow Saunders ($18,000). Pillow asked his friends Governors James D. Porter and John Calvin Brown for help and went to the Tennessee General Assembly for assistance with some of the many suits and liens against Clifton. Pillow, in effect, was drowning in debt.[60]

As Pillow grew more desperate, Harris—his friend and former litigant—returned to Memphis from exile, and the two decided to open a Memphis law practice in late 1867 or early 1868. Pillow had no more resources to dump into farm operations. Basement-level cotton prices and the lack of capital investment proved self-destructive as did Pillow's practice of absentee ownership, not to mention the natural blows of flooding and drought. Even the

Ku Klux Klan proved a threat to securing and retaining laborers. Governor William G. Brownlow and a group of former Tennessee military leaders, including Pillow and Forrest, turned this aside, although they did take the opportunity to remind the Tennessee General Assembly that "the large mass of white men in Tennessee are denied the right to vote or hold office and urge that disenfranchisement be removed to heal all the wounds of our State."[61]

Pillow also involved himself actively in the controversial Mississippi Valley Immigration Company and pushed through the formation of a Chinese Immigration Corporation to be capitalized at $1 million (and twice that, if circumstances allowed). Pillow's trump card was a pledge of financial aid by Forrest, president of the Meridian & Memphis Railroad. Pillow and Harris also combined to revive the moribund Confederate Historical Association (founded in 1866).[62]

On October 4, 1869, Mary Elizabeth Martin Pillow died suddenly, and with her passed the essential stability of Gideon J. Pillow's life. She bore him fourteen children, four of whom died in infancy; Gideon Jr. perished in a steamboat accident; George M., an alcoholic, frightened his parents and six grown but unmarried sisters with continued suicide attempts.[63]

Six years later he married a twenty-eight-year-old widow and daughter of a wealthy cotton planter, Mary Eliza Dickson, an attractive young woman, heavily in debt, but with significant claims against the U.S. government for confiscating some of her cotton. Pillow championed her in court, and since he found her irresistible, nothing would suit except to return to Clifton Place and show her off to the Maury County folk and take her to Washington to meet President Grant. Grant was initially curt and cold to the newlyweds, but after he had apologized, Pillow dismissed the incident in a letter, writing that his behavior was "due to your pressing engagements." It took nine more pages before Pillow reminded Grant of Mary Eliza's cotton claims.[64]

Gideon J. Pillow would live thirteen more years, dying virtually alone on October 8, 1878, at Mound Plantation, Arkansas. Misery accompanied Pillow to an agonizing death from yellow fever and burial in an "Arkansas swamp." These latter years brought legal actions within the family and by thirty-seven major creditors, driving the old general into bankruptcy. He lost everything: Clifton Place, Mound Plantation, his north Mississippi land, and his beautiful city home on Adams Street in Memphis. He had lost his wife Mary and half of his fourteen children. A male friend of Mary Eliza would pay to have Pillow reinterred in Memphis, but it would be one hundred years before a monument marked his grave.[65]

In 1875, with Harris and Forrest in the audience, Pillow had spoken at the decoration of the graves of Union soldiers at the National Cemetery near Memphis. He spoke of the "great pain" it had given him to take up arms against the United States, then, perhaps with a half-smile, he went on, saying "even the dread of the gallows did not scare me away from treason," bringing on laughter and applause. He continued, "still we can claim the honor that we are all Americans. . . . It is my government and I would not live under any other."[66]

Notes

The only modern biography of Pillow, *The Life and Wars of Gideon J. Pillow* (1993, reprint 2011) by Nathaniel C. Hughes Jr. and Roy P. Stonesifer Jr. served as the basis for this essay and is cited subsequently as Hughes and Stonesifer, *Pillow*. The late Mr. Hughes was revising his manuscript at the time of his death. Despite the similarity remaining between this essay and the book-length biography regarding the Battle of LaFayette, Georgia, and the sparse references to other works, the editors believed for the reasons stated in the preface that the article merited inclusion in this volume. Where possible, the notes have been expanded, especially in regard to the original source of a quotation.

1. Jill K. Garrett, "General Gideon J. Pillow and the Pillow Family" (unpublished manuscript in possession of Jill K. Garrett, Columbia, TN).
2. Nathaniel C. Hughes Jr. and Roy P. Stonesifer Jr. *The Life and Wars of Gideon J. Pillow* (1993; repr., Knoxville, TN, 2011), 2–4.
3. Ibid., 2–9.
4. Robert M. McBride, "The Gideon J. Pillow Everybody Knows" (unpublished manuscript in possession of Jill K. Garrett, Columbia, TN); Hughes and Stonesifer, *Pillow*, 12–21.
5. Hughes and Stonesifer, *Pillow*, 26–28, 30–47.
6. Ibid., 54, 56–60, 62–63, 65–86, 88–93, 95–101, 104.
7. The court-martials of Pillow and Scott took place in Mexico City in March 1847 and Baltimore in April 1848 respectively. K. Jack Bauer, *The Mexican War, 1846–1848* (New York, 1974), 363; Hughes and Stonesifer, *Pillow*, 105–30.
8. Kendall D. Gott, *Where the South Lost the War: An Analysis of the Fort Henry-Fort Donelson Campaign, February 1862* (Mechanicsburg, PA, 2002), 15; Hughes and Stonesifer, *Pillow*, 130–40.
9. Hughes and Stonesifer, *Pillow*, 131–38 (quote on p. 132).
10. William K. Scarborough to author, Jan. 3, 1993; Hughes and Stonesifer, *Pillow*, 141–42 (quotes on p. 142).
11. Hughes and Stonesifer, *Pillow*, 149, 152–54.
12. Previous pages based on Hughes and Stonesifer, *Pillow*, 155–58, 160, 162–208 (quote on p. 155). For a more detailed account of the fighting at Belmont, see Nathaniel C. Hughes Jr., *The Battle of Belmont: Grant Strikes South* (Chapel Hill, NC, 1991).

13. Hughes and Stonesifer, *Pillow,* 209–11, 213–14, 215–17, 220–38 (quotes on pp. 235, 236). For a full scholarly study of this Confederate disaster, see Benjamin F. Cooling, *Forts Henry and Donelson: The Key to the Confederate Heartland* (Knoxville, TN, 1987).

14. Hughes and Stonesifer, *Pillow,* 238–39.

15. Garrett, "General Gideon J. Pillow"; Hughes and Stonesifer, *Pillow,* 246–47. Colonel Cook would die in the war in June 1864.

16. Hughes and Stonesifer, *Pillow,* 241–42, 244–45, 249.

17. Ibid., 248, 250 (quote on p. 250). For Pillow's furious, but futile, struggle with the Confederate War Department, see pp. 247–51.

18. Ibid., 251, 253–57. For a more detailed account of the battle, see Peter Cozzens, *No Better Place to Die: The Battle of Stone's River* (Urbana, IL, 1990).

19. U.S. War Department, *The War of the Rebellion: A Compilation of the Official Records of the Union and Confederate Armies,* 128 vols. (Washington, DC, 1880–1901), ser. 1, vol. 20, pt. 2:498 (hereafter cited as *OR;* all references are to series 1 unless otherwise indicated); Pillow to Bragg, Jan. 12, 1863, Gideon J. Pillow Papers, Record Group (RG) 109, War Department Collection of Confederate Records, National Archives and Records Service, Washington, DC (hereafter cited as NA); General Orders No. 6, Army of Tennessee, Jan. 14, 1863, Gideon J. Pillow Military Service Record, RG 109, NA.; *OR,* ser. 4, vol. 2:305–6; Circular Order, Jan. 16, 1863, Brig. Gen. Gideon J. Pillow's Command Special Order Book, RG 109, NA; Douglas C. Purcell, "Military Conscription in Alabama during the Civil War," *Alabama Review* 34 (Apr. 1981): 94; Roy W. Black, Sr., ed., "William J. Rogers' Memorandum Book," *Papers of the West Tennessee Historical Society* 9 (1955): 79. For a discussion of Pillow and the Army of Tennessee Conscript Bureau, see Hughes and Stonesifer, *Pillow,* 259–75.

20. *OR,* vol. 52, pt. 2:426; Hughes and Stonesifer, *Pillow,* 260–61.

21. *OR,* vol. 23, pt. 2:921; B. F. Cheatham to J. A. Seddon, Oct. 10, 1863, Gideon J. Pillow Military Service Record, RG 109, NA; Hughes and Stonesifer, *Pillow,* 265, 269, 273–74.

22. Hughes and Stonesifer, *Pillow,* 276–78 (quote on p. 278).

23. J. B. Jones, *A Rebel War Clerk's Diary at the Confederate States Capital,* 2 vols. (Philadelphia, 1866), 2:140; Samuel Cooper to Pillow, Feb. 5, 1864, Gideon J. Pillow Military Service Record, RG 109, NA.

24. Hughes and Stonesifer, *Pillow,* 278–79 (quote on p. 279).

25. Ibid., 279–80 (quote on p. 280).

26. *OR,* vol. 32, pt. 3:683; Hughes and Stonesifer, *Pillow,* 279–81.

27. Hughes and Stonesifer, *Pillow,* 280–81 (quote on p. 281).

28. Ibid., 281–82.

29. *OR*, vol. 38, pt. 4:772; Hughes and Stonesifer, *Pillow*, 282–83.

30. Tennessee Civil War Commission, *Tennesseans in the Civil War*, 2 vols. (Nashville: 1964–65), 1:85; Hughes and Stonesifer, *Pillow*, 283.

31. Hughes and Stonesifer, *Pillow*, 283–84.

32. William T. Alderson, ed., "The Civil War Reminiscences of John Johnston," *Tennessee Historical Quarterly* 13, no. 4 (Dec. 1954): 342; *OR*, vol. 38, pt. 2:795–96; R. M. Kelly, "A Brush with Pillow," in *Sketches of War History, 1861–1865: Papers Read Before the Ohio Commandery of the Military Order of the Loyal Legion of the U.S.*, 9 vols. (Cincinnati, 1888–1908), 3:324; William S. Speer, *Sketches of Prominent Tennesseans* (Nashville, 1888), 343; James A. Sartain, *History of Walker County Georgia*, vol. 1 (Dalton, GA, 1932), 1:113.

33. *OR*, vol. 38, pt. 3:995, 998, 1005; J. M. Henry, "Detailed and Authentic History of the Battle of LaFayette, June 24, 1864," *Walker County (GA) Messenger*, July 29, 1927; Alderson, "Civil War Reminiscences of John Johnston," 342.

34. A company of Federals were also out scouting toward Summerville on June 23 but returned to LaFayette that evening "without seeing anything." Kelly, "A Brush with Pillow," 324.

35. Kelly, "A Brush with Pillow," 330–31.

36. Henry, "Battle of LaFayette"; *OR*, vol. 38, pt. 2:795–800; Kelly, "A Brush with Pillow, 323–24.

37. Henry, "Battle of Lafayette"; *OR*, vol. 38, pt. 3:998. For an additional account of this engagement, see W. S. Nye, "The Battle of LaFayette," *Civil War Times Illustrated* 6 (June 1966): 34–40.

38. *OR*, vol. 38, pt. 3:998–1004, 1009–10; Alderson, "Civil War Reminiscences of John Johnston," 342; Sartain, *History of Walker County Georgia*, 1:114. "Col. Armistead had been shot in some of his fingers," reported Private John Johnston, "and was standing near the road as we passed him, with his hand raised in the air, shouting out lustily that he had been shot and calling for help. This impressed me as being rather ludicrous and childish conduct for the commander of a brigade."

39. Private John Johnston remembered that they sat or lay waiting—"another hour of long waiting." Alderson, "Civil War Reminiscences of John Johnston," 342.

40. *OR*, vol. 38, pt. 3:1005; John B. Lindsley, ed., *The Military Annals of Tennessee*, 2 vols. (1896; repr., Wilmington, NC, 1995), 2:730; Alderson, "Civil War Reminiscences of John Johnston," 342–43; F. M. Stewart to E. S. Hammond, June 28, 1864, Confederate Collection, Tennessee State Library and Archives, Nashville.

41. Kelly, "A Brush with Pillow," 326.

42. *OR*, vol. 38, pt. 2:795–96; ibid., pt. 4:794; Kelly, "A Brush with Pillow," 328; Henry, "Detailed and Authentic History of the Battle of Lafayette."

43. Kelly, "A Brush with Pillow," 326; *OR*, vol. 38, pt. 3:998–1010.

44. Charles G. Joy, "The Stampede at LaFayette, Ga.," *Confederate Veteran* 20, no. 10 (Oct. 1912): 474; *OR*, vol. 52, pt. 1:102–4; ibid., vol. 38, pt. 3:794, 1008, ibid., vol. 38, pt. 2:777–78; Henry, "Battle of LaFayette"; Kelly, "A Brush with Pillow," 324; Union Soldiers and Sailors Monument Association, Louisville, *Union Regiments of Kentucky* (Louisville, KY, 1897), 152, 173, 186–87; Sartain, *History of Walker County Georgia*, 1:231–32.

45. Alderson, "Civil War Reminiscences of John Johnston," 345.

46. *OR*, vol. 38, pt. 3:996, 1007; Speer, *Sketches of Prominent Tennesseans*, 343.

47. *OR*, vol. 38, pt. 4:601, 794, 996–97; ibid., pt. 2:494–95, 795–96; ibid., pt. 3:1000–10; Kelly, "A Brush with Pillow," 321–22.

48. *OR*, vol. 38, pt. 3:996–97; ibid., pt. 2:494–95, 777–78, 795–96; Thomas B. Van Horne, *History of the Army of the Cumberland: its Organization, Campaigns, and Battles written at the request of Major-General George H. Thomas chiefly from his private military hournal and official and other documents furnished by him*, 3 vols. (Cincinnati, 1875), 2:95; Kelly, "A Brush with Pillow," 330; *The Union Army: A History of Military Affairs in the Loyal States 1861–65—Records of the Regiments in the Union Army—Cyclopedia of Battles—Memoirs of Commanders and Soldiers*, vol. 6, *Cyclopedia of Battles—Helena Road to Z* (Madison, WI, 1908), 546. The 12th Mississippi Cavalry was also referred to as the 16th Confederate Cavalry Regiment.

49. *OR*, vol. 38, pt. 3:996.

50. Alderson, "Civil War Reminiscences of John Johnston," 345–56.

51. *OR*, vol. 38, pt. 5:112; ibid., pt. 4:633.

52. Hughes and Stonesifer, *Pillow*, 290–91.

53. *OR*, vol. 39, pt. 2:709. Rousseau's Alabama raid never received the attention, nor the admiration, it merited. With no pretense of being a cavalry commander, he managed to pull off one of the most successful Union cavalry strikes of the war.

54. Hughes and Stonesifer, *Pillow*, 292–93.

55. *OR*, vol. 45, pt. 2:689–90; Nimrod Porter Diary, Dec. 16, 1864, Southern Historical Collection, University of North Carolina Library, Chapel Hill; John C. Burch to G. W. Brent, Dec. 16, 1864, George W. Brent Papers, William R. Perkins Library, Duke University Library, Durham, NC; Hughes and Stonesifer, *Pillow*, 295.

56. Hughes and Stonesifer, *Pillow*, 295–96 (quote on p. 296).

57. Ibid., 296–98.

58. Ibid., 299.

59. *New York Times*, Jan. 10, 1866; Hughes and Stonesifer, *Pillow*, 300–6.

60. Hughes and Stonesifer, *Pillow*, 306.

61. Ibid., 307–8.

62. Ibid., 309–10.

63. Ibid., 310.

64. Pillow to Grant, Mar. 21, 1873, Gideon Johnson Pillow Letter, Special Collections, University of Tennessee Libraries, Knoxville; Hughes and Stonesifer, *Pillow*, 309–15, 317.

65. Hughes and Stonesifer, *Pillow*, 321–22.

66. Pillow to W. F. Cooper, 1875, Cooper Family Papers, Tennessee State Library and Archives, Nashville; Archelaus M. Hughes Diary, June 5, 1875, Tennessee State Library and Archives, Nashville; *New York Times*, June 4, 1875.

Brigadier General John Hunt Morgan and Mrs. Rebecca Gratz Bruce Morgan. Library of Congress.

Banner in the Dust: John Hunt Morgan's Last Kentucky Raid

James M. Prichard

By the spring of 1862, John Hunt Morgan had emerged as one of the most daring Confederate cavalry leaders in the Western Theater. His colorful raids behind Union lines led the Kentuckian to be hailed as "The Thunderbolt of the Confederacy." Launched in the summer of 1862, his First Kentucky Raid created panic throughout the Bluegrass State as well as Indiana and Ohio. He boldly carried the war north of the Ohio in the summer of 1863 with a daring raid across southern Indiana and Ohio. However, Morgan's luck finally deserted him, and the great raider, along with most of his command, was finally cornered and forced to surrender.

Although his great Ohio raid ended in disaster, his escape from captivity seemed straight out of the works of Sir Walter Scott. Confined in the Ohio State Penitentiary in Columbus since his capture the previous summer, Brigadier General John Hunt Morgan and six of his officers tunneled their way to freedom on November 27, 1863. Making his way through Kentucky, the noted raider reached the Confederate lines safely and was hailed as a Southern hero. After a reunion with his wife, Morgan journeyed to the Confederate capital in Richmond, where he was welcomed by the mayor before a large crowd of citizens and soldiers on January 8, 1864. Mayor Joseph Mayo praised the Kentuckian as the Francis Marion of the new struggle for Southern independence.[1]

A man of action, Morgan was not a compelling orator. Yet his response to the grand welcome was fitting but brief. He afterwards met with President Jefferson Davis and soon conferred with prominent Kentuckians about leading a bold strike into the heart of the Bluegrass State. He also pressed the Confederate high command to transfer the remnants of his old division, effectively destroyed during the Ohio raid, from General Joseph E. Johnston's Army of Tennessee in Georgia. Despite his best efforts, and considerable public support, Morgan secured the services of only one battalion of "Morgan's

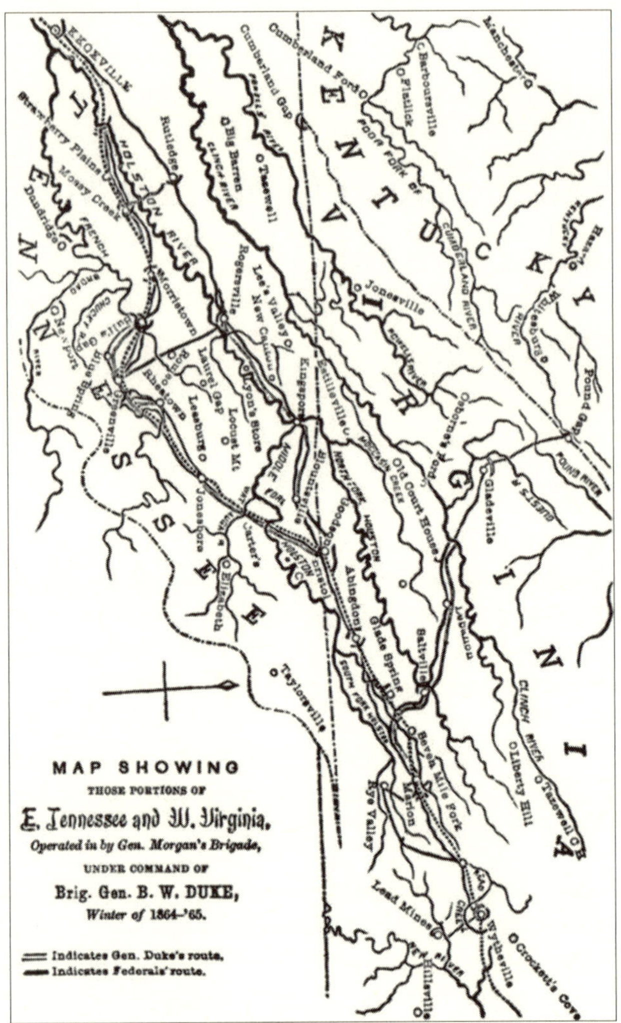

John Hunt Morgan's area of operations in 1864. From Basil W. Duke, *A History of Morgan's Cavalry* (Cincinnati: Miami, 1867), 543.

Men" led by Captain John D. Kirkpatrick. Although greatly disappointed, Morgan was fortunate to be ordered to southwestern Virginia, where Confederate forces had maintained a presence along the Kentucky border since late 1861.[2]

Upon his arrival in the mountainous region on March 27, 1864, the Kentuckian established his headquarters at Abingdon on the Virginia & Tennessee Railroad. Morgan's new field of operations formed part of Major

General Simon Bolivar Buckner's Department of East Tennessee. Since the fall of Knoxville and Cumberland Gap in the autumn of 1863, Federal forces in that region posed a constant threat to the Confederacy's vital salt works, lead mines, and rail line in western Virginia. Morgan's service with Buckner, however, was destined to be brief.[3]

Following his appointment as general-in-chief of all Federal forces, Lieutenant General Ulysses S. Grant launched a spring offensive that would hammer the Confederacy on all fronts. In addition to major drives against Richmond and Atlanta, he ordered multiple strikes against western Virginia. The Confederate commander of the Department of Western Virginia, Major General John C. Breckinridge pushed hard to prepare his sector for defense. Given the growing threat against the region, Morgan's command was transferred to Breckinridge's department on May 2.[4]

While Morgan's efforts to rebuild his old command had largely failed, he soon received welcomed reinforcements. The news of his arrival in the region electrified the Kentuckians of Colonel Henry L. Giltner's cavalry brigade. Giltner's veterans, who had served on the border since 1862, had passed through a grueling winter campaign with Lieutenant General James Longstreet's command in East Tennessee. However, their ranks had recently been increased by the addition of the remnants of George B. Hodge's Kentucky brigade, veteran riders who had recently fought with Major General Joseph Wheeler in Tennessee and Georgia.[5]

An able officer, Giltner petitioned the authorities in Richmond for a transfer to Morgan's new command. Like all Kentucky "orphans" scattered throughout the Confederacy, Giltner and his men knew that under Morgan they would soon be fighting on their native soil. Request granted, by early May his brigade joined Morgan's border command.[6]

At the same time, Captain Kilpatrick's battalion formed the nucleus of a second brigade composed of new recruits and members of Morgan's old command. Placed under the command of Colonel Robert A. Alston, one of Morgan's veteran officers, this second brigade placed the raider at the head of an effective fighting force. The command was further increased by a third brigade composed of the dismounted men of Giltner's and Alston's brigades. This "foot cavalry" was ably led by Colonel D. Howard Smith, one of Morgan's veteran officers who was recently exchanged after being captured during the Ohio raid.[7]

Morgan's new command was soon tested. In cooperation with Brigadier General William E. "Grumble" Jones's Brigade of Virginia cavalry, Morgan's force repulsed a Federal cavalry raid against the Virginia & Tennessee Railroad at Wytheville, Virginia, on May 11.[8] Days later, on May 15, Breckinridge defeated a large Federal force at New Market in the Shenandoah Valley. Because of the North's overwhelming superiority in manpower, however, fresh

Federal columns were soon on the march against the isolated mountain department. At this critical hour Breckinridge, along with 2,600 much needed men, was ordered to reinforce Robert E. Lee's hard-pressed army near Richmond on May 17.[9]

Brigadier General "Grumble" Jones suddenly found himself in temporary departmental command with a much reduced force and facing a Federal column of 8,500 men under Major General David Hunter who threatened Confederate control of the Shenandoah Valley. At the same time, another Union strike force organized in Kentucky prepared to raid southwestern Virginia. Commanded by Brigadier General Stephen G. Burbridge, that column, estimated by Confederates to be 2,100 strong, was determined to destroy the vital salt-producing facilities at Saltville, Virginia.[10]

Undaunted by these dire threats, Morgan saw an opportunity to strike at the very heart of Kentucky. He was convinced that taking the offensive would force Burbridge, who had stripped Kentucky of troops for the Saltville raid, to reverse his course in order to defend the vulnerable Bluegrass Region of his adopted state. In a meeting with Jones, he obtained permission to raid Kentucky, and he notified the Confederate high command in Richmond of his plans on May 31. Morgan, with about 2,600 men, intended to strike the state's major rail lines between Cincinnati and Lexington and between Frankfort and Louisville. He also planned to strike the vital Louisville & Nashville Railroad, the main supply line for William T. Sherman's Union forces in Georgia. He fully expected to be pursued by Burbridge, he continued, but was confident he could safely return to Virginia through southeastern Kentucky or East Tennessee.[11]

By the time Morgan notified Richmond, Burbridge's column had advanced to within striking distance of the Kentucky-Virginia line. Instantly putting his forces in motion, Morgan encountered an advance unit of Burbridge's command at Pound Gap, the gateway to Kentucky, on June 1.[12] The Federals were brushed aside after a brisk action, and Morgan began to march with lightning speed for the Bluegrass. The Confederate column marched through the valley of Troublesome Creek, a stream that by all accounts lived up to its name. After passing through Perry and Breathitt Counties, Morgan struck the headwaters of the Red River in Wolfe County and rode into Hazel Green on June 6.[13]

The march of the dismounted brigade was one of the most remarkable feats of the war. Colonel Smith's "foot cavalry" covered over two hundred miles in less than eight days. In his official report to Morgan, Smith boasted: "The conduct of this band of patriots on this trying occasion excited my highest admiration and pride." He added that "their conduct was not exceeded by the veteran army of the first Napoleon when they scaled the Alps and descended to meet the legions of Southern Europe."[14]

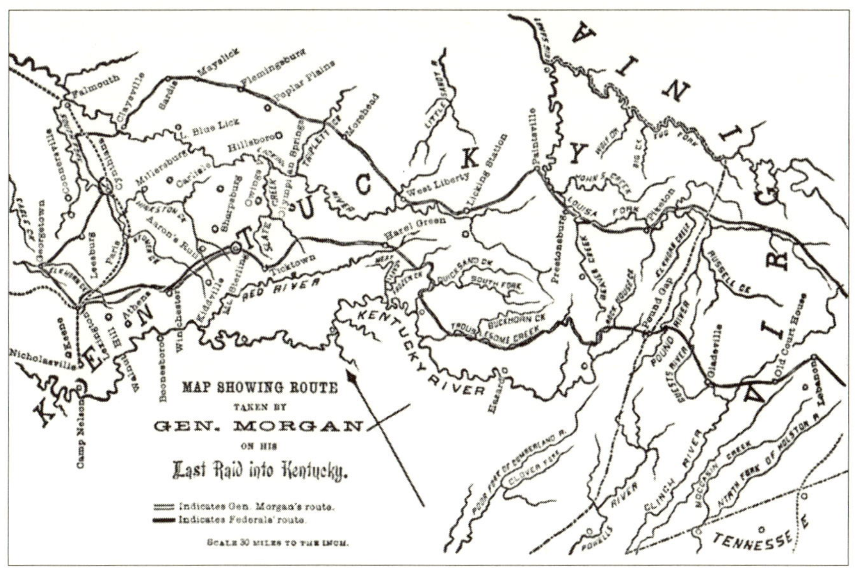

Route of John Hunt Morgan's last raid. From Basil W. Duke, *A History of Morgan's Cavalry* (Cincinnati: Miami, 1867), 521.

Upon reaching Hazel Green, Morgan ordered Captain James T. Willis of the 4th Kentucky Cavalry Regiment and Captain Bart W. Jenkins, who commanded an independent company, to push ahead with fifty men and strike the railroad between Frankfort and Louisville. At the same time Major John T. Chenoweth of the 10th Kentucky Mounted Rifles Battalion, numbering seventy-five men, was ordered to strike the Kentucky Central Railroad between Cincinnati and Lexington. A third detachment of sixty-one men, composed of Lieutenant Colonel George M. Jesse's 6th Confederate Cavalry Battalion and Captain Pete Everett's detail from the 3rd Kentucky Mounted Rifles Battalion, was sent to make a demonstration at Maysville on the Ohio River. As these units, all from Giltner's brigade, fanned out toward their objectives, Morgan halted his main column to allow Smith's "foot cavalry" to close up.[15]

During the course of the brief halt, Morgan relieved Colonel Alston of command of his mounted brigade. Colonel Smith was made his successor, and Lieutenant Colonel Robert M. Martin, a hard-fighting veteran of Morgan's old command, assumed control of the dismounted brigade. Determined to strike the Federal base at Mt. Sterling, Morgan resumed his advance on the morning of June 7.[16] Captain Edward O. Guerrant of Giltner's staff was elated: "We have completely fooled the Yankees, who have gone to Saltworks, Va, 3,500 strong, & left Ky. open to us, with a poor prospect of accomplishing anything in Va. Morgan's strategy is splendid."[17]

By midnight the column was within twelve miles of Mt. Sterling, which was defended by some 240 men, detachments of the 12th Ohio Cavalry Regiment and the 40th Kentucky Mounted Infantry Regiment, the majority of whom were considered unfit for active duty. Unknown to the approaching Confederates, however, they had lost the element of surprise. On June 7, Captain Edward C. Barlow of the 40th Kentucky, who acted as provost marshal of town, received a report that a Rebel force, no doubt the Jesse-Everett detachment, had scattered a company of Kentucky State Guard cavalry at Owingsville. Later that night a twelve-man detail of the 12th Ohio Cavalry, which had been sent with dispatches for Burbridge's command, returned to town and reported they had clashed with a large Confederate detachment advancing from the mountains.[18]

Barlow immediately conferred with fellow Kentuckian Captain Thomas R. Rorer, who commanded the Kentucky camp about one mile east of the town on the Owingsville Road. Both officers determined to make a stand and sent word to Captain Thomas H. Parkinson, commander of the smaller Ohio camp, to prepare for action. Barlow then ordered his detachment of forty-seven men to form a mounted line in the heart of the town. The Kentuckian recorded in his diary that when his men learned of the enemy advance they "cheered, and all said they would stick by me to the last."[19]

While the Federals prepared to fight, Morgan's column approached Mt. Sterling in the pre-dawn darkness. The command left the Ticktown Pike east of town and continued to advance along wooded pathways toward the Union camps. Reaching his objective at first light, Morgan sent Lieutenant Colonel Thomas Johnson's 2nd Kentucky Mounted Rifles Battalion to block all possible escape routes from the town. He then ordered Major John B. Holliday's 3rd Kentucky Mounted Rifles Battalion to charge the smaller of the two Union camps near the Owingsville Road. Holliday's battalion quickly overran the Ohioans, taking some sixty to seventy prisoners. At the same time, Lieutenant Colonel Ed Trimble's 10th Kentucky Cavalry Regiment charged the larger, stubbornly defended Kentucky camp.[20] In Mt. Sterling, Captain Barlow observed Johnson's battalion surrounding the town and recalled: "I soon seen I had my hands full, rode up and down the line of my men encouraging them and sending them from one Street to and other [*sic*]."[21]

Supported by Kirkpatrick's battalion of Smith's brigade, Trimble began to force the Federals back through the streets of the town. The fighting that followed was fierce but brief. Two of Trimble's company commanders, Captains David Swango and Anderson Moore, were shot dead in the streets. Lieutenant Joseph Jordan, the adjutant of Holliday's battalion, had his horse shot out from under him. Lieutenant Colonel Johnson, who left Mt. Sterling to fight for the Confederacy in 1861, was badly shaken when his mount dropped dead under enemy fire.[22] Supported by the 4th Kentucky Cavalry, which advanced into town on foot, the Confederate attackers soon forced the Federals to surrender. Giltner's units, which had borne the brunt of the fighting, were promptly ordered back to the Owingsville Road where they swept through the captured Union camps like locusts. The hungry, ragged Rebels soon made quick work of the food, clothing, and supplies they found there.[23]

At the same time members of Smith's brigade began to plunder the town. Morgan's "old hands," Captain Guerrant of Giltner's staff noted contemptuously in his diary, called their actions "bumming."[24] The deeply religious Kentuckian added that he was "ashamed to be caught in such company. God's retributive justice will certainly overtake us and the innocent will suffer with the guilty."[25]

Captain Barlow recorded in his diary: "I was robbed of every thing I had in my pocketts including my wedding ring, a lot of gold pens & some other valuebles [*sic*]. I was forced to draw [off] my boots, but fortunately they were to[o] small for any of them and I was permitted to put them [back] on[.]" Barlow had seen Morgan in Georgetown, during his first raid through Kentucky in 1862. Now when he was brought before the Confederate commander to be paroled, Barlow noted that "he had very much changed in appearance and his manners." The Union prisoner found him physically "bloated" and in a foul mood—far from the chivalrous knight of the past.[26]

While the raiders swarmed through the business district, Dr. Richard R. Goode, Morgan's chief medical officer, took two armed soldiers and made his way to the home of William Mitchell, the cashier of Farmers Bank. They forced Mitchell to direct them to the home of bank clerk George E. Miller, where both men were ordered to proceed to the bank and open the vault. Goode seized over $59,000 in bank funds and an additional $10,000–$15,000 from special deposits; they carried the loot away in two black carpet bags.[27]

These acts of robbery and plunder mirrored the actions of Morgan's command during the great raid through Indiana and Ohio the previous summer. At that time Morgan allowed his men to live off the land and plunder stores. He instructed his officers to enter Northern banks and seize all government funds deposited there.[28] Many of Morgan's men, including members of Giltner's brigade, regarded Mt. Sterling as a Union town. However, others—particularly several officers in Giltner's brigade—were disgusted at the sight of Morgan's cavaliers behaving like brigands on Kentucky soil. A mortified Lieutenant Colonel Johnson approached Morgan with the daughter of the bank cashier and demanded an immediate investigation of Goode's actions. Major O. S. Tenney, Morgan's provost marshal, later recalled that the cavalry chieftain seemed surprised by the report and promised to investigate the matter once the division reached Lexington.[29]

However, Mathias Gossett of Mt. Sterling, whose home served as Morgan's headquarters, later recalled that Morgan's staff officers, who no doubt included Dr. Goode, carried several satchels and carpet bags into his residence. After permitting the men to rest several hours, Morgan ordered Giltner to hold the town and await the arrival of Martin's dismounted brigade. He then rode out at the head of Smith's brigade late that afternoon and halted at Winchester where he established his new headquarters at the home of Mrs. Emma Lewis. She later recalled that the Rebel chieftain carried a large black satchel into her home, and that this item—along with two heavy satchels—was afterwards placed under his bed.[30]

Giltner questioned the wisdom of dividing the command and reportedly declared that Morgan had made "a grievous mistake."[31] In Morgan's defense, his scouts had reported that Burbridge's force remained deep in the mountains. Given this intelligence, he no doubt felt justified in paving the way for his next objective, the Federal base at Lexington. Yet poor intelligence had given Morgan a false sense of security. For in reality, a grimly determined Burbridge was closing in on the Rebel raiders.[32]

Immediately after learning that Morgan had entered Kentucky, Burbridge conferred with his officers and ordered Brigadier General Edward Hobson to return immediately to central Kentucky and organize a defensive force. At the same time, he instructed Colonel John Mason Brown to shadow Morgan's column with his small brigade. Seeking to deceive any of Morgan's scouts in the vicinity, he feinted toward Pound Gap with the rest of his force. But he soon countermarched his men to the mouth of Beaver Creek in Floyd County.[33]

Here he selected a strike force of men and horses able to withstand a grueling forced march. Moving on to Prestonsburg, which he reached on the night of June 7, Burbridge set out in pursuit of Morgan's command the following morning. Farther down the Licking River Valley, Brown continued to follow Morgan's trail. Upon reaching McCormick's Gap in present-day Menifee County, he was surprised to find the key defile unguarded. Twelve miles east of Mt. Sterling on the Ticktown Pike, Brown encountered a Unionist who provided a detailed description of the Confederate positions in Mt. Sterling.[34]

Brown was surprised to learn that the enemy pickets had been carelessly placed at the very edge of their main camp. The young officer immediately halted his command and rode back to report to Burbidge who, on hearing the report, immediately determined to attack. The Kentuckian reorganized his command and created an advance brigade under Brown composed of the latter's regiment, the 45th Kentucky Mounted Infantry, and the 12th Ohio Cavalry and 11th Michigan Cavalry Regiment.[35]

As the Federals advanced through the darkness, the weary raiders at Mt. Sterling slept quietly in their camps. Martin's exhausted "foot cavalry," who had arrived during the afternoon, was camped in Wilson's Woods along a ridge just east of town. Incredibly, Lieutenant Colonel Courtney B. Brent, a Virginian who commanded the thirty-man rear guard, established his picket posts less than a half-mile from camp on the Ticktown Pike. He probably believed an advance post in Ticktown, some six miles away, offered sufficient advance warning for the camp. This might have been true in other circumstances, but Brown's advancing troopers had swept through Ticktown at 3:00 A.M. and captured the post without firing a shot.[36]

Brown reached Mt. Sterling in the pre-dawn darkness and scattered Brent's pickets in every direction. The 45th Kentucky dashed through the smaller camp north of the pike killing many of Martin's troopers before they could rise from their bedrolls. Major George R. Diamond, one of Martin's battalion commanders, leaped to his feet in his nightshirt and cut his way out with a sabre.[37] At the same time Lieutenant Colonel Robert H. Bentley's battalion of the 12th Ohio Cavalry rode through the larger camp south of the pike at a full gallop and pushed on to strike Giltner's camp on the Owingsville Road.[38]

Those Confederates who survived the initial onslaught began to rally. Lieutenant John W. Headley and other officers formed their men behind a plank fence some seventy-five yards from Tickton Pike and began to rake the Federals with buckshot and rifle fire. Caught in the narrow pike between high plank fences, Major Erastus C. Moderwell's battalion of the 12th Ohio Cavalry was quickly forced back.[39] At this point Colonel Charles S. Hanson reportedly rode up at the head of his brigade and shouted to his comrade Brown: "Ah Mars John, you are catching hell, but you are too proud to run!" Unfortunately for Brown, Hanson then ordered Lieutenant Richard W. McReynolds to send his two-gun section of Battery C of the 1st Kentucky Light Artillery into action.[40]

The Kentucky cannoneers galloped down the narrow pike and immediately came under heavy fire. One of the horses in the lead team was shot dead, which brought the advance to an abrupt halt and blocked the pike for twenty crucial minutes. McReynolds brought his other gun up, but barely got off one round of canister before Martin's Confederates counterattacked "with desperate fury."[41] All the artillery horses were shot down as the Rebels overran the position. Assisted by Captain Adam Trebein of Hanson's staff, McReynolds and his men managed to safely haul away the caisson. Martin's Rebels, however, soon swarmed over the gun and began to drag it toward the Confederate lines.[42]

At this point Major Moderwell and Captain James Hicks counterattacked with sixty Ohioans armed with Spencer repeating rifles.[43] Ordered to abandon their prize of war and fall back, four members of the 4th Kentucky Cavalry, temporarily attached to Diamond's dismounted battalion, vainly attempted to spike the gun. Young Humphrey Marshall Jr., the son of a Confederate congressman from Kentucky, scooped up double handfuls of mud and stuffed the cannon barrel before falling back.[44]

The Ohioans swiftly recaptured the gun, but in the course of the fighting, Major Moderwell fell gravely wounded. Coming upon Lieutenant Colonel Brent of the Rebel rear guard, he fired and wounded his foe but not before taking a bullet in his stomach. Incredibly, Brent's shot drove a writing pen deep into Moderwell's gut, which continued to exit his body in pieces from time to time for years after the war. At this point the firing was so intense that efforts to bear Moderwell to the rear were quickly abandoned.[45]

Positioning themselves behind a stone wall, the Ohioans poured a heavy fire into the Rebel ranks. Captain William H. Hunter, who succeeded Moderwell in command, fell wounded, but Lieutenant Colonel Martin, who had been shot in the foot during the charge against the gun, soon ordered his men to fall back. The remnants of the shattered dismounted brigade made their way back through the town and retreated toward the Winchester Pike.[46]

Giltner's troops were as completely surprised by the enemy attack as Martin's men and were driven through their camp on the Owingsville Road. Lieutenant Colonel Moses Pryor quickly formed the 4th Kentucky Cavalry into line to cover the withdrawal. Falling back to the Maysville Pike, Giltner led his troopers around the town to the tollgate on the Winchester Pike where he met the survivors of Martin's brigade. Of the eight hundred men who made their way through the mountains only three hundred were accounted for. The rest were either dead, captured, or scattered through the countryside.[47]

Captain Guerrant observed that Martin was "very much exasperated at the result of the disaster & the dispersion or annihilation of his Brigade" but also equally confident the Federals could be hurled back.[48] Accordingly, he and Giltner determined to counterattack immediately. Supported by the 2nd Kentucky Mounted Rifles Battalion, Martin led his "foot cavalry" against the Federals on the Ticktown Pike while Giltner advanced down the Winchester Pike back toward town. Upon reaching the home of W. Halley Smith, Giltner dismounted his men, placing the 3rd Kentucky Mounted Rifles Battalion on the right of the road. The 4th Kentucky Cavalry was placed on the opposite side of the road with the 10th Kentucky Cavalry anchoring the far left of the line.[49]

Following the initial fighting in the camps, the 12th Ohio Cavalry was ordered to guard the Winchester Pike on the outskirts of the town. After their pickets were driven back, the Ohioans took up positions along a fence line facing a large garden. The advancing troopers of the 4th Kentucky Cavalry quickly sheltered along a fence line beneath some saplings opposite the garden and opened a heavy fire. Here, one Ohioan recalled, the 12th Ohio Cavalry endured the "sharpest conflict of the day" as the Confederate fire literally splintered their fence rail cover. The Ohioans, however, lay flat on the ground and poured a murderous return fire with their Spencer repeating rifles.[50] "The fire was as rapid and terrible as any I ever experienced," Captain Guerrant recorded in his diary. "The balls filled the air & tore through the branches of the trees perfectly savagely, & apparently with unusual vengeance. One struck a man just by me & it could have been heard 200 y'ds."[51]

Over fifty-two men of the 4th Kentucky Cavalry fell killed or wounded in less than thirty minutes. Convinced they could not recapture the town without artillery, Giltner's men were forced to fall back down the Winchester Pike where they soon encountered Martin's men, likewise repulsed along the Ticktown Pike. Some eight to ten miles beyond Mt. Sterling, the column encountered General Morgan at the head of Smith's brigade riding to their support. According to Guerrant, an agitated Morgan considered returning to Mt. Sterling to give battle, but Giltner and Martin convinced him the town could not be taken without artillery.[52]

At Winchester, the survivors of the "foot cavalry" were mounted and returned to their respective units in Giltner's and Smith's brigades. Martin's ill-fated command dissolved. After a brief halt, Morgan pressed on with Smith's brigade determined to attack Lexington. At 2:00 A.M. he reached the outskirts of the city where he dispatched a party under a flag of truce with a surrender demand—which was promptly refused. Morgan dismounted his troopers and immediately attacked. Ordered to lead the advance, Captain Tom Quirk's company of Major Jacob T. Cassell's 2nd Kentucky Cavalry Battalion soon engaged the Federal pickets.[53]

Lexington seemed ripe for the taking. The majority of the troops Burbridge left behind had been detailed to defend the military base at Camp Nelson in nearby Jessamine County. As the Rebel raiders approached Morgan's hometown, only the recently organized 30th Kentucky (US) Mounted Infantry Regiment, some three hundred recruits of the 100th U.S. Colored Infantry, and Battery E of the 1st Kentucky Light Artillery opposed them. Colonel Wickliffe Cooper of the 4th Kentucky (US) Cavalry Regiment, who was home on leave, was placed in command of the small city garrison. Lieutenant Colonel Edward R. Wier Jr. of the 35th Kentucky (US) Mounted Infantry Regiment assisted him, as did the officers of the court-martial proceedings he presided over and Captain William W. Woodward of Burbridge's staff.[54]

As Morgan's men swept into the city under cover of darkness, Cooper ordered all his available forces to fall back to Fort Clay. Located on the Versailles Pike, the earthen fort was garrisoned by Battery B of the 1st Wisconsin Heavy Artillery. While the Rebels were able to capture two guns of the 1st

Kentucky Light Artillery, one piece, commanded by Lieutenant Samuel A. Miller, got off a round down Main Street and scattered the raiders in all directions. Hauled by thirty determined black infantry recruits, Miller's gun afterwards reached the fort safely.[55]

Morgan ignored the Federal fortifications and captured the government stables, which contained over two thousand government horses and over five thousand "magnificent horses that had been sent from the country for protection."[56] One detachment also raided the stables of John M. Clay, the youngest son of the late Kentucky statesman Henry Clay, and made off with $25,000 worth of racehorses, including the celebrated Skedaddle. After torching both the government stables and the railroad depot, Morgan's men plundered the stores, seizing clothing, boots, and shoes. Morgan later boasted that by dawn his men were well supplied, well clothed, and superbly mounted.[57]

According to a subsequent account of the raid in the *Lexington (KY) Observer and Reporter,* the raiders set some private structures ablaze and robbed many citizens, both Union and Confederate sympathizers, of their valuables. The Branch Bank of Kentucky, the report continued, was also robbed of "about $10,000 in gold, silver and greenbacks."[58] As in Mt. Sterling, according to Confederate eyewitness accounts, another member of Morgan's staff committed the robbery. Private George W. McCullough of Kirkpatrick's battalion afterwards stated that while in Lexington, Major Robert Williams, Morgan's chief ordnance officer, had ordered him to search for candles. He observed a light flickering in the bank and upon entering saw Captain Edward P. Byrne, Morgan's artillery chief, handing sacks of specie to Private Humphrey Castleman. Byrne ordered McCullough to carry off another bag and keep it safe until called for.[59]

While Smith's men overran Lexington, Giltner's brigade was halted on the outskirts of town. Guerrant afterwards recorded in his diary that the men "were all crazy to go to town," adding that "they complained loudly of doing all the fighting but getting no spoils."[60] At dawn the Federal guns in Fort Clay began to fire on Morgan's men and Giltner's command was ordered to march around the city to keep his men out of range. Orderly Sergeant George D. Ewing of Giltner's staff later described a close call for Morgan himself:

> As the staffs of Morgan and Giltner were leaving Lexington, in passing through a small grove of locust trees, the guns of the fort, in easy range, opened fire on us, striking a tree about twenty feet above the ground, cutting it off. General Morgan was immediately under the tree and spurred his horse to avoid the falling top. He facetiously remarked that it seemed that the manners of the negroes

> had not been improved by Puritanical instruction, and no doubt their morals suffered in like proportion by evil associations.[61]

His command reunited, Morgan led his raiders out of Lexington around 7:00 A.M. on the Georgetown Pike. Guerrant noted that while some of Giltner's men were guilty of plundering, members of Smith's brigade, the "Calico Brigade" as he derisively referred to them, "eclipsed" them. He described the sight of many of Smith's "bummers" riding through the Bluegrass countryside laden with plunder:

> They were laden to the guards with calico by the bolt, silks, satins, baby shoes, breeches by the dozens . . . silver plate, silver watches, gold watches, silver prize cups & pitchers strung on a string, boots by the bag full, etc. . . . I was so thoroughly disgusted and ashamed by my association with such a command that I resolved to sever my connection with it at the earliest opportunity. I sought by every means to keep our brigade separate from the other, and to draw a distinct line of demarcation between the two.[62]

The subsequent arrival of the raiders in Georgetown later that day was followed by numerous acts of robbery and pillage. This time some members of the 2nd Brigade joined in, forcing Colonel D. Howard Smith, a Georgetown resident, to order Colonel Giltner to restrain his men. Nevertheless, discipline within Morgan's ranks continued to deteriorate. Captain Guerrant was disgusted by the sight of Captain Byrne, roaring drunk and brawling in the street with another officer.[63] Private George Dallas Mosgrove, Giltner's headquarters clerk, afterwards recalled, "I regret to record the fact that while we were partaking of the generous hospitality of the town some of the soldiers were pillaging it."[64]

The raiders galloped out of Georgetown on the Frankfort road at 2:00 P.M., but Morgan soon halted the command three or four miles to the west and hastily convened a council of war. Kentucky's capital had been a primary objective for Morgan at the onset of the raid. At this point, however, he decided to change course and march on Cynthiana so as to make his way back to Virginia through the Licking River Valley. The possible factors in his decision to about-face no doubt stemmed from the fact that his largest brigade, Martin's, had been virtually destroyed at Mt. Sterling, and now Burbridge's entire force was hot on his trail. In addition, both officers and men had been pushed to the limits of human endurance.[65]

Morgan ordered Captain John A. Cooper's company of Kirkpatrick's battalion to make a demonstration toward Frankfort and then put his force in motion toward Cynthiana. Cooper's "demonstration," which took place later that evening, consisted of a full-scale attack on Fort Boone, Frankfort's principal defense. The city was garrisoned by fewer than 183 of the Franklin County militia commanded by Kentucky Adjutant General Daniel W. Lindsey and Colonel George W. Monroe of the 22nd Kentucky Infantry Regiment who was home on leave. In one of the most colorful episodes of the raid, Governor Thomas E. Bramlette, State Attorney General and future Supreme Court Justice John Marshall Harlan, and other government officials seized arms and joined the small militia detachment assigned to defend the earthen fort overlooking the capital. Driven off by small arms and artillery fire after three separate charges, Cooper torched the nearby military barracks and set out to rejoin Morgan that night.[66]

While Cooper carried out his mission, Morgan's main column endured a grueling night march. Captain Guerrant noted in his diary:

> We rode all night, a long, tiresome ride. Many of the men asleep, all broken down. O how tired did I get of going, going, going, my eyelids heavy as curtains of lead: with hardly strength enough to hold them up, and despite every effort I would sometimes fall asleep, too sound to dream, & ride along until some other sleeper, or some passing "bummer" jostled me unceremoniously awake. So we went along, half the time in this world, & half the time dead asleep in another.[67]

As Morgan advanced on Cynthiana, the Federals undertook desperate measures to defend the Kentucky Central Railroad and block the path to Cincinnati. After leaving Burbridge's main column on June 5, Brigadier General Hobson reached Cincinnati on June 8. He immediately crossed the river to Covington, Kentucky, where he learned the railroad lines had been cut between there and Lexington. The Kentuckian was stunned to discover that only 230 men, mostly militia, were available to defend the eight–mile-long line of fortifications in northern Kentucky. He assembled a scratch force composed of 130 men of the 50th Veteran Reserve Corps, 50 of the 47th Kentucky Mounted Infantry, and 30 militia and sent them down the Kentucky Central Railroad to hold the depot at Falmouth.[68]

Calling on Major General Samuel P. Heintzelman, who commanded the Northern Department, Hobson obtained the men of the 1st and 2nd Kentucky Infantry Regiments, who were awaiting their discharge, and quickly placed them in the defensive works in northern Kentucky and at the arsenal at Newport Barracks. Following the arrival of Colonel Conrad Garis's 168th Ohio Infantry Regiment (National Guard) on June 9, Hobson promptly ordered that officer to continue to Cynthiana to protect the railroad bridges in that vicinity. When the 171st Ohio Infantry Regiment (National Guard) arrived the following day, Hobson set out by rail to reinforce Garis's command at Cynthiana.[69]

Morgan's column was considerably slowed by the over two hundred Union prisoners captured at Mt. Sterling. The command reached the vicinity of Cynthiana at daybreak on Saturday, June 11. Morgan prepared to attack the Federal defenders immediately and ordered Smith's brigade to prepare to strike the town from the east. Giltner's brigade was ordered to attack the town directly from the west. Colonel Garis's recently arrived Ohioans scrambled to defend the town. Although Garis had seen brief service in West Virginia at the start of the war, his men were largely untried one hundred-day volunteers armed with Harper's Ferry muskets.[70]

After Smith's advance units drove in his pickets, Garis formed his men in line of battle. Smith quickly dismounted his men and struck the Ohioans in front and flank. The Federals fell back into the town and took up defensive positions in the railroad depot, the courthouse, and the new Rankin House Hotel. At the sound of the first fire, Giltner's men charged the town from the west and drove a large party of Federals from their position behind a stone fence. They captured some seventy-five to one hundred of the fleeing Ohioans, but Giltner's men still came under heavy fire when they reached the main streets of the town.[71] Guerrant recalled that "they raked the streets everywhere & no head was safe around a corner."[72]

After nearly two hours of constant fighting, the Federals held their Rebel foes at bay. Morgan finally ordered his men to burn them out. The smoke and heat of the spreading flames soon overcame the Ohioans, who were running low on ammunition anyway. Colonel Garis stepped out from the hotel to surrender his command but was shot down and dangerously wounded. His men immediately threw down their arms and gave themselves up. By 8:00 A.M. Cynthiana was in Confederate hands. D. Howard Smith described his losses as "inconsiderable," while Giltner made no mention of casualties in his official report.[73] The 168th Ohio suffered 7 killed and 18 wounded including Garis and Lieutenant Colonel George W. Barrere. Over 280 men were taken prisoner.[74]

Tragically, the fires that forced the Federals to surrender quickly spread and destroyed much of the town's business district. Cynthiana also lost one of its leading citizens, Captain George W. Berry, the provost marshal of Kentucky's 6th Congressional District. The sixty-one-year-old Harrison County resident offered his services as a volunteer aide on Garis's staff and suffered a mortal head wound in the fighting at the depot. Ironically, his son, Captain Robert Berry, was the acting commissary of Smith's brigade. According to one source, he rode into the fight unarmed because he did not want to risk shooting his own father. Young Berry visited his dying father at the depot before returning to his command.[75]

The train bearing Brigadier General Hobson's command had rolled to a stop at the charred remains of Kellar's Bridge, one mile north of Cynthiana, as Garis's men were making their final stand. The 171st Ohio had just left the cars and fallen into line when a citizen rushed toward them and reported that Cynthiana was under attack. The sound of firing in the distance instantly confirmed the report. Colonel Joel F. Asper ordered two companies to seize a small nearby hill and look for any sign of the enemy.[76]

They had not long to wait. The advance of Lieutenant Colonel Trimble's 10th Kentucky Cavalry of Giltner's brigade, which had been pursuing some of Garis's fleeing men, soon galloped toward the hilltop position. The Ohioans drove them off with a volley. Trimble, whose regiment was actually no larger than a battalion, immediately sent a courier requesting support. He then formed a skirmish line that advanced through an open field against the Federal position.[77]

Hobson likewise formed a skirmish line composed of another company of the 171st Ohio and the convalescents of the 52nd Kentucky Mounted Infantry Regiment, which soon drove Trimble's Kentuckians back. Giltner rushed his entire brigade to Trimble's support, dismounted his men, and soon advanced against Hobson's position in line of battle. The advancing Confederates drove back Hobson's skirmishers as well as Captain John C. Wilson's detachment of the 47th Kentucky Mounted Infantry, which had been placed in an advanced position. Hobson formed a line of battle on a wooded knoll near the bluffs over the Licking River and his Ohioans poured a heavy fire into the advancing Confederates.[78]

Giltner, who went into action with five hundred men, kept up the attack for nearly five hours. The Ohioans fought with such steady determination that Captain Guerrant was convinced they were veterans and not "100 day men."[79] Private Mosgrove recalled: "The combat became most desperate. On the slope I saw Jesse Fallis, of the Fourth Kentucky, stretched on his back, his feet to the foe, his face ghastly pale in death."[80] Guerrant recorded in his diary: "The mortality in our ranks was becoming serious. Many a brave fellow poured out his blood on that stubborn field. . . . [Lieutenant Joseph] Jordan's company of Holliday's battn lost six men along one ridge. But if our loss was heavy, the Enemy's loss was far greater."[81]

Giltner frequently sent couriers to Morgan requesting reinforcements but received no response. Guerrant was convinced that the men of Smith's brigade were too busy "[p]lundering & pillaging the ruins & remains of the best rebel town of our Native State."[82] In time, Giltner's largest unit, the 4th Kentucky Cavalry, ran out of ammunition and was forced to withdraw. With 250 men, Giltner continued to press the attack and succeeded in driving back Hobson's right flank; however, the attackers began to run critically low on ammunition.[83]

Fortunately, Morgan's men arrived at the gallop and completed the encirclement of Hobson's position. Giltner's weary fighters raised a shout and resumed their advance. But the sudden appearance of a white flag in the enemy's lines ended further bloodshed. "Genl. Hobson surrendered himself & his whole force . . . to Brigr. Genl. Morgan," Guerrant noted in disdain, "whose men did not fire a gun & who arrived upon the field himself just in time to receive the surrender."[84]

Morgan's victory at Cynthiana proved a Pyrrhic one that had cost him precious time. Following Hobson's surrender, he advised Giltner that he had received reports that Burbridge was closing in. Morgan ordered a stunned Giltner to march his men back through Cynthiana and prepare to meet the enemy on the Paris Pike. At the same time, Morgan ordered Colonel Smith to cover the western approaches to the town along the Leesburg Road. Guerrant noted in his diary that Morgan's resolve to give battle "surprised and confounded most everyone." Some, he said, regarded Morgan's decision "as little short of madness."[85]

Was Morgan drunk on the eve of battle? While known to partake, he was never known to be intoxicated on active duty. In wartime recollections written solely for his children, however, Lieutenant Thomas W. Bullitt recalled that he was stunned to see Morgan "very deeply intoxicated" at the start of the Ohio Raid. He noted: "The incident impressed me most painfully and awoke grave apprehensions in my mind." The following day, Bullitt continued, Morgan's command was repulsed in a series of futile assaults on the Federal works at Tebbs Bend, Kentucky. For years after the war, the Louisville veteran wondered whether Morgan's condition had cost the lives of so many of his officers and men that day. Nevertheless, not a single shred of evidence has emerged of Morgan being intoxicated at any point during his last Kentucky raid.[86]

A bewildered Giltner advanced to the home of John Kimbrough atop a rise that commanded the eastern approach to the town. He placed the 4th Kentucky Cavalry to the left of the Paris Pike and ordered Holliday's battalion to form on the right. The rest of his brigade lay on their arms beside their horses a few hundred yards to the rear.[87]

That afternoon, Giltner accompanied only by his chief courier, Orderly Sergeant Ewing, inspected his picket lines. The worried commander unburdened himself to the youth: "Ewing, I very much fear there is a serious disaster not far ahead. General Morgan is a very likeable man, and a genius at raiding; but he is such an optimist. I have advised him to leave here at once, but he persists in remaining and fighting Burbridge's command with near empty guns. In all probability he will attack us by daylight to-morrow."[88]

Not long after they returned from the inspection, Giltner and Ewing were approached by Morgan and his staff. "Morgan asked Giltner if he had been out to the guard lines," Ewing recalled, "and then said that he expected Burbridge would attack by early morning." Giltner protested that his men had no more than two rounds of ammunition apiece and doubted they could hold the enemy long. Without hesitation, Morgan replied: "It is my order that you hold your position at all hazards!" According to Ewing, Morgan then angrily snapped, "we can whip him with empty guns!" and rode back to town.[89]

As night fell, Private Mosgrove overheard an informal council of war discussion among high-ranking officers in Morgan's absence. By this time, Smith, who had determined the rumors of an enemy advance from the west were false had, at Morgan's command, taken up position on the Ruddles Mill Road along the same rise just south of Giltner's position. Mosgrove was surprised to hear that Morgan had countermanded his original order and instructed his brigades to withdraw to the west side of the Licking River. He marked well that a high-ranking officer, whom he refused to identify, ridiculed Morgan's order and advocated holding their present position. The men needed rest, he insisted, and the other officers readily agreed.[90] The stage was now set for disaster.

Following his victory at Mt. Sterling, Burbridge wisely allowed his men to rest after their grueling ride through the mountains. The following day, Friday, June 10, he resumed pursuit of his celebrated foe, arriving in Lexington that afternoon. Colonel Israel Garrard's cavalry brigade from Camp Nelson reinforced him there. Upon learning that Morgan was at Georgetown, the Federal commander determined to block any move against the vital railroad bridge at Paris. The Union column moved out of Lexington at midnight and reached Paris at dawn on Saturday, June 11. From this point, Burbridge sent out scouting parties that returned after dark reporting that Morgan had defeated Hobson and captured Cynthiana.[91]

Sending Colonel Brown's brigade on a reconnaissance northward toward Millersburg and Carlisle, Burbridge rode out of Paris at 11:00 P.M. with 2,500 men. At 2:30 A.M. on June 12, his extreme advance guard under Major John B. Tyler of the 52nd Kentucky Mounted Infantry clashed with Morgan's pickets about two-and-a-half miles east of Cynthiana. The main Federal column pushed forward and approached Giltner's position on the Paris Pike at sunrise. Burbridge immediately formed a line of battle with the 40th Kentucky Mounted Infantry Regiment and the 12th Ohio Cavalry of Colonel Hanson's brigade on the right of the pike and the 39th Kentucky Mounted Infantry Regiment and the 11th Michigan Cavalry of Colonel David A. Mims's brigade on the left. Colonel Garrard's brigade—the 7th Ohio Cavalry Regiment, the 9th Michigan Cavalry Regiment, and the first battalion of the 16th Kentucky Cavalry Regiment—was held in reserve.[92]

Burbridge dismounted his two Kentucky regiments in the center and ordered them forward with the 12th Ohio Cavalry and 11th Michigan Cavalry, still mounted, covering their flanks. At the same time, Giltner brought up the 6th Confederate Cavalry Battalion and the 2nd Kentucky Mounted Rifles Battalion to support the 4th Kentucky Cavalry on the left of his line and sent the 10th Kentucky Mounted Rifles Battalion and the 10th Kentucky Cavalry to strengthen his right. These tough mountain Rebels, along with Holliday's battalion, poured a heavy fire into Mims's advancing ranks from behind a stone wall and rail fence. Ironically Mims's 39th Kentucky Mounted Infantry was composed of mountaineers from the same region of eastern Kentucky as their Confederate foes. On this portion of the field, it was truly brother against brother.[93]

As the battle grew in intensity, Captain George T. Atkins, the quartermaster of the 4th Kentucky Cavalry, rode up to Giltner and asked how the fighting proceeded. "We are going to get the damned ass kicked off us," Giltner snapped. "What?" a startled Atkins asked. Giltner replied that his men were too low on ammunition to stand long. Atkins offered to carry the report to Morgan which only prompted Giltner to sneer, "I'll see him damned first; I told him about it last night."[94]

Nevertheless, Giltner's men gave the Federals a warm reception. Colonel Mims afterwards reported that his men advanced through a cornfield up the hill "under a terrible fire." Fortunately, the Confederate volleys must have been too high as the 39th Kentucky Mounted Infantry lost only one man killed and three or four wounded by the time they neared the crest.[95] At the same time, Hanson's dismounted Kentuckians swept up the hill from the right side of the pike, while the Michigan and Ohio troopers on each flank threatened to turn the entire Confederate line. Giltner ordered his men to abandon Kimbrough hill and fall back to another rise some three hundred to four hundred yards to the rear.[96]

Shortly before the battle opened, Colonel Smith, whose pickets had been driven in by the enemy, immediately dispatched a courier to Morgan's headquarters in town. Smith had been ordered to hold Ruddles Mill Road against a potential enemy flank attack and was reluctant to march to Giltner's aid without orders. While a lack of ammunition hampered Giltner, Smith was weakened by the absence of Major Cassell's 2nd Kentucky Cavalry Battalion, which was on the Augusta Road guarding Federal prisoners. Sent toward the sound of the guns, Smith's acting adjutant general Lieutenant Arthur W. Andrews quickly returned with an ominous report of Giltner heavily engaged and running low on ammunition. At virtually the same time, Lieutenant Headley, who had attached himself to Smith's staff after the destruction of Martin's brigade at Mt. Sterling, observed the 11th Michigan Cavalry swinging around toward their front.[97]

Smith attempted to cover the Ruddles Mill Road sector while extending his line to the left to link with Giltner. As his battalions moved up on the right of Giltner's new line, however, a gap remained between the two brigades. At this juncture, Morgan appeared on the field and sent his remaining units into action. Lieutenant Colonel James W. Bowles's 1st Kentucky Cavalry Battalion, with the balance of Captain Kirkpatrick's 3rd Kentucky Cavalry Battalion, swept past the fences near the Redmon House and charged the Federal line. Lieutenant Headley was surprised by the sudden appearance of Lieutenant Colonel Martin who galloped to the front, his wounded foot propped on a pillow, ordering the men forward.[98]

The Confederate charge coincided with a change in the Union battle formation. Taking personal control of the right of his line, Burbridge ordered Colonel Garrard to command the left and send his brigade into action. With Mims's advance stalled, Garrard ordered the 16th Kentucky Cavalry to dismount and form on the left of the mountain men of the 39th Kentucky Mounted Infantry. At the same time, he ordered the 7th Ohio Cavalry to gallop to the front and prepare to advance. The arrival of these fresh troops on the field drove Bowles's battalion back to a stone fence near the Ruddles Mill Road where they made a determined stand. Bowles rode up and down the line encouraging his men as they poured a heavy fire into Captain Solomon L. Green's advance battalion of the 7th Ohio.[99]

The Ohioans were hurled back losing two killed, sixteen wounded, and seventeen horses. Garrard later reported the fire "so well directed that one horse received seven shots."[100] Green reformed his riders as the 16th Kentucky Cavalry arrived on foot. Garrard threw the Kentuckians forward and sent three fresh companies of the 7th Ohio Cavalry to attack Smith's flank. The Confederates continued to fire into the advancing line of the 16th Kentucky Cavalry until they saw the Ohioans bearing down on their right. At this point Bowles's men abandoned the stone wall and fled in all directions.[101]

Captain Theodore F. Allen of the 7th Ohio afterwards noted in his diary: "The 7th was to [*sic*] fast for them & closed in rapidly with Sabre & pistol; Killing, wounding and capturing many."[102] Overtaking the regiment's advance element, Allen, as senior officer, took command and charged into Cynthiana. The Ohioan, at the head of twenty men, quickly seized the vital Licking River Bridge while the 9th Michigan and the 12th Ohio Cavalry swept around Giltner's left scattering the two companies of Kirkpatrick's battalion sent to bolster the line.[103]

Giltner ordered the 4th Kentucky to hold the advancing enemy in check while his remaining battalions mounted their horses and fell back toward the town. As the Confederate line disintegrated, Morgan and his staff set out to join Cassell's battalion on the Augusta Road. Private Mosgrove afterwards recalled seeing his commander "skimming along at an easy pace, looking up at our broken lines and—softly whistling."[104] The cavalry chieftain sent word to Giltner to join the retreat, but by the time the order arrived the 9th Michigan had cut off the Augusta Road. With the bridge also in enemy hands, the five hundred fugitives quickly became a panicked mob. Mosgrove left a vivid description of the scene: "The confusion was indescribable—pandemonium reigned supreme. There was much shooting, swearing and yelling—some from sheer mortification were crying."[105]

Facing death or capture, the trapped Confederates plunged into the Licking River under heavy fire. Many men and horses were hit before they reached the opposite bank. Clambering out of the water, Giltner and Smith's men made a desperate effort to cut their way out. Captain Allen of the 7th Ohio recalled capturing several prisoners on the river bank before leading the pursuit after the fleeing foe. He shot one Rebel in the back and toppled another off his horse with a shot through the back of his head.[106]

Effectively cut off from Morgan's command, Giltner eluded his pursuers and led his men toward Georgetown. Of the four hundred to five hundred troopers in his column only sixty were armed. The rest had left their weapons at the bottom of the river or tossed them aside when they ran out of ammunition. Virtually helpless and scared, scores of unarmed men struck out in small parties all along the line of march. By the time he halted to regroup at Payne's Depot, Giltner had only two hundred men left. He moved on through Nicholasville after nightfall and by continuous marches gradually circled back to the north toward Richmond. Striking the mouth of the Red River, he made his way through the mountains via Estill Furnace and Boonville.[107]

Immediately after his victory, Burbridge ordered Colonel Hanson to take his brigade to Mt. Sterling, where he set out in pursuit of the retreating Rebels on June 14. Hanson's men rode hard through Winchester and Richmond before halting at Irvine. He prepared to rest his men and horses until he received a report that Giltner had passed through the vicinity the day before. He immediately selected three hundred of his best troopers and set out in hot pursuit on the evening of June 16.[108]

Striking the South Fork of the Kentucky River, Giltner's fugitives made their way to Harlan County and crossed the Cumberland Mountains into Virginia on June 19. Two hundred "Kentucky Cavaliers" had managed to finish the odyssey with Giltner. Hanson, who barely missed his quarry, had to turn back empty-handed at Harlan courthouse the very same day. The hard-fighting Kentuckian afterwards reported that during his pursuit from Cynthiana to the Virginia line and back, his command covered over 470 miles in eleven days.[109]

While Giltner eluded his pursuers through southeastern Kentucky, Morgan led some two hundred to three hundred men on a retreat up the Licking River Valley in the northeastern foothills. Taking flight at Cynthiana, he proceeded to Claysville where he immediately paroled all of his prisoners. Passing through Harrison and Bracken Counties, the column halted at Sardis in Mason County. Captain Atkins afterwards recalled that Captain Quirk's advance guard plundered a country store reportedly owned by a Unionist. Private Mosgrove, another eyewitness, confessed: "It was enough to bring the blush of shame to the cheek of any honest cavalier, and was especially mortifying and humiliating to all proud Kentuckians, and more's the pity we were nearly all Kentuckians."[110] Quirk's men were soon forced to move on, but other men in the column broke ranks and seized all the plunder that remained. Morgan led his men on through Flemingsburg where he abandoned his wagons and wounded. He then pushed on to Morehead in Rowan County where his weary men camped for the night.[111]

Seeking to overtake the retreating raiders, Colonel Garrard and his troops followed in their wake. When Garrard reached Morehead, however, he found the Rebel camp deserted. He pushed his men to the summit of nearby Clack Mountain only to see Morgan's rear guard disappear in the distant hills. With his horses nearly broken down, the Ohioan reluctantly called off the pursuit.[112]

Pushing on to West Liberty, Morgan made his way through the mountains to Prestonsburg and Pikeville. Having outdistanced their pursuers, Morgan's riders finally passed through the Breaks of Sandy and reached Virginia safely. On June 20, the day after Giltner's column reached Virginia, Morgan rode into his headquarters at Abingdon.[113]

On July 20 Morgan submitted his official report of the raid to the authorities in Richmond. He glossed over the disaster to Martin's brigade at Mt. Sterling and described the fight at Cynthiana as a defeat due to overwhelming odds rather than the disastrous rout it had actually been. The recruits gained on the expedition offset his losses, he claimed, and he boasted that his men were now well mounted, equipped, and supplied at the expense of the enemy. More importantly, he continued, the Federal threat against southwestern Virginia had been thwarted. He also claimed to have temporarily disrupted the recruitment of black troops in central Kentucky. The cost to his command he concluded had been 80 killed, 125 wounded, and 150 captured or missing.[114]

Morgan had indeed forced Burbridge to abandon his strike against Virginia—but he paid a far higher price than he was willing to admit. Captain Guerrant disputed reports from Morgan's headquarters that the command had not been shattered. He recorded that the division rode into Kentucky with 2,600 men and returned with 900—which left over 1,700 men unaccounted for.[115] On July 23, Morgan admitted to Richmond that some 600 men remained in Kentucky and that an additional 300 had made their way to Major General Nathan Bedford Forrest's command in northern Mississippi. He also reported that many of the men who made their way back to Virginia refused to rejoin their units, preferring instead to plunder loyal Confederate citizens in the border region.[116] Most telling was a report from Colonel William Henry Norris to Richmond, dated September 15, that stated Giltner had entered Kentucky with 1,640 men and now had 603 present for duty. Moreover, only 292 men remained present of the 800 "Morgan's Men" who entered Kentucky.[117]

In addition to the depleted state of his command, Morgan faced determined opposition from those officers outraged by the bank robberies and widespread looting during the raid. Lieutenant Colonel Tom Johnson of Giltner's brigade was untiring in his efforts to bring the guilty parties to justice. "I hope to God all who had a hand in the robbing and stealing may be sorely punished," he told his sister after the raid. "I will apply to quit the command if this thing is not corrected."[118]

Johnson, according to some accounts, pressed the matter with such force that his life was threatened.[119] Morgan assured his officers that he would thoroughly investigate the bank robberies. After charging his inspector general with that task, however, he granted that officer a thirty-day furlough. Frustrated by the perceived delay, Colonel Alston sent a formal letter of complaint to Richard Hawes, the provisional governor of Kentucky. Four days later, on August 18, 1864, Colonel Giltner, supported by Alston and Lieutenant Colonel Martin, submitted a formal request for investigation to the Confederate secretary of war in Richmond. In a carefully worded cover letter, Morgan admitted that robberies had occurred in Kentucky but assured his superiors that he had taken steps to investigate the matter.[120]

Morgan's stock, not very high in Richmond before the raid, plummeted rapidly. During the Kentucky foray, Brigadier General "Grumble" Jones had been killed and his forces routed by Major General Hunter's column at Piedmont in the Shenandoah Valley. Ignoring the threat posed by Burbridge, General Braxton Bragg declared to President Jefferson Davis that Morgan, through his absence in Kentucky, doomed Jones to defeat.[121] On August 30, Morgan was suspended from command and a military court of inquiry ordered to convene in Abingdon on September 10. In addition to the bank robberies, the court was also ordered to investigate whether Morgan had entered Kentucky without proper authority.[122]

Morgan welcomed the court of inquiry, informing the secretary of war that he awaited the opportunity to refute the charges and restore "discipline and subordination" in his command.[123] Boldly ignoring the order to relinquish his command, however, he took the field against Federal forces in East Tennessee. On the morning of September 4, 1864, he was shot down during a surprise attack on his headquarters in Greenville. So he returned to Abingdon not to stand trial but for burial. Yet his tragic death may have been a merciful end that saved the Morgan legend for posterity.[124]

In the weeks that followed Morgan's funeral, the court of inquiry convicted Captain Byrne, Morgan's chief of artillery, for his role in the Lexington bank robbery, stripped him of his rank, and dismissed him from the service before the entire command. Private James P. Stott of Tennessee was convicted of being an accomplice of Dr. Goode in Mt. Sterling and sentenced to wear a ball and chain. Private Castleman, a member of a prominent Kentucky family, was charged with assisting Byrne in Lexington and, shackled to a ball and chain, confined in the Abingdon jail. According to one source, however, Federal strikes against southwestern Virginia disrupted the proceedings before judgment was reached regarding Castleman.[125]

Dr. Goode, Morgan's chief surgeon, was more fortunate. He broke out of jail in Abingdon and fled through the mountains to Kentucky before he could be tried for the Mt. Sterling robbery. It was afterwards rumored that he lived a comfortable life in Europe on the stolen loot. At the same time, Captain Quirk was stripped of his rank for his role in the Sardis store robbery during the retreat from Cynthiana.[126]

Morgan's last raid had been a bold gamble that promised to restore his damaged reputation after the Ohio raid. As he had on his legendary first Kentucky raid, he struck when the Bluegrass Region was lightly defended. In 1862, however, the forces that rallied to meet him consisted primarily of slow moving infantry and poorly trained "Home Guards." In 1864 he faced a large mounted force led by a relentless, tough opponent.

Historians have generally blamed the poor quality of Morgan's command as one of the chief causes of the raid's disastrous outcome. Most of the division, however, primarily Giltner's and Martin's brigades, largely comprised seasoned veterans. While the large number of newcomers in Smith's brigade got the blame for wholesale plundering, the fact remains that similar acts had occurred during Morgan's past operations, particularly in Ohio.[127]

More importantly, little emphasis has been placed on the fact that Morgan's opponent, Brigadier General Stephen G. Burbridge, had in fact out-generaled the legendary raider. The Union commander's feint toward Virginia thoroughly fooled Morgan's scouts. This factor, coupled with Burbridge's lightening pursuit, made possible the bloody surprise at Mt. Sterling. Equally important, Burbridge's decision to send Hobson to defend central Kentucky paved the way for Morgan's final rout at Cynthiana. Hobson's determined stand at Kellar's Bridge cost Morgan precious time and drastically reduced his remaining ammunition.

As historian James A. Ramage contends, Morgan could have saved his command from disaster at Cynthiana by refusing to give battle and continuing the retreat to Virginia. Ramage notes, however, that Morgan exhibited the same characteristic overconfidence that led to the destruction of his command during the 1863 Ohio raid.[128] A gambler at heart, Morgan attempted to bluff his way to victory at Cynthiana, despite the fact that his Federal foe held all the high cards. In an August conversation with Brigadier General Basil W. Duke, his brother-in-law and right arm, Morgan saw his defeat at Cynthiana solely as the result of bad luck. Had he been victorious, he lamented to Duke, he could have held Kentucky for months and achieved successes "unparalleled in his entire career."[129]

As it stood, his defeat not only weakened the defenses of southwestern Virginia but robbed the Confederacy of mounted troops that could have operated against the Louisville & Nashville Railroad—the primary lifeline for Sherman's forces hammering at the gates of Atlanta.[130] Instead the man who won glory as "The Thunderbolt of the Confederacy" returned to Virginia leaving his once-proud banner in the hands of Union Brigadier General Burbridge.

Notes

1. *Richmond Whig*, Jan. 12, 1864.
2. Ibid.; James A. Ramage, *Rebel Raider: The Life of General John Hunt Morgan* (Lexington, KY, 1986), 200–207.
3. Ramage, *Rebel Raider*, 211; William C. Davis, *Breckinridge: Statesman, Soldier, Symbol* (Baton Rouge, LA, 1974), 409, 414.
4. Richard R. Duncan, *Lee's Endangered Left: The Civil War in Western Virginia, Spring of 1864* (Baton Rouge, LA, 1998), 8–10; U.S. War Department, *The War of the Rebellion: A Compilation of the Official Records of the Union and Confederate Armies*, 128 vols. (Washington, DC: 1880–1901), ser. 1, vol. 39, pt. 2:567 (hereafter cited as *OR*; all references are to series 1 unless otherwise indicated).
5. Edward O. Guerrant, *Bluegrass Confederate: The Headquarters Diary of Edward O. Guerrant*, ed. William C. Davis and Meredith L. Swentor (Baton Rouge, LA, 1999), 418, 427; Bruce S. Allardice and Lawrence Lee Hewitt, eds., *Kentuckians in Gray: Confederate Generals and Field Officers of the Bluegrass State* (Lexington, KY, 2008), 147, 287.
6. Guerrant, *Bluegrass Confederate*, 410, 412.
7. Basil W. Duke, *A History of Morgan's Cavalry* (New York, 1969), 520–22. The 2nd Kentucky Cavalry, Morgan's original regiment, as well as most of the units that composed his division, ceased to exist after the Ohio raid. Though most historians have continued to use defunct unit designations, the remnants of Morgan's former division were reorganized into four battalions of Kentucky cavalry, of which Kirkpatrick's was the 3rd.
8. Ramage, *Rebel Raider*, 211–12.
9. Davis, *Breckinridge*, 428–29, 433.

10. Ramage, *Rebel Raider,* 212–15.

11. *OR,* vol. 39, pt. 1:64–65. Morgan does not list the number of men he led into Kentucky in his official report of the raid. The total of 2,600 was given by Captain Guerrant in his wartime diary. See Guerrant, *Bluegrass Confederate,* 494.

12. Ramage, *Rebel Raider,* 213.

13. Guerrant, *Bluegrass Confederate,* 457–59.

14. Janet E. Hewett, ed. *Supplement to the Official Records of the Union and Confederate Armies,* 100 vols. (Wilmington, NC, 1994–2004), 7:179 (hereafter cited as *ORS*).

15. Ramage, *Rebel Raider,* 217; Guerrant, *Bluegrass Confederate,* 458–59.

16. Ramage, *Rebel Raider,* 216; *ORS,* 7:179. The reason for Morgan's relieving of Colonel Alston remains a mystery.

17. Guerrant, *Bluegrass Confederate,* 459.

18. George Dallas Mosgrove, *Kentucky Cavaliers in Dixie: The Reminiscences of a Confederate Cavalryman* (1895; repr., Jackson, TN, 1957), 137; Captain Edward C. Barlow Diary, June 7, 1864, accessed June 21, 2015, www.barlowgenealogy.com/BOB/ECBarlowDiary.html.

19. Mosgrove, *Kentucky Cavaliers,* 137; Barlow Diary, June 8, 1864.

20. Guerrant, *Bluegrass Confederate,* 461–63.

21. Barlow Diary, June 8, 1864.

22. Guerrant, *Bluegrass Confederate,* 461–63.

23. Mosgrove, *Kentucky Cavaliers,* 139–40.

24. Guerrant, *Bluegrass Confederate,* 464.

25. Ibid.

26. Barlow Diary, June 8, 1864.

27. A native of Germany, Goode had served as Morgan's chief surgeon since May 1863. Richard R. Goode, Compiled Service Records of Confederate General and Staff Officers and Nonregimental Enlisted Men, Roll 108, M331, National Archives and Records Service, Washington, DC (hereafter cited as NA); "Farmers Bank vs. Thomas Johnson," Case No. 1971, Kentucky Court of Appeals, Kentucky Department for Libraries and Archives, Frankfort (hereafter cited as KDLA). Lieutenant Colonel Johnson was one of three of Morgan's officers sued by the bank after the war. See also "Farmers Bank vs. Jacob T. Cassell," Case Nos. 19594 and 19595, Jefferson County Circuit Court, KDLA, and "Farmers Bank vs. James F. Witherspoon," Case No. 483, Kentucky Court of Appeals, KDLA. Both Major Cassell and Lieutenant Witherspoon were officers in Colonel D. Howard Smith's brigade.

28. Ramage, *Rebel Raider,* 170–72.

29. "Farmers Bank vs. Thomas Johnson," Kentucky Court of Appeals, KDLA.

30. "Farmers Bank vs. James F. Witherspoon," Kentucky Court of Appeals, KDLA.

31. G. D. Ewing, "Morgan's Last Raid into Kentucky," *Confederate Veteran* 31, no. 7 (July 1923): 254–56.

32. Ramage, *Rebel Raider,* 218.

33. *OR,* vol. 39, pt. 1:23.

34. Ibid., 23, 44.

35. Ibid.

36. John W. Headley, *Confederate Operations in Canada and New York* (New York, 1906), 189, 193; C. B. Brent, Compiled Service Records of Confederate General and Staff Officers and Nonregimental Enlisted Men, Roll 32, M331, NA; *Louisville (KY) Daily Journal,* June 29, 1864; F. H. Mason, *The Twelfth Ohio Cavalry . . . in the War of the Rebellion* (Cleveland, OH, 1871), 31.

37. Mosgrove, *Kentucky Cavaliers,* 142–43; John B. Wells III and James M. Prichard, *10th Kentucky Cavalry, C.S.A.* (Baltimore, 1996), 64.

38. Mason, *Twelfth Ohio Cavalry,* 34.

39. Headley, *Confederate Operations,* 189; Mason, *Twelfth Ohio Cavalry,* 34–35.

40. Headley, *Confederate Operations,* 189; Mason, *Twelfth Ohio Cavalry,* 34–35; *Louisville (KY) Daily Journal,* June 29, 1864.

41. Mason, *Twelfth Ohio Cavalry,* 35.

42. *OR,* vol. 39, pt. 1:39–40.

43. Mason, *Twelfth Ohio Cavalry,* 35.

44. H. Marshall Jr., 4th Kentucky Cavalry, Compiled Service Records of Confederate Soldiers who Served in Organizations from the State of Kentucky, Roll 29, M319, NA.

45. Mason, *Twelfth Ohio Cavalry,* 35; Joseph K. Barnes, *The Medical and Surgical History of the Rebellion, 1861–65,* 6 vols. (Washington, DC, 1870–88), vol. 2, pt. 2:597.

46. Mason, *Twelfth Ohio Cavalry,* 35–36; Headly, *Confederate Operations,* 190–92.

47. Ewing, "Morgan's Last Raid," 254–56; Guerrant, *Bluegrass Confederate,* 466–68.

48. Guerrant, *Bluegrass Confederate,* 466–68.

49. Ibid., 468–69.

50. Mason, *Twelfth Ohio Cavalry,* 39–41.

51. Guerrant, *Bluegrass Confederate,* 469.

52. Ibid.; *ORS,* 7:173–74; Headley, *Confederate Operations,* 194–95.

53. Headley, *Confederate Operations*, 195; *ORS*, 7:181.

54. *Report of the Adjutant General of the State of Kentucky*, 2 vols. (Frankfort, KY, 1867), 1:521, 2:300–301; *Louisville (KY) Daily Journal*, June 22, 1864; 100th U.S. Colored Infantry, Compiled Military Service Records of Volunteer Union Soldiers Belonging to the 56th through 138th Infantry Units, United States Colored Troops (USCT), 1864–1865, NA. A search of the service records of the 100th U.S. Colored Troops reveals that the recruits for this regiment, the first all-black regiment raised on Kentucky soil, were collected at Lexington in June of 1864 prior to being forwarded to Nashville.

55. *ORS*, vol. 22:45.

56. *OR*, vol. 39, pt. 1:68.

57. Ibid.; Henry Clay Simpson Jr., *Josephine Clay: Pioneer Horse Woman of the Bluegrass* (Louisville, KY, 2005), 60. John M. Clay followed the raiders to Georgetown where he paid Morgan $900 to recover his thoroughbred.

58. *Lexington (KY) Observer and Reporter*, June 11, 1864.

59. *OR*, vol. 39, pt. 1:78.

60. Guerrant, *Bluegrass Confederate*, 471.

61. Ewing, "Morgan's Last Raid," 254–56.

62. Guerrant, *Bluegrass Confederate*, 472.

63. D. Howard Smith to Henry L. Giltner, June 10, 1864, D. Howard Smith Papers, Special Collections, Kentucky Historical Society Library, Frankfort; Guerrant, *Bluegrass Confederate*, 473.

64. Mosgrove, *Kentucky Cavaliers*, 149.

65. *OR*, vol. 39, pt. 1:68–69; Guerrant, *Bluegrass Confederate*, 473–74.

66. *OR*, vol. 39, pt. 1:48–55.

67. Guerrant, *Bluegrass Confederate*, 474.

68. *OR*, vol. 39, pt. 1:33.

69. Ibid., 33–34.

70. Mosgrove, *Kentucky Cavaliers*, 150–52; *OR*, vol. 39, pt. 1:34; Conrad Garis, Soldiers Who Served in Organizations from the State of Ohio, Indexes to the Carded Records of Soldiers Who Served in Volunteer Organizations During the Civil War, compiled 1899–1927, documenting the period 1861–1866, Roll 37, M552, NA. Garis had previously served as a lieutenant in the 20th Ohio Infantry.

71. Mosgrove, *Kentucky Cavaliers*, 152; *ORS*, 7:181. Guerrant, *Bluegrass Confederate*, 475.

72. Guerrant, *Bluegrass Confederate*, 475.

73. Whitelaw Reid, *Ohio in the War: Her Statesmen, Her Generals, and Soldiers,* 2 vols. (Cincinnati, 1868), 2:698.

74. Ohio Roster Commission, *Official Roster of the Soldiers of the State of Ohio in the War of the Rebellion,* 12 vols. (Cincinnati, 1886), 9:385.

75. William A. Penn, *Rattling Spurs and Broad Brimmed Hats: The Civil War in Cynthiana and Harrison County, Kentucky* (Midway, KY, 1995), 108–11.

76. *OR,* vol. 39, pt. 1:34; Mosgrove, *Kentucky Cavaliers,* 154.

77. *OR,* vol. 39, pt. 1:34; Mosgrove, *Kentucky Cavaliers,* 154.

78. *OR,* vol. 39, pt. 1:35.

79. Guerrant, *Bluegrass Confederate,* 470.

80. Mosgrove, *Kentucky Cavaliers,* 154–55.

81. Guerrant, *Bluegrass Confederate,* 476.

82. Ibid.

83. *ORS,* 7:174–75.

84. Guerrant, *Bluegrass Confederate,* 478.

85. Ibid.

86. Thomas W. Bullitt, "Some Recollections of the War," Bullitt Family Papers, Special Collections, The Filson Historical Society, Louisville, KY.

87. Ibid.; Mosgrove, *Kentucky Cavaliers,* 159.

88. Ewing, "Morgan's Last Raid," 254–56.

89. Ibid.

90. Mosgrove, *Kentucky Cavaliers,* 158–59. Captain George T. Atkins indicated that the unidentified officer was a member of Morgan's staff. He also shared post-raid camp rumors he heard—but were never substantiated—to the effect that Morgan chose to stay in Cynthiana to pursue a local belle and that he and his staff officers went on a "carouse" the night before Burbridge attacked. George T. Atkins to E. O. Guerrant, July 15, 1896. E. O. Guerrant Papers, Archives, Special Collections Research Center, University of Kentucky, Lexington.

91. *OR,* vol. 39, pt. 1:24–25.

92. Ibid.

93. Ibid., 37, 40; Wells and Prichard, *10th Kentucky Cavalry,* 66.

94. *OR,* vol. 39, pt. 1:37.

95. Atkins to Guerrant, July 15, 1896, E. O. Guerrant Papers.

96. *OR,* vol. 39, pt. 1:40; Guerrant, *Bluegrass Confederate,* 479–80.

97. *ORS,* 7:182–83; Headley, *Confederate Operations,* 198.

98. *ORS*, 7:182–83; Headley, *Confederate Operations*, 198; Mosgrove, *Kentucky Cavaliers*, 161.

99. *OR*, vol. 39, pt. 1:46–47.

100. Ibid.

101. *OR*, vol. 39, pt. 1:46–47.

102. Captain Theodore F. Allen Diary, June 12, 1864, Special Collections, The Filson Historical Society, Louisville, KY.

103. Ibid.; *OR*, vol. 39, pt. 1:47. Jno. Robertson, comp., *Michigan in the War*, rev. ed. (Lansing, MI, 1882), 710.

104. Mosgrove, *Kentucky Cavaliers*, 162.

105. Ibid., 161.

106. Allen Diary, June 12, 1864.

107. Guerrant, *Bluegrass Confederate*, 482–489.

108. *OR*, vol. 39, pt. 1:40–43.

109. Ibid.; Guerrant, *Bluegrass Confederate*, 490–91.

110. Mosgrove, *Kentucky Cavaliers*, 163.

111. Ibid., 164–65; Duke, *Morgan's Cavalry*, 528.

112. *OR*, vol. 39, pt. 1:48.

113. Ibid., 69; Mosgrove, *Kentucky Cavaliers*, 165.

114. *OR*, vol. 39, pt. 1:67–69.

115. Guerrant, *Bluegrass Confederate*, 494.

116. *OR*, vol. 39, pt. 2:272.

117. Ibid.; *OR*, vol. 39, pt. 1:84.

118. "Farmers Bank vs. Thomas Johnson," Kentucky Court of Appeals, KDLA.

119. Deposition of Major Henry T. Stanton, recorded in "Farmers Bank vs. Thomas Johnson," Kentucky Court of Appeals, KDLA.

120. *OR*, vol. 39, pt. 1:74–75, 77–80.

121. Ibid., 76.

122. Ibid., 80.

123. John Hunt Morgan to James A. Seddon, Sept. 1, 1864, quoted in Duke, *Morgan's Cavalry*, 535–36.

124. Ramage, *Rebel Raider*, 230–31, 234–38.

125. Depositions of Major Thomas J. Chenoweth and Ben Robertson, recorded in "Farmers Bank vs. Thomas Johnson," Kentucky Court of Appeals, KDLA; Humphrey Castleman, 2nd (Duke's) Kentucky Cavalry, Compiled Service

Records of Confederate Soldiers who Served in Organizations from the State of Kentucky, Roll 10, M319, NA.

126. Ibid.

127. Ramage, *Rebel Raider,* 170–72.

128. Ibid., 224–25.

129. Duke, *Morgan's Cavalry,* 532.

130. Albert Castel, *Decision in the West: The Atlanta Campaign of 1864* (Lawrence, KS, 1992), 277, 344.

Major General William H. T. Walker. Courtesy of Lawrence Lee Hewitt.

A Ghost on Horseback: The Many Wounds and Curious Death of General William H. T. Walker

Stewart L. Bennett

DURING THE EARLY MORNING OF JULY 22, 1864, CONFEDERATE MAJOR GENERAL William H. T. Walker scanned the lush hills and valleys of rural Georgia just outside of Atlanta. Now, after marching the better part of the night, Walker and his division approached the rear of the unsuspecting Union army. Walker readied his men for the coming attack but imminent surprise awaited him. On this day, Walker and his division would find themselves in the thick of the fighting that would become a turning point in the day's battle. On this fateful morning, while Walker surveyed the land before him, a shot rang out from the woods. It would be remembered as the shot that started the Battle of Atlanta. The same bullet that killed the major general ended his long and storied career. From here, Walker's Division moved into battle without their leader or, at least, that is what many believe. True, Walker would breathe his last on this fateful day. But how he died and where he died is still a matter of speculation and, like the rest of Walker's life, controversial. There was more to Walker than where he met his ending near Atlanta. A complicated sort, he lived a life of controversy often attributed to his many physical and psychological wounds.

As a soldier, Walker was never a stranger to confrontation, whether in camp or on the battlefield. For this, he suffered his share of mental or psychological wounds. Walker also spent much of his life suffering from various medical maladies. To understand his complexity, as well as the mental and physical ailments that contributed to it, the story must start at the beginning.

Born in 1816, William Henry Talbot Walker grew up in Augusta, Georgia, where his father was an attorney. When his father became a U.S. senator, young William certainly benefited from political connections. Unfortunately, the nearly bankrupt Senator Walker died in 1827 before his son's application reached West Point. Nonetheless, his son was admitted because of financial need and six letters of recommendation for appointment from members of the Georgia delegation to Congress. Walker would make good in the area of perseverance, always one of his greatest strengths, and graduate from West Point in 1837 near the bottom of his class. As a second lieutenant he would serve with the 6th Infantry, experience combat, and sustain his first physical war wounds at the hands of the Florida Seminoles.[1]

In December of 1837, Colonel Zachary Taylor led Walker and some eight hundred American troops in what would be remembered as the Battle of Okeechobee, the severest fight of the Second Seminole War. Taylor and his men attacked the Seminoles, who happened to be posted on an island in Lake Okeechobee. Walker and his comrades traversed several hundred yards of chest-deep water in order to carry out their mission. In the end, the Seminoles were defeated. The American troops won the battle with severe casualties, with Colonel Taylor receiving the praise.[2]

This battle, however, did not turn out well for the young second lieutenant from Georgia. While moving his men toward the enemy, Walker received three wounds: one shot to the leg, another to the neck, and a third to his shoulder, and he also broke his arm. In spite of his injuries, Walker continued advancing. Finally, while checking on the condition of a fellow officer, a fourth shot struck Walker in the chest. Subsequently the medical staff gave up hope on his recovery and expected him to die. However, according to one account, Walker, "laughed at their predictions and recovered," showing great strength of will in overcoming so many injuries. His personal strength and perseverance made the difference. Fortunately, he was allowed to regain much of his health before his next military challenge and injuries during the war with Mexico.[3]

The Mexican War tested the stamina of many a soldier, and Walker was no exception. During the bombardment of Vera Cruz, he chaffed for a fight. Writing home to his wife, Walker admitted: "How I do wish they would come on the plain and fight us with muskets. . . . I am dying to pay them back for all this work." Though he would receive a slight wound at the Battle of Churubusco when a cannonball exploded close by, it would not be until later in the war that a wound threatened his life. At the Battle of Molino Del Rey, Walker suffered "several wounds, all pronounced fatal."[4]

Once again, the physicians gave Walker up for dead. And once more he managed to regain his health, "to spite the doctors," as he is believed to have said. He lived to fight another day, but would be bedridden in Mexico for ten months before he was considered well enough to return to the United States. As a result of these events, his troops nicknamed Walker "Old Shot Pouch." With time, Walker would heal from his physical wounds brought on by his past military actions. However, looming on the horizon was another war that would test his invincibility.[5]

If the Second Seminole War and the war with Mexico were any indication, Walker could expect to sustain many more battle wounds if he saw much action during the American Civil War. Curiously, indeed almost miraculously considering his past history, Walker fought in numerous battles without sustaining a single wound until that fateful day outside of Atlanta. At Chickamauga, Walker commanded the Reserve Corps, composed of five brigades divided into two divisions. Though the smallest of General Braxton Bragg's five corps, his troops played a major role throughout the two-day engagement. Though Walker passed through the battle unscathed, it was nevertheless rumored that he had, indeed, been killed. Lieutenant Colonel Frank Erdelmeyer of the 32nd Indiana Infantry Regiment was a victim of this misbelief, noting in his after action report that "passing over the field, we found the dead body of General Walker." Walker quickly sent a letter to his wife dispelling the erroneous reports of his death.[6] In another instance, it was rumored that Walker had again been wounded. This time, the incident was believed to have taken place at New Hope Church on May 26, 1864. Again, Walker was quick to notify his wife that he was unharmed.[7]

One soldier seemed to grasp why Walker could be reported dead or hurt so often once he witnessed the general in action. Georgia Private Walter A. Clark, 1st (Ramsey's) Georgia Infantry Regiment, watched Walker as he rode past the troops on his way to the front. "Another shot from the battery struck immediately behind him, barely missing his horse," he recalled. "Glancing around at the dust it had raised and turning to us with a smile on his face, he said, 'Go it boots,' and galloped on to the head of the division." Clark suddenly understood: "On this, as well as on every other occasion when under fire, he seemed not only absolutely indifferent to danger, but really to enjoy its presence." Brigadier General William L. Cabell recalled that "battle always brought to his eyes an unusual glitter and he thought [Walker] the bravest man he had ever known." Regardless of his indifference to battlefield dangers and his proven courage, Walker still suffered wounds without the aid of battles, bullets, or shrapnel.[8]

The effects of asthma as a young child may have been one. Of small stature and weak constitution—so others found—Walker reported sick or too sick for his studies early on at West Point. This pattern continued during his early military career, in both peace and war. Walker fell in and out of poor health, frequently requesting sick leave from his military responsibilities. At one point, before his service in the Confederate army, Walker was stricken with a serious attack of asthma, which made him question his own chances of recovery. The best his physician offered at the time was, "three drinks of brandy or whiskey per day and three . . . pieces of red pepper." But he survived both the illness and the cure.[9]

Not only was Walker sidelined by the severe bouts of asthma, but the loss of sleep they caused took its toll on his body and emotions. Walker would admit to an adjutant general in the late 1850s that "an attack of asthma . . . has kept me out of my bed for seven nights." Later, he would complain: "Nearly five nights out of seven I am not able to lay down at night." Colonel Richard Taylor served under Walker in Virginia in 1861 where he witnessed his commander's ailments firsthand. Taylor recalled, "Always a martyr to asthma, he rarely enjoyed sleep but in a sitting position; yet he was as cheerful and full of restless activity." As the war continued, few, if any, would notice Walker's cheerfulness.[10]

Walker's chronic asthma could also be aggravated by his physical location and emotional stability. Walker despised his assignment in Pensacola, Florida, early in his Confederate service. He truly wanted to be in Virginia—where the action was. The stress of the situation brought on a severe bout of asthma. The asthma, along with the difficult climate and humid summer, did nothing to improve his ailing health, and by August, Walker was allowed to transfer, according to Bragg, "with regret and reluctance." Walker was now on his way to a new assignment in Virginia.[11]

Walker soon found that the weather in Richmond could not alleviate his health problems. The rainy Richmond weather also brought with it another bout of asthma. It was rumored that Walker had smoked saltpeter for this ailment in the past, but while in Richmond, he kept ether and laudanum close by if needed. Walker's problems with sickness continued to plague him from one assignment to the next. While posted in Savannah, Georgia, his health failed again when he was stricken with pneumonia. Later, while serving in Mississippi, Walker suffered another asthma attack. It is interesting that the sickly Walker did not contract malaria in the hot, humid, and dusty environs of Mississippi. All his various ailments distorted Walker's physical appearance. One soldier described the "permanent evidences of his sufferings a . . . painfully spare frame and a pale cadaverous complexion, which always suggested a ghost on horse back."[12]

Walker's numerous physical wounds and his continuous battles with asthma understandably affected his reactions in various situations. However, it was the emotional wounds, his argumentative nature and perceived affronts to his honor and leadership abilities that may have caused Walker the deepest of all wounds. When Walker arrived at his new assignment in Richmond, after leaving Pensacola, he started out on the wrong foot. In no way did he endear himself to Richmond society when he engaged in a rather heated argument with South Carolina Senator Robert W. Barnwell during dinner at the fashionable Richmond residence of Congressman James Chesnut Jr. and his wife Mary. Many a guest were discomfited that night with the two men hurling verbal barbs at each other. The senator "fired off at regular intervals, and Shot-Pouch Walker literally raved."[13]

Sadly, this initial social faux pas was only the beginning. Walker did not leave his arguments at Richmond dinner tables. He soon found himself quarreling with President Jefferson Davis himself. Walker believed himself slighted when Davis removed him from command of a brigade of Louisianans. Davis believed it best to realign the Confederate army whereby the soldiers of a brigade and their commander would be from the same state whenever possible. As a result of this bureaucratic change, Walker was removed from the Louisiana brigade, which he had spent months training and, instead, offered a Georgia brigade. Louisianan Colonel Taylor was given Walker's old command. Walker, a Georgian, now commanded Georgia troops, but that did not seem to bring him any comfort. It also did not help that Taylor was promoted and given his old command and that he also happened to be the brother of the president's first wife. So Walker submitted a resignation letter to Secretary of War Judah P. Benjamin. He felt slighted to find junior officers promoted over him and now his command, which he had spent months training, had been given to one of his "junior colonels." To make matters worse, Walker rebuked the president at the end of his letter. "The sacred cause for which I drew my sword I will fight for in my native state but I will not condescend to submit any longer to the insults and indignities of the Executive."[14]

When Benjamin responded to Walker, defending the president and criticizing Walker's "disrespectful and insulting comments," the volatile general fired back that Benjamin could "lose the respect of the country" in defending "an Executive who chooses to do this and to do that, in the face of the public opinion of the army and the country." The situation might have healed sooner had not their letters been printed and reprinted in many of the Southern papers, not uncommon with political correspondence at the time.[15]

Davis, who usually suffered from the effects of the Richmond press, found himself unusually allied with the *Daily Examiner* against Walker's actions. Many citizens could not understand Walker's position. "After all, it is only transferring Walker, a Georgian, to a Georgia [brigade]," wrote one, "and giving Walker's [brigade], which is from Louisiana, to Dick Taylor *of that ilk*. Walker says he has disciplined and trained this [brigade] and now Taylor will have all of the benefit of his work. Forgetting their country–quarreling for their own glory. For shame!"[16]

The talents of such an officer could not be wasted in time of war, and Georgia Governor Joseph E. Brown appointed Walker a major general in charge of Georgia's state troops. But the Confederacy needed him more, and it would appear that President Davis and Walker were willing to try and work together. Walker returned to the Confederate army as a brigadier general in February of 1863, but only after he withdrew "the insubordinate and disrespectful language used by him in his correspondence with the Honorable Judah P. Benjamin."[17]

Although back in the Confederate army, Walker did not return to Virginia. At first, he found himself supporting the defenses around Charleston and Savannah in the District of Georgia. But in early May he and his men were sent to Mississippi to reinforce General Joseph E. Johnston's army there and help contest the Union campaign against Vicksburg. It was here that Walker received his promotion to the rank of major general. Though it appeared that Walker had found his stride and appreciation, it did not last. Unfortunately, he continued to cripple his opportunities for redemption and the recognition of his leadership qualities by other commanders and subordinates with his fiery temper and uncompromising attitude.[18]

Assigned to the Army of Tennessee in August, Walker finally received the chance he had been waiting for: a major battle with the Union army in northwest Georgia. Even before the battle had been launched, the Confederate army and Walker had a chance possibly to cripple Union Major General Thomas L. Crittenden's corps. Unfortunately for the Southerners, Confederate Lieutenant General Leonidas Polk faltered. During Polk's council of war prior to the attack on Crittenden, Walker disagreed with Polk's arrangement and placement of troops for the attack. And he refused to be satisfied regardless of how often Polk tried to explain his plans. When Major General Benjamin Franklin Cheatham tried to engage Walker about the matter, he too became frustrated, and within minutes walked away. He told Brigadier General St. John R. Liddell, who commanded a division under Walker, "he would not serve two hours under Walker to save his life." Walker finally gave up the argument with Polk, but only after "having exhausted rhetoric and expletives. He came grumblingly away, greatly to the relief of General Polk who was completely badgered."[19]

The Battle of Chickamauga took place September 19–20, 1863, soon after Polk's frustrating meeting with his generals. Walker commanded the Reserve Corps during the battle. During the fury of the second day's fighting, Walker found the five brigades of his corps going into battle against fortified Union lines in what he considered ill-advised attacks ordered by Lieutenant General Daniel Harvey Hill. In the midst of the conflict, Walker and Hill began arguing over the splintered placement of Brigadier General States Rights Gist's Brigade, commanded by Colonel Claudius C. Wilson, and Brigadier General Edward C. Walthall's Brigade. Walker showed no qualms expressing his resentment (verbally and loudly) about how Hill had misused his corps. Walker soon complained to Polk, in Hill's presence, about the latter's placement of his command, lamenting that he (Walker) no longer had a command. As Hill stormed off in a rage, Walker, according to Liddell, remarked: "The man is mad, and in a mad fit will expose himself to the sharpshooters and will get killed." Even though Walker would soon after apologize to Hill, the damage between the two had been done. Despite the apology, Walker did not let that

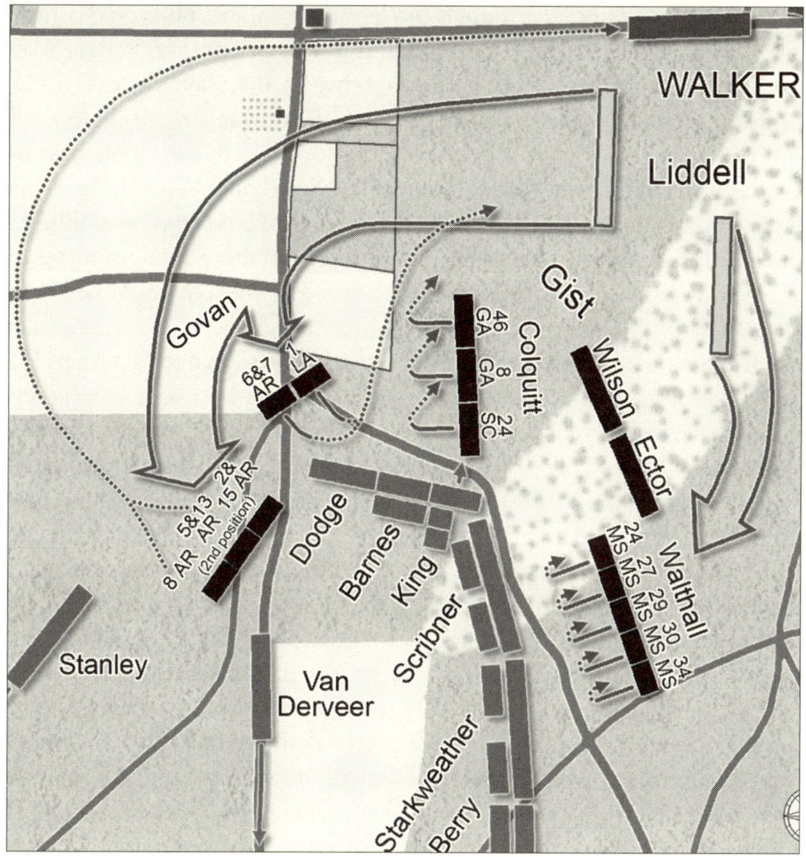

Battle of Chickamauga, late morning, September 20, 1863. From *The Maps of Chickamauga* by David Powell and David Friedrichs (New York: Savas Beatie, 2009), 165. Used with permission.

stop him from issuing his opinion of Hill's leadership actions in his official report of the battle.[20]

Walker's fiery temper may have been directed toward those he believed had slighted him, but others saw it as a serious character flaw that could flare up at any moment in the heat of battle or in camp against anyone—another general or the president of the Confederacy. Even Liddle, Walker's subordinate, had little good to say about his commander during much of their time together. Liddell recalled that Walker was viewed as a "crackbrained fire-eater, always captious or caviling about something whimsical and changeable. . . . The only satisfaction that I had was that our official relations would end with the next battle."[21]

It was an accumulation of the many bouts of sickness, battle wounds, and his attitude concerning being overlooked for promotion that would continue to affect Walker's ability to progress further in command. He would continue to argue with others and feel slighted in one way or another. Walker would also continue to suffer through illnesses, some brought on by stress.

Walker felt aggrieved about being passed over for promotion upon the death of Lieutenant General Polk at Lost Mountain. Given their past disagreements, it might have been easier to swallow had President Davis been responsible for the slight. However, Walker discovered that people he had considered friends did not recommend him for the promotion. Enraged and hurt, Walker lamented: "Here are 3 of my old army acquaintances, men I have served with for over a quarter of a century, two of the 3 professing great friendship, who sit quietly and see me overslaughed." While it was true Walker had resigned before and been allowed back into the ranks of the Confederate army, and that he was a major general, the promotion opportunity created by Polk's death was offered to Major General Alexander P. Stewart, who was junior in rank to Walker. This was possibly the cruelest slight of all. Nonetheless, Walker continued in command of his division, waiting for further developments and new challenges as he moved toward Atlanta and his final wound.[22]

The winds of change moved swiftly through the Army of Tennessee as it fought and maneuvered south through Georgia during the Atlanta Campaign of 1864. Walker's Division was reduced from four brigades to three, but the greatest change for the army was the dismissal of its leader, General Joseph E. Johnston. The change in leadership took place almost at the gates of the "Gate City" of Atlanta. The president chose Lieutenant General John Bell Hood to command the army, although some expected Lieutenant General William J. Hardee to take the helm.[23]

General Hood's taking command of the army came as mixed news for Walker. On the one hand, Walker appreciated Johnston; yet on the other he had "never . . . approved of our falling back but have been in favor of a fight." Soon after Hood's promotion, Hardee requested a transfer, but Davis denied it. This situation, the promotion of Hood over Hardee, which Walker seemed to relish, may have brought thoughts of poetic justice to his mind. "Hardee ranks Hood. I wonder how he fancies this *overslaughing* business. . . . He ought to revolve around my headqrs. awhile and get a little consolation from one who has suffered so many similar eclipses as to have lost all light."[24]

The new commander quickly lived up to his reputation as a fighter, and he planned a bold maneuver for July 22, 1864, in which both Hardee and Walker would play significant roles. In meeting with his cavalry commander Major General Joseph Wheeler, Hood learned that Union Major General James B. McPherson's Army of the Tennessee, positioned in lines east of the city of Atlanta, was exposed on its left flank, that it was indeed "standing out in air." Not only was the flank vulnerable, but the massive Union wagon train was parked in and around Decatur, only a short distance from Atlanta.[25]

Major General John Schofield, Hood's friend from his old West Point days, had his small Federal Army of the Ohio to the north of Atlanta not far from McPherson. Better yet for Hood, Major General George H. Thomas's much larger Army of the Cumberland was located northwest of Schofield about twelve miles away, a difficult and long way off if McPherson needed help. If a large portion of Hood's forces could actually strike McPherson's flank or rear, the rout or destruction of the Army of the Tennessee would actually be possible. This could mean the destruction of at least a quarter of Sherman's strength, and it would clear the area east of Atlanta of Federals and reopen the Georgia Railroad to Augusta. A successful attack would also deliver a staggering blow to President Abraham Lincoln's reelection chances.[26]

Hardee played a leading role in the plan: he was expected to move his men, including Walker's Division, out of their entrenchments soon after dusk, march them south, and finally, as Hood later wrote, "completely turn the left of McPherson's Army." Hardee's troops would then strike McPherson's men from the rear, thus rolling up the Army of the Tennessee from the left to the right. Wheeler's cavalry would simultaneously capture the Union wagon train near Decatur. Cheatham's corps would join in the rout, striking the enemy from the front, taking prisoners as they went. The combined blows were expected to seed consternation and confusion all along McPherson's line. If fortune smiled on the Confederacy this day, the Army of the Tennessee would be rolled up and forced upon Schofield's Army of the Ohio, also taking this army out of action. These disasters would force Thomas's Army of the Cumberland back toward Peachtree Creek. While the complete destruction of Sherman's forces was not guaranteed by this plan, it had the real possibility of forcing Sherman north of the Chattahoochee River, thus buying Hood and the city of Atlanta precious time.[27]

Hardee's route of march included the McDonough Road southward to the Fayetteville Road, then eastward to Middle McDonough Road, via Cobb's Mill on Entrenchment Creek. The jumping-off point for the attack on McPherson's flank and rear has been reported as a distance between ten to eighteen miles. Fifteen miles was the most commonly given and was the actual distance if measured from the start of Hardee's troop movement at the entrenchments to where the troops commenced their attack on the flank and rear of McPherson's army.[28]

Once Walker had his men out of their fortifications and marching southward, he focused on what lay ahead. He quickly concluded that he must stop at the Leyden House where Hood had made his headquarters. Walker felt the need to tell Hood that he understood his commander's heavy responsibilities as well as the condition of the Confederate army after the many retreats during the campaign. With characteristic brashness, he felt obliged before going into battle to let Hood know he was with him "in heart and purpose." Walker left the meeting with Hood "full of enthusiasm" and "aglow with martial fire from that moment." Perhaps this had been a convocation of fighting spirits, or it could have been simply pure politicking, currying favor with the commander. Maybe it would help obtain that elusive promotion down the line.[29]

Another meeting took place on the morning of July 22, including Hardee, Walker, Wheeler, and Major General Patrick Cleburne, to finalize the plans for the assault that day. It was at this meeting that Hardee and Wheeler discussed the Union army's location. Wheeler explained that there were no enemy forces between Cobb's Mill and Decatur. Local citizens who were also present at this meeting confirmed this assessment. On the subject of possible impediment to the attacking columns, close cross-examination of one citizen revealed that a pond at least a mile long and ten feet deep in places intersected the right of the attacking Confederate line.[30]

The good news though, Wheeler said, was that at "some points our line was nearly parallel to McPherson's entrenchments which faced Atlanta, and which my troops were facing and fighting the day before." Wheeler's reconnaissance had paid off. The road was clear and the attack, though not on schedule due to slow troop movements and environmental impediments, still had promise. "When I left General Hardee to prepare for the attack," Wheeler wrote concerning his departure on his mission, "we knew we were in rear of General McPherson's line, at least in rear of his left." Hardee had indeed successfully bypassed McPherson's flank and positioned the bulk of his corps to the Union rear, but there was still a vast Georgia woodland wilderness between the two armies.[31]

Walker was ready. During the march one soldier observed that "Fighting Billy" was "one of the thinnest men he had ever seen," and likened him to "a fence rail, dressed in complete uniform, closely buttoned up warm as it was, topped by a long pale face, almost hidden, however, by a bushy black beard, and above all a huge black felt hat with a big black feather curling around it. . . . Long and tall as he looked, as he sat on his horse, straight as a ram rod."[32]

Walker's task was to march his division into position to the right of Cleburne's Division and to the left of Major General William Bate's Division. Walker and his men continued north on the Middle McDonough Road, followed by Cleburne and his men. Not long after, the Confederate divisions encountered a fork in the road with the left being the Flat Shoals Road. Cleburne's Division passed along this road, a route that would lead him directly to Leggett's Hill. The right-hand turn was the Fayetteville Road, the same road Wheeler had taken on his journey toward Decatur, which Walker and his column wearily followed northeast. After marching about a quarter of a mile, Walker and his men moved left off the Fayetteville Road just before crossing Sugar Creek, therefore maneuvering to the right side of the creek.[33]

Walker's troops were now marching off the road and stumbling through the tangled underbrush wilderness. Walker's Division was supposed to dress toward Cleburne's right, yet Walker was also to have his right flank against Bate's left. But now because of the dense forest, Walker could no longer see Bate's Division. And it was at this point that Bate's and Walker's Divisions had to fight their first battle of the day, the battle against topography. The morass of dense woods included ground cover punctuated by massive briar patches. This tangle made many places almost impenetrable for troop movements. Terry's Mill Pond was, as citizens had mentioned, deep and large, and of particular concern, most inconveniently shaped—it stretched a half mile to the north. And even more bothersome, the pond was almost as wide as it was long, with a protruding point that greatly hindered movement of Confederate troops to the west of the pond. Finally, the swamps around and near the pond also slowed progress for the Southerners. Walker's horse reportedly got mired deep in the mud when nearing the pond.[34]

At one point, Walker had had enough. His division had been delayed by their western movement around Terry's Mill Pond. To add to their problems, one of Walker's regiments came upon a giant briar patch that nettled their attack. Walker rode over to explain his situation to Hardee, who was under the strain of command and the fact his attack was running behind schedule. So when Walker approached him about the terrain issues, Hardee exploded at him before he could explain. "General Hardee turned roughly and rudely upon him," recalled a witness, "and said loudly in the presence of staff officers and orderlies: 'No, Sir! This movement has been delayed too long already. Go and obey my orders!'" As Walker rode off, he asked Joseph Cumming: "Major, did you hear that?" Cumming responded, "Yes, General Hardee forgot himself." Walker then angrily again answered, "I shall make him remember this insult. If I survive this battle, he shall answer to me for it."[35]

Hardee quickly sent a staff officer to Walker to apologize, even mentioning that he would have come himself but matters deemed it difficult at the time. But this apology by courier did not appease the emotionally wounded general; Walker remained upset. Confederate leaders felt the weight of their responsibilities this day and some broke under the pressure. Although Walker was still outraged by Hardee's actions, the Georgian would never live to follow through on his threats.[36]

While official accounts place Walker with his troops at the time of his death, much controversy shadows what happened during his final moments. There are two possible scenarios historians and others interested in the subject find viable. The first is historian Wilbur G. Kurtz's narrative about Walker's death as told by a man by the name of Case Turner. According to Kurtz, Hardee, Walker, and Cleburne met at William Cobb's home around sunrise on July 22 to discuss the final movements of the march. While there, Kurtz stated that the farmer who had mentioned the obstacles in the Confederate path may have possibly been Case Turner. This same Case Turner, Kurtz admitted, was the one upon which "the rest of the narrative hinges."

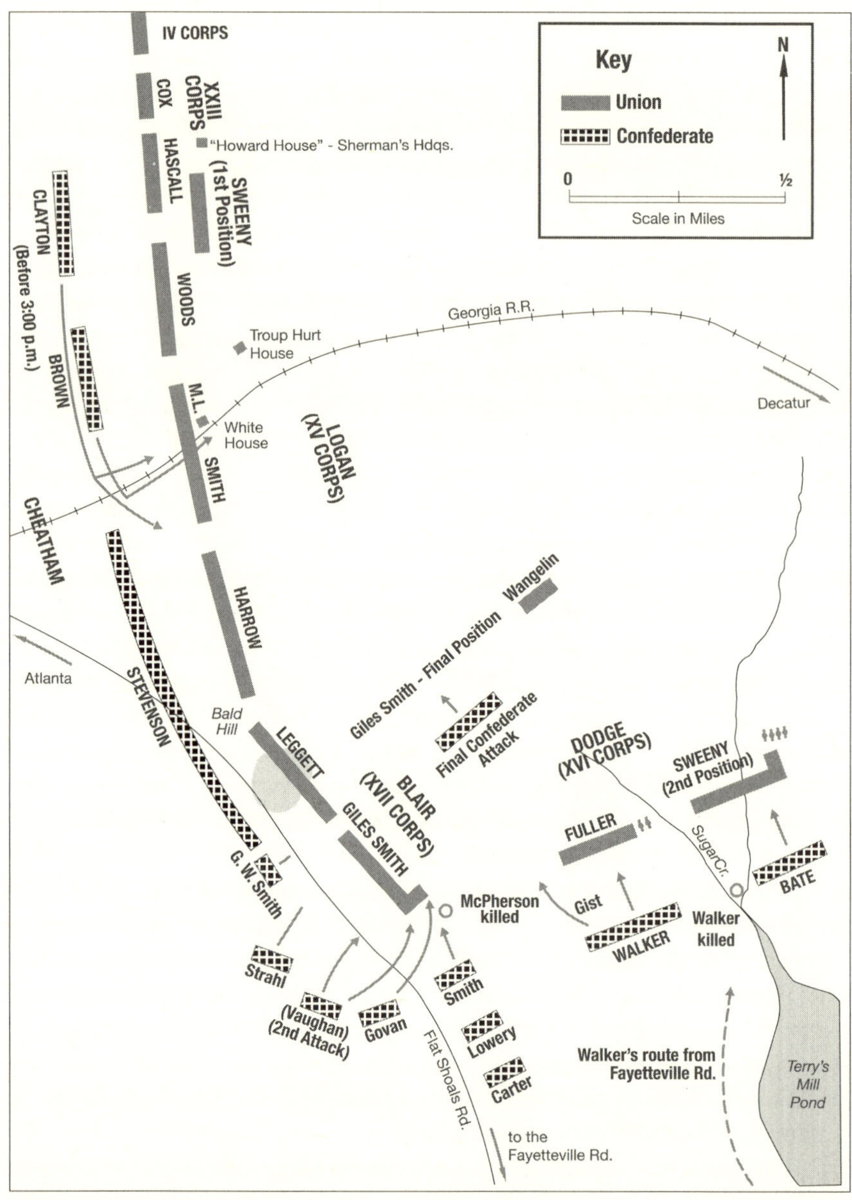

Battle of Atlanta.

Supposedly, Turner worked for Cobb at the mill and was assigned to Walker (whether willingly or not) to help guide the division through the woods, fields, and thickets toward the Union line near Atlanta.[37]

As Walker and his staff moved forward guided by Turner toward the west of Sugar Creek, Turner objected that the course they were on would lead them straight into the pond. Walker, finding no such place on his map, continued to move his men forward. Besides, pond sizes varied and many could usually be waded through and across. Upon final approach to the south side of Terry's Mill Pond, Walker found what many might call a "pond" but others might see as a "lake." Not only was this body of water large and deep, but it branched out toward the west further impeding Walker's Division from its timely march toward destiny. As Walker and his staff rode around the arm of the pond, they found themselves mired in the swampy mud. Although difficult, they managed to make their way out of the morass. In a fit of his signature anger in such times as this, it was said that he "drew forth from a holster a long revolver, and threatened to shoot Turner right out of the saddle!" Supposedly, Major Cumming quickly mediated between the two, thus saving Walker one bullet and Turner his life.[38]

Walker now rode north and, after clearing the pond area, to the northeast. At this point, Walker, presumably ahead of his escort, stopped above the mill pond on the rise of a hill to examine the position before him peering through his field glasses. "A shot rang out from the hill side," says the Turner narrative, "two or three hundred feet in front and overlooking the stream valley. General Walker fell from his saddle! He had been shot by a Federal picket, posted behind a small earthwork on the hill side in such a position as to command a view of the valley, and the head of the pond." There are no records of what happened immediately after Walker was allegedly shot. In any event since Walker was dead, Turner believed his services were no longer needed. So he lost no time riding his mule back from the Confederate line as quickly as possible and toward the mill pond out of harm's way.[39]

Case Turner told an interesting and informative story, if the story was in fact reported correctly. Though Kurtz heard the story, it was not from the primary source, Case Turner, but instead, from a veteran of the 42nd Georgia Infantry named J. W. McWilliams. Although McWilliams and his regiment fought at the Battle of Atlanta, they were not in the fighting near Walker's Division and, therefore, nowhere near Walker's death. Instead, McWilliams's relating of the Case Turner account was, he said, because he had "heard the story often enough, and knew well the localities named, to retain a vivid recollection of all the details . . . in the absence of stated official verbiage, the tale comes as a refreshing bit of [illegible] information that cannot fail to be convincing." But what can be learned regarding the background of Case Turner?[40]

Turner's testimony is crucial, but there is little that we know of him. According to Kurtz, not much about Turner's past is known, except for his involvement in the earlier Indian wars. At that time, he had been wounded by a bullet to his arm pit. After the surgeon removed it, Turner kept the bullet as a memento, and he was known to tell the story of his wound and would show the bullet to anyone who cared to listen. Wherever Case Turner went, the bullet went also. All his friends and acquaintances had heard the story.

According to Kurtz, those who "failed to see the bullet and hear its story, it was, because they were blind and deaf!" It is possible the Walker story became a new and interesting tale in which Turner may have been a guide but embellished the tale. Maybe Turner was not there at all. Even Kurtz shed doubt on Turner's credibility when he bluntly stated: "Case–and he is said to have been just that." This appears to call into question Turner's own truthfulness and possibly his reputation.[41]

Nor was Turner mentioned in any of the official writings and correspondence by Walker's staff at the time of his death or soon after the battle. We have yet to find anything that these participants might have written that mentions Turner. The closest we come to such testimony was the address given by Major Cumming years later at the unveiling of the monument to Walker in Atlanta. In his address, Cumming did mention the dense growth of the environment around them and that Walker sent some of his staff, including Major Cumming, Captain William H. Ross (acting assistant adjutant general), and Captain James R. Troup (assistant adjutant general) to his three brigades to "preserve intervals and alignment." This left only Captain M. H. Talbot (volunteer aide-de-camp) and Lieutenant J. W. Bass (assistant adjutant and inspector general) and a person he recalled as Walker's "volunteer aid." It is upon this information of the volunteer aid that Kurtz asks, "Could this have been Case Turner, the guide?"[42]

It may or may not have been, but it was enough evidence for Kurtz to accept the McWilliams testimony of Case Turner, and as time progressed, Turner's version become the story of Walker's death most accepted by historians. For Kurtz, "a single musket-shot, fired by a Federal picket from the woods, not only toppled Walker from his saddle, his field-glasses still in his hands—but began the Battle of Atlanta."[43]

Other accounts appear to follow Case Turner's, but with certain twists. Private Eugene P. Speer of the 46th Georgia Infantry Regiment explained that Walker did ride out to the brow of a hill accompanied by staff officers including Cumming, Ross, and Lieutenant Thomas H. Kenan (aide-de-camp). "A shot struck Ross's horse and another grievously wounded the General's while yet another pierced his body through and through. It proved instantly fatal . . . the General reeled, fell forward and struck the ground heavily on his head." Supposedly, South Carolina soldiers of Gist's Brigade ran out and secured Walker's body. Speer recalled seeing the body soon afterward, mentioning that it was placed in an ambulance and sent to the rear of the army.[44]

So Speer believed Cumming was, in fact, with Walker during the incident; however, Cumming denies it. Speer also mentioned that Walker and the group rode out to the front during a lull during battle with Union forces, and not as the first shot of the Battle of Atlanta as stated earlier by Kurtz. Speer recalled that the "Federals were in strength in a wood opposite, and the flight of rifle shot across this space was incessant at times, while fragments of exploding shell sawed the air disagreeably . . . filling our position each minute with a tumult of wounds and disorder." It would seem strange for Walker to ride to the front when "in the bright sunlight the gleam of uniforms and busy ramrods could be easily distinguished in the thickets beyond."[45]

Walker rode out, according to Speer, during a lull in the battle and while the Union forces appeared to be retreating. So it is reasonable to believe that "Old Shot Pouch" would have led the men forward during such an opportunity. It was during this movement, however, that Speer recalled Union soldiers, possibly a dozen or more, hidden in a hollow halfway between the opposing lines of battle. He believed "a volley was probably agreed upon and concentrated on the officer whose uniform and decorations denoted his high rank. It came, a cruel, cowardly fusillade, and proved fatal to an old commander." This account puts Walker amidst already heavy fighting when he was killed by several shots, not a single one from a lone picket, while he was moving Gist's Brigade forward.[46]

Yet another account must be taken into consideration. In this version, Walker's Division did encounter the pond and other obstacles; however, the general managed to live long enough to lead his troops up to the Union 16th Corps. As mentioned before, Walker had sent Cumming, Ross, and Troup to the three separate brigades; however, it appeared that Gist and his brigade were having serious problems moving forward and in the correct direction. Following the death of Brigadier General Clement H. Stevens on July 20, command of Stevens's Brigade fell to Colonel James C. Nisbet. On July 22, the brigade was on the division's right when the colonel noted at that time: "Gist's Brigade became completely separated from the rest of our division. Major General Walker went to find it." While waiting on Walker and Gist, Nisbet received orders to move his brigade with Bate's Division to his right. Understanding the circumstances he was in, Nisbet rode over to tell Bate the situation, asking him not to move yet because of the tardiness of Gist's Brigade. Nisbet also mentioned the gap that had developed on the left because of Gist's delay. However, Bate would not relent. Too much time lost, he said, and it was imperative the attack proceed without further delay. When Bate moved out, Nisbet moved with him. But because of his insecurity about his left, Nisbet put Lieutenant Colonel Algernon Sydney Hamilton in command of the center while Major Newton Hull took command of the right. Nisbet himself rode to the left, no doubt under duress. Bate's Division and part of Walker's were at that point on the move toward the Union line, despite the gap between Walker's left and Cleburne's Division. The last Nisbet knew of Walker, the general was "killed leading the South Carolina brigade. It was in the woods not far from where McPherson lost his life."[47]

Walker did indeed find his way to Gist's Brigade, but owing to the delays, his brigades attacked in piecemeal fashion with disastrous results, especially for Gist's. During the assault of Gist's Brigade, Walker realized that his troops were embroiled in a desperate struggle and rode to the front of the men to rally them. One soldier of the 24th South Carolina Infantry Regiment recalled: "Without hesitation, Gen. Walker rode among them, in the middle of the 'iron hail' and complimented the gallant regiment for their bravery. Gen. Walker's clarion voice reached out to every soldier, calmed their fears and urged them onward. Gen. Walker waved his hat and extolled the bravery of every man! 'Soldiers: Remember Stevens! Remember him! One more charge and the day is won! Follow me!' With a wild cheer those gallant men responded."[48]

Then Walker met his fate. Walker's grey horse was struck by Union fire and fell hard upon the ground. At that moment, the general stood upright and several enemy bullets pierced his body, fatally wounding him. "Bring off the general!" the soldiers hollered, and John Bagley of the 24th South Carolina carried Walker's body from the line of fire and off the field.[49]

Unlike the other eyewitness accounts for Walker's death, Union soldiers figured in this one. Union Colonel Charles Sheldon of the 18th Missouri Infantry Regiment remembered changing his regiment's line of fire so that it faced the 24th South Carolina and released a hail of lead into the oncoming Rebels. This fire stopped the South Carolinians in their tracks. And it was at this point that Sheldon believed he saw Major General Walker riding through the field before them waving his hat and rallying the troops. Soon thereafter, however, Sheldon spotted Walker's horse but no rider.[50]

Union Brigadier General John W. Fuller also wrote of the situation in his lines, especially in Sheldon's area where Walker was believed to have been shot. As he explained: "Just then a fine-looking officer brought another regiment out of the woods. He rode forward, hat in hand, to rally his men. . . . The officer who was so conspicuous was immediately shot down, and the whole mass swayed back into the forest. As the last of them were retiring voices were heard shouting 'Bring off the general.' Some prisoners told us that the general was Walker, the commander of the division."[51]

Major General Grenville M. Dodge was in command of the 16th Corps on July 22 and was near Fuller during most, if not all, of the fighting that took place in that sector. "Where I stood in my line," Dodge remembered, "I could see the entire Confederate force, and all of my own, something that very seldom occurs, and, of course, the scene . . . was a magnificent one." Dodge recalled Walker's troops breaking the center of Fuller's brigade, but Fuller rallied his men and saved the Union line. "It was but a moment later," Dodge said, "that I saw Walker, who commanded the division that was attacking Fuller, fall from his horse, and the division broke and went into the woods."[52]

It is true that another Confederate officer, Brigadier General Gist, had been shot around the same time as Walker. Gist's wound was to the hand and wrist and he was able to continue the fight for about two hours until the loss of blood finally caused him to faint. The time difference between the falling of the two generals should dispel any confusion concerning the mention of the Confederate troops bringing off the general from the field of battle. Even though the chain of command remained intact after Walker's death, without him to lead the division, and given the already piecemeal commitment of the brigades to battle, the fact remained that the division was used up. What was left of Walker's Division fell back and reformed, only to spend the rest of the battle in reserve.[53]

In reviewing the separate accounts of Walker's demise, it would appear that those by Kurtz, members of the 24th South Carolina, and Union generals Dodge and Fuller offer the most in-depth information. While Walker's staff—Cumming, Ross, or Troup—did not refute McWilliams's story of Case Turner, it still raises questions. One cannot escape the lack of credibility Turner appears to have as a storyteller to all and sundry willing to listen or not, and even Kurtz tended to question his own source's integrity. What gave the Turner story its most credibility was Kurtz himself. During the time that Kurtz developed the Turner story, many in Georgia, especially in Atlanta, viewed him as the foremost authority on the Atlanta Campaign and Atlanta history. He had been involved in various history projects; however, he was arguably best known for his position as historian for the epic movie *Gone With the Wind*. Writer Margaret Mitchell was once quoted speaking of Kurtz as "our greatest authority on the Civil War in this section. He has studied every campaign, been over every battlefield, mapped out the position of the troops. . . . Mr. Kurtz is the real authority." Kurtz would later work as the historian and technical advisor for such films as Disney's *Song of the South* and *The Great Locomotive Chase*. Many historians accepted his views as authoritative because the Civil War history community accepted him as the premier Atlanta historian in the field. So the account of Walker's death, as Kurtz believed it and wrote it, was accepted.[54]

After considering other possible accounts of Walker's death, the fact that a participant would so often write that Walker fell leading his troops is significant. This fact does not help to determine if the location mentioned was in front of the troops, with Walker leading near Terry's Mill Pond, or against the 16th Corps's defenses. Many statements could go either way. This has also been true of the writings of some historians.[55] The statements made by the soldiers of the 24th South Carolina and those of Federals Sheldon, Fuller, and Dodge help to bring some credence to the possibility of Walker's dying as he led Gist's Brigade against the Union lines during the heat of battle. No Union accounts of Walker being shot and killed near the pond are known to exist.

In any event, the ghost on horseback had fallen to rise no more. There would be no serious combat wounds to question, no doctors to prove wrong, no longer any slights in promotion to argue over, no arguments to correct, or illnesses to overcome. William H. T. Walker was finally at rest. One soldier recalled tying Walker's handkerchief around the major general's chin as he was taken from the field and placed in the ambulance. His body was brought back to Augusta, Georgia, soon after the battle where he was buried. Walker's Division died with him. Soon after the Battle of Atlanta, the division was, as it had been in the battle itself, piecemealed out—but this time to Cheatham's, Cleburne's, and Bate's divisions within the Confederate army. The Army of Tennessee's commander, General Hood, wrote of Walker's death and his bravery but would mistakenly add the unfortunate sting of misremembering the dead general's name as W. H. S. Walker.[56]

As the years passed and many Confederate veterans returned to Atlanta, they would eventually remember Major General William H. T. Walker with a monument, placed where some presumed he had died. But like Walker's death, the placement of the memorial to him also became controversial. Years later the monument was moved to a different location believed to be closer to where he had fallen. Today, the Walker monument, lodged virtually unseen between roads on all sides, looks tired and old; it is a monument all but forgotten. It stands as a quiet reminder of a bygone day and to a general who, like so many others, may also become a dying memory.

In retrospect, Walker could be seen as a military hero to the United States and the Confederacy. He devoted himself to the position and duty at hand. His efficiency paid off for himself, at times, but especially for his men's benefit. Combat, health, and emotional wounds scarred him in many ways throughout his life and career. His fiery temper made him volatile. His perpetual arguments with leadership, subordinates, and peers often denied him career advancement and influence. It is possible that Walker might have overcome some but not all of the many wounds he had accumulated over the years. He was a complicated and controversial man. It was the way he lived his life, and maybe it is fitting that the way he died or did not die is a consistent last chapter to a complicated saga.

Notes

1. Russell K. Brown, *To the Manner Born: The Life of General William H. T. Walker* (Macon, GA, 2005), 1–4, 8–9.
2. Richard Taylor, *Destruction and Reconstruction: Personal Experiences of the Late War in the United States* (Edinburgh and London, 1879), 17–18.
3. Brown, *To the Manner Born*, 12; Taylor, *Destruction and Reconstruction*, 18 (quote).
4. Jeffrey Mosser, "I Shall Make Him Remember This Insult," *Civil War Times Illustrated* 32 (Mar.—Apr. 1993), 49; Taylor, *Destruction and Reconstruction*, 18.
5. Taylor, *Destruction and Reconstruction*, 18; Stephen Davis, "A Georgia Firebrand: Major General W. H. T. Walker, C.S.A." *Georgia Historical Quarterly*

64, no. 4 (Winter 1979): 448–49; John H. Eicher and David J. Eicher, *Civil War High Commands* (Stanford, CA, 2001), 21. Even civilians used the nickname, "Shot-Pouch" for the wounded Walker. Mary Chesnut, *Mary Chesnut's Civil War,* ed. C. Vann Woodward (New Haven, CT, 1981), 149, 152, 235.

6. U.S. War Department. *The War of the Rebellion: A Compilation of the Official Records of the Union and Confederate Armies.* 128 vols. Washington, DC, 1880–1901, ser. 1, vol. 30, pt. 1:547 (hereafter cited as *OR;* all citations are to series 1 unless otherwise indicated); Brown, *To the Manner Born,* 180–81.
7. Brown, *To the Manner Born,* 240–41.
8. Walter A. Clark, *Under the Stars and Bars, or Memories of Four Years Service with the Oglethorpes, of Augusta, Georgia* (Augusta, GA, 1900), 109; W. A. Clark, 1st (Ramsey's) Infantry, Compiled Service Records of Confederate Soldiers Who Served in Organizations from the State of Georgia, Roll 143, M266, National Archives and Records Service, Washington, DC.
9. Brown, *To the Manner Born,* 7, 19, 74.
10. Ibid., 79; Taylor, *Destruction and Reconstruction,* 18.
11. Brown, *To the Manner Born,* 99–100.
12. Jack D. Welsh, *Medical Histories of Confederate Generals* (Kent, OH, 1995), 227; Brown, *To the Manner Born,* 125, 157; Henry E. Handerson, *Yankee in Gray: The Civil War Memoirs of Henry E. Handerson, with a Selection of His Wartime Letters* (Cleveland, OH, 1962), 33.
13. Chesnut, *Mary Chesnut's Civil War,* 151–52.
14. Brown, *To the Manner Born,* 111–12.
15. Davis, "Georgia Firebrand," 451.
16. Chesnut, *Mary Chesnut's Civil War,* 235. Confederate Brigadier General St. John R. Liddell would later write that the Louisiana brigade, in fact, preferred Walker over Taylor, but the brigade reluctantly submitted to Davis's order. See St. John Richardson Liddell, *Liddell's Record,* ed. Nathaniel Cheairs Hughes Jr. (Dayton, OH, 1985), 184.
17. Brown, *To the Manner Born,* 137–39; Ezra J. Warner, *Generals in Gray: Lives of the Confederate Commanders* (Baton Rouge, LA, 1959), 323.
18. Brown, *To the Manner Born,* 140, 147, 153.
19. Ibid., 166; Liddell, *Liddell's Record,* 140.
20. Liddell, *Liddell's Record,* 144–45; Judith Lee Hallock, *Braxton Bragg and Confederate Defeat, Vol. 2* (Tuscaloosa, AL, 1991), 74; Hal Bridges, *Lee's Maverick General: Daniel Harvey Hill,* (Lincoln, NE, 1991), 222; *OR,* vol. 30, 2:241–42.
21. Liddell, *Liddell's Record,* 137.
22. Brown, *To the Manner Born,* 253–255.

23. Richard M. McMurry, *John Bell Hood and the War for Southern Independence* (Lexington, KY, 1982), 8–10. During discussions before the change, Davis had asked General Robert E. Lee his opinion about Hood as a replacement for Johnston. "Hood is a good fighter," Lee said, "very industrious on the battle field, careless off, and I have had no opportunity of judging of his action, when the whole responsibility rested upon him. I have a high opinion of his gallantry, earnestness and zeal. Gen. Hardee has more experience in managing an army." Robert E. Lee, *The Wartime Papers of R. E. Lee*, ed. Clifford Dowdey (Boston, 1961), 821–22.

24. Brown, *To the Manner Born*, 257.

25. John Bell Hood, *Advance and Retreat: Personal Experiences in the United States and Confederate States Armies* (New Orleans, 1880), 173.

26. Ibid., 176; Stephen Davis, *Atlanta Will Fall: Sherman, Joe Johnston, and the Yankee Heavy Battalions* (Wilmington, DE, 2001), 138.

27. *OR*, vol. 38, pt. 3:631; Stanley F. Horn, *The Army of Tennessee* (1941; repr., Wilmington, NC, 1987), 354.

28. Nathaniel Cheairs Hughes Jr., *General William J. Hardee: Old Reliable* (Baton Rouge, LA, 1965), 226; Wilbur G. Kurtz, "Major-General W. H. T. Walker," *Atlanta Constitution*, July 27, 1930, sec. "Civil War Days in Georgia," 6; T. B. Roy, "General Hardee and the Military Operations Around Atlanta," *Southern Historical Society Papers* 8 (Sept. 1880), 356; Thomas Robson Hay, "The Atlanta Campaign [pt. 1]," *Georgia Historical Quarterly* 7, no. 1 (Mar. 1923), 40.

29. Brown, *To The Manner Born*, 263; Hood, *Advance and Retreat*, 181–82; Robert E. L. Krick, *Staff Officers in Gray: A Biographical Register of the Staff Officers in the Army of Northern Virginia* (Chapel Hill, NC, 2003), 323.

30. Albert Castel. *Decision in the West: The Atlanta Campaign of 1864* (Lawrence, KS, 1992), 391; Roy, "General Hardee," 359–60.

31. Roy, "General Hardee," 365; *OR*, vol. 38, pt. 3:952. In his official report dated October 9, 1864, Wheeler wrote that he moved in pursuant to orders from Hood to attack the enemy from the rear in conjunction with Hardee, while Hardee moved upon the enemy flank for the same purpose.

32. Philip Daingerfield Stephenson, *The Civil War Memoir of Philip Daingerfield Stephenson, D.D.*, ed. Nathaniel C. Hughes, Jr. (Conway, AR, 1995), 221.

33. Kurtz, "Major-General W. H. T. Walker," 6, 16; Wilbur G. Kurtz, "The Death of Major General W. H. T. Walker, July 22, 1864," *Civil War History* 6, no. 2 (June 1960), 177.

34. Kurtz, "Death of Major General W. H. T. Walker," 177–78.

35. Hughes, *General William J. Hardee*, 229; Brown, *To the Manner Born*, 265.

36. Hughes, *General William J. Hardee*, 229.

37. Kurtz, "Major-General W. H. T. Walker," 16.

38. Ibid. If Major Cumming was present for this episode, he never mentioned it in his speech for the unveiling of the Walker monument years after the war.

39. Ibid.

40. Ibid., 6.

41. Ibid., 16.

42. Joseph B. Cumming, *Address of Joseph B. Cumming at the Unveiling of the Monument to Maj. Gen'l. William Henry Talbot Walker on the Battle Field of Atlanta, July 22, 1902* (Augusta, GA, 1902), 8–9; Kurtz, "Death of Major General W. H. T. Walker," 179; Krick, *Staff Officers in Gray*, 288, 315, 352, 357.

43. Kurtz, "Death of Major General W. H. T. Walker," 179.

44. Eugene P. Speer, "General W. H. T. Walker: An Account of His Death at the Battle Before Atlanta, July 22, 1864—His Altercation with Hardee, Etc," *Newnan (GA) Herald*, May 29, 1883; Krick, *Staff Officers in Gray*, 337.

45. Speer, "General W. H. T. Walker."

46. Ibid.

47. James Cooper Nisbet. *Four Years on the Firing Line*. (Jackson, TN, 1963), 211–12, 216.

48. Eugene W. Jones Jr., *Enlisted for the War: The Struggles of the Gallant 24th Regiment, South Carolina Volunteers, Infantry, 1861–1865* (Hightstown, NJ, 1997), 181.

49. Ibid.

50. Ibid., 181, 183; *OR*, vol. 38, pt. 3:476.

51. John W. Fuller, "A Terrible Day: The Battle of Atlanta, July 22, 1864," in *Battles & Leaders of the Civil War*, vol. 5, ed. Peter Cozzens (Urbana, IL, 2002), 5:551.

52. Grenville M. Dodge, *The Battle of Atlanta and Other Campaigns, Addresses, etc.* (Council Bluffs, IA, 1910), 56; Grenville M. Dodge, "Battle Of Atlanta: The Terrible Struggle of July 22, 1864—Hood's Desperate Attempt to Turn Sherman's Left, and Drive Him Back from Atlanta," *National Tribune* (Washington, DC), Sept. 1, 1904.

53. Jones, *Enlisted for the War*, 181, 183.

54. Susan Myrick, *White Columns in Hollywood: Reports from the Gone With the Wind Sets* (Macon, GA, 1994), 5; Rebecca Nash Paden and Joe McTyre, *Images of America: Cobb County* (Charleston, SC, 2005), 64.

55. See, for example, Thomas L. Connelly, *Autumn of Glory: The Army of Tennessee, 1862–1865* (Baton Rouge, LA, 1971), 449; Clement A. Evans, ed. *Confederate Military History*, 12 vols. (Atlanta, 1899), 6:329.

56. William R. Ross, "Battlefield Letters to Mother and Sweetheart," *Atlanta Journal Magazine*, Apr. 25, 1943, 8–9; Connelly, *Autumn of Glory*, 451; Hood, *Advance and Retreat*, 181.

Major General Edward C. Walthall. Courtesy of Lawrence Lee Hewitt.

"He exhibited the highest soldierly qualities": Edward C. Walthall

Keith S. Bohannon

On December 19, 1864, General John Bell Hood assessed the grim situation of the Confederate Army of Tennessee from his headquarters in Columbia, Tennessee. The Battle of Nashville on December 15–16 had resulted in a decisive Union victory, Federal forces capturing thousands of men and dozens of cannon. Although Hood had intended in the case of failure at Nashville to retreat no further south than the Duck River, he decided on the night of December 19 after consulting with Major General Nathan Bedford Forrest that the army's disorganized state "made it necessary to recross the Tennessee [River] without delay."[1]

The next morning Hood sent for Major General Edward C. Walthall, whose headquarters were at the home of Nimrod Porter near Columbia. As Walthall approached army headquarters, he encountered Hood on horseback. Major David W. Sanders, Walthall's acting assistant adjutant general, recalled many years later the ensuing conversation. Hood said that things were "in a bad condition" and that Forrest, commanding the rear guard, could not "keep the enemy off us any longer without a strong infantry support." Forrest had requested three thousand infantry under the command of Walthall. Hood warned Walthall that the rear guard would be "a post of great honor, but one of such great peril that I will not impose it on you unless you are willing to take it."

Sanders remembered Walthall's reply as follows: "General I have never asked for a hard place for glory, nor a soft place for comfort, but take my chances as they come. Give me the order for the troops and I will do my best. Being the youngest Major General in the army, I believe my seniors may complain that the place was not offered them, but that is a matter between you and them."

"Forrest wants you, and I want you," Hood replied. And when Forrest rode up in the midst of the conversation, the cavalry general supposedly said: "Now we will keep them back."[2]

Why did Hood and Forrest choose Walthall to command the infantry portion of the rear guard during the Army of Tennessee's darkest hour? Hood claimed in his memoirs that at that point Walthall was "one of the most able division commanders in the South." This essay attempts to explain why Hood and Forrest held such high opinions of Walthall.[3]

Although Edward C. Walthall had neither attended West Point nor served in the U.S. Army, he did have a modicum of martial training and background. At age fifteen, Walthall entered St. Thomas Hall, a military academy located in Holly Springs, Mississippi. While at St. Thomas, Walthall and the other cadets received instruction from Commandant Claudius W. Sears, a West Point-trained former U.S. Army officer and future Confederate general. Later in the mid-1850s, Walthall served for two years in the Mississippi state militia system as an aide-de-camp to the governor. In 1859, Secretary of War John B. Floyd requested that Walthall attend the annual examination of the U.S. Military Academy as a member of the board of visitors. Although Walthall's positions on the Mississippi governor's staff and the West Point board of visitors were likely due as much to political considerations as military expertise, they still suggest some knowledge of martial affairs.[4]

At the time of secession, Walthall was the attorney for Mississippi's Tenth Judicial District, a position he had filled since 1856. The twenty-nine-year-old lawyer owned $7,000 in personal estate, including six slaves. He lived with his wife, Mary L. Jones Walthall, whom he had married the previous year.[5]

Soon after Mississippi's secession from the Union, Walthall resigned his public office and helped organize the "Yalobusha Rifles," and was elected first lieutenant. The company mustered into Confederate service on April 27, 1861. A few weeks later, when the Rifles were at Camp Clark in Corinth, Mississippi, they became Company H of the 15th Mississippi Infantry Regiment. Walthall became the regiment's lieutenant colonel on July 31, 1861.[6]

In mid-August 1861, the 15th Mississippi traveled to Knoxville, Tennessee, where it joined a brigade commanded by Brigadier General Felix Kirk Zollicoffer. Zollicoffer's command met disaster at the Battle of Mill Springs, Kentucky, on January 19, 1862 (see map on page 18). Walthall commanded the 15th Mississippi during the engagement, with the Mississippians fighting in the center of the Confederate line and sustaining more casualties than any other Southern unit. Despite the humiliating rout of the Confederate forces at Mill Springs, Walthall received praise for his personal conduct. A Natchez newspaper claimed "his skill, coolness, and unflinching courage" had been conspicuous, while Major General George B. Crittenden said that the 15th Mississippi had been "gallantly led" by Lieutenant Colonel Walthall.[7]

A few weeks after the debacle at Mill Springs, Walthall wrote President Jefferson Davis requesting permission to raise a regiment for the war with the assistance of other officers from the 15th Mississippi. Davis supported the proposal, aware of Walthall's conduct at Mill Springs and during the subsequent retreat out of Kentucky. Walthall proceeded to Grenada, Mississippi, where on April 11, 1862, he was elected colonel of the newly organized 29th Mississippi Infantry Regiment. As part of a brigade commanded by Brigadier General James R. Chalmers, Walthall and the 29th Mississippi served through General Braxton Bragg's Kentucky Campaign, seeing action at Munfordville on September 14, 1862.[8]

After Bragg's army had returned to Middle Tennessee on November 13, 1862, following the Kentucky Campaign, Bragg appointed Walthall to command a newly organized brigade of Mississippi and Alabama troops. Eight days later, Bragg forwarded the names of Walthall, Zachariah Deas, and Arthur Manigault to the secretary of war for promotion to brigadier general. These men, he explained, were "bold, energetic and capable" and had "served the country well." This was the first of numerous wartime instances of Bragg's praising Walthall. Walthall, who undoubtedly viewed his commander as a mentor in military affairs, in return displayed unwavering loyalty to Bragg.[9]

Several regimental officers of the 29th Mississippi also praised their departing colonel, proclaiming in a farewell resolution that they appreciated his military qualifications and "untiring energy" in instilling discipline, as well as his "gentlemanly, affable and courteous disposition." Walthall regretted that the "condition of his throat and lungs" prevented him from delivering a farewell address to the regiment, but through a letter admitted pride in his advancement, claiming it was more a compliment to the regiment and its record than to himself.[10]

Walthall left the army on a thirty-day sick leave at the advice of Bragg a few days before the Battle of Murfreesboro. After spending several weeks with his wife at her parents' home in Mecklenburg County, Virginia, Walthall returned to the Army of Tennessee at Shelbyville, Tennessee on January 17, 1863. There Walthall found waiting for him the promotion to brigadier general, to take rank from December 13, 1862. Brigadier General Chalmers had supported the promotion, pointing out Walthall's "knowledge of tactics . . . discipline . . . [and] care and attention to his men."[11]

During the Tullahoma Campaign, Walthall's command retreated with the rest of the army out of Middle Tennessee. In the fourth week of July 1863, Bragg sent Walthall and his men to Atlanta to protect it from enemy cavalry

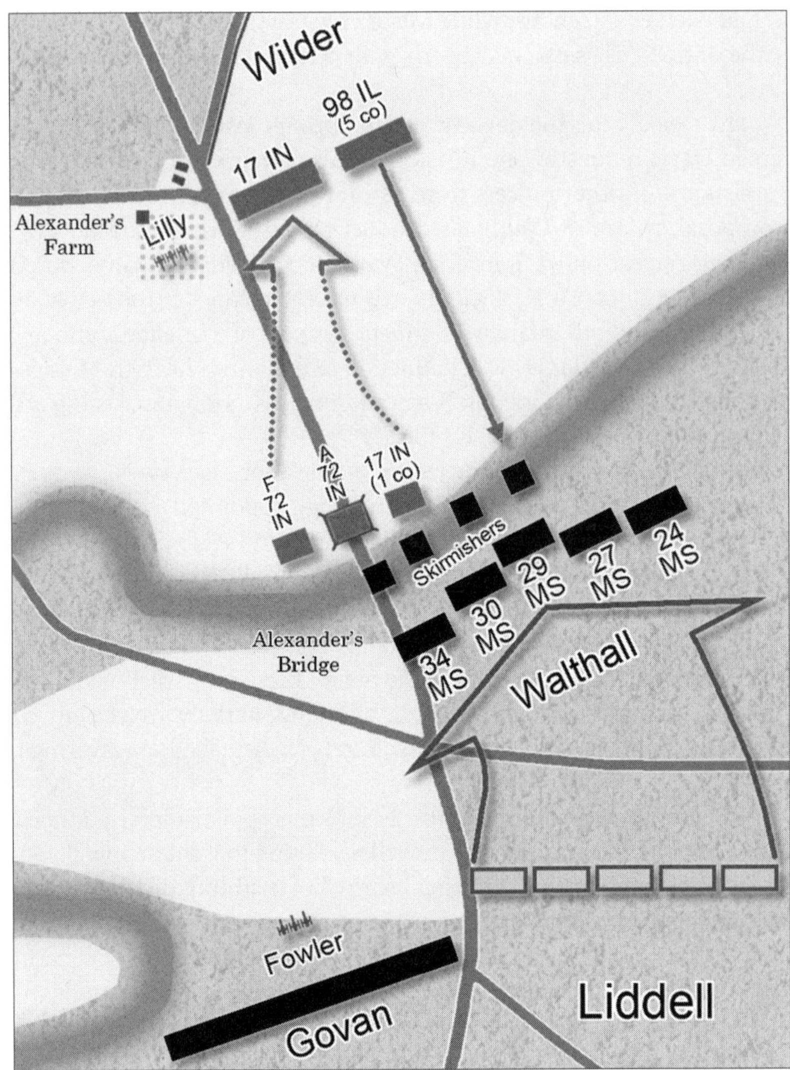

Alexander's Bridge. From *The Maps of Chickamauga* by David Powell and David Friedrichs (New York: Savas Beatie, 2009), 39. Used with permission.

raids. When Walthall's regiments returned to the Army of Tennessee at the end of August 1863, they became part of a division under Brigadier General St. John R. Liddell. Walthall assured his parents back in Holly Springs at this time that his "faith in our ultimate success is still as strong as in the beginning." He continued: "God will not suffer this nation to be conquered."[12]

Walthall's Brigade saw heavy action at the Battle of Chickamauga. On September 18, his Mississippians assaulted Alexander's Bridge on Chickamauga Creek, sustaining dozens of casualties before breaking off the engagement and crossing the creek at a ford about one mile below the bridge. The next day, Walthall's men attacked twice alongside Brigadier General Daniel C. Govan's Brigade, the first time overrunning a Union battery and capturing hundreds of prisoners.[13]

On the morning of September 20, Lieutenant General Leonidas Polk detached Walthall's Brigade from its division and the Mississippians attacked in support of Brigadier General States Rights Gist's Brigade (see map on page 66). According to Lieutenant General Harvey Hill, Walthall's and

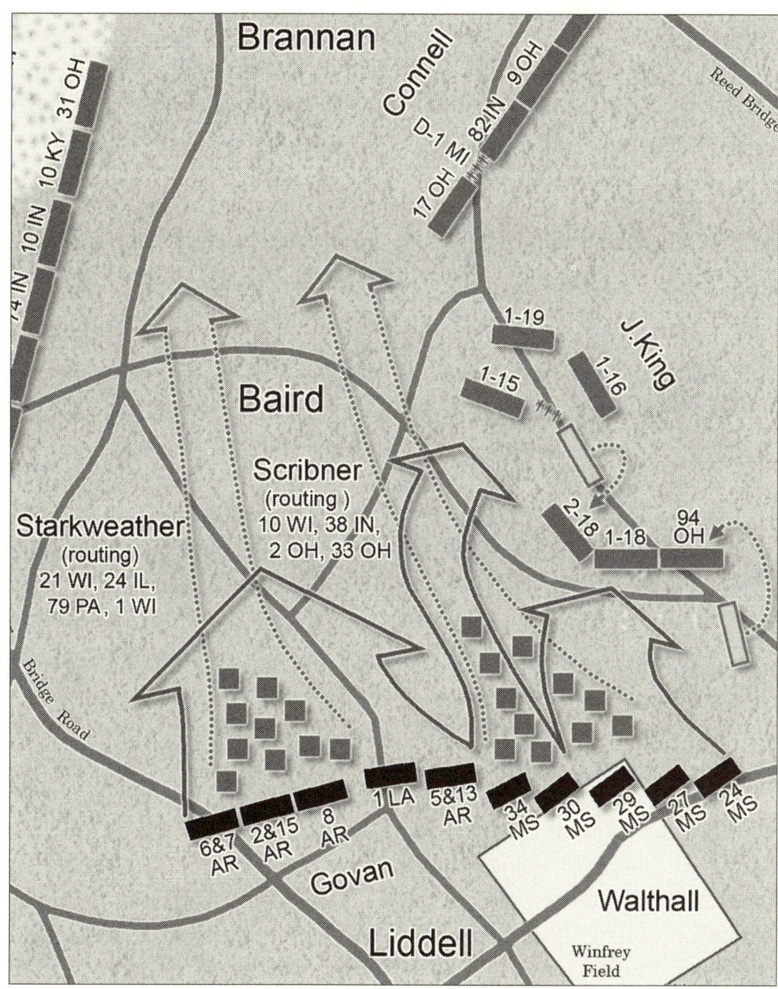

Battle of Chickamauga, late morning, September 19, 1863. From *The Maps of Chickamauga* by David Powell and David Friedrichs (New York: Savas Beatie, 2009), 63. Used with permission.

Gist's men encountered a front and flank fire which threw them "into confusion and drove them back precipitately." Later that afternoon, Walthall attacked a second time in conjunction with Govan's Brigade. The two brigades advanced westward across the LaFayette Road on the northern end of the battlefield before encountering enfilading artillery fire and being struck in the flank by Union infantry. The Federal counterattack drove the Confederates back eastward in confusion. One of Walthall's men remembered that after he and his comrades broke and ran, Walthall rallied them and "cursed us," saying that "as Mississippians we had disgraced the cradles in which we were rocked, and demanded we at once advance on the enemy."[14]

Although Liddell admitted that the costly assaults conducted by Walthall's Brigade at Chickamauga bore no "brilliant results," its commander still elicited praise in official reports. Liddell noted that his brigade commanders, Walthall and Govan, provided "prompt co-operation in every movement and quick apprehension of the constantly reoccurring necessities that arise on a battle-field."[15]

Walthall also received favorable notice in Southern newspapers after the battle. A soldier writing to the *Memphis Appeal* characterized him as always "with his troops, encouraging them by word and deed." Walthall's fitness for command, the writer continued, "has been exemplified in camp and on the field" and "his element seems to be where the bullets are thickest."[16]

When Bragg laid siege to the Federals in Chattanooga after Chickamauga, Walthall's Mississippians occupied a position on Missionary Ridge for several weeks before being ordered to support Confederates occupying the top of Lookout Mountain. Walthall's men took positions on the west side of Lookout Mountain near the northern slope with pickets extending along Lookout Creek below. On the morning of November 24, Union forces crossed Lookout Creek and assaulted a portion of Walthall's Brigade on the western slopes of the mountain. The greatly outnumbered Mississippians retired slowly across the rugged, boulder-strewn ground and around the northern end of the mountain, sustaining heavy casualties. Eventually the Mississippians formed part of a defensive line a few hundred yards south of the Cravens House, which the Confederates held until after nightfall.

In his report of the Battle of Lookout Mountain, Walthall criticized his acting division commander, Brigadier General John K. Jackson. He hinted that Jackson did nothing to address Union batteries across Lookout Creek trained on the Confederates. Although Walthall received several dispatches from Jackson during the fighting, at no time did the brigade commander encounter his immediate superior. Walthall saw Jackson only after the fighting had ended when he claimed the division commander was on his way to see Bragg.

Walthall's report, along with those of two other brigadiers critical of Jackson's absence during the engagement, prompted a "bellicose corre-

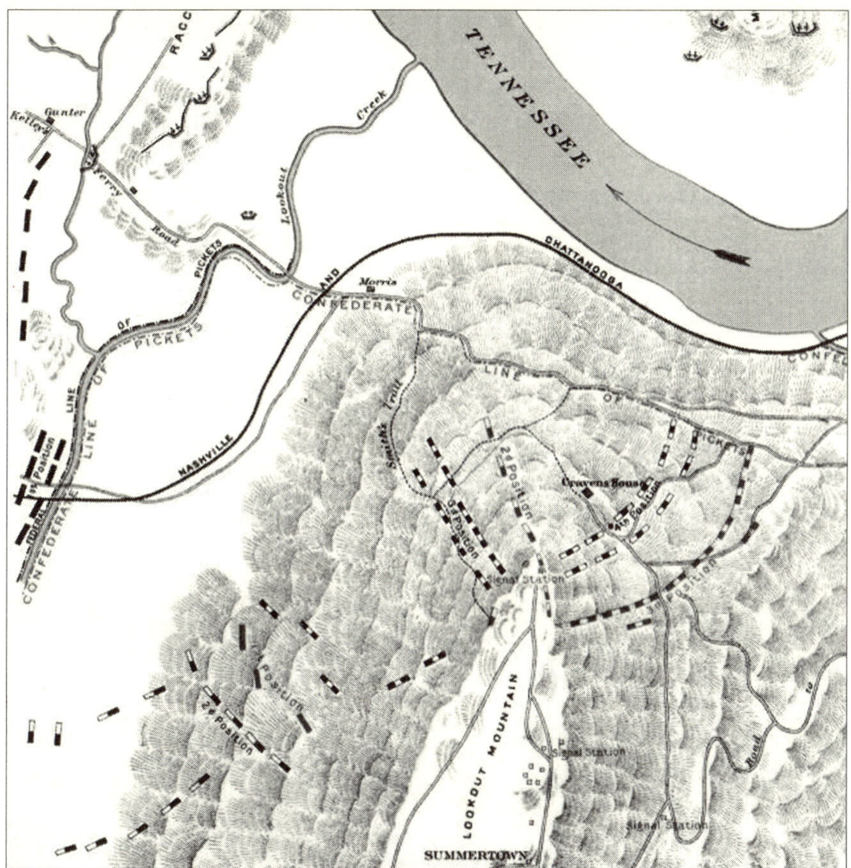

Battle of Lookout Mountain. From *Atlas to Accompany the Official Records of the Union and Confederate Armies* (1891–95), plate L, no. 4.

spondence" between Jackson and Walthall in the spring of 1864. For a time, remembered one of Walthall's staff officers, it appeared that the generals would resort to the "code duello," but eventually friends of Jackson realized the veracity of the reports and urged him to drop the matter, which he did.[17]

His brigade's performance at Lookout Mountain remained a sensitive topic for Walthall the rest of his life. In 1882, he carried on a heated correspondence for several months with Colonel Daniel R. Hundley of the 31st Alabama Infantry Regiment who claimed in the *Philadelphia Weekly Times* that Federals had surprised the Mississippians at Lookout Mountain. Walthall objected to this, repeatedly telling Hundley to study the official reports of the battle. Brigadier General Edmund Pettus, whose brigade had fought with Walthall that day, eventually acted as an arbiter between Walthall and Hundley, ruling in the Mississippian's favor. The debate ended, but Walthall entrusted the bound correspondence with Hundley and Pettus, which he called "the Lookout Book," to a former staff officer in case controversy over the matter ever arose again.[18]

The day after the Battle of Lookout Mountain, the Federals in Chattanooga attacked the Confederate lines on Missionary Ridge. Walthall, now serving directly under Major General Benjamin F. Cheatham, helped slow the advance of the soon-to-be victorious Federals. When Walthall saw the

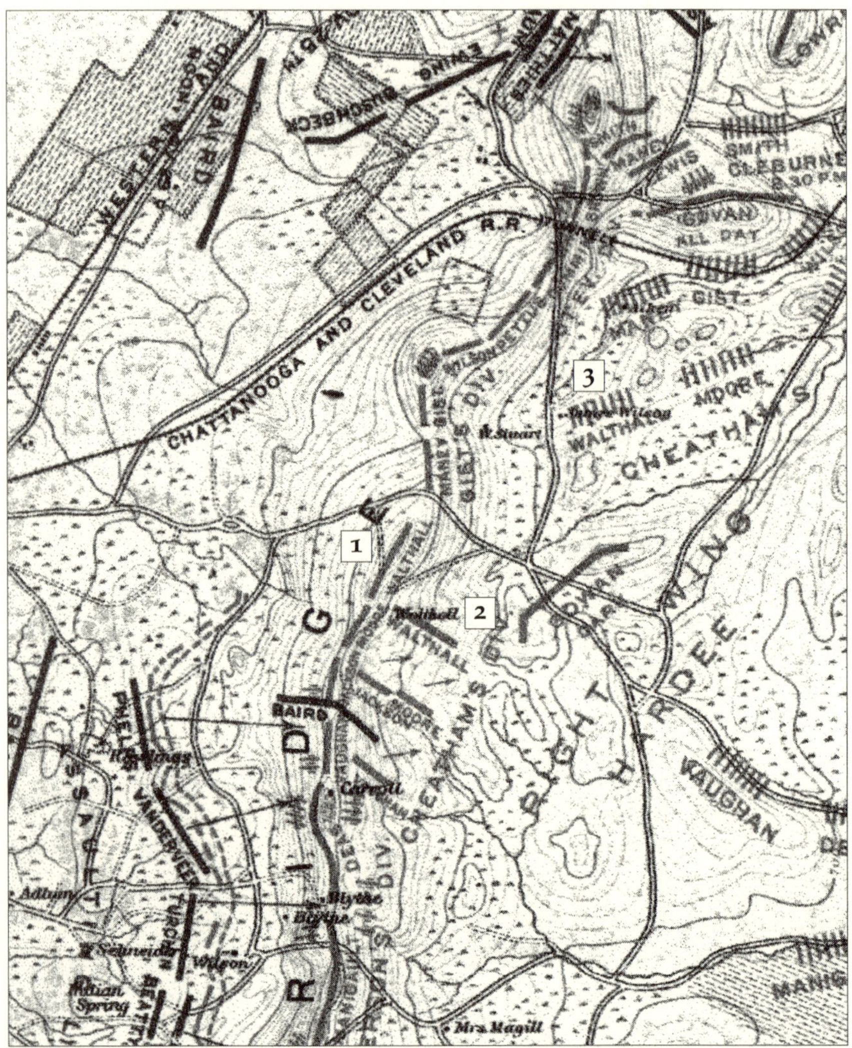

Battle of Missionary Ridge. The numbers indicate Walthall's Brigade (1) prior to Union assault, (2) after the breakthrough, and (3) withdrawing from the battle. From "Map of the Battlefields of Chattanooga: Battle of Missionary Ridge," by the Chickamauga and Chattanooga National Park Commission, 1901.

enemy drive Southerners off Missionary Ridge and then advance northward along the crest, the Mississippian received orders to form his brigade at right angles to the Confederate breastworks to stop the Federals. While Walthall's regiments executed this change of front under heavy fire, a minié ball passed through Walthall's heel, the general "playfully remarking" to one of his regimental commanders, "Colonel, they have hit me," and displaying his torn boot. Cheatham, according to one of his staff officers, claimed that Walthall's change of position under fire was "one of the most brilliant of the war, and his report of it exceedingly modest."[19]

Walthall remained in the saddle at Missionary Ridge despite being wounded until his brigade had withdrawn to Chickamauga Station. There Bragg advised Walthall to go to Atlanta for treatment. In Bragg's report of the fighting around Chattanooga, he included Walthall in a list of division and brigade commanders distinguished for their coolness, gallantry, and successful conduct.[20]

Walthall spent eight weeks in Atlanta under the care of his wife, who had been there assisting in the care of wounded Confederates. Even when apart, the Walthalls remained in constant contact; in a November 21, 1863, letter, Mary noted that her husband wrote every day, sometimes six or eight pages. At the end of March 1864, Walthall was still lame and expected to limp for several more months.[21]

During his recovery in Atlanta, Walthall pondered advice from Lieutenant General Polk and Major General Forrest that he apply to command two cavalry brigades in northern Mississippi. Walthall sought opinions from associates, and on February 11, a friend in Richmond wrote that he had spoken about the matter to the president. Davis revealed that several other generals with experience commanding cavalry had been recommended for the same position. The president concluded that since Walthall already had "a good & gallant command of infantry" he should remain where he was.[22]

Walthall clearly agonized over whether to accept Polk's offer of a position in Mississippi, apparently turning it down twice and then wondering whether he had made a mistake. Louis J. Dupree of the *Knoxville (TN) Register,* a close friend of Walthall, informed Bragg on February 25, 1864, that while his friend's "ambition and hopes cluster around the fortunes of Mississippi," the general worried that taking the position from Bragg's old enemy Polk would alienate the former commander of the Army of Tennessee. Dupree confided to Bragg that "Walthall's attachment to you overrides all these considerations."[23]

Bragg advised Walthall not to take Polk's offer, and Walthall replied on March 11 that Bragg's views were "in perfect harmony" with his own. "I would have gone to Miss. only when I was convinced I could do more good [there] than here," Walthall admitted, "& had such been your opinion

I should have adopted it." The day before, he had written his mother on the topic, admitting that while he would like to fight for his own home, he knew "nothing of that service [cavalry] & have concluded I can do more good where I am."[24]

On the last day of March, Walthall assured his sister-in-law in Holly Springs that his "faith in the justice of our cause & our final success have never wavered." He also mused about his upcoming thirty-third birthday. "I have a horror of being a middle-aged man," he said, "because it is the halfway house to old age, helplessness, [and] decay." Then in a playful turn, he consoled himself by noting that he had "no gray hairs, except for a few stragglers" and that "no envious crow" had left a foot print in the corner of his eye. His wife assured him that he remained "young looking" and "many pretty girls say more than that."[25]

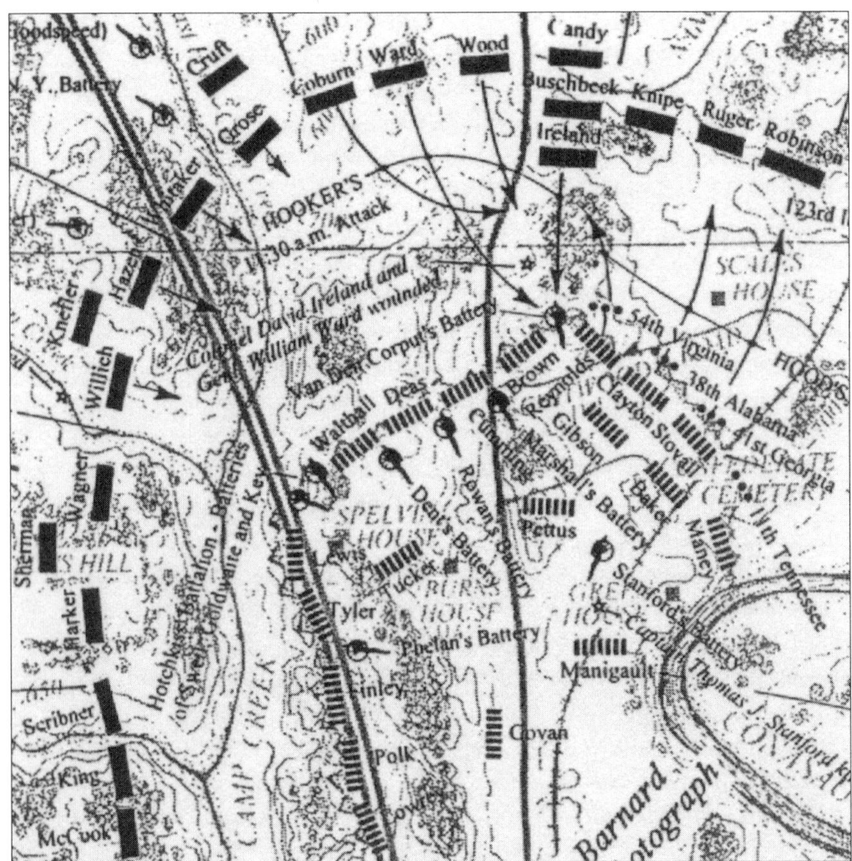

Battle of Resaca, May 15, 1864. Courtesy of the Kennesaw Mountain Historical Association.

During the opening phase of the Atlanta Campaign, Walthall's Brigade saw heavy action at the Battle of Resaca, May 14–15. The Mississippians held an entrenched position supporting an artillery battalion posted on a bald knob. Walthall's men occupied a critical point in the Southern line from which the trenches stretched to the east and south. On May 14, the Mississippians repulsed repeated Union infantry attacks, while enduring heavy artillery and rifle fire that afternoon and much of the following day. Throughout the battle, Walthall constantly exposed himself to enemy fire along every part of the line while encouraging his men, earning praise in the official report of his corps commander, Lieutenant General Hood. But Walthall had several close calls at Resaca, receiving a slight wound on the forehead from a minié ball and having a highly prized bay mare shot from under him.[26]

As General Joseph E. Johnston's army retreated to Cassville, and the vicinity of Dallas, Lieutenant General Polk repeatedly noted the "very great need" for an officer to command a recently formed division in his Army of the Mississippi, then serving alongside the Army of Tennessee in Georgia. On June 1, Polk asked the War Department that either Walthall or Brigadier General Winfield S. Featherston be promoted to fill the position. Both officers, Polk noted, had already been nominated for promotion to major general. Bragg, now chief military advisor to President Davis, responded to this request by his old foe by reminding Secretary of War James A. Seddon that it was improper for official applications for promotion to come from anyone other than Army of Tennessee commander, General Johnston.[27]

Despite his implicit criticism of Polk, Bragg praised his protégé Walthall, noting that the Mississippian's "distinguished merit" was "fully recognized & appreciated." On June 2, the president told Johnston that if there were a sufficient number of brigades to form an additional division in Polk's Corps that he should assign Walthall to its command and the president would nominate him for promotion. Three days later, Johnston reassured the president that from his view of the Army of the Mississippi, another major general was necessary to the efficiency of Polk's Corps, and he thought the president's selection of Walthall was an excellent one. Walthall received the promotion (temporary at the time, per Davis's nomination) on June 10, 1864, to rank from June 6.[28]

Walthall took command of a division recently formed from troops that had been stationed in the Mobile area. The division had suffered from uneven leadership. Brigadier General James Cantey, Walthall's immediate predecessor as division commander, was not competent to command a division and had exercised poor leadership at Resaca. An officer on Cantey's staff who personally liked him admitted that he was "by no means a success" from a military point of view. On June 12, 1864, Johnston had written Davis requesting Walthall take over Cantey's division, pointing out that Polk "regards this promotion as important as I do." Walthall's assignment suggests that the army's high command did not believe Cantey's three brigade commanders were capable at that point of leading a division.[29]

Walthall's first brigade consisted of five Arkansas Mounted Rifle Regiments serving as infantry under Brigadier General Daniel H. Reynolds. Although Reynolds had only been in brigade command since March 1864, he had distinguished himself at Chickamauga. Reynolds rightfully thought highly of the veteran regiments in his brigade, confiding in his diary in the first week of June 1864 that they were some of the best troops in the army and could bear almost anything and be cheerful.[30]

The second brigade, comprised of three Alabama regiments and one from Mississippi, had been under Brigadier General Cantey. When Cantey rose to division command, the brigade's senior colonel, Virgil S. Murphy, led it until the end of June 1864 when he fell ill. The brigade then came under the temporary command of Colonel Edward A. O'Neal. O'Neal had commanded a brigade in the Army of Northern Virginia on the first day of the Battle of Gettysburg with disastrous consequences. In subsequent months, General Robert E. Lee and O'Neal's division commander had sought to block O'Neal from obtaining a general's commission and permanent brigade command. A frustrated Colonel O'Neal had subsequently transferred with his old regiment to Cantey's Brigade in the Army of Tennessee.[31]

Brigadier General William A. Quarles commanded the third brigade in Walthall's Division, comprised of one Alabama, two Louisiana, and six understrength Tennessee regiments. Quarles had commanded the brigade since September 1863, but his first experience leading it in battle came at Pickett's Mill on May 27, 1864, the day the regiments joined the Army of Tennessee in north Georgia. During the engagement, Quarles helped lead one of his regiments in an attack that bolstered the Confederate right flank, earning the thanks of Major General Patrick Cleburne. After the war, a veteran claimed that "every soldier in the brigade loved and served" under Quarles as "a son does a father." Quarles likewise held his command in high esteem, writing that it was "one of the best, if not the best, brigade in the service."[32]

A week after assuming division command, Walthall found his division entrenched at the base and across the top of Big Kennesaw Mountain. There for two weeks, Walthall's men endured periodic shellings, as well as heavy skirmishing on June 27, when they repulsed lines of attacking Union infantry. While Walthall was a stranger at this time to the majority of his men, one of them remembered three decades after the war that his "splendid presence and military bearing at once secured the admiration of his new command, and this first impression quickly ripened into a feeling of absolute confidence."[33]

Walthall's first test commanding his division in battle outside of a fortified position came in the third week of July, after Davis removed Johnston as commander of the Army of Tennessee. Johnston's replacement, General John Bell Hood, immediately planned to attack the Federal Army of the Cumberland under Major General George Thomas as they crossed Peachtree Creek north of Atlanta. On July 20, Hood ordered corps commanders William J. Hardee and Alexander P. Stewart to advance their divisions en echelon from the right against the Federals south of Peachtree Creek, pushing back an enemy that hopefully had not fortified. Stewart placed Walthall's Division in the center of his corps.

When the advance began, Walthall's Division, minus Quarles's Brigade which was detached on picket duty, marched out of earthworks in column before forming line of battle in the vicinity of Mt. Zion Church along the Pace's Ferry (now Howell Mill) Road. Because of orders to guide on the division to their right, Walthall's men marched northeastward at this point before encountering Federals. O'Neal's brigade, on Walthall's right, charged over rough ground and dense underbrush before striking an advanced Union line and capturing several hundred prisoners. In the midst of the fighting, O'Neal's center broke and fell back in disorder, forcing Walthall to send reinforcements to restore the line. A second Confederate charge,

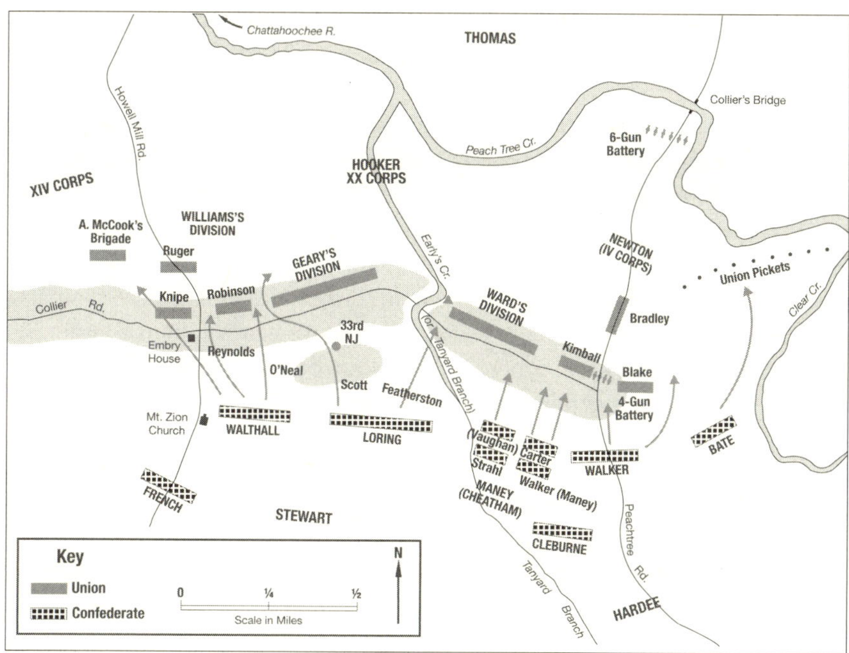

Battle of Peachtree Creek.

which O'Neal claimed had no support on its right flank, failed to carry the entrenched Federal position in its front. Walthall's other brigade, the Arkansans under Reynolds, fought on O'Neal's left. Reynolds's men held an advanced position until after dusk when they retired to their works. O'Neal's brigade suffered 279 casualties in the battle, while Reynolds lost 67 men.[34]

In his official report of Peachtree Creek, Walthall claimed that although his men achieved lodgments in the enemy's line, a "want of general cooperation and equal success at other points" compelled them to withdraw. Lieutenant General Stewart, who witnessed the advance of Walthall's brigades, wrote laconically that the men "behaved entirely to my satisfaction." Stewart's biographer suggests that the corps commander spent the battle on the left of his corps watching Walthall's command since Walthall and O'Neal were new to division and brigade command.[35]

Stewart's Corps played no part in the fighting two days after Peachtree Creek when Hood lashed out at the Federal advance east of Atlanta. On July 28, Hood sent Lieutenant General Stephen D. Lee, appointed the day before to corps command, to seize a road juncture south and west of Atlanta in the vicinity of Ezra Church. Stewart's Corps accompanied Lee. After marching along the Lick Skillett Road to an area south of Ezra Church, Lee's men found Federals hastily entrenched along high ground to the north. Although Lee had orders not to attack unless the enemy exposed himself, the aggressive new corps commander sent his divisions against the Federals.

When Stewart received word that Lee's Corps had attacked and needed assistance, he moved Walthall's Division out the Lick Skillett Road to the vicinity of the Poor (Alms) House. There Walthall formed Reynolds's Brigade on the right and O'Neal on the left, with Quarles in reserve. Shortly after 2:00 P.M., Walthall advanced the brigades of Reynolds and O'Neal against the enemy. In the midst of the fighting, Walthall personally conducted two regiments from Quarles's Brigade to support an artillery battery in rear of the division's center, the only Southern cannon along that section of the line. The balance of Quarles's Brigade moved to the left of Walthall's Division and with a yell launched a "bold and bloody" assault against the Federals. As they advanced, several members of Quarles's Brigade remembered seeing O'Neal's men lying down, intimating that the Alabamians subsequently did little to support the right flank of Quarles.[36]

Some of Walthall's men got quite close to the partially entrenched enemy in the assaults; Reynolds claimed within thirty to forty yards, while Quarles said "from twenty-five to fifty paces." Captain Stephen A. Cowley of Quarles's staff wrote a friend that it had been "the happiest moment" of his life to see the men charge within thirty yards of the enemy line, but then "the beauty of the advance transformed itself into reality [with] men falling like grain before the Reaper." After retiring some distance and continuing the fight for several more hours, Walthall's shattered brigades withdrew in what Brigadier General Arthur Manigault described as a state of "utter confusion and rout." (A member of O'Neal's brigade, writing for a newspaper, claimed instead that his brigade fell back "in good order" only after its ammunition was exhausted.) Walthall's Division had suffered a loss of 152 officers and nearly 1,000 men, "considerably over one-third" of the division's strength. Walthall told Lieutenant Colonel Hickerson H. Barksdale of the 3rd Mississippi Cavalry Regiment, a unit temporarily attached to the division, that the Federal fire at Ezra Church was the heaviest that he had ever encountered.[37]

Walthall attributed his men's repulse at Ezra Church to the great natural strength of the enemy's line, arguing that "double the force could not have accomplished what my division was ordered to undertake." He also expressed frustration at the ability of the Federals to pour fire into the unprotected flanks of his division's line. During the fighting Walthall had brought to the attention of Lee and Stewart a large gap that extended from the right of his line to the closest brigade in an adjacent division, but it is unclear if Lee ever sent up promised support.

When Walthall informed Stewart that his reduced brigades could not take the Federal position at Ezra Church, the corps commander ordered him to withdraw. Before executing this order, Walthall learned that Stewart had been wounded and command of the corps had devolved temporarily upon him. Later in the afternoon Walthall requested that Hood send reinforcements. Hood advised Walthall at 5:00 P.M. that he could call upon the divisions of Major General William B. Bate and Major General Samuel G. French if needed, but that the Confederates must "hold the enemy in check." The main fighting had ended by that point, and after dark the Confederates withdrew into the works around Atlanta.[38]

Walthall turned command of Stewart's Corps over to Major General Cheatham the day after the Battle of Ezra Church. Although the official reports contain no criticism of Walthall's leadership on July 28, Hood understandably felt that an officer who had commanded a division for just over a month did not have enough experience to lead a corps.[39]

Walthall's brigades spent the next few weeks manning the siege lines of Atlanta with his division's right resting near the Marietta Road. During part of this time, Lieutenant J. Irwin Kendall of Cantey's staff served as Walthall's aide. Kendall remembered him as being "every inch a soldier . . . inspiring everyone who came near him with the deepest respect and confidence." Walthall seldom said anything, Kendall claimed, and under fire was especially cool and collected. In the final days of the siege, between August 18 and September 1, Walthall's Division served as a general reserve near Hood's headquarters, with brigades being sent to assist in the repulse of Federal raids against the Macon & Western Railroad and to reconnoiter north of Atlanta.[40]

Following the evacuation of Atlanta by Stewart's Corps on September 1, the Army of Tennessee enjoyed a brief period of rest. Hood then marched his men north to cut the Western & Atlantic Railroad, Major General William T. Sherman's supply line from Chattanooga to Atlanta. During the first two weeks of October, Walthall's brigades struck the Western & Atlantic at several points, capturing a small Union garrison at Moon's Station and wrecking sections of the railroad. By the third week of October, Walthall's Division and the balance of Hood's army had marched into northern Alabama, with Walthall reaching South Florence on November 14.[41]

Walthall's men crossed the Tennessee River on a pontoon boat five days later and followed Hood into Tennessee. Struggling over poor roads in frigid weather, the division accompanied Stewart's Corps to the outskirts of Columbia, skirmishing on November 27 before the Federals withdrew to the north side of the Duck River. The next morning at daylight, Walthall advanced a skirmish line into Columbia and found it vacated.

At dawn on November 29, Walthall's Division followed that of Major General William W. Loring to Davis's Ford on the Duck River in a flanking attempt to cut off the retreating Federals. After a forced march on what Walthall described as a "circuitous route" with a halt and deployment in line of battle at Rutherford Creek, his brigades reached a point about a mile above Spring Hill after night. With the Confederate high command gripped by confusion, Walthall's weary men stood in ranks until finally bivouacking alongside the Franklin Turnpike. During the remainder of the night, the Federals marched north across the front of Hood's army.[42]

The following morning, Walthall's Division moved rapidly up the Columbia Pike toward Franklin. Chaplain James H. McNeilly in Quarles's Brigade remembered Walthall riding up to Major General Forrest during the advance. The angry and disgusted cavalry general supposedly exclaimed to Walthall—who was one of the Forrest's favorite generals—that if on the previous day he had just had one of Walthall's brigades to throw across the pike and intercept the retreating Federals, he could "ha' tuck the whole d—— shebang."[43]

Upon reaching the hills south of Franklin, a location which Federal soldiers briefly occupied, Hood sent Stewart's Corps on a flanking march to the east around Breezy Hill until the troops were within a mile and a quarter south of the town. Stewart subsequently met with Hood, who asked if he would be able to move his corps north of Franklin. Stewart answered yes, knowing of several fords over the Harpeth River. Following Hood's departure, Stewart naturally expected to receive an order to move around the Federal flank.[44]

But instead of conducting a flank attack, Stewart received orders to prepare his corps for a frontal assault against the entrenched Federals. Walthall's Division, numbering 1,878 rifles, formed line of battle in the center of Stewart's Corps. Walthall deployed the brigades of Quarles and Reynolds in the front line with Cantey's Brigade, now under Brigadier General Charles M. Shelley, in reserve. Chaplain McNeilly claimed to have seen a "sharp colloquy" between Walthall and Loring around this time regarding the placement of their commands. Loring, whose brigades were on Walthall's right, claimed that the Mississippian was responsible for the lines of the two divisions overlapping. Walthall ended the discussion by stating that it was "no time for a personal quarrel" and that Loring would know where to find him after the battle. Whether the two ever resumed the argument is unknown.[45]

At roughly 4:00 P.M., Walthall advanced his men, making sure they conformed to the movements of Loring's Division on their right. After marching a short distance, Walthall halted his line, which had become disordered by the broken ground and underbrush. The advance resumed after Walthall brought Shelley's men up to the front line, noting that "both officers and men seemed fully alive to the importance of beating the enemy at any cost."[46]

When the enemy's advanced line collapsed, the survivors retreated to the main Federal line. Walthall's men charged across open ground in pursuit, taking heavily casualties from an intense frontal and oblique fire. Upon reaching thick Osage orange hedge tops in front of the enemy's works, through which "no organized force could go," the main body of Walthall's Division fell back in confusion. Some officers and men, including Brigadier General Shelley, nonetheless made it through the entanglements to the Federal earthworks in the vicinity of Carter's cotton gin. There they fought until late in the night, the ditch in front of the Union earthworks becoming filled, in the words of one of Shelley's Alabamians, with "heaps of bloody corpses."[47]

The Battle of Franklin wrecked Walthall's Division and the Army of Tennessee. Walthall's three brigades sustained 580 casualties, with Quarles's Brigade ending the engagement commanded by a captain. Walthall had two horses shot from under him, and his face was "a little skinned" from the fall of one of the animals. One member of Walthall's staff was killed, another severely wounded, and the rest dismounted by their horses being shot shortly after the start of the engagement.[48]

In the days immediately following the Franklin disaster, Hood pushed his depleted army to the outskirts of Nashville, where it attempted to lay siege to the Federal occupiers. Stewart's Corps held the left flank of the Army of Tennessee with Walthall's Division entrenching in the center. On the night of December 10, the Confederates withdrew south to another line.

Stewart sent Walthall orders on the morning of December 15 to pull his division, (numbering only 1,374 rifles) and that of Major General French from the main Confederate line and deploy it behind a stone fence on the east side of the Hillsboro Pike. (French had left the army on December 13 due to failing eyesight, and Stewart attached his brigades to Walthall.) Along Walthall's new line, which ran southward at a right angle from the main Confederate position, the Mississippian placed from right to left the brigades of Sears, Reynolds, Quarles (under Brigadier General George D. Johnston), and Shelley. Stewart further ordered cannon from Major Daniel Trueheart's Battalion and infantry detachments from Walthall's Division numbering between 100 and 150 men into five earthen redoubts. These "self-supporting detached works," as Hood described them, had been constructed over the previous few days on high points to protect the left rear of the army. Lastly, Stewart posted the other brigade of French's Division under Colonel Daniel Coleman on Walthall's far left.

Walthall made these dispositions anticipating an imminent attack in heavy force upon his line. Although Hood and Stewart ordered several brigades of reinforcements to bolster the Confederate left, Federal assaults launched around 11:00 A.M. carried two of the detached redoubts, capturing cannon and driving off Coleman's brigade. Walthall then detached Reynolds to shore up the threatened left flank and called for reinforcements. Several brigades from Major General Edward Johnson's Division arrived to assist Reynolds, but the much larger attacking Federal force drove back the Confederates.[49]

As Union troops enveloped the left flank of Walthall's Division while simultaneously assaulting its front, Walthall ordered a retreat. Stewart subsequently praised Walthall for maintaining his position "until the last possible moment." A cannoneer in Seldon's Alabama Battery wrote the next day that Walthall personally gave the order to retreat when a Federal battle line was only two hundred yards away. He had no choice, as several brigades on his left had been routed. At this point, the cannoneer remembered, it was a "perfect stampede for a mile" as the Confederates fled toward the southwest. In addition to capturing hundreds of prisoners, victorious Federals seized all but one of the twelve cannon of Trueheart's Artillery Battalion, assigned to Walthall. A tearful Captain Edward W. Tarrant, reporting the loss of his guns to his division commander, received consolation and assurance from Walthall that "he saw my position, that I had done everything that a man could do, and that he had no fault to find with me."[50]

Before dawn the next morning, Walthall took up position in the center of a new line. The right of Walthall's command rested on the Granny White Pike, while the left connected with Bate's Division near the foot of Shy's Hill. During the forenoon, Walthall's men repulsed a "feeble assault" in their front while being subjected to a heavy cannonade. During the morning and afternoon, Stewart ordered Walthall to send Brigadier General Matthew D. Ector's and Reynolds's Brigades to the rear, where they subse-

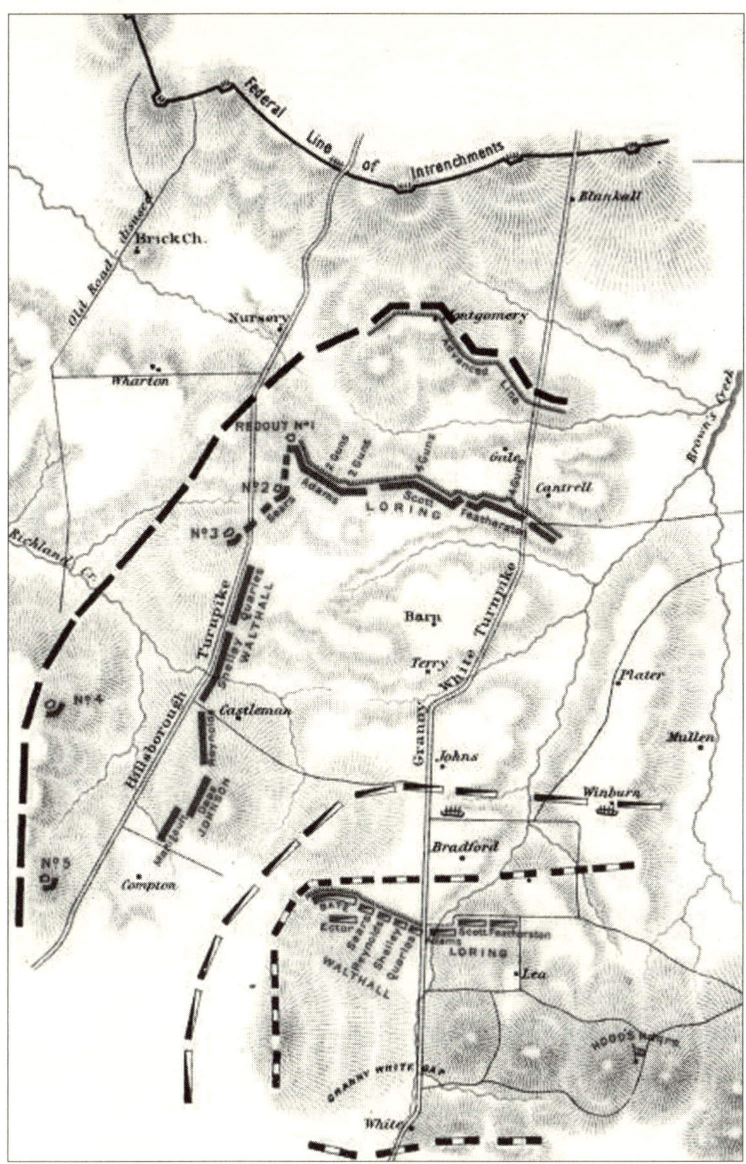

Battle of Nashville. From *Atlas to Accompany the Official Records of the Union and Confederate Armies* (1891–95), plate LXXIII, no. 2.

quently did valiant service attempting to hold open a retreat route through the hills to the rear of the Confederate army. Although the balance of Walthall's men repulsed another Federal attack in their front, the massed enemy in front of Shy's Hill portended disaster. Stewart instructed Walthall that if Bate fell back, to "keep your left connected with him, falling back from your left toward right and forming a new flank line extending to hills in rear."[51]

It proved impossible for Walthall to follow Stewart's orders when the Federals carried Shy's Hill, shattering Bate's line. Facing encirclement, Walthall conducted an immediate withdrawal to the southeast toward the Franklin Turnpike. The distance involved in the retreat over rugged ground resulted in great disorder, and efforts to rally the demoralized men were only partially successful. Division level returns compiled immediately after the engagement reveal the extent of the panic; out of a total of 839 casualties in Walthall's command, 17 were killed, 127 wounded, and 695 captured.[52]

During the next two days Walthall's men retreated through Spring Hill before fortifying a line north of the Duck River to cover the army's passage on a pontoon bridge in the vicinity of Columbia. Walthall's regiments then crossed the river on December 19 and encamped a short distance from Columbia on the Pulaski Pike, enduring a harsh winter rainstorm. Early the next morning, Walthall rode to Hood's quarters. There, as we have seen, the army commander directed Walthall to organize a special infantry command to act as part of the rear guard along with Forrest's cavalry. Walthall would report to Forrest, whom Hood placed in charge of the entire rear guard. The main army was retreating toward Pulaski at this time, Hood's ultimate goal being to cross the Tennessee River in the vicinity of Bainbridge, Alabama.[53]

Hood told Walthall that he would have five infantry brigades in addition to three from his own division. Walthall ordered temporary consolidations of all these skeletal brigades to make them "more wieldy and compact." Brigadier General Joseph B. Palmer commanded his brigade and that of Brigadier General James A. Smith (commanded by Colonel Charles H. Olmstead). Brigadier General George Maney's Brigade (commanded by Colonel Hume R. Feild) and the brigade of the late Brigadier General Otto H. Strahl (under Colonel Carrick W. Heiskell) were under Colonel Feild. Brigadier General Reynolds led his brigade and also Ector's (commanded by Colonel Coleman). Featherston commanded his brigade and that of Quarles (under Brigadier General George D. Johnston). Each brigade's ordnance, cook, and tool wagons, along with ambulances, accompanied the rear guard. Although Forrest had asked Hood for four thousand infantry, Walthall's force numbered less than half of that number, with many of the men poorly clad and several hundred of them barefoot.[54]

The same day that Walthall assumed command of this rear guard, Union forces on the north bank of the Duck River shelled Columbia. Forrest responded by asking for a flag of truce. Forrest, Walthall, and several staff officers subsequently conferred with Union Brigadier General Edward Hatch on opposite sides of the Duck River where abutments of the former turnpike bridge stood. Forrest requested that the shelling end because only civilians and sick and wounded Confederates were in the town and proposed an exchange of prisoners. Hatch stopped the bombardment, but said he had no authority to grant a prisoner exchange.

When several hundred Union soldiers crossed the swollen Duck River above Columbia on the morning of December 22, Walthall ordered his advanced brigade under Colonel Feild to reconnoiter and skirmish with the enemy while the balance of the Southern infantry formed in line across the Pulaski Pike. The Federals eventually compelled Feild to fall back to Walthall's main force. Forrest then ordered Walthall to retreat twelve miles south to Lynnville in the direction of Pulaski.[55]

At some point, probably early on December 22, Walthall and Forrest said goodbye to the family of Major William Galloway on 9th Street in Columbia, where Forrest had visited on occasion earlier in the war. Walthall signed the autograph book of Laura Galloway, writing only his name, rank, and the date. Forrest also signed the album, writing "Miss Laura" that he hoped "she may never have to morn over another defete of the confederate army."[56]

Two days later, Walthall's men skirmished with the enemy before receiving orders to hold the crossing of Richland Creek, south of Lynnville, should the Southern cavalry be forced to fall back across the creek before dark. That night around eight o'clock, the infantry rear guard retired to an outer line of earthworks around Pulaski. At dawn on Christmas day, Walthall's men passed through Pulaski and followed a nearly impassible road leading southwest toward the Tennessee River crossing at Bainbridge, Alabama. Moving the Confederate army's long trains of wagons and artillery through the quagmire of mud along this road slowed the retreat considerably, and the rear guard soon felt increasing pressure from pursuing Union cavalry.

Four miles southwest of Pulaski, Forrest laid an ambush for the Federals at Anthony's Hill. The infantry brigades of Featherston and Palmer, with dismounted cavalrymen on each flank, waited behind hastily constructed log earthworks along a densely wooded ridge. The balance of Walthall's infantry continued south with the wagon train for three miles before halting and building a reserve line with fence rails.

A half mile to the north of Featherston and Palmer, a small force of mounted Confederates engaged the Federals and then withdrew into the narrow valley where the advanced infantrymen lay hidden. When the dismounted Union troopers got close to the concealed Confederates around dusk, Featherston and Palmer's men opened up in concert with a masked battery of Forrest's horse artillery. The Federals retreated with the yelling Confederates in pursuit capturing prisoners, several hundred horses, and a piece of artillery. Around dusk, Walthall's men commenced a "long, cold cheerless march, through half ice and half water" southward down a winding road to Sugar Creek before going into camp an hour before midnight.[57]

Early on the morning of December 26, Forrest sent word to Walthall that the infantry would likely have to dispute again the advance of Union cavalrymen. A dense fog allowed for the concealment of the brigades of Ector,

Reynolds, Strahl, and Maney near the bank of Sugar Creek with some of Forrest's cavalry deployed on their right flank. Reynolds, whose diary suggests that he may have commanded the small infantry contingent at Sugar Creek this day, noted that when the hidden Southerners exchanged fire with the Federals at close range, the Union line broke and retreated. Confederate infantrymen and several cavalry regiments pursued the Federal troopers for some distance, capturing sixteen prisoners and twenty horses while killing and wounding a considerable number of men and horses. That evening Walthall's men resumed the southward march, finally camping sixteen miles north of the Tennessee River.

The next day Walthall reported once again to Lieutenant General Stewart, who ordered the Mississippian to guard a ford over Shoal Creek, two miles north of the Tennessee River, until the Confederate cavalry got across. At 10:00 P.M., Stewart told Walthall to leave a brigade at Shoal Creek and move the rest of his command to occupy earthworks covering the pontoon bridge over the Tennessee River.

At 3:00 A.M. on December 28, Walthall issued orders for his frozen and exhausted soldiers to move at daylight over the pontoon bridge. The orders demanded a prompt and phased withdrawal, with brigades leaving behind skirmish lines as they moved toward the river. Walthall's men were the last element of the shattered Army of Tennessee to cross the Tennessee River. Days later, when Walthall composed his report of the retreat, he noted that the troops had exhibited fine conduct throughout the ordeal, despite the ground often being covered with snow and many men lacking shoes and blankets. General Reynolds complemented Walthall's rear guard in his December 27, 1864, diary entry, calling them the "Old Guard," undoubtedly a comparison with the reserve of elite troops in Napoleon's Grande Armée.[58]

A paucity of sources, particularly brigade and regimental reports from the infantry portion of the Confederate rear guard, make it impossible to ascertain how much tactical control Walthall exercised day to day during the retreat. Several sources suggest that Forrest planned the ambushes at Anthony's Hill and Sugar Creek. Nonetheless, Forrest undoubtedly spent much time with his mounted command, which usually operated at some distance from the infantrymen, leaving Walthall in charge of the frozen, ragged, and half-barefoot foot soldiers.[59]

Forrest offered restrained praise for Walthall in his official report of the 1864 Tennessee Campaign, claiming that during the retreat the Mississippian furnished "much valuable service" and "exhibited the highest soldierly qualities." In his postbellum memoir, Hood also praised Walthall, saying that he had been confident during the retreat that the rear guard "would prove equal to any emergency which might arise." Stewart, who probably had not been privy to the decision to place Walthall with the rear guard, gave his thanks to Walthall and his other division commanders for the "cordial co-operation and skillful management" of their respective commands during the campaign.[60]

Despite these accolades, not everyone in the Army of Tennessee complemented Walthall in the aftermath of Hood's disastrous campaign. Walthall remained in command of French's Division during this time, an arrangement that at least one of French's staff officers regretted. In a letter written from Tupelo on January 10, 1865, Cadet Edward T. Freeman, French's acting assistant adjutant and inspector general, wrote to French that serving under Walthall was "not very pleasant" and "all are looking for you back anxiously." Freeman also drew an unfavorable comparison between French's chief of artillery, Major George Storrs, who saved all his cannon at Nashville, and Walthall, who lost his. Unfortunately, Freeman did not elaborate any further except to claim that French's men "felt like outsiders" under Walthall "and are treated more or less so accordingly." Whether Freeman's sentiments reflected those of others in French's Division, or were simply an attempt to curry favor with French, is unknown.[61]

Hood's invasion took an immense physical and mental toll on the Army of Tennessee. Walthall, whose constitution had previously been robust, suffered permanent ill-effects. Like many others, he also apparently began to lose faith in the Confederacy's chances of gaining independence. When a Southern staff officer encountered Walthall on February 26, 1865, the general stated that "from the way that things are going now, I am afraid that the Lord is a Union man."[62]

During February and early March 1865, Walthall and the remnants of the Army of Tennessee passed through the Carolinas. March 10 found Walthall with 354 members of his command on a troop train in Goldsboro, North Carolina, en route to Kinston; many of his men were lacking cartridge boxes and some even without arms. Instead of going to Kinston, however, Walthall's tiny division of roughly 241 effective men joined a polyglot force of Confederates at Smithfield under General Joseph E. Johnston. On March 18, Johnston's command, which included the remnants of the Army of Tennessee under Lieutenant General Stewart, marched south from Smithfield toward Bentonville to attack a wing of Sherman's Union army advancing eastward along the Goldsboro Road.[63]

Shortly after sunrise on March 19, Walthall's two brigades, the Arkansans under Reynolds and Quarles's old brigade under Brigadier General George D. Johnston, left their camps and marched south. When they arrived at the point of deployment in the late morning, Walthall led them into position, accompanied by Reynolds, Johnston, Major General Daniel Harvey Hill (now commanding Lee's Corps), and others. As Walthall's men began maneuvering to take position, a Union artillery shell struck Reynolds's horse, passing through the animal and tearing off a portion of the general's calf. Knowing that Reynolds was "the idol" of his brigade, Walthall rode up to the prone Arkansas troops. One of Reynolds's soldiers remembered him saying: "Boys, you have lost your commander, but you shall not suffer for the want of one. I'll command you myself." As a result of the Federal cannon fire, Walthall's two brigades moved out of the open and deployed instead in the woods with instructions to protect artillery batteries in their front.[64]

Walthall's Division formed the extreme left flank of the Army of Tennessee, connecting on its left with other Confederates under General Bragg. Many years after the war, Walthall described his feelings upon receiving the word to advance that afternoon. Although the general and his men knew there was "no longer any hope for the South," Walthall rode down the line of his division and "there burst forth from the tattered and torn" ranks "the old familiar cheer that had so often greeted him." The orders to charge, he recounted, "were the saddest word[s] he ever spoke."[65]

Walthall led his men forward under a slight fire of enemy artillery. Stewart, who witnessed the charge, remembered it as "an inspiring sight . . . to see the firm, steady lines, their intrepid commander, in whom all had unbounded confidence, towering above them on his own horse." Colonel Henry Bunn, who had succeeded to the command of Reynolds's Arkansans, recalled Walthall turning to him during the advance and saying, "I have been in all, or nearly all the battles fought by the Army of Tennessee, and have seen many brave sights, but nothing comparable to this."[66]

After marching several hundred yards through an open field, Walthall's men entered a briar-filled ravine, where they halted to dress the lines. Upon leaving the ravine, the men continued charging south, driving before them a Union skirmish line and eventually crossing the Goldsboro Road. The division's most intense fighting, according to Colonel Bunn, occurred late in the afternoon and up until dusk, when the men exchanged heavy volleys of musketry with prone Union troops in line along the edge of a swamp. This ended the most serious fighting at Bentonville for Walthall's Division, which suffered seventy casualties in the battle.[67]

The departure of Major General Loring from the army due to sickness left Walthall in command of a corps for several days after Bentonville. A week after the battle, Bragg passed "poor Walthall" and inquired about his old command. Walthall pointed to a small squad, telling his beloved superior that "my Division now numbers two Brigadiers and 63 men for duty." Walthall's Division, Bragg told Jefferson Davis, was a sample of the whole force left to confront the Federals in North Carolina.[68]

By the first week of April 1865, rumors circulated throughout Johnston's army about an impending reorganization. Walthall's eighteen-year-old brother and aide-de-camp, George, wrote their mother on April 1 that the consolidation of commands would result in many supernumerary officers being "thrown out." Walthall's friends had told him "he will certainly get a Div, but he says there are several here whose commissions are older than his and there can [only] be so many and no more." The youth then revealed his older brother's anxieties by explaining in a confused and conflicted fashion that the "Genrl says he does not intend to ask for a command, if he never gets one, and wants to call on Genrl Johnston, but is so afraid, some body will say that he is trying for a command, he of course cares about it, but does not give himself any uneasiness about it." General orders regarding the reorganization issued on April 9 left Walthall in command of a division, but not one composed of his old troops. Instead, he received two brigades of Georgia and South Carolina regiments that had formerly been under Major General Lafayette McLaws. Walthall surrendered his new division with the balance of the army before the end of the month.[69]

Edward C. Walthall's military career provides an outstanding example of the professionalization of the citizen soldier in the midst of war. Despite the absence of any formal military education or service, Walthall became a "master of drill" and, unlike many volunteer officers, consistently stressed discipline and obedience to orders. According to Captain Edward T. Sykes, formerly Walthall's assistant adjutant general, "the basic principle underlying Walthall's matchless command over his soldiers was the recognition by them of his unquestioned gallantry, his exact and equal justice, and his superb personality."[70]

Walthall had proven himself as a capable brigade commander by the summer of 1864, when a shortage of experienced upper echelon generals in the Army of Tennessee thrust him into command of a division. While Walthall had molded his old brigade of Mississippi regiments into a fine fighting force over time, the brigades he inherited in June 1864 varied considerably in the competence of their leadership and their experience in battle. None of the attacks made by Walthall's Division during the battles of Peachtree Creek, Ezra Church, and Franklin overran an enemy position, but these failures cannot be attributed solely to Walthall. While Walthall's inexperience in division command was likely a factor in his division's performance in the July 1864 battles, the strength of the Union positions, the incompetence of Colonel O'Neal and possibly others, and the inability of Confederate corps and army level generals to coordinate attacks also contributed to the lack of success.

Praise for Walthall's abilities and contributions consistently appears in the official reports of his superiors, including all three commanding officers of the Army of Tennessee. Shortly after the war, Colonel John B. Sale, who had been Bragg's secretary and assistant adjutant general in 1864–65, claimed that authorities in Richmond recognized Walthall "as being the best division commander in the Army of Tennessee" and slated him "for the first vacancy occurring in the grade of lieutenant generalship of that Army," though Sale was not precise in stating when authorities reached this decision. Several tributes published following Walthall's death in 1898 quote Joseph E. Johnston as saying that if the war had lasted longer, Walthall would have been placed in command of the Army of Tennessee. Even though this is questionable, especially given Walthall's lack of a professional military background, its repeated appearance in print speaks to the Mississippian's high reputation. In retrospect, we might modify Colonel Sale's assertion that Walthall was the Army of Tennessee's best division commander by instead saying that Walthall evolved over time into one of the army's finest generals, particularly following his eminent contribution made in conjunction with Forrest in saving Hood's army in the frigid retreat out of Tennessee in December 1864.[71]

Notes

The author would like to thank Dr. A. M. (Mac) Mellor for his generous assistance with this essay.

1. John Bell Hood, *Advance and Retreat: Personal Experiences in the United States and Confederate States Armies* (1880; repr. New York, 1993), 332; Thomas Jordan and J. P. Pryor, *The Campaigns of General Nathan Bedford Forrest and of Forrest's Cavalry* (1868; repr. New York, 1996), 645–46; Charles Todd Quintard, *Doctor Quintard, Chaplain, C.S.A., and Second Bishop of Tennessee: The Memoir and Civil War Diary of Charles Todd Quintard*, ed. Sam Davis Elliott (Baton Rouge, LA, 2003), 200–201.
2. David W. Sanders, "Hood's Tennessee Campaign," *Confederate Veteran* 15, no. 9 (Sept. 1907), 401. This account by Sanders first appeared in print in 1881.
3. Hood, *Advance and Retreat,* 306.
4. Paul D. Hardin, "Edward Cary Walthall: A Mississippi Conservative" (master's thesis, Duke University, 1940), 7–8; Records of Commissioned Officers of Mississippi Militia, 1848–1861, Registers of Military Commissions, Series 224, Mississippi Department of Archives and History, Jackson (hereafter cited as MDAH); John B. Floyd to Edward C. Walthall, Mar. 29, 1859, Edward C. Walthall Papers, Library of Congress, Washington, DC (hereafter cited as LC); James L. Morrison Jr., *"The Best School in the World," West Point in the Pre-Civil War Years, 1833–1866* (Kent, OH, 1986), 24. On Walthall at St. Thomas Hall, see Goodspeed Brothers, *Biographical and Historical Memoirs of Mississippi, Embracing an Authentic and Comprehensive Account of the Chief Events in the History of the State and a Record of the Lives of Many of the Most Worthy and Illustrious Families and Individuals,* 2 vols. (Chicago, 1891), 2:325–26.

5. U.S. Census Office, *Eighth Census of the United States, Free Schedule* (Washington, DC, 1860), Yalobusha County, MS: 183; U.S. Census Office, *Eighth Census of the United States, Slave Schedule* (Washington, DC, 1860), Yalobusha County, MS: 486; E. T. Sykes, *Walthall's Brigade: A Cursory Sketch, with Personal Experiences of Walthall's Brigade, Army of Tennessee, C.S.A., 1862–1865,* Publications of the Mississippi Historical Society (Centenary Series) vol. 1, pt. 2 (Jackson, MS, 1916), 487.
6. Edward C. Walthall, 15th Mississippi Regiment, Compiled Service Records of Confederate Soldiers Who Served in Organizations from the State of Mississippi, Roll 236, M269, National Archives and Records Service, Washington DC (hereafter cited as NA); Ben Wynne, *A Hard Trip: A History of the 15th Mississippi Infantry, CSA* (Macon, GA, 2003), 38, 46, 47.
7. Wynne, *A Hard Trip,* 64.
8. Edward C. Walthall to Jefferson Davis, Feb.7, 1862, #11055–1862, Letters Received by the Confederate Secretary of War, 1861–1865, Record Group 109, War Department Collection of Confederate Records, NA; Edward C. Walthall, 29th Mississippi Regiment, Compiled Service Records of Confederate Soldiers Who Served in Organizations from the State of Mississippi, Roll 236, M269, NA; Sykes, *Walthall's Brigade,* 517; Edwin Bearss, "Edward Cary Walthall," in *The Confederate General,* ed. William C. Davis and Julie Hoffman, 6 vols. (Harrisburg, PA, 1991), 6:105.
9. U.S. War Department, *The War of the Rebellion: A Compilation of the Official Records of the Union and Confederate Armies,* 128 vols. (Washington DC, 1880–1901), ser. 1, vol. 20, pt. 2:508 (hereafter cited as *OR;* all references are to series 1 unless otherwise indicated).
10. "Testimonial to Col. E. C. Walthall" and "Letter from Col. Walthall to the 29th," *Jackson Weekly Mississippian,* Nov. 30, 1862; Sykes, *Walthall's Brigade,* 516.
11. The Confederate Senate confirmed Walthall's promotion on April 23, 1863. Edward C. Walthall, Compiled Service Records of Confederate General and Staff Officers and Nonregimental Enlisted Men, Roll 258, M331, NA; Sykes, *Walthall's Brigade,* 497.
12. Edward C. Walthall to father and mother, Sept. 5, 1863, E. C. Walthall Papers, Department of Archives and Special Collections, J. D. Williams Library, University of Mississippi, Oxford (hereafter cited as UM); Sykes, *Walthall's Brigade,* 525.
13. *OR,* vol. 30, pt. 2:252, 272–74.
14. Ibid., 142, 274–76; "A Participant," "The Battle—Participation of Liddell's Division," *Memphis Appeal,* Oct. 7, 1863; Robert A. Jarman, "The History of Company K, 27th Mississippi Infantry," *Aberdeen (MS) Examiner,* Feb. 28, 1890.
15. *OR,* vol. 30, pt. 2:254–55.

16. "A Participant," "The Battle—Participation of Liddell's Division."

17. *OR*, vol. 31, pt. 2:692–97; Sykes, *Walthall's Brigade*, 539.

18. E. C. Walthall Scrapbook, Edward Cary Walthall Papers, MDAH. A handwritten copy of Walthall's official reports of Lookout Mountain and Missionary Ridge is in the Braxton Bragg Papers, LC.

19. Sykes, *Walthall's Brigade*, 543; Christopher Losson, *Tennessee's Forgotten Warriors, Frank Cheatham and His Confederate Division*, (Knoxville, TN, 1989), 128; William F. Dowd, "Lookout Mountain and Missionary Ridge," *Southern Bivouac* 4, no. 4 (Dec. 1885), 399; James D. Porter, *Tennessee*, vol. 10 of *Confederate Military History Extended Edition*, ed. Clement A. Evans, 17 vols. (Wilmington, NC, 1987), 119.

20. Sykes, *Walthall's Brigade*, 542; *OR*, vol. 31, pt. 2:666.

21. E. McGuire to Mary Walthall, Dec. 1, 1863, Edward C. Walthall Papers, LC; Mary Walthall to Cary Freeman, Nov. 21, 1863, and Edward C. Walthall to Kate Freeman, Mar. 31, 1864, E. C. Walthall Papers, UM; Sykes said that Walthall used crutches for four weeks after returning to his brigade. Sykes, *Walthall's Brigade*, 542.

22. Bragg's chief of cavalry, Major General Joseph Wheeler, also apparently felt that Walthall would make a good brigade commander, writing on October 12, 1863, that such men as Walthall, Patton Anderson, and Arthur Manigault (all pro-Bragg men, as was Wheeler) "are what the cavalry needs." [?] Phelan to Edward C. Walthall, Feb. 11, 1864, Edward C. Walthall Papers, LC; *OR*, vol. 30, pt. 2:666.

23. Edward Walthall to Braxton Bragg, Mar.11, 1864, and Louis J. Dupree to Braxton Bragg, Feb. 25, 1864, Braxton Bragg Papers, William P. Palmer Collection, Western Reserve Historical Society, Cleveland, OH.

24. Walthall to Bragg, Mar. 11, 1864, Bragg Papers, Western Reserve Historical Society; Edward C. Walthall to Mother, Dalton, Georgia, Mar. 10, 1864, E. C. Walthall Papers, UM.

25. Edward C. Walthall to Kate W. Freeman, Mar. 31, 1864, E. C. Walthall Papers, UM.

26. Sykes, *Walthall's Brigade*, 567–68; *OR*, vol. 38, pt. 4:761.

27. *OR*, vol. 38, pt. 4:748, 753; Braxton Bragg to Samuel Cooper, May 31, 1864, found in Edward C. Walthall, Compiled Service Records of Confederate General and Staff Officers and Nonregimental Enlisted Men, Roll 258, M331, NA.

28. Braxton Bragg to Samuel Cooper, May 31, 1864, and Joseph E. Johnston to Jefferson Davis, June 5, 1864, found in Edward C. Walthall, Compiled Service Records of Confederate General and Staff Officers and Nonregimental Enlisted Men, Roll 258, M331, NA. On September 12, 1864, Walthall wrote Confederate Adjutant and Inspector General Samuel Cooper to accept the ap-

pointment of major general. Edward C. Walthall, Compiled Service Records of Confederate General and Staff Officers and Nonregimental Enlisted Men, Roll 258, M331, NA; *OR*, vol. 38, pt. 4:755; Edward C. Walthall to Samuel Cooper, September 12, 1864, Edward C. Walthall Papers, LC; Jefferson Davis, *The Papers of Jefferson Davis*, ed. Lynda L. Crist, Kenneth H. Williams, and Peggy L. Dillard, vol. 10, *October 1863–August 1864* (Baton Rouge, LA, 1999), 449–50.

29. John Smith Kendall, ed., "Recollections of a Confederate Staff Officer," *Louisiana Historical Quarterly* 29 (Oct. 1946): 1182. On Cantey at Resaca, see Robert Patrick, *Reluctant Rebel, The Secret Diary of Robert Patrick, 1861–1865*, ed. F. Jay Taylor (Baton Rouge, LA, 1959), 159–63; James Cooper Nisbet, *Four Years on the Firing Line*, ed. Bell Irwin Wiley (1963; repr., Wilmington, NC, 1987), 179–82; Daniel H. Reynolds Diary, May 14, 1864, Daniel H. Reynolds Papers, Special Collections Department, University of Arkansas Libraries, Fayetteville. For an overly critical assessment of the Cantey-Walthall division, see Steven H. Newton, *Lost for the Cause: The Confederate Army in 1864* (Mason City, IA, 2000), 123.

30. Lawrence L. Hewitt, "Daniel H. Reynolds," in *The Confederate General*, ed. William C. Davis and Julie Hoffman, 6 vols. (Harrisburg, PA, 1991), 5:84–85; Reynolds Diary, June 4, 6, 1864.

31. General Hood wrote Adjutant and Inspector General Cooper on August 14, and again on September 13, 1864, that Cantey was sick "and not likely to return" to command his brigade. Brigadier General Charles Shelley took permanent command of the brigade on October 2, 1864. Shelley's sister wrote in a September 10, 1864, letter that Walthall had nominated her brother "to take command of Cantey's Brigade, and he was very strongly recommended for promotion by General Lee, Hood, and all the others . . . Cantey was removed for some cause—Charlie thinks drunkenness." Illene D. Thompson and Wilbur E. Thompson, *The Seventeenth Alabama Infantry: A Regimental History and Roster* (Bowie, MD, 2001), 80, 86; Robert K. Krick, "Three Confederate Disasters on Oak Ridge: Failures of Brigade Leadership on the First Day of Gettysburg," in *The First Day at Gettysburg: Essays on Confederate and Union Leadership*, ed. Gary W. Gallagher (Kent, OH, 1992), 120–23; John B. Hood to J. A. Seddon, Aug. 14, 1864, found in C. M. Shelley, Compiled Service Records of Confederate General and Staff Officers and Nonregimental Enlisted Men, Roll 224, M331, NA; *OR*, vol. 39, pt. 2:833; Larry Stephens, *Bound for Glory: A History of the 30th Alabama Infantry Regiment, C.S.A.* (Ann Arbor, MI, 2005), 277–78.

32. Arthur W. Bergeron Jr., "William Andrew Quarles," in *The Confederate General*, ed. William C. Davis and Julie Hoffman, 6 vols. (Harrisburg, PA, 1991), 5:66–67; *OR*, vol. 38, pt. 4:725; John B. Lindsley, ed., *The Military Annals of Tennessee*, 2 vols. (1896; repr., Wilmington, NC, 1995), 2:517; "Quarles'

Brigade-A Few Incidents," undated newspaper clipping, Hunter-Taylor Papers, Confederate Military Manuscripts, Series B: Holdings of the Louisiana State University, Reel 9, University Microfilms Publications; Thomas A. Head, *Campaigns and Battles of the Sixteenth Regiment, Tennessee Volunteers* (Nashville, TN, 1885), 327.

33. *OR*, vol. 38, pt. 3:922–23; A. F. Smith, untitled article, *Confederate Veteran* 6, no. 7 (July 1898): 307.

34. *OR*, vol. 38, pt. 3:925–26, 938, 941–42. For a positive assessment of O'Neal's brigade at Peachtree Creek, see George C. Osborn, ed., "Civil War Letters of Robert W. Banks: Atlanta Campaign," *Georgia Historical Quarterly* 27, no. 2 (June 1943): 216.

35. *OR*, vol. 38, pt. 3:871, 925–26; Sam D. Elliott, *Soldier of Tennessee: General Alexander P. Stewart and the Civil War in the West* (Baton Rouge, LA, 1999), 207.

36. *OR*, vol. 38, pt. 3:927, 931; Edward Y. McMorries, *History of the First Regiment Alabama Volunteer Infantry C.S.A.* (Montgomery, AL, 1904), 77; Daniel P. Smith, *Company K, First Alabama Regiment, or Three Years in the Confederate Service* (1885 repr., Baltimore, 1984), 101.

37. *OR*, vol. 38, pt. 3:927, 931, 939; Stephen A. Cowley to Hubbard T. Minor, Aug. 6, 1864, Hubbard T. Minor Papers, U.S. Army Military History Institute, Carlisle, PA; Arthur Middleton Manigault, *A Carolinian Goes to War: The Civil War Narrative of Arthur Middleton Manigault*, ed. R. Lockwood Tower (Columbia, SC, 1983), 235; "The 29th Alabama," *Columbus (GA) Daily Sun*, Aug. 10, 1864; Hickerson H. Barksdale to brother, Aug. 10, 1864, William R. Barksdale Papers, MDAH.

38. *OR*, vol. 38, pt. 4:921.

39. Ibid., pt. 3:928; ibid., pt. 5:925.

40. Ibid., pt. 3:928; Kendall, "Recollections of a Confederate Staff Officer," 1187.

41. *OR*, vol. 39, pt. 1:825–26; Elliott, *Soldier of Tennessee*, 226–35.

42. *OR*, vol. 39, pt. 1:719–20; Eric A. Jacobson and Richard A. Rupp, *For Cause and For Country: A Study of the Affair at Spring Hill and the Battle of Franklin* (Franklin, TN, 2006), 159. In 1903, a veteran of Forrest's command claimed to have witnessed several Southern generals, including Walthall, drinking heavily at Hood's headquarters at the home of Absalom Thompson on the night of November 29, 1864. Historians have been rightfully skeptical of this account. Walthall's strong views on the importance of temperance appear in Edward C. Walthall to Braxton Bragg, Mar. 11, 1864, Braxton Bragg Papers, William P. Palmer Collection, Western Reserve Historical Society.

43. James H. McNeilly, untitled article, *Confederate Veteran* 22, no. 2 (Feb. 1914): 60; James H. McNeilly, "Franklin—Incidents of the Battle," *Confederate Veteran* 26, no. 3 (Mar. 1918): 117.

44. Robert Dacus of Reynolds's Brigade wrote many years after the war that Walthall told Hood that with two brigades he could execute a flank attack on the Federals. If true, the exchange might have taken place at the same time Hood met with Stewart. Elliott, *Soldier of Tennessee,* 237; *OR,* vol. 45, pt. 1:720; Robert H. Dacus, *Reminiscences of Company "H," First Arkansas Mounted Rifles* (Dardanelle, AR, 1897), 15.

45. "Record of Walthall's Division at Franklin and Nashville in late 1864," *Confederate Veteran* 7, no. 6 (June 1899): 265; *OR,* vol. 45, pt. 1:720; McNeilly, "At the Battle of Franklin," 117.

46. *OR,* vol. 45, pt. 1:720.

47. A division ordnance return states that the command fought for two hours, but this undoubtedly refers to the main body and not those men who made it to the enemy's main line. *OR,* vol. 45, pt. 1:720; "Army Correspondence, Letter from the 29th Alabama," *Mobile (AL) Advertiser and Register,* Dec. 21, 1864; "Record of Walthall's Division," 265; Wiley Sword, *Embrace an Angry Wind* (New York, 1992), 219–20.

48. Walthall's younger brother George, a cavalry private serving as a temporary aide to the general, noted that one of the general's horses was shot three times during the battle, the third shot killing it. After losing the second horse, Walthall took the mount of a subordinate, but not before appointing several appraisers to fix the value of the steed. Major General Samuel G. French remembered encountering Walthall as their divisions came out of the fighting. When French put his hand on the shoulder of Walthall's mortally wounded animal, it "plunged violently forward and fell dead, throwing the General far over his head." *OR,* vol. 45, pt. 1:721, 726; George M. Walthall to mother, Dec 2, 1864, E. C. Walthall Papers, UM; Robert W. Banks, *The Battle of Franklin, November 30, 1864* (1908; repr., Dayton, OH, 1982), 52–53; Samuel G. French, *Two Wars: The Autobiography and Diary of Gen. Samuel G. French, CSA* (Nashville, TN, 1901), 296.

49. Some confusion exists as to who commanded French's Division on December 15. Brigadier General Sears indicated in a 10:00 A.M. dispatch that day that he was in command, but Stewart's official report suggests that he had attached the division to Walthall. "Record of Walthall's Division," 265; *OR,* vol. 45, pt. 1:709, 723; ibid., pt. 2:672, 691, 693.

50. *OR,* vol. 45, pt. 1:709; Kate Cumming, *Kate: The Journal of a Confederate Nurse,* ed. Richard B. Harwell (Baton Rouge, LA, 1959), 251–52; Edward W. Tarrant, "With Walthall at Nashville," *Confederate Veteran* 13, no. 2 (Feb. 1905), 66.

51. *OR,* vol. 45, pt. 1:723–24; ibid., pt. 2:696.

52. *OR,* vol. 45, pt. 1:721–23; "Record of Walthall's Division," 265.

53. *OR,* vol. 45, pt. 1:724.

54. Field returns dated December 21, 1864, for six of the brigades record an effective strength of 1,655 men. Major Sanders claimed that Hood allowed Walthall to choose the composition of the rear guard and that the entire force numbered 1,601 effectives. *OR*, vol. 45, pt. 1:726; ibid., pt. 2:714, 715; John Allan Wyeth, *Life of Lieutenant-General Nathan Bedford Forrest* (New York, 1908), 567, 568; Sanders, "Hood's Tennessee Campaign," 401; David W. Sanders, "Autobiography of Maj. D. W. Sanders," *Confederate Veteran* 18, no. 8 (Aug. 1910), 371.

55. Sanders, "Hood's Tennessee Campaign," 402; *OR,* vol. 45, pt. 2:722.

56. Laura Galloway autograph book, 1994 catalog of *Southern Historical Showcase* (Nashville, TN), 3.

57. Captain John W. Morton, commanding Forrest's artillery, suggests that Forrest and Walthall were together during this engagement, although he does not provide a location. *OR,* vol. 45, pt. 1:727; Reynolds Diary, Dec. 25, 1864; Wyeth, *Life of Lieutenant General Nathan Bedford Forrest,* 571; Sanders, "Hood's Tennessee Campaign," 403; John Watson Morton, *The Artillery of Nathan Bedford Forrest's Cavalry* (Nashville, TN, 1909), 296–97; Lindsley, *Military Annals of Tennessee,* 2:191.

58. *OR,* vol. 45, pt. 1:724, 726–28; Sanders, "Hood's Tennessee Campaign," 404; Reynolds Diary, Dec. 26, 27, 1864; Wyeth, *Life of Lieutenant General Nathan Bedford Forrest,* 572.

59. Reynolds Diary, Dec. 26, 1864; Charles H. Olmstead, *The Memoirs of Charles H. Olmstead,* ed. Lilla Mills Hawes, in *Collections of the Georgia Historical Society,* Vol. 14 (Savannah, GA, 1964), 171

60. *OR,* vol. 45, pt. 1:711, 758–59; ibid., pt. 2:699; Hood, *Advance and Retreat,* 306–7.

61. *OR,* vol. 45, pt. 2:774; Robert E. L. Krick, *Staff Officers in Gray: A Biographical Register of the Staff Officers in the Army of Northern Virginia* (Chapel Hill, NC, 2003), 328.

62. *Memorial Addresses on the Life and Character of Edward C. Walthall Delivered in the Senate and House of Representatives, Fifty-Fifth Congress, Second and Third Sessions* (Washington, DC, 1899), 78–79; Robert D. Smith, *Confederate Diary of Robert D. Smith,* ed. Jill K. Garrett (Columbia, TN, 1997), 170. On Walthall's postbellum health problems, see Hardin, "Edward Cary Walthall," 112.

63. *OR,* vol. 47, pt. 1:1104, 1105; ibid., pt. 2:1368.

64. Robert Dacus of Reynolds's Brigade claims that the unwillingness of the Alabamians under Johnston to deploy in Cole's field caused Walthall to shift the positions of his two brigades. In the subsequent maneuvering, Reynolds received his wound. Nathaniel Cheairs Hughes Jr., *Bentonville: The Final Battle of Sherman and Johnston* (Chapel Hill, NC, 1996), 53, 54; Dacus, *Reminiscences of Company "H,"* 24; *OR,* vol. 47, pt. 1:1104. For a detailed tactical description of

Walthall's Division at Bentonville, see Mark Bradley, *Last Stand in the Carolinas: The Battle of Bentonville* (Campbell, CA, 1996), 166–67, 203–5.

65. *Memorial Addresses on the Life and Character of Edward C. Walthall,* 25.

66. "Gen. E. C. Walthall," *Confederate Veteran* 6, no. 7 (July 1898), 306; Bradley, *Last Stand,* 204.

67. Bradley, *Last Stand,* 205–7, 262–66; *OR,* vol. 47, pt. 1:1060; ibid., pt. 2:1105.

68. *OR,* vol. 47, pt. 3:698; Jefferson Davis, *The Papers of Jefferson Davis,* ed. Lynda Lasswell Crist, Barbara J. Rozek, and Kenneth H. Williams, vol. 11, *September 1864-May 1865* (Baton Rouge, LA, 2004), 470.

69. George Walthall to mother, Apr. 1, 1865, E. C. Walthall Papers, UM; *OR,* vol. 47, pt. 3:773.

70. Sykes, *Walthall's Brigade,* 515–17; Krick, *Staff Officers in Gray,* 357.

71. Sykes, *Walthall's Brigade,* 488; Edgar S. Wilson, "Senator Edward Cary Walthall," *Memphis Commercial Appeal,* Apr. 20, 1904; W. H. R., "Brigadiers in Togas With Colonels and Even Privates Representing the Southern States," undated newspaper clipping, Folder 117, E. C. Walthall Papers, UM; Krick, *Staff Officers in Gray,* 259.

General Braxton Bragg. Library of Congress.

Unlucky in War: Braxton Bragg's Return to Field Duty at Wilmington, North Carolina, 1864–65

Chris E. Fonvielle Jr.

THE EDITOR OF THE *CHARLOTTESVILLE (VA) DAILY CHRONICLE* WROTE IN LATE October 1864: "We suspect General Bragg is going to Wilmington. Goodbye Wilmington." This audacious prediction spread like wildfire across the state when the *Richmond Enquirer*, a more widely distributed newspaper, reprinted the quotation on October 26. Clearly President Jefferson Davis's assignment of General Braxton Bragg, his own military adviser, to command at Wilmington, North Carolina, was a highly controversial move. Arguably the most despised general officer in the army, Bragg would be in control of the Confederacy's last open major seaport and most important city. At the same time, his appointment to the leadership position at Wilmington revealed the internal politics of the Davis administration and the high command, and ultimately contributed to Confederate defeat.[1]

Wilmington is nestled on a high, sloping sand ridge on the east side of the Cape Fear River where it meets the northeast branch. The Cape Fear River is the only waterway in North Carolina that flows directly into the Atlantic Ocean, twenty-eight nautical miles south of Wilmington. Access for the remaining watersheds into Albemarle and Pamlico Sounds are cut off by a long line of barrier islands known as the Outer Banks. Founded in 1732, Wilmington grew from a small trading post in colonial days to the state's busiest seaport and largest city by 1840. Twenty years later it boasted a population of 9,552 people, one third of whom were African American. The city featured an active mercantile trade, five banks, three railroads, two commercial shipbuilding yards, two iron and copper works, a sword factory, turpentine distilleries, cotton presses, and sawmills. One of the rail lines—the Wilmington & Weldon—was reportedly the longest in the world upon its completion in 1840 and stimulated the town's growth. The shipyards, owned by James Cassidey & Son and Benjamin and William Beery, manufactured and repaired both steamships and sailing vessels. The Beery brothers' business, known as the Confederate Navy Yard during the war, built the Richmond-class ironclad *North Carolina,* while Cassidey's constructed a similar model, the CSS *Raleigh.*

Wilmington's maritime trade during the antebellum period was small compared to the South's principal seaports of New Orleans, Charleston, and Norfolk, but it grew exponentially during the Civil War. For more than three years, commerce vessels smuggled much-needed supplies from Europe into the Confederacy by way of the Tar Heel port. Five days after Major Robert Anderson surrendered Fort Sumter in Charleston Harbor on April 14, 1861, President Abraham Lincoln proclaimed a naval blockade of the seven seceded Southern states. Eight days later he revised the blockade to include Virginia, which left the Union on April 17, and North Carolina, even though it had not yet joined the Confederacy. Angered by Lincoln's call for seventy-five thousand troops to put down the "rebellion" and his declaration of economic warfare, the Old North State passed an ordinance of secession on May 20, 1861.

The blockade was initially worth little more than the paper on which the president's scribe wrote it. An effective dragnet of Southern harbors was virtually impossible, as the U.S. Navy comprised only ninety ships, forty-two of which were operational and mostly stationed in foreign waters. Moreover, at 3,549 miles, the lengthy shoreline from Cape Henry, Virginia, to the Florida Keys, to the Rio Grande River in Texas forced Union blockading vessels to focus their efforts against the South's major seaports: New Orleans, Charleston, Mobile, Savannah, Norfolk, and Wilmington.

The Confederacy responded to "Mr. Lincoln's blockade" by establishing maritime trade relations overseas. Even though European governments vowed to remain neutral during the war, the lure of huge profits attracted many of their citizens to become private investors and speculators in the smuggling trade. They justified their involvement by citing international maritime law that defined a naval blockade as an act of war between two belligerent nations that was in fact effective. Yet the Lincoln administration denied that international law applied, defining the seceded Southern states as merely being out of their proper structure while engaged in a rebellion against the United States.

Great Britain became the Confederacy's biggest trading partner. Parliament turned a blind eye as merchants and manufacturers began selling and trading supplies, provisions, and equipment to Southern commission merchants, individual Southern states, and the Confederate government. In exchange for cotton or cotton bonds, British businessmen exported a mass of war materiel and supplies to the Confederacy: rifle-muskets, artillery, ammunition, swords, bayonets, knives, uniforms, accoutrements, footwear, medicines, blankets, bacon, medicines, tools, and other assorted military items. To a lesser degree, Confederate agents also purchased similar materiel in Austria, France, Belgium, and Prussia.

Wilmington quickly emerged as one of the Confederacy's main seaports for the blockade running trade. Geography favored the commerce vessels that operated there. It was close to the British transshipment points of Bermuda and Nassau in the Bahamas. As blockade-runners approached the Cape Fear River, two entryways—Old Inlet and New Inlet—provided them with a choice of entrance and exit, and lessened their chances of detection, capture, or destruction by Union blockading ships. As a result, they enjoyed an incredible success rate of 80 percent. An undetermined number of sailing vessels and at least 106 different steamships brought more war supplies, as well as civilian goods, into the Confederacy by way of Wilmington than any other Southern seaport. Approximately half of everything the Confederacy used and consumed came through the Union blockade.[2]

Military arms and supplies imported for the government were generally transported on the Wilmington & Weldon Railroad to Virginia. Wilmington became so important as a port of entry for military supplies for the Army of Northern Virginia that General Robert E. Lee stated in early January 1863: "It ought to be defended to the last extremity."[3]

To protect Wilmington, the Cape Fear River, the railroads, and the inlets that blockade-runners used, Confederate engineers designed and constructed a vast network of forts, batteries, and fieldworks. With the exception of Charleston, Wilmington became the most heavily defended Southern seaport along the Atlantic coast. Artillery batteries ringed the city, while a series of outer defenses guarded it from an overland attack. Fort Anderson, located at Brunswick Point halfway between Wilmington and Old Inlet, guarded the water and land approaches on the west side of the river. Military constructors built the strongest and best armed forts at Old Inlet and New Inlet to provide covering fire for Confederate commerce vessels. Fort Caswell, Fort Campbell, Battery Shaw on Oak Island, and Fort Holmes on Bald Head Island overlooked Old Inlet, also known as the Western Bar. To safeguard New Inlet, engineers built the largest and most powerful seacoast fortification in the Confederacy—Fort Fisher. The fort and its auxiliary works were located near the end of Confederate Point (called Federal Point before the war), a narrow peninsula bounded by the Cape Fear River on the west and the Atlantic Ocean on the east. The sand spit tapered to a point at New Inlet. The imposing two-sided earthwork comprised a series of elevated gun batteries mounting forty-seven pieces of seacoast artillery connected by a broad rampart. Fort Fisher's land face stretched 682 yards from the river to the sea and then

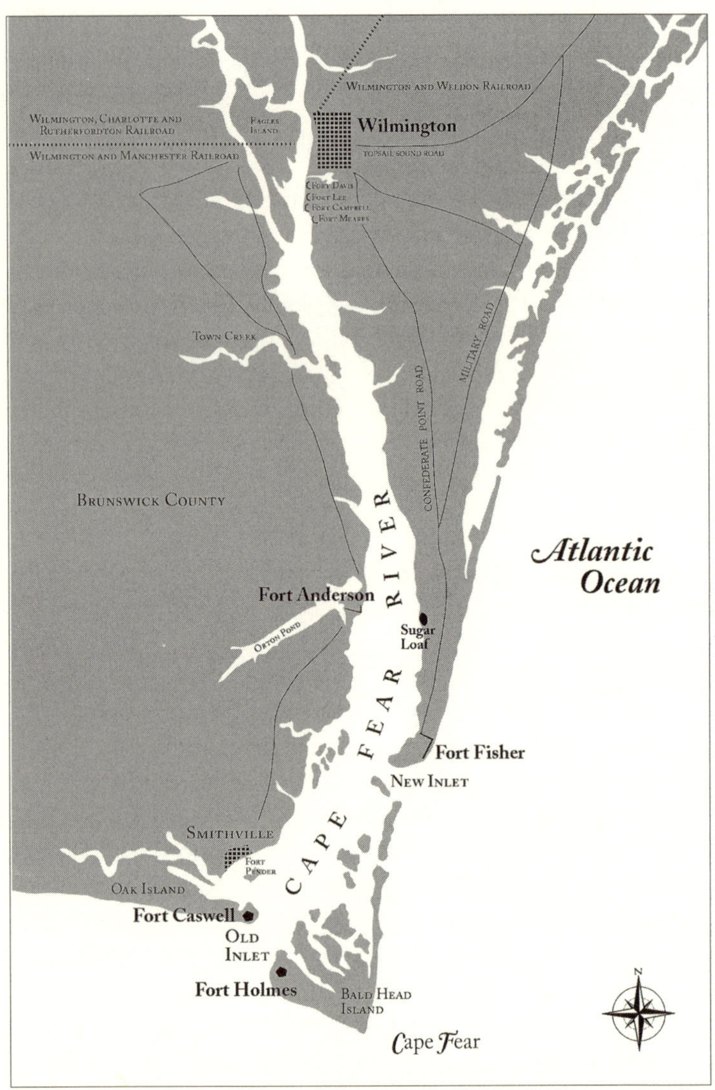

Wilmington and its defenses. Courtesy of Chris E. Fonvielle Jr.

turned southward along the ocean's shoreline for almost 1,900 yards. Both Confederate and Union observers alike considered Fort Fisher impregnable against a naval attack and dubbed it the "Malakoff of the Confederacy," in reference to the formidable Russian fortifications at Sevastopol during the Crimean War. Fort Fisher was crucial to Wilmington's protection. "No more tremendous earthworks exist on this continent than those that bulwark the inlets of the Cape Fear River," one observer boasted.[4]

Commanding the District (later the Department) of the Cape Fear, was Major General William Henry Chase Whiting, one of the most talented engineers in the Confederacy. An army brat whose father was a career U.S. Army artillery officer, Whiting was born in Biloxi, Mississippi, but raised in the northeast. After graduating at the top of his class at West Point in 1845, he served with distinction in the U.S. Army's elite Engineer Corps. Whiting offered his services to the newly established Confederate States of America in early 1861, and the government initially assigned him to help his mentor and friend, General Pierre G. T. Beauregard, develop Charleston's defenses. After the capture of Fort Sumter in April, then-Major Whiting accepted a commission from Governor John W. Ellis of North Carolina to serve as inspector general of the state's coastal defenses.

Major General William Henry Chase Whiting. Courtesy of Chris E. Fonvielle Jr.

Whiting remained in the Tar Heel State for only four weeks, designing defenses on the Outer Banks and at Wilmington. What he desired, however, was a field command. When the opportunity came in late May, he joined General Joseph E. Johnston's staff as chief engineer. For his good work transferring troops by rail from Harper's Ferry to join the fighting at Manassas in late July 1861, Whiting received a battlefield promotion to brigadier general from President Jefferson Davis. The following spring and summer, Whiting commanded a division in Johnston's and then Robert E. Lee's army in the defense of Richmond. The president praised Whiting as "heroic and highly gifted." Johnston so depended on Whiting's wise counsel that he nicknamed him "Solomon." General Lee called him a "good engineer and a hard laborer." Despite the accolades, a dark side to Whiting's personality soon emerged that thrust him into disfavor with the Confederate high command.[5]

Whiting's critics claimed that his high rank and rare intellect (one of his staff members called him a genius) went to his head, and he sometimes came across as brusque and obstinate. His supporters described him as bold and extremely self-confident. Whatever the case, Whiting expressed frustration with people who did not share his views and opinions on military matters. He openly criticized Jefferson Davis. When the president proposed to reorganize the Confederate army in 1861 by placing regiments from the same state into brigades to be led by officers from those states, Whiting called the policy "inconceivable folly." He suggested that Davis refrain from meddling in army affairs. The criticism infuriated the chief executive, as did unsubstantiated rumors the following year that Whiting wanted him deposed and General Joe Johnston installed as military dictator.

Davis had soon had enough of Whiting, whom he found to be imperious, insolent, and insubordinate. Whiting turned to Lee for support but found none, as the commanding general also considered Whiting disputatious. When Lee restructured the army in the autumn of 1862, he quietly transferred Whiting to the District of the Cape Fear, headquartered in Wilmington. However problematic Davis and Lee may have found Whiting, they still held his engineering skills in high regard. Whiting considered himself a victim of army politics, but dutifully accepted his fate.[6]

In truth, Wilmington was the ideal place for Whiting. The city needed stronger fortifications to protect the blockade running trade and to defend against an enemy assault, and Whiting knew the area well. Besides, he had married an "agreeable and pretty young belle" named Katherine Davis Walker from Wilmington. Local military men familiar with Whiting greeted his arrival to the city in mid-November 1862 with excitement. "We justly regarded the general as one of the few eminently fit appointments the War Department had made," one devotee stated. A soldier remarked that Whiting "is a good man and a brave General, and we will do our part to sustain him in his determination to defend the place to the last." To keep Whiting and his loyalists content, the War Department promoted him to major general on April 22, 1863, backdated to rank from February 28.[7]

Some Wilmingtonians, on the other hand, were not pleased with Whiting's return to their port town. "He was not popular with many of the citizens," observed one army officer, "as he was arbitrary and paid little attention to the suggestions of civilians." At the same time, he added, "[Whiting] was a gentleman at heart, incapable of anything mean or low, and of undaunted courage." Yet throughout the war, Whiting sparred with both residents and civil authorities, especially Davis and Zebulon B. Vance, North Carolina's governor for most of the war.[8]

As more and more blockade-runners came and went at Wilmington, Whiting called attention to the port's growing importance to both North Carolina and Confederate authorities. Constantly in need of additional soldiers, laborers, and resources to construct and defend the works, Whiting wrote hundreds of letters requesting assistance from Davis, Lee, Vance, Beauregard, and other leaders. Whiting had good reason to be concerned about Wilmington's security. By the spring of 1862, Federal army and navy forces had captured and occupied North Carolina's Outer Banks and two-thirds of the coastal plain and river towns from Virginia to White Oak River, only sixty miles north of Wilmington. With the Union army ensconced in New Bern and a North Atlantic Blockading Squadron fuel and supply substation in nearby Beaufort, Wilmington faced constant threat.

A Union attack on the Tar Heel port was a long time coming. The U.S. Navy had targeted it as early as the summer of 1861. When the blockade strategy board issued its recommendations in September, Wilmington was on the list of places to be hit. Acting Rear Admiral S. Phillips Lee, commander of the North Atlantic Blockading Squadron from 1862 to 1864, insisted that only a well-planned and well-executed combined operation could capture Wilmington. A unilateral naval attack was impractical, since shoals and shallow waters along the Cape Fear coast would prevent warships from getting close enough to shore to effectively bombard the forts and batteries guarding Old and New Inlets.

In the spring of 1862, U.S. Secretary of the Navy Gideon Welles lobbied to gain political and logistical support for an assault on Wilmington. While dismal defeats plagued the Army of the Potomac in Virginia, the navy experienced considerable success in coastal operations. Between March and May, navy and army forces captured several principal seaports, including New Bern and Beaufort, North Carolina; Jacksonville and Fernandina, Florida; and New Orleans, Louisiana. Port Royal, South Carolina had fallen into Union hands the previous November, and Savannah, Georgia, lost its status as a blockade running port when Federal forces captured Fort Pulaski in April 1862.

With momentum clearly in his favor, Secretary Welles proposed a strike on Wilmington in May 1862. His plan failed to attract much attention because the Army of the Potomac, led by Major General George B. McClellan, was at the time slowly but surely advancing to the gates of Richmond. After McClellan's defeat in the Peninsula Campaign that summer, Welles again tried to persuade the army to go after Wilmington. In the autumn of 1862, he planned an assault to coincide with Major General Ambrose E. Burnside's advance on Richmond by way of Fredericksburg. Admiral Lee selected several ironclads for an attack on Fort Caswell at the mouth of the Cape Fear River, foremost among them the famed *Monitor* that had battled the CSS *Virginia* in Hampton Roads, Virginia, the previous March in the first duel between ironclads. The operation also called for conventional warships to bombard Fort Fisher near New Inlet and for Union infantry to advance from New Bern to hit Wilmington's comparatively weak north side. The campaign collapsed when Robert E. Lee thrashed Burnside's army at Fredericksburg in mid-December and the *Monitor* sank in a gale off Cape Hatteras, North Carolina, on New Year's Eve 1862. The "Sailors' Grave," as nineteenth-century mariners called North Carolina's treacherous coastline, had claimed yet another vessel.[9]

Admiral Lee proposed other ideas for taking Wilmington over the following two years, which Welles supported. "To close the port of Wilmington is undoubtedly the most important and effective demonstration that can be made," the secretary exclaimed. "If of less prestige than the capture of Richmond, it would be as damaging to the Rebels." Yet the War Department, led by Secretary Edwin Stanton, showed little interest in providing a large expeditionary force to strike a backwater port it considered of little strategic value compared to Richmond, Vicksburg, and Chattanooga. The army's apathy toward Wilmington and the lack of resources compelled the Navy Department to pick and choose its targets. Attention shifted to Charleston, the birthplace of secession and the war and the center of popular and political interests.[10]

In the spring of 1863, Union navy and army forces initiated a campaign against Charleston that would last 587 days. The Union high command put Wilmington on the back burner. This enabled Confederate blockade-runners to regularly penetrate the blockade there more easily, importing vital military arms, equipment, and provisions. "As the siege of Charleston continues, so the importance of [Wilmington] grows every day," Whiting proclaimed. "I do not know now that there is another place, excepting perhaps Richmond, we should not sooner see lost than this." Many others agreed. "Having sealed up nearly every other seaport, the Yankees are bent upon the destruction of Wilmington. No one can readily imagine its enormous value to the Confederacy," reported the *Augusta (GA) Constitutionalist*. "The supplies brought from abroad have been immense. Outside of its maritime importance, the fact of its being a railroad center, just in the rear of General Lee, makes its position of prime necessity."[11]

Despite Whiting's anxiety over Wilmington's safety, Davis, Lee, and Secretary of War James A. Seddon perceived no imminent danger to the seaport. If and when the threat became real, they reasoned, troops could be rushed to meet the attackers. Until then the War Department promised only to try and meet Whiting's needs. The situation changed when Rear Admiral David G. Farragut's warships sealed Mobile Bay, Alabama, the last haven for blockade-runners in the Gulf of Mexico, in a dramatic naval battle on August 5, 1864. The closure of Mobile left Wilmington as the only major port effectively open to trade with the outside world. "The success of the enemy in closing the port of Mobile will very probably encourage them to make efforts on Wilmington," Seddon informed Whiting.[12]

Positive that an assault was all but certain, Whiting needed no convincing. "The thing is so," he remarked to one confidant, "neither General Lee nor General Anybody can hold this place with the present force if attacked with any vigor." Yet Lee was disinclined to send reinforcements from his beleaguered, if strongly entrenched, army in Virginia until the intentions of the enemy became known. He believed the build up of Union warships at Hampton Roads, Virginia, as intelligence sources reported, planned to reinforce siege forces at Charleston. Lee also thought that Whiting exaggerated the danger to Wilmington and asked the War Department to rebuke him for his constant correspondence that only increased the risk of the enemy becoming more acquainted with the seaport's defenses and launching an attack.[13]

Whiting's "cries of wolf" in the twenty-three months that he had headed the District of the Cape Fear now came back to haunt him. As the Union threat to Wilmington grew more ominous, his detractors moved to oust him from command. Foremost among them was Governor Vance, who had lost confidence in Whiting because of his alleged alcohol abuse at inopportune times, most recently in the defense of Petersburg, where the general had been sent in May 1864 to help Beauregard defend the city. "In case a real attack should be made upon Wilmington, I earnestly urge that General Beauregard should be sent there," Vance wrote Lee, "and this not only because of the great confidence felt in him, but also because of the very little reposed in General Whiting." Lee shared Vance's concerns about Whiting "in an equal degree." "He is a man of unquestionable ability, versed in the particular knowledge suited to his position," the commanding general acknowledged, "but whether he would be able at the required time to apply these qualifications and to maintain the confidence of his command is with me questionable." At the same time, Lee did not know of a more qualified officer to replace Whiting. He had considered transferring Beauregard to Wilmington should an attack there materialize, but that was now out of the question as Davis had recently reassigned him to duty in Georgia.[14]

When he learned of Vance's request, Whiting complained to the governor that he had done him an injustice. Vance responded candidly, saying: "Only one thing has ever occurred to impair the universal confidence which you inspired by your diligence in fortifying the town, and that was a very general impression that you drank too much; that your nervous system had been injured by it." Whiting vehemently denied the accusations, but perception now shaped his reality. It did not help his case that the Virginia media also questioned his credentials for defending Wilmington at such a critical hour for the Confederacy. "Are the officers in command at Wilmington attending to it?" asked the editor of the *Richmond Sentinel.* "No officer is worthy of position there who is capable of neglecting a duty," he observed, perhaps making subtle reference to the recent debate over Whiting's questionable performance at Petersburg. "[Wilmington] is the post of responsibility and is soon to be a post of danger. We need in the commander a sleepless vigilance, a far seeing sagacity, an indefatigable industry, a cool head and a brave heart." It was a tall order for any man to fill.[15]

A somber Whiting told a friend: "I desire [Wilmington's] safety so much and so sincerely that I am willing at any time to serve under any more able or capable of my seniors who may be more acceptable to the people of Raleigh &c., and to aid any such with my entire efforts, or to waive in favor of any junior who may be wished for. It's an ungrateful duty this, and no bed of roses, and the prospect not particularly cheerful ahead.[16]

President Davis finally weighed in to resolve the matter by replacing the controversial Whiting with an even more controversial officer: General Braxton Bragg. "The condition and threatening aspect of affairs in the District of the Cape Fear renders it, in my judgment, desirable that you should exercise immediate command over the troops and defenses of Wilmington and its approaches," Davis informed Bragg on October 15, 1864. In ordering Bragg to Wilmington, the president expected him to organize a successful defense of the Confederacy's last lifeline, while at the same time working harmoniously with the mercurial Whiting.[17]

To most Southerners, Braxton Bragg's reassignment was one of the most baffling decisions Jefferson Davis made during the war. Here was an officer as confounding a combination of promise and disappointment as the Confederacy turned out. His resume was replete with battlefield indecisiveness and failure, to say nothing of the contentious personal relations he suffered with fellow officers. One government bureaucrat tempered his comment about Bragg's awful army associations when he wrote that many officers merely found the general "very distasteful."[18]

It has not always been so. Indeed, Bragg's military career began with great expectations. He had been an exemplary cadet at the U.S. Military Academy at West Point, where he graduated fifth in the class of 1837. He served with distinction in both the Second Seminole War and the Mexican War, during which he was awarded three brevets. As a captain of artillery, Bragg gained recognition at the Battle of Buena Vista in February 1847, when General Zachary Taylor ordered him to "double shot those guns and give 'em hell." From then on Bragg's name became synonymous with double shotting artillery and giving the Mexicans hell. It made him famous.

Bragg rose to the rank of lieutenant colonel before resigning from the army in January 1856. According to an old army acquaintance, William T. Sherman, Bragg retired rather than obey a transfer order from then Secretary of War Jefferson Davis in the Franklin Pierce administration that would have sent him into Indian Territory. "Bragg hated Davis bitterly" after this, Sherman claimed. Instead of returning to his hometown of Warrenton, North Carolina, where he was born on March 22, 1817, Bragg moved to Louisiana and married the wealthy Eliza Brooks Ellis. He found success in the Pelican State as both a sugar planter and civil engineer. When Louisiana seceded from the Union, the governor named Bragg a major general of state forces. Six weeks later, on March 7, 1861, Bragg was appointed brigadier general in the Confederate army by the newly elected president and his old nemesis—Jefferson Davis. In an amazing ascent in rank, Bragg rose from brigadier general to full general in the regular Confederate army, a position held by only seven other men, in only thirteen months.[19]

Bragg cut a striking figure in his double-breasted gray wool uniform coat with gold braid on the cuffs and stars enveloped by a wreath on the collar, denoting his rank as a general officer. According to one observer, the general was "a tall, thin man, with eyes deeply sunken beneath the most lowering lashes, thin blue lips, nervous and inconstant, scant gray hair and beard, a narrow forehead; there are few men in the South so striking in person." Even so, he added, "[Bragg's] appearance was pale and haggard." By all accounts, Bragg had remarkable intelligence and good character and was highly regarded in the army as a strict disciplinarian, skillful organizer, and efficient administrator. "All the officers who knew Bragg thought he was perhaps the best disciplinarian in the United States Army," claimed one Union general during the Civil War. Ulysses S. Grant wrote in his postwar presidential memoirs that "Bragg was a remarkably intelligent and well informed man, professionally and otherwise. He was also thoroughly upright."[20]

By 1862, Bragg had helped organize and commanded the Army of the Mississippi, later renamed the Army of Tennessee. In a bold strategic move in September of that year, Bragg raided into Kentucky, coinciding with Lee's invasion of Maryland. Bragg penetrated farther north than any other commander of the Confederacy's Western Department. Despite an auspicious start, the campaign unraveled after an inconclusive engagement at Perryville, compelling Bragg to retreat into Tennessee. The bloody draw at Perryville was followed by a series of stinging defeats for Bragg, each succeeded by vitriolic intra-army disputes. Setbacks on the battlefield led to a crushing loss of confidence in Bragg's leadership. His failure to exploit an advantage won by his army in the first day of fighting at Stones River near Murfreesboro on December 31, 1862, led to his withdrawal three days later and the abandonment of much of Tennessee the following summer. After reinforcements from Lieutenant General James Longstreet's Corps arrived from Virginia in September 1863, Bragg attacked Federal forces at Chickamauga, Georgia, but again blundered by not following up what appeared to be a sweeping Confederate victory.

Bragg instead settled for a siege of Chattanooga, one of Tennessee's principal railroad hubs, a course of action his army was ill-prepared to conduct. His gross mismanagement and humiliating defeat at the Battle of Missionary Ridge on November 25, 1863, strained the already frayed relationships with his senior subordinates. Typically, he blamed others for his own shortcomings, denouncing Major General John C. Breckinridge. Bragg also realized there might well be a storm of criticism against him and a formal investigation into his poor performance in the battle, and so offered his resignation to the president. "I deem it due to the cause and to myself to ask for relief from command." Much to both Bragg's surprise and sorrow, Davis accepted it. The general's critics quickly pounced. "The army will be relieved to get rid of him," one claimed. "He has a winning way of earning everybody's detestation. Heavens know how they hate him."[21]

Not everyone hated Bragg, of course. Once Bragg's nemesis, Jefferson Davis was now his biggest supporter. To appease his distressed friend, the president brought Bragg to Richmond in late February 1864 to serve as his military adviser, "charged with the conduct of military operations in the armies of the Confederacy." Detractors worried Davis might even appoint him secretary of war. Why Davis felt inclined to uphold Bragg under such a withering storm of criticism engendered wild speculation and caustic conversations. The falsehood that Davis and Bragg were brothers-in-law, or that Varina Howell Davis had intervened on the general's behalf because of her "warm personal" friendship with Eliza Brooks Bragg, were suggested as explanations for the chief executive's action. John B. Jones, a clerk in the War Department, wrote in his tell-all wartime diary that the contrary president enjoyed a "secret satisfaction" in ignoring strong popular sentiment against Bragg, but that he also felt "bound in honor to sustain him." A Confederate army officer assessed the situation more candidly: "Mr. Davis was a man who never forgot his friends nor forgave his enemies. He seemed determined to sustain Bragg at all events."[22]

No doubt Davis believed Bragg would offer him valuable counsel, although Lee remained his most trusted confidant. Yet Davis was roundly and bitterly criticized for making the dubious appointment. The editor of the *Richmond Whig* blasted the president, writing sarcastically: "When a man fails in an inferior position, it is natural and charitable to conclude that the failure is due to the inadequacy of the task to his capabilities, and wise to give him a larger sphere for the proper exertion of his abilities." Hounded mercilessly by critics, Davis commiserated with his unpopular general: "You have the misfortune of being regarded as my personal friend, and are pursued therefore with malignant censure by men regardless of truth." By most accounts, Bragg served Davis faithfully and judiciously as adviser in the end.[23]

Davis's decision to transfer Bragg to Wilmington in October 1864 prompted skepticism given the general's knack for sowing disharmony and causing debacle wherever he went, not to mention the seaport's great importance. The president's motivation was unclear. He made no mention of the contentious appointment in his extensive postwar memoir, *The Rise and Fall of the Confederate Government.* To be sure, the general had made enemies in Congress and in the War Department. "Gen. Bragg is going away, probably to Wilmington. The combination against him was too strong," wrote Jones. Even Davis acknowledged "the prejudices existing against Bragg."

Perhaps the president was counting on the critical response Virginia newspaper editors gave the story to deflect attention away from himself. "The attacks on Bragg are meant principally for Mr. Davis," one observer pointed out. The administration was coming under heavy criticism as the fortunes of war turned against the Confederacy. The closure of Mobile to blockade running in early August was followed by the capture of Atlanta by Major General William T. Sherman's army on September 2, General Phil Sheridan's scorched earth campaign in the Shenandoah Valley, and Grant's renewed offensive against Lee at Petersburg. The prospects for Confederate victory and independence looked bleak by the autumn of 1864, and the public sensed that Bragg's reassignment to Wilmington would not change that. Always the dutiful subordinate to Davis, Robert E. Lee did nothing to challenge the dubious appointment.[24]

Bragg did have his defenders. James Fulton, editor and publisher of the *Wilmington Daily Journal,* wrote that

> while legitimate criticism of the conduct of public men is the right, and often the duty, of the press, it by no means follows that there can be either justification or excuse for making that the cover of vulgar malice or unreasonable prejudice. We who are in Wilmington and nearest the danger are unmoved by the leave-taking of the *Chronicle,* and equally so by the ready echo of the *Enquirer* [in reporting that 'General Bragg is going to Wilmington. Goodbye Wilmington']. General Bragg is in his *native* State, and we believe justly enjoys the confidence of her people. They know him to be well qualified for his place, and unselfishly devoted to the cause, and they are willing to trust their safety in his hands, with a confident feeling that Wilmington will not be lost by any deficiency on his part.[25]

The general's new leadership position did not preclude continuing his role as the president's military adviser, it merely expanded his realm of responsibility. Davis intended for Bragg to successfully defend Wilmington, while at the same time keeping tabs on Whiting. For his part, Bragg believed his departure from Richmond only temporary and his official position there secure until his return. Colonel John B. Sale, Bragg's secretary, would remain behind in the capital city to keep him informed of military affairs.

Bragg traveled by train to the Carolina seaport, arriving either late October 21 or early the following morning. With little fanfare, he appeared at Whiting's headquarters during the morning hours of October 22 and assumed command. Informed by the War Department that he was to be superseded, Whiting had been expecting Bragg but was still gravely disappointed when he showed up. "I do not know what he was sent to Wilmington for. I had hoped that I was considered competent," Whiting confided to Lee. "I acquiesced with feelings of great mortification." Colonel William Lamb, Fort Fisher's commander and Whiting's protégé, was also chagrined by the change in leadership. "This was a bitter disappointment to my command, who felt that no one was so capable of defending the Cape Fear as the brilliant officer who had given so much of his time and ability for its defense."[26]

Soon after assuming command, Bragg reported to the president that Whiting seemed "much worried and disconcerted," yet "very industrious and zealous, and deeply interested in the success of his labors here." Indeed, the strength and condition of Wilmington's defenses, which Bragg toured with Whiting, were "judiciously located and well constructed. They are prepared to oppose a powerful resistance to any naval attack, and will hold any considerable land force in check for a considerable time, if the garrisons will do their duty," he told Lee. So as not to wound the deposed Whiting's pride too much, Bragg retained him "as second in command, in discharge of his former functions of administration and detail."[27]

Despite having expended so much time and energy preparing for an attack, Whiting apparently failed to persuade Bragg of Wilmington's utmost significance to the Confederacy, and Bragg expressed little confidence. "If the harbor is lost, [it] can only be recovered by means much greater than would suffice to hold it," he suggested to Lee. "Whether the importance of the harbor is such as to justify the withdrawal of means from other points, also endangered, or whether our information leads to the conclusion that this point is the one to be assailed, your own judgment can best decide."[28]

Perhaps Governor Vance sensed Bragg's seeming indifference when he wrote Davis about another officer with a more vested interest in the fate of the Tar Heel State. Although his earlier request for Beauregard to supersede Whiting at Wilmington had been declined, Vance now asked Davis to give a command in the eastern part of the state to Major General Daniel Harvey Hill, "an officer whose abilities in the field are highly esteemed in North Carolina." Davis forwarded Vance's letter to Lee for advice. "General Hill is brave, watchful, and patriotic, [but] I think while General Bragg is at Wilmington he had better be in command of that whole district, and have so recommended to the Secretary of War," Lee responded. "I fear there may be a want of harmony between the two." With Davis' wholehearted approval of Lee's recommendation, Secretary Seddon assigned Bragg to lead the Department of North Carolina, a responsibility the general officially assumed on November 17, 1864.[29]

Unlike Bragg, at least according to his critics, Seddon appreciated Wilmington's "very great" importance to the Confederacy. As the Union threat to the seaport increased in the autumn of 1864, the Confederate high command debated its significance compared to that of Richmond. "I am reluctant to contemplate the consequences which would follow from the loss of the capital or to estimate the relative expediency of endangering either," Seddon observed. "I submit the propriety of sending more forces to Wilmington to the better judgment of the general commanding." While Lee agreed to dispatch any troops the secretary might direct, he believed they were as much needed around Petersburg and Richmond as at Wilmington at present. "It is the want all over the country," Lee acknowledged. The difference between Richmond and Wilmington was that three times as many Federal troops were engaged in the siege of the capital as troops defending it. "There is no enemy as yet on the shores of Wilmington," he pointed out. "To attack it, troops must be drawn from elsewhere, when I trust re-enforcements can be sent from the point from which the pressure is relieved. In the meantime, the North Carolina troops, brave as any in the Confederacy, if all are brought out that can be and properly organized and instructed, are capable of protecting it."[30]

If intelligence sources were correct about a forthcoming Union strike on Wilmington, many more troops than the approximately five thousand mostly Tar Heel soldiers, including "Home Guards" and Senior Reserves, now garrisoning the forts, batteries, and lines of defenses would be needed to safeguard it. "What has been so long threatened and so much talked about seems to have come at last," reported the *Wilmington Daily Journal*. "The long deferred attack on Wilmington would appear to be at hand."[31]

Secretary of the Navy Welles exploited Farragut's victory at Mobile Bay to convince Lincoln of the necessity of going after the Tar Heel seaport. "Could we seize the forts at the entrance of Cape Fear and close the illicit traffic," he argued, "it would be almost as important as the capture of Richmond and a step in that direction." Lincoln now concurred, recognizing that its fall would both sever the Confederacy's principal maritime trade route and pacify northern shippers and merchants who were pressuring the administration to combat Wilmington-based commerce raiders. The CSS *Tallahassee* and CSS *Chickamauga* had wreaked considerable damage to merchant marine vessels off the north Atlantic coast that summer.[32]

A quick victory at Wilmington might also reap political benefits for the president by reigniting popular support from war-weary Northerners. Things were so bad on the battlefront in mid-1864 that Lincoln predicted he would not be re-elected in November unless the tide of war turned more favorably for the Union. His popular Democratic opponent, George B. McClellan, the former U.S. Army commander whom Lincoln had dismissed from the service in 1862 for poor leadership, posed a stiff challenge. Political considerations aside, Lincoln deferred final approval of a campaign against Wilmington to the new U.S. Army commander Lieutenant General Ulysses S. Grant, in whose judgment about such matters he placed great faith.

Grant initially expressed little enthusiasm for Welles's proposal to attack Wilmington, as it would require him to provide a large expeditionary force to assist the navy. In his opinion he needed more soldiers to maintain the pressure on Lee. Since the late spring of 1864, Grant's operational forces—the Army of the Potomac and the Army of the James—had been battling Lee's Army of Northern Virginia for possession of Petersburg and Richmond. As the summer wore on, the fighting at Petersburg had devolved into a stalemate that neither side had been able to break. Grant's repeated frontal assaults against Lee's vastly outmanned but strongly entrenched army, followed by efforts to outflank his defenses, gained little ground and came at a great cost in blood and lives. Like two angry fighting dogs, the opposing armies were locked in mortal combat with no end in sight.

Hunger, attrition, and desertion began taking a heavy toll on "Lee's Miserables," as the gray-clad soldiers sometimes grimly referred to themselves. Lee's lifeline through Wilmington, however, provided just enough sustenance to keep most of them hunkered down in the trenches. Lee warned that if Wilmington fell, he "could not maintain his army" and would have to evacuate his position. "If Lee's army can be fed—as long as it can be fed—Richmond is safe," asserted diarist Jones. "Its abandonment will be the loss of Virginia, and perhaps the cause." Clearly, the survival of the Confederacy depended upon the survival of the Army of Northern Virginia, and the survival of the Army of Northern Virginia depended largely upon the survival of Wilmington as a blockade running seaport.[33]

Welles argued that the deadlock in Virginia could be broken by closing Wilmington to blockade running, thus denying Lee's army its desperately needed supplies. Grant, however, did not believe he could afford to dispatch the estimated ten thousand troops for an attack 240 miles away on the North Carolina coast. He eventually came around, agreeing to supply troops "when the time was right."[34]

When an attack on Wilmington had not materialized by late November, Davis requested General Bragg meet a more immediate threat. If local affairs permitted, he was to assemble all available forces and proceed to Augusta, Georgia, to try to stem General Sherman's advance. After occupying and destroying Atlanta in September 1864, Sherman cut his communication and supply lines to march his force of sixty thousand men across the state to Savannah on the Atlantic coast. Davis wanted Bragg to reinforce the forces of Beauregard, William J. Hardee, and Richard Taylor to prevent the Confederacy from being further dismembered. After turning over command of the department to Whiting, Bragg departed Wilmington on November 23 with 2,700 "of the best troops" from Fort Fisher and Fort Holmes. For his part, Whiting was glad to have been restored to his old command, if only temporarily, and although greatly depleted of defenders, he believed the reported attack on Wilmington would be delayed until Sherman reached the sea.[35]

Sherman's rapidly advancing army cut a swath of destruction across Georgia, and Confederate forces, unable to halt the juggernaut, soon conceded loss of the state. "Sherman may possess the land at pleasure," Jones penned in his diary. With the capture of Savannah now seemingly inevitable, Davis determined to protect the Carolinas and Virginia. Under the circumstances, he thought it best for Bragg to return to Wilmington where he would be "more useful to the public defense than any longer continuance at Augusta." Therefore, Bragg resumed his command of the Department of North Carolina on December 17. Diarist Jones saw things differently, believing Davis needed to get Bragg out of Augusta for political reasons as much as anything. "Gen. Bragg will be crucified by the enemies of the President for staying at Augusta while Sherman made his triumphant march through Georgia," he wrote. "So ends Gen. Bragg's campaign against Sherman."[36]

Bragg's return coincided with the arrival of a massive Federal fleet off Fort Fisher. The attack so long feared had finally come. In preparing for Wilmington's defense, Bragg assumed the immediate command of all the troops in and about the city as well as its defenses, in addition to his administrative duties as head of the Department of North Carolina. Whiting quickly repaired to the point of attack at Fort Fisher as a volunteer adviser and combatant, but left Colonel Lamb in command of the fort. He, like many Southerners, felt great apprehension about the coming battle and its consequences. The prevailing supposition in Richmond, at least, was that if Wilmington fell, the capital would be next. "Between Bragg and Lee, Sherman and Grant, old North Carolina is in a pretty fix," Whiting confided to one of his officers. Jones wrote that Confederate authorities "hoped that Gen. Bragg [would] do more than chronicle the success of the enemy this time."[37]

Commanding the Union naval task force off Fort Fisher was Rear Admiral David Dixon Porter, an authoritative, ambitious, and acerbic fifty-one-year-old veteran of sea service. A scion of professional naval officers, Porter had won his laurels fighting on the Mississippi River, quickly emerging as one of the navy's best and brightest. He led a mortar flotilla in the capture of New Orleans in April 1862 and headed the Mississippi Squadron in the taking of Vicksburg in July 1863. Porter cooperated closely with Grant and Sherman in the Vicksburg Campaign, which Grant professed "could not have been successfully made" without the navy's able assistance. Porter remained as head of the Mississippi Squadron until he was ordered east to assume command of the North Atlantic Blockading Squadron in early October 1864.

In assigning Porter to lead the North Atlantic Blockading Squadron, Welles rejected S. Phillips Lee, who had headed the squadron for two years, as too "timid and cautious" for the hard duty required to take the strongly defended seaport of Wilmington. Welles had initially offered the command to Farragut, but the rear admiral turned him down, explaining that the long, hard campaigning in the Gulf had left him exhausted and desperately in need of some "shore rest." After carefully considering other worthy candidates, Welles concluded Porter was "probably the best man for the service." Arriving at squadron headquarters in Hampton Roads, Virginia, in mid-October 1864, the admiral selected sixty-four warships, including five well-armed steam frigates and the USS *New Ironsides,* the navy's strongest ironclad vessel, to attack the target—Fort Fisher.[38]

To complement Porter's fleet, the largest assembled during the war, Grant detached a 6,500-man expeditionary force led by Major General Godfrey Weitzel, former chief engineer in the Army of the James, but now commander of the 25th Army Corps. Grant's instructions to Weitzel called for him to assist the navy in capturing Fort Fisher and closing New Inlet, the favored entryway into the Cape Fear River for blockade-runners trading at Wilmington. Much to Grant's chagrin, Weitzel's superior officer, Major General Benjamin F. Butler, decided to accompany the army and in effect take over command. Bad blood existed between Porter and Butler, going back to the New Orleans expedition in 1862 where they had argued over Porter's role in the Crescent City's capture. They intensely disliked each other, and the acrimonious relationship did not bode well for the success of such an important mission at the Cape Fear.

Informed of the enemy's arrival off Wilmington, Lee immediately dispatched one of his largest divisions, more than 6,400 troops under Major General Robert F. Hoke, to help defend the life-sustaining seaport. Leaving Petersburg on December 21, 1864, the gray-jacketed reinforcements traveled slowly but surely by rail toward southeastern North Carolina.

The Federals initiated their attack early on Christmas Eve morning, with a powder ship as the novel feature of their strategy. Convinced that a giant floating bomb could blow down the sand walls of the mighty stronghold, Butler had packed a steamship, the USS *Louisiana,* with 215 tons of gunpowder planning to detonate it close by the fort. Such an experiment had not been attempted before, but Butler was convinced it would work and revolutionize warfare against harbor defenses, for which he could claim credit. The admiral tried to steal Butler's thunder by deploying the *Louisiana* to its task before the army commander arrived. A party of volunteer sailors towed it toward shore, anchored it, and set the timing devices. But instead of exploding simultaneously, the casks of gunpowder blew up haphazardly causing no damage whatsoever to the fort. Confederate sentinels reported to Colonel Lamb that a blockade-runner must have run aground and been sabotaged by its captain and crew rather than allow it to be captured.

When the powder ship turned out to be a dud, Porter blamed Butler for wasting valuable time, money, and energy on such a preposterous idea. Determined to reduce Fort Fisher the old-fashioned way, Porter then unleashed a massive naval bombardment, the likes of which had never been seen before. During the daylight hours of December 24–25, 1864, his warships fired unremittingly at the sand bastion. Nevertheless, the stout Confederate defenses and defenders held their own.[39]

Having learned that his ambitious project had gone awry, Butler was in no mood to cooperate with his nemesis when he finally reached the Cape Fear late on Christmas Eve. The following morning, he put only a third of his infantry ashore to assault Fort Fisher. They met no resistance from Hoke's Division, only one brigade of which had even reached Wilmington. Weitzel personally led a reconnaissance force down the beach toward the fort, but soon reported that Porter's bombardment, despite the severity, had not damaged the imposing works or armament enough to warrant a sure-to-be-bloody frontal assault. Butler needed only the slenderest of reasons to abort the mission, and so he withdrew his troops and sailed back to Virginia. His precipitous departure left six hundred of his soldiers behind on shore; stranded by heavy rains and cold winds, they endured two days before the navy finally rescued them.[40]

An aggressive advance under the cover of darkness might well have captured the marooned men, but Bragg made no attempt. His inaction angered Whiting and Lamb, who observed the weather-beaten Federal troops dug in along the beachfront only two miles above Fort Fisher. At his headquarters in Wilmington, Bragg bided his time waiting for Hoke's reinforcements to show up. Their arrival held up by deteriorating transportation, Bragg blamed the railroads for the "criminal delays," continuing with the somewhat ironic observation that "no army can be supported and no cause sustained where such imbecility obtains."[41]

In the meantime, Bragg had sent his wife away by "special train" on the Wilmington & Weldon Railroad, which alarmed city residents and reportedly provoked a general exodus. He also made plans to abandon the forts at Old Inlet in case Fort Fisher fell. "Should it become necessary to evacuate Fort Fisher, Forts Holmes, Caswell, and Campbell must be abandoned also," he declared. Bragg's fall back scheme infuriated Whiting, who considered it symbolically weak and pessimistic. The departmental commander, on the other hand, saw it as a necessary contingency plan. It all came to nothing as the Confederates emerged victorious in the first battle of Fort Fisher, but portended badly for Wilmington's survival.[42]

Fort Fisher had withstood the greatest naval bombardment in history. Those who had witnessed it would never forget it and insisted that those who had not could never truly appreciate the ferocity, grandeur, and excitement of it. "Such a rain of shot and shell never before fell upon any spot of earth since gunpowder was invented," one war correspondent reported. The Federal fleet had unleashed at least 20,271 projectiles against the fort—one shell every two seconds, or fifteen shells per defender—during the bombardment. Whiting asserted that "it was, no doubt, the most terrific of any war yet known." Heavy as the bombardment had been, Fort Fisher still stood and Wilmington remained open to trade with the outside world. On the night of December 27, the *Wild Rover* ran the blockade into New Inlet, followed closely by the *Banshee* early the following morning, both steamships carrying vital supplies for Lee's army.[43]

Wilmingtonians rejoiced over the news of the Confederate victory at Fort Fisher. Many of them credited Bragg for spoiling the Federal attack—perhaps because Bragg and his buddies claimed as much—and they showered him with praise. He received similar accolades from the media. "General Bragg is about the best abused man in the country, or rather has been, and yet this abused man is a brave soldier, a pure patriot, and a skillful general," wrote the editor of the *Wilmington Daily Journal*. "We remember the sneer of some Virginia papers when General Bragg was sent to this point and yet when the attack came, his conduct and bearing justified the confidence of the whole community." As a token of their appreciation, a group of admirers presented Bragg with a brand new gray wool uniform adorned with fancy gold braid. In his own show of appreciation to Colonel Lamb and his garrison for their success, Bragg visited Fort Fisher on December 27–28 and then returned a week later with a group from the Ladies Relief Society for a picnic.[44]

Both Whiting and Lamb realized that they had been fortunate to have prevailed. Yet neither harbored any illusions about having seen the last of the Yankees. "It can scarcely be possible that after such extraordinary preparations the enemy has altogether abandoned, or even long postponed, his designs upon this port," Whiting informed the secretary of war. General Lee also chimed in, noting that information he received made him "think it probable the attack on Wilmington will be renewed."[45]

Bragg did not share Whiting and Lee's anxiety about another strike. Having received reports that Porter's armada had sailed for Beaufort, North Carolina, he believed the Federals had given up their plans for taking Wilmington. Even so, Whiting asked Bragg to keep Hoke's Division, or at least a portion of it, near Fort Fisher. Reaching Wilmington on Christmas Day, Brigadier General William W. Kirkland's Brigade had been rushed to Confederate Point to man a strong line of earthen fieldworks around Sugar Loaf Hill only four-and-a-half miles north of the fort. Whiting believed its appearance had been largely responsible for the enemy's retreat and would do much to deter another assault. Bragg disagreed and on New Year's Eve withdrew Kirkland's Brigade and a contingent of Senior Reserves from Sugar Loaf to reunite them with Hoke's remaining three brigades that finally pulled into Wilmington. They were now bivouacked at Camp Whiting, half-a-mile east of the city. With colors flying and bands playing, Kirkland's troops marched through the town where the people enthusiastically received them as "their victorious defenders."[46]

Whiting seethed over Bragg's actions. A fellow officer begged him not to get into a quarrel with the commanding general. "We must bear with all," he cautioned, but Whiting's flinty temperament soon bristled against Bragg as it had Davis, Lee, and Vance previously. When Whiting "respectfully requested that all movements and dispositions of troops in this district for the defense of the Cape Fear . . . will be communicated to and through me," Bragg lashed out at him for overstepping his authority. Writing on Bragg's behalf, an assistant adjutant general shot back: "He regrets to have to call your attention to the tenor and language of that communication as neither respectful nor subordinate from a junior to his commanding officer." In response, Whiting lamented "that the commanding general should place so harsh a construction upon my language." The dispute dissipated, but the two officers were hardly reconciled.[47]

As for the Federals, the failed combined operation to take Fort Fisher sparked a firestorm of controversy that led to Butler's dismissal from command of the Union Department of Southeastern Virginia and North Carolina, and a Congressional investigation into why the campaign had gone so badly. While politicians wrangled, Grant got serious about capturing Wilmington. Although indifferent to the first expedition, the commanding general's interest now intensified.

The Federal defeat at Fort Fisher was offset by the capture of Savannah by Sherman's forces on December 21, 1864. The cocksure Sherman presented the city to President Lincoln as a Christmas gift. For his part, Grant was glad to see Sherman safely on the coast and eager to transfer his large army by sea to Virginia for a final push against Lee's forces. But Sherman had other plans, proposing instead to march his soldiers overland to the Old Dominion by way of the Carolinas, destroying supply depots and railroads and "smash things generally" along the way, as he had done so effectively in Georgia. Once he reached North Carolina, he could "make a bee-line" for Raleigh or Weldon on the Wilmington & Weldon Railroad, placing his forces in an advantageous position to strike the beleaguered Army of Northern Virginia. "Then the game is up with Lee," Sherman predicted, since his advance would force Lee away from Petersburg and into open country where the two commanding Union generals together could trap him in a pincer movement. If need be, Sherman could attack Wilmington from the rear or retreat to the coast in case he found himself in trouble. Indeed, neither he nor Grant knew what kind of opposition Sherman might face in the Tar Heel State.[48]

Sherman's ambitious plan and his confidence in it pleased Grant. The crowning benefit might well be the collapse of the Confederacy. At the very least the commanding general believed that a successful campaign would keep the South and its armies in disarray. Grant wrote to Sherman on December 27, 1864, authorizing him to "make preparations to start on your Northern expedition without delay. Break up the rail-roads in South & North Carolina and join the Armies operating against Richmond as soon as you can."[49]

Having agreed to Sherman's bold Carolinas Campaign, as historians call it, Grant determined to guarantee its success by furnishing his army with provisions, supplies, and reinforcements, as well as a haven on the seacoast halfway between Savannah and Petersburg in case Sherman needed to retreat. Wilmington now took on a whole new meaning for Grant. Possession of the Cape Fear River and the city's three railroads would best enable him to assist Sherman's army.

To cooperate with the contentious Porter, Grant assigned the capable but affable Brigadier General Alfred Howe Terry, respected commander of the newly formed 24th Army Corps in the Army of the James, to command the Wilmington expeditionary force. Terry's Provisional Corps, as it was officially designated for the campaign, comprised the same handpicked troops from Butler's ill-fated expedition: Brigadier General Adelbert Ames's Second Division, 24th Army Corps, and two brigades of U.S. Colored Troops, 25th Army Corps, commanded by Brigadier General Charles J. Paine. Terry also took along his old unit, the 2nd Brigade, First Division, 24th Army Corps. Together with artillery and support personnel, the increased force numbered about 9,600 officers and men. Terry's transports and Porter's warships, slightly scaled down to fifty-eight in number, reached Fort Fisher late on the night of January 12, 1865.[50]

From his vantage point atop the fort's ramparts, Colonel Lamb watched the twinkling lights of the great armada as the ships appeared one by one. The dreaded fleet had returned, and headquarters in Wilmington had not warned Lamb of its approach down the coast as he expected. Instead it fell to Lamb to notify Bragg that the enemy had come back. "When the news came up at midnight that the fleet had again appeared," one Confederate noted, "the band of Hoke's Division was in town serenading, the officers were visiting, and the men scattered about—Bragg, no doubt, asleep in fancied security." Informed of Lamb's telegraph, Bragg quickly dispatched orders for one brigade of Hoke's Division to travel by steamboat to Sugar Loaf and the others to march there at once.[51]

While Porter's warships renewed their bombardment of Fort Fisher early on the morning of January 13, 1865, Terry's infantry landed without opposition. Hoke's brigades arrived on Confederate Point during the day, but too late to contest the Union troops as they came ashore and who were now entrenching about halfway between Sugar Loaf and Fort Fisher. "It seems incomprehensible that Gen. Bragg should have allowed the Federal troops, on both attacks, to have made a frolic of their landing on the soil of North Carolina," Colonel Lamb railed. "Six thousand soldiers from Lee's army within call, and no one sent to meet the invader and drive him from the soil."[52]

Hoke's absence and Bragg's unpreparedness also enraged Whiting, who boarded a steamboat and headed downriver to rejoin Lamb and his men at Fort Fisher on the afternoon of January 13. Upon his arrival, Whiting greeted Lamb with a stunning comment: "Lamb, my boy, I have come to share your fate. You and your garrison are to be sacrificed." He told his protégé that when he left Wilmington, Bragg and his staff were discussing a line of retreat from the area. "Don't say so, General," Lamb replied, "we shall certainly whip the enemy again."[53]

After positioning his troops over the following two days, during which the fleet shelled the fort continuously in what turned out to be the second largest bombardment of the war, Terry launched the infantry attack late on the afternoon of January 15. Ames's division took the lead. A landing party of more than twenty-two hundred volunteer sailors and U.S. Marines from various ships in Porter's fleet also participated in the ground action.

The Confederate defenders, personally led by Lamb and Whiting, rushed from their underground bombproofs, where the enemy's intense bombardment had forced them to take refuge, to meet the ground assault. They succeeded in turning back the poorly-armed and disorganized naval column that had advanced along the beachfront, but soon became locked in hand-to-hand combat with Ames's troops, who soon secured a lodgment on and inside the fort. The savage, close-quarters fighting raged for more than five hours before the heavily outnumbered, outgunned, and exhausted Southerners were driven from the fort. At 10 P.M. on January 15, with both Lamb and Whiting seriously wounded, about two thousand men of the garrison surrendered.[54]

The battle's outcome might have turned out differently had General Bragg been aggressive. Throughout the battle, Whiting sent urgent telegraphs to Bragg's field headquarters at Sugar Loaf, pleading with him to send reinforcements to the fort or to strike the Federal army with Hoke's Division. "The enemy are assaulting us by land and sea. Their infantry outnumber us," Whiting telegraphed Bragg shortly after Union troops entered the fort. "Can't you help us?" A little later Whiting informed Bragg that the Confederates still held the fort, but were "sorely pressed." "Can't you assist us from the outside?" he wanted to know.[55]

Bragg had made only a halfhearted attempt to reinforce Fort Fisher by sending troops down the Cape Fear River about sunrise on the morning of January 15. Fewer than five hundred soldiers of Brigadier General Johnson Hagood's Brigade of fifteen hundred South Carolinians had landed before heavy cannon fire from Union gunboats on the ocean side drove off the troop transport. Bragg later claimed that Hoke made a "heavy demonstration" upon the enemy's entrenched line below Sugar Loaf with the brigades of Kirkland and Thomas L. Clingman, but found them "in a very strong position and force ready to receive them." According to Bragg's official report, Hoke had personally advanced with his skirmishers close to the Federal position and was fired upon, taking two minié balls in his coat. Hoke deemed a full-scale assault "impracticable" with his "small command," and Bragg concurred, insisting that "he could not have succeeded." They made no other attempt to support the fort by dispatching additional reinforcements or attacking the rear of the Federal army. Instead, the man Jefferson Davis had personally sent to save Wilmington kept Hoke's soldiers sitting on their rifle-muskets within striking distance of the enemy.[56]

In a telegraph to the president, Bragg described the fall of Fort Fisher as an "unexpected blow." "The defense of the fort ought to have been successful against this attack," he maintained. To his credit, he held himself accountable, saying: "The responsibility is all mine, and I shall bear it as resolutely as possible." Yet the commanding officer in whom the Confederacy's chief executive had placed so much faith in safeguarding the Confederacy's lifeline also stated that Fort Fisher's capture was inevitable. "It had to fall eventually," Bragg declared rather indifferently in a letter to his brother Thomas a few days after the battle. In his mind, neither he nor anyone else could have prevented the outcome. "Blockade running has cured itself. I knew its demoralizing influence, and even before I came here, had urged on the President to remove these officers and troops, replacing them by veterans. . . . I was at work on these evils, gradually correcting them, but meeting with the usual denunciation. Time was not allowed . . . the expedition brought against [Fort Fisher] was able to reduce it in spite of all I could do."[57]

After receiving the shocking news about Fort Fisher, both Davis and Lee implored Bragg to counterattack. "Can you retake the fort?" Davis asked. "If anything is to be done you will appreciate the necessity of its being attempted without a moment's delay." Bragg refused to consider the idea, fearful that the enemy's warships alone would destroy his assaulting force before it reached the fort. His abandonment of Fort Fisher raised howls of protest from both soldiers and civilians alike, but they fell on deaf ears. They did succeed, however, in confirming Bragg's reputation for not being "a fighting general." "I am not given to croaking about our generals, but I must say I think the blame of the fall of Fort Fisher rests on [Bragg's] shoulders," asserted one Confederate officer. "The enemy should have been attacked by Hoke whether he could carry the works or not. [We] have no confidence in Gen'l Bragg."[58]

Colonel Lamb also expressed indignation over Bragg's inaction. "No assault could have succeeded under a competent commander," he stated. "The fort was treated with utter neglect by the Commanding General." Whiting expressed even greater anger in a letter written from his prison cell at Fort

Columbus on Governor's Island, New York. "That I am here, and that Wilmington and Fisher are gone, is due wholly and solely to the incompetency, the imbecility and the pusillanimity of Braxton Bragg," he maintained. In his official report, Whiting contended that

> the result might have been avoided, and Fort Fisher still held, if the commanding general had done his duty.
>
> I charge him with this loss; with neglect of duty. . . .
>
> I charge him, further, with making no effort whatever to create a diversion, in favor of the beleaguered garrison, during the three days' battle, by attacking the enemy; though that was to be expected.

Whiting demanded that the Confederate government investigate Bragg, "in justice to the country, to the army, and to myself." It was the wish of a dying man fighting for a dying cause. Less than two months after the fall of Fort Fisher, Whiting died as a prisoner of war from complications of his wounds.[59]

Reports of Fort Fisher's capture and the closure of blockade running at Wilmington spread quickly across the South. "The news of the fall of Wilmington, and the cessation at that port, falls upon the ears of [Richmond] with stunning effect," declared Jones in his diary. "We thought the port of Wilmington was to be kept open," the editor of the *Wilmington Daily North Carolinian* declared. "President Davis knew its value; Gen. Lee felt its worth. Why was not a sufficient force sent to prevent its fall?" Confederate Vice President Alexander Stephens proclaimed that "the fall of this fort was one of the greatest disasters which had befallen our Cause from the beginning of the war." Francis Lawley, an English journalist covering the war for the London-based newspaper *The Times*, reported that Fort Fisher's capture produced in the Confederacy "a mingled feeling of dismay and indignation against President Davis and his Administration at Richmond."[60]

Bragg's incompetence played into the hands of his Union opponents, and they now had a good foothold in the Cape Fear. They soon aimed their gun sights at Wilmington with plans to assist General Sherman's march through the Carolinas to attack the underbelly of Lee's beleaguered army in Virginia. News of the Union victory at Fort Fisher cheered Sherman. "The capture of Fort Fisher has a most important bearing on my campaign and I rejoice in it for many reasons, because of its intrinsic importance and because it gives me another point of security on the seaboard," Sherman told Grant. "I hope General Terry [and Admiral Porter] will follow it up by the capture of Wilmington."[61]

Having sacrificed Fort Fisher ostensibly to save Wilmington, General Bragg now chose to abandon the forts at the mouth of the Cape Fear River as no longer worth defending. Wilmington-bound blockade-runners that entered through Old Inlet could not proceed upstream more than a few miles now that Union forces controlled both Fort Fisher and New Inlet.

Bragg immediately ordered the garrisons at the lower forts to withdraw upriver. Although unwilling to adequately support Fort Fisher, the department head now committed to halting any further enemy advance by establishing a new defensive line anchored at Sugar Loaf on the east side of the Cape Fear River and Fort Anderson on the west. Shocked by the loss of Fort Fisher and Bragg's inaction during the battle, despondent Tar Heel soldiers evacuated Fort Holmes on Bald Head Island on January 16, 1865, and Fort Caswell and its auxiliary works on Oak Island the following day. The departing soldiers burned barracks and warehouses and blew up magazines. Fort Caswell suffered extensive damage when ordnance personnel detonated one hundred thousand pounds of gunpowder.

Together with the garrison from Fort Pender at Smithville, the troops withdrew to Fort Anderson, where they joined the small garrison of North Carolinians and the bulk of Hagood's Brigade, which had been sent there after its ill-fated attempt to reinforce Fort Fisher. "We are now here at Fort Anderson, what is left of us, and it is said we are going to make a stand here," wrote Captain William Henry Tripp of the 40th Regiment North Carolina Troops.[62]

The capture of Fort Fisher and the abandonment of the forts at the mouth of the river allowed the Federals to quickly gain control of the Cape Fear estuary. By the afternoon of January 16 the USS *Tacony* and the USS *Sassacus* had bumped their way through New Inlet and turned their bows upriver. Other vessels followed in their wake. The navy also seized two unsuspecting blockade-runners—the *Charlotte* and *Stag*—that were unaware of Wilmington's closure and entered the river through Old Inlet in the early morning hours of January 20.[63]

Porter assembled a flotilla of about thirty ships on the Cape Fear River. Gunboats soon began shelling both Fort Anderson and Sugar Loaf to draw their fire as they attempted to harass the enemy and learn the number of cannons they had. On January 19, they bombarded Sugar Loaf in support of a reconnaissance in force by Terry's corps. Terry failed to breach Hoke's lines but came away with a good idea of their strength. While the Union navy probed the Confederate river defenses, the army sent out patrols from Smithville, which Union forces occupied on January 18, to reconnoiter the Brunswick County roads leading toward Fort Anderson.

From a military standpoint, Wilmington still retained some importance after its closure as the Confederacy's last major blockade running seaport. Bragg's army distracted the attention of a sizable Union corps that would otherwise be battling General Lee's army in Virginia. While Lee could ill-afford to leave Hoke's Division at the Cape Fear, its presence there might prove beneficial. At the very least, Wilmington needed to be held until government stores and property could be removed to Raleigh as a place of safety. More importantly, Richmond instructed Bragg to do everything in his power to keep Terry's Provisional Corps in check at the Cape Fear to prevent it from reinforcing Sherman. "If Wilmington was abandoned to-morrow, Sherman's road would be open to form the intended junction with Grant," claimed one strategist. "In a very few days he could have a supporting force here on the Cape Fear River." It was imperative that Hagood hold Fort Anderson, and Hoke the Sugar Loaf lines. Bragg informed Richmond that Wilmington would be held "so long as our means enable us."[64]

By late January 1865, Grant was so intent on capturing the Carolina seaport that he left the Virginia battlefront and traveled to the Cape Fear to confer with Porter and Terry about the best way of accomplishing it. Accompanying him were Assistant Secretary of the Navy Gustavus V. Fox and Major General John McAllister Schofield, commander of the 23rd Army Corps, Army of the Ohio. For several hours on the night of January 28, the five men studied maps and charts of the Cape Fear region on board Porter's flagship, the USS *Malvern.* Grant explained that he wanted to open the railways between the North Carolina coast and Goldsboro in order to meet Sherman with reinforcements and supplies once he entered the state.[65]

For his part, Sherman was ready to invade the Carolinas targeting Columbia, South Carolina, and then Fayetteville, North Carolina, both of which contained Confederate arsenals. Sherman's objective, however, was Goldsboro, the capture of which would be advantageous for three main reasons. First, the city was the junction of two major lines of transportation and communication—the Wilmington & Weldon Railroad and the Atlantic & North Carolina Railroad to Morehead City and New Bern. Second, from Goldsboro Sherman could strike Raleigh where Confederate supplies from Wilmington were being sent. Third, Sherman's occupation of Goldsboro would threaten Lee's army in Virginia and compel the enemy to evacuate Wilmington. "If Lee lets us get [Goldsboro], he is gone up," Sherman predicted. "[From there] I can easily take Raleigh, when it seems Lee must come out of his trenches or allow his army to be absolutely invested."[66]

After consulting with his "war committee," Grant agreed that Wilmington offered the best route for making contact with Sherman at Goldsboro. New Bern possessed a deeper harbor more favorable for a supply base, but the Atlantic & North Carolina Railroad needed extensive repairs. Grant assumed that the presence of Bragg's army at the Cape Fear indicated that Wilmington's three rail lines—the Wilmington & Weldon, the Wilmington & Manchester, and the Wilmington, Charlotte & Rutherford—were still operational. A bold strike might capture them before the Confederates could remove locomotives and cars or destroy the rails and trestles. Terry's occupation of Fort Fisher gave Sherman a haven on the seacoast in case he had to retreat, but Wilmington would make an ideal supply depot and a place to concentrate troops south of Goldsboro if need be. Grant therefore considered "the capture of Wilmington of the greatest importance."[67]

Having reconnoitered the defenses guarding Wilmington's approaches for more than a week now, Porter and Terry suggested advancing against the city by way of Fort Anderson. "There is only one important work between us and Wilmington—Fort Anderson, which is very strong," Porter pointed out. Nevertheless, the mainland of Brunswick County on the west side of the Cape Fear River, would offer the army more space to maneuver than the narrow peninsula on the east bank. Porter and Terry's plan for attacking Fort Anderson was pretty straightforward. While Porter's warships bombarded the main artillery batteries along the riverfront, the army could make a frontal assault against the fort's center or attempt to outflank it by going around Orton Pond, a five-mile long freshwater lake on the fort's far west end. Just as at Fort Fisher, cooperation between the navy and army forces would be crucial to capturing the Brunswick stronghold. Grant liked the plan. "It is the best and only thing to be done," he stated emphatically.[68]

According to Porter, the campaign to capture Fort Anderson and Wilmington would require at least thirteen thousand soldiers, about forty-five hundred more than Terry commanded in the vicinity of Fort Fisher. "[Wilmington] is too important a place for the rebels to give up without a struggle for it," Porter stated. Terry's Provisional Corps had suffered more than one thousand casualties in the recent battle, diminishing its numbers to approximately eighty-five hundred men. Grant had already prepared for such a contingency by transferring Schofield's 23rd Army Corps, about twenty-one thousand troops, from Tennessee to Alexandria, Virginia. He planned to use Schofield's men to either support Terry at the Cape Fear or reinforce Sherman. Grant now concluded that there was greater need in North Carolina, so he ordered Schofield to bring his corps to the state as quickly as possible. Grant was back in Virginia by January 30, and the following day requested the War Department to assign Schofield as commander of the newly created Department of North Carolina.[69]

As Schofield prepared his campaign against Wilmington, Sherman advanced northward from Savannah on February 1, 1865. After a brief delay due to cold temperatures, Schofield's Third Division, commanded by Major General Jacob D. Cox, set sail from Virginia in early February. At the same time, the army sent Brigadier General Thomas F. Meagher's Provisional Division to bolster the occupation forces at New Bern under Brigadier General Innis N. Palmer for an advance toward Goldsboro from that direction. The remainder of the 23rd Army Corps shipped out in the following two weeks as transports and the weather permitted.[70]

The massive Union build up on Confederate Point, and in eastern North Carolina generally, greatly concerned General Bragg. He told Governor Vance that he believed the concentration of enemy forces indicated an impending advance against both Wilmington and Raleigh. Bragg urged the governor to forward all the troops he could muster for Wilmington's defense. In the meantime, he quietly began removing both government and private property from Wilmington and threatened to destroy cotton, tobacco, naval stores, and other commodities that would be of use or value to the enemy. He also imposed a blackout of military news, refusing to publicly discuss affairs at Fort Anderson and Sugar Loaf. The policy of silence frustrated the families and friends of soldiers stationed at those points who wanted desperately to hear something more than wild rumors on the streets and the rumbling of cannon fire downriver. "Is it a military necessity to keep our people ignorant of every occurrence connected with their interests?" asked the editor of the *Wilmington Daily North Carolinian*. "The stereotyped phraseology of 'all quiet below' will have no effect on us. We place no confidence in such reports."[71]

Bragg maintained his strict silence, but the disapproving glances he got from residents as he walked about the city bothered him. His next move fanned the flames of their discontent even higher. As if indifferent to Wilmington's fate, Bragg temporarily relinquished field command to Major General Hoke on February 10 and boarded a train for Richmond. From a public relations standpoint, the trip was an untimely disaster. Public opinion of Bragg plummeted, as more and more citizens came to see him as an incompetent leader with a poor sense of judgment and duty. The general's explanation—that the high command had summoned him to Richmond to reorganize his staff—did not assuage their suspicions of him leaving at such a critical hour. In his defense, he had requested a postponement to the meeting.[72]

To most Wilmingtonians, Bragg's departure seemed more like an excuse for him to remove himself from harm's way, and they viewed it as a sign that he planned to abandon Wilmington as he had Fort Fisher. In early January 1865, citizens had presented Bragg with a new, beautifully tailored uniform to show their appreciation for the successful defense of Fort Fisher during the Christmas battle, but now they realized how wrong they had been to have placed such faith in him. Lieutenant Zaccheus Ellis of the 1st Battalion North Carolina Light Artillery spoke for soldiers and civilians alike when he said that both "have no confidence whatever in Gen'l Bragg." Another critic remarked that "General Bragg's presence has been felt as a harbinger of disaster, an omen of impending evil—like a dark, cold, dreary cloud."[73]

The same day that Bragg left for Richmond, Schofield, Cox, and Terry met with Porter in a council of war on board the USS *Malvern*, to "forge a thunderbolt" as one reporter termed it. Time was now pressing: Sherman's army had been on the march northward into South Carolina for ten days. After consultation, Schofield decided to begin active operations without waiting for the remainder of his corps to reach the Cape Fear. He believed he could capture both Fort Anderson and Wilmington with the 14,500 troops he had on hand. "[Sherman] does not want you to wait for his movements in your advance, but to commence your movements as soon as you get ready," one general officer informed Schofield. "[He] attaches great importance to the effect that your advance will produce."[74]

The Federals launched their combined operation on February 11, with Schofield again pushing Terry's corps toward Hoke's entrenched position at Sugar Loaf. After a heavy firefight, Paine's U.S. Colored Troops established a new line to hold Hoke in check to prevent him from sending reinforcements to Fort Anderson. On February 16, transports ferried Cox's division across the Cape Fear River to Smithville. Early the following morning, Cox advanced his six thousand troops toward Fort Anderson ten miles upstream. Porter's gunboats, including the light draft monitor *Montauk* that had been transferred from the Charleston blockading squadron in late January, steamed up the Cape Fear River to cover the wings of both Terry and Cox's commands.

Porter's heavy bombardment of Fort Anderson on February 17–18 enabled Cox to approach to within six hundred yards of the work, but it failed to silence the Confederates' artillery. The narrow river channel restricted the gunboats' maneuverability and placed the brunt of responsibility for capturing the fort on the army.

Cox and Schofield's reconnaissance of Fort Anderson early on the morning of February 18 dissuaded them from attempting a frontal assault against the imposing earthen defenses. Instead, as the navy intensified its shelling on shore, Schofield demonstrated in front of Fort Anderson with two of Cox's brigades, while Cox personally led his two remaining brigades on a forced march around Orton Pond. By nightfall, Cox's rapidly moving units had brushed aside a small contingent of Confederate cavalry and positioned itself above the fort with plans to advance at first light.

Brigadier General Johnson Hagood, Fort Anderson's commanding officer, faced a desperate situation. His garrison of about two thousand soldiers was much too small to oppose Cox's flanking force, Schofield's two brigades in front of the fort, and Porter's flotilla of gunboats on the Cape Fear River. Hagood believed that he should abandon the work, but such a drastic move would require his superior officer's authorization. Major General Hoke, however, was reluctant to give it because of Bragg's standing orders that, except in an emergency, the positions must be held. A retreat from Fort Anderson would compromise the Sugar Loaf defenses by allowing Porter's warships to advance upriver. Repositioned above Hoke's lines, the navy could make an amphibious landing or bombard them. Evacuating both Fort Anderson and Sugar Loaf would also threaten the security of Wilmington. Under the circumstances, though, Hoke had little choice. As one Confederate observed: "We could do nothing but fall back." Both Hagood and Hoke were in full retreat toward Wilmington before sunrise on February 19.

Federal forces occupied both Fort Anderson and Sugar Loaf early that same morning. One Northern war correspondent remarked: "Fort Anderson is ours. The river is ours. Wilmington is virtually ours." Federal troops on both sides of the Cape Fear River closely pursued the Confederates, who fought a series of delaying actions to the outskirts of Wilmington. After clearing the river of mines and obstructions off Fort Anderson, Porter's flotilla also steamed forward, keeping pace with and providing covering fire for the army wings. By the afternoon of February 21, Cox's brigades had advanced to the Brunswick River, within sight of church spires in Wilmington to the east.[75]

With Union troops poised on the edge of Wilmington, its fall seemed inevitable. As Hoke pondered his next move, a train bearing General Bragg pulled into the depot. Hoke's report and his own assessment of the dire situation convinced Bragg that Wilmington must be abandoned at once. "Gen. Bragg says he is greatly outnumbered by the enemy's two corps near Wilmington," recorded Jones in Richmond "Of course he will evacuate." Bragg's first order of business was the destruction of government property, cotton, and tobacco. "Sad accounts of mismanagement in the evacuation of Wilmington, which I suppose is also to be laid to Bragg's account," one North Carolinian overheard. "50,000 lbs. of bacon were burnt & boxes on boxes of shoes tumbled into the water, whilst our barefooted troops marched out hungry & without rations before the face of the victorious enemy."[76]

In the predawn hours of February 22, despondent Confederate soldiers withdrew from Wilmington and headed northward toward Kinston. A thick pall of black smoke from smoldering fires and a deathlike stillness enveloped the city as they trudged through the darkened streets. "[It was] so black and compact as to appear to come from the infernal regions," observed a Tar Heel musket-bearer. "Lights could be seen from but a few windows, and these appeared to be the last rays of departing hope."[77]

In the wake of Bragg's retreating army, Union troops occupied Wilmington early that morning. It was George Washington's birthday, and they considered their victory a good sign. The city's fall gave Federal forces control of the Cape Fear River, which they soon ascended as far as Fayetteville. Sherman's vanguard reached that town on March 11, with Union soldiers from Wilmington arriving the next day. Supplies and provisions also made their way upriver, enabling Sherman to continue his advance toward Goldsboro without detouring to the coast.

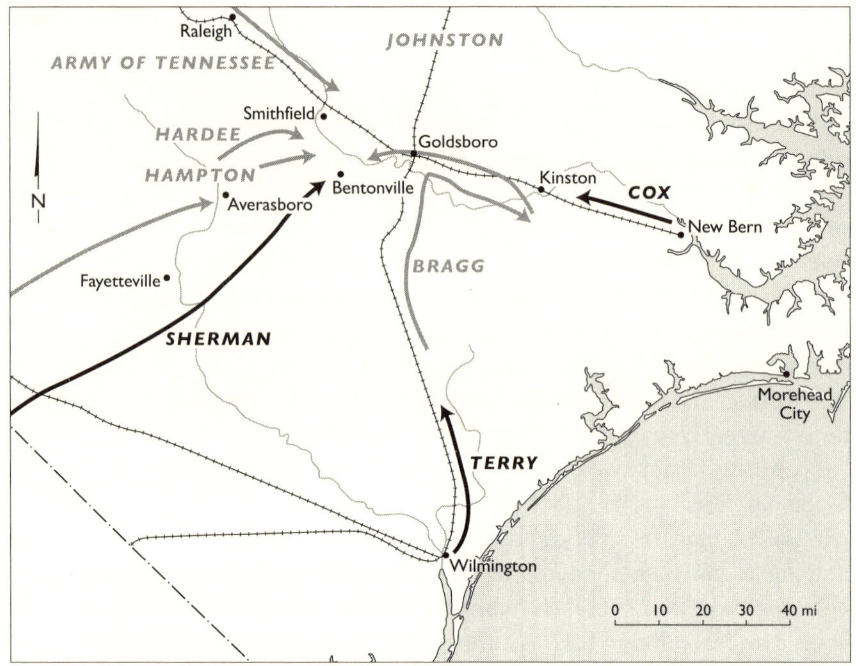

Braxton Bragg's movements after evacuating Wilmington.

Before Sherman reached Goldsboro, a Confederate army, including Bragg's troops from Wilmington, commanded by General Joseph E. Johnston, struck him at Bentonville. For three days, March 19–21, the opposing forces traded blows in what turned out to be the largest land battle of the Carolinas Campaign. After suffering heavy casualties he could ill afford, Johnston retreated toward Greensboro. Sherman quickly regrouped and pushed on to Goldsboro.

Schofield and Terry, along with troops that arrived from New Bern, linked forces with Sherman at that juncture, bolstering Sherman's army to eighty-eight thousand, more than enough soldiers to meet any Confederate threat. Sherman was also positioned near the North Carolina coast, which the Union navy now effectively controlled. The railroads for supplies and reinforcements from both Wilmington and New Bern were soon repaired and operational. Well-armed, well-fed, well-rested, and battle-hardened, Sherman's mighty legion stood ready to advance up the Wilmington & Weldon Railroad toward Virginia.

With Grant renewing the offensive on March 29, and his rear vulnerable to an attack from Sherman, General Lee saw little choice but to withdraw from his lines around Petersburg. As he had predicted, with the fall of Wilmington, Lee could no longer maintain his army. Now threatened by two superior armies, he had to move. Grant followed, battling Lee to Appomattox Courthouse, where the Army of Northern Virginia surrendered on April 9, 1865. Without renewing hostilities after his defeat at Bentonville, Johnston, along with the remnants of Hoke's Division, surrendered to General Sherman at Durham Station, North Carolina, two weeks later.

The Union victory at Wilmington severed the Confederacy's last lifeline and helped assure the success of Sherman's Carolinas Campaign. The importance of the capture of Fort Fisher and the Confederacy's most important seaport and city had been paramount. "We had some very important naval victories during the war, but none so important as Fort Fisher," boasted Admiral Porter. "It's fall sealed the fate of the Confederacy." Historians believe the Civil War's outcome was determined by Sherman's capture of Atlanta, Sheridan's Shenandoah Valley Campaign, and President Lincoln's reelection. The end by then was but a matter of time. Maybe so, but the Union victories at Fort Fisher and Wilmington hastened the downfall of the Confederacy.[78]

And what of Braxton Bragg's role in the loss of these two vital points? Perhaps he wrote his own epitaph in a letter to Jefferson Davis shortly after the Battle of Bentonville, by which time he had been largely discredited and his reputation was at an all-time low.

> Finding myself with nothing but a small division in the field and virtually ignored in regard to that and all other command, orders being constantly sent to my subordinates without notification to me, I asked and was allowed to turn over Hoke's Division to him. I have retired to this point [Raleigh], where I have nothing to do but mourn over the sad spectacle hourly presented of disorginisation, demoralisation, and destruction . . . You hear of victories and routes, I see disasters, disorderly retreats and utter confusion on our part, with combinations and numbers against us which must prevail . . . With no duty to perform I shall remain quietly here, awaiting events. . . . My position is both mortifying and humiliating, but the example of you more trying one warns me to bear it with resignation.[79]

Notes

1. Few wartime copies of the *Charlottesville (VA) Daily Chronicle* are extant, including the late October 1864 issue with the prediction that Braxton Bragg was being sent to Wilmington. The *Wilmington Daily Journal* of October 31, 1864, however, noted that "the Charlottesville 'Chronicle' of last week says: 'We suspect that General Bragg is going to Wilmington. Good bye Wilmington.'" The

editor of the Wilmington paper went on to write: "The above appeared in the *Richmond Enquirer* of the 26th, and we re-produce it here."

2. Chris E. Fonvielle Jr., *The Wilmington Campaign: Last Rays of Departing Hope* (Campbell, CA, 1997), 1–22.

3. Robert E. Lee, *Lee's Dispatches: Unpublished Letters of General Robert E. Lee to Jefferson Davis and the War Department of the Confederate States of America, 1862–65,* ed. Douglas Southall Freeman (New York, 1915), 69.

4. William Lamb, "Fort Fisher. The Battles Fought There in 1864 and '65," *Southern Historical Society Papers* 21 (1893), 261–62; William Lamb, "The Defense of Fort Fisher," in *Battles and Leaders of the Civil War: Being for the Most Part Contributions by Union and Confederate Officers Based upon "The Century War Series,"* eds. Robert Underwood Johnson and Clarence Clough Buel, 4 vols. (New York, 1884—88), 4:643; *Augusta (GA) Constitutionalist,* Sept. 22, 1864.

5. William C. Davis and Julie Hoffman eds., *The Confederate General,* 6 vols. (Harrisburg, PA, 1991), 6:132–33; Jefferson Davis, *The Rise and Fall of the Confederate Government,* 2 vols. (New York, 1881), 2:646; U.S. War Department, *The War of the Rebellion: A Compilation of the Official Records of the Union and Confederate Armies,* 128 vols. (Washington, DC, 1880–1901), series 1, vol. 25, pt. 2:643 (hereafter cited as *OR;* all references are to series 1 unless otherwise indicated).

6. Robert Tansill, *A Free and Impartial Exposition of the Causes which Led to the Failure of the Confederate States to establish their Independence* (Washington, DC, 1865), 20; A Late Confederate Officer, "Wilmington During the Blockade," *Harper's New Monthly Magazine* (Sept. 1866): 497; C. B. Denson, "William Henry Chase Whiting: An Address Delivered in Raleigh, N.C. on Memorial Day (May 10), 1895, Containing a Memoir of the Late Major-General William Henry Chase Whiting of the Confederate Army," *Southern Historical Society Papers* 26 (1898): 150–51; *OR,* vol. 5:1011–12; ibid., vol. 18:770.

7. James Lowndes to "Cousin Harriet," Oct. 23, 1861, James Lowndes Papers, South Caroliniana, University of South Carolina, Columbia; *Wilmington Daily Journal,* May 27, 1863; Whiting to Cooper, Apr. 30, 1863, Letters Sent, Gen. W. H. C. Whiting's Command, Chp. 11, 335, April–June 1863, Record Group 109, War Department Collection of Confederate Records, National Archives and Records Service, Washington, DC.

8. A Late Confederate Officer, "Wilmington During the Blockade," 497; Joe A. Mobley, *War Governor of the South: North Carolina's Zeb Vance in the Confederacy* (Gainesville, FL, 2005), 159–60.

9. Fonvielle, *The Wilmington Campaign,* 51–52. The "Sailors' Grave" is generally referred to today as the Graveyard of the Atlantic. By 2014, underwater

archaeologists and historians had discovered more than five thousand shipwrecks, one thousand of which have been identified, in North Carolina's inland sounds and waterways and along the coast.

10. Gideon Welles, *Diary of Gideon Welles, Secretary of the Navy under Lincoln and Johnson*, 3 vols. (Boston, 1911), 2:146.

11. Whiting to Seddon, Aug. 24, 1863, *OR*, vol. 29, pt. 2:670; *Augusta (GA) Constitutionalist*, Sept. 22, 1864.

12. Seddon to Whiting, Sept. 5, 1864, *OR*, vol. 42, pt. 2:1236.

13. Whiting to Holmes, Sept. 26, 1864, *OR*, vol. 42, pt. 2:1295.

14. Samuel A'Court Ashe, *History of North Carolina*, 2 vols. (Raleigh, NC, 1925), 2:935; Vance to Lee, Sept. 5, 1864, *OR*, vol. 42, pt. 2:1235; Lee to Vance, Oct. 8, 1864, *OR*, vol. 42, pt. 3:1142.

15. Vance to Whiting, Sept. 28, 1864, *OR*, vol. 42, pt. 2:1299; *Richmond Sentinel*, Oct. 10, 1864.

16. Whiting to Holmes, Sept. 26, 1864, *OR*, vol. 42, pt. 2:1295–96.

17. Davis to Bragg, Oct. 15, 1864, *OR*, vol. 42, pt. 3:1149.

18. J. B. Jones, *A Rebel War Clerk's Diary at the Confederate States Capital*, 2 vols. (Philadelphia, 1866), 2:209.

19. Davis and Hoffman, *The Confederate General*, 1:113–17; Fonvielle, *The Wilmington Campaign*, 84.

20. *Wilmington Daily Journal*, Dec. 16, 1863; Grady McWhiney, *Braxton Bragg and Confederate Defeat*, vol. 1, *Field Command* (Tuscaloosa, AL, 1969), 33, 97.

21. Bragg to Cooper, Nov. 29, 1863, *OR*, vol. 31, pt. 2:682; Mary Chesnut, *Mary Chesnut's Civil War*, ed. C. Vann Woodward (New Haven, CT, 1981), 496.

22. General Orders No. 23, Feb. 24, 1864, *OR*, vol. 32, pt. 2:799; Catherine Ann Devereux Edmondston, *"Journal of a Secesh Lady": The Diary of Catherine Ann Devereux Edmondston, 1860–1866*, eds. Beth B. Crabtree and James W. Patton (Raleigh, NC, 1979), 617; *Wilmington Daily Journal*, Oct. 16, 1863; Jones, *A Rebel War Clerk's Diary*, 2:157, 395; A Late Confederate Officer, "Wilmington During the Blockade," 502.

23. Jones, *A Rebel War Clerk's Diary*, 2:157–58; E. Merton Coulter, *The Confederate States of America 1861–1865* (Baton Rouge, LA, 1950), 379–80.

24. Jones, *A Rebel War Clerk's Diary*, 2:221, 310.

25. *Wilmington Daily Journal*, Oct. 31, 1864.

26. General Orders No. 1, Oct. 22, 1864, *OR*, vol. 42, pt. 3:1160; Whiting to Lee, Feb. 19, 1865, *OR*, vol. 46, pt. 1:442; Denson, "William Henry Chase Whiting," 173; William Lamb, *Colonel Lamb's Story of Fort Fisher* (Carolina Beach, NC, 1966), 10; Bragg to Davis, Oct. 25, 1864, *OR*, vol. 42, pt. 3:1171.

27. Bragg to Davis, Oct. 25, 1864, *OR*, vol. 42, pt. 3:1171; *Richmond Daily Dispatch*, Oct. 23, 1864; Bragg to Lee, Oct. 25, 1864, *OR*, vol. 42, pt. 3:1171–72.

28. Bragg to Lee, Oct. 25, 1864, *OR*, vol. 42, pt. 3:1172.

29. Vance to Davis, Oct. 25, 1864; Lee to Davis, Nov. 8, 1864; Davis to Seddon, Nov. 10, 1864; Cooper to Davis, Nov. 18, 1864; General Orders No. 1, Wilmington, N.C., Nov. 17, 1864, all in *OR*, vol. 42, pt. 3:1163, 1164, 1218.

30. Seddon to Adjutant General, Nov. 22, 1864, *OR*, vol. 42, pt. 3:1214; Lee to Adjutant and Inspector General's Office, Nov. 30, 1864, *OR*, vol. 42, pt. 3:1215.

31. *Wilmington Daily Journal*, Oct. 22, 1864.

32. Welles, *Diary of Gideon Welles*, 2:146; Fonvielle, *The Wilmington Campaign*, 80–82.

33. Lamb, *Colonel Lamb's Story of Fort Fisher*, 35; Jones, *A Rebel War Clerk's Diary*, 2:447; Ashe, *History of North Carolina*, 2:939; *Fayetteville (NC) Observer Semi-Weekly*, Jan. 16, 1865.

34. Fonvielle, *The Wilmington Campaign*, 60–61.

35. Davis to Bragg, Nov. 22, 1864; General Orders No. 23, Hdqrs. Dept. of North Carolina, Nov. 23, 1864; Whiting to Hébert, Nov. 23, 1864; Whiting to Lee, Nov. 29, 1864, all in *OR*, vol. 42, pt. 3:1225, 1226, 1227, 1233; Jefferson Davis, *The Papers of Jefferson Davis*, ed. Lynda Lasswell Crist, Barbara J. Rozek, and Kenneth H. Williams, vol. 11, *September 1864—May 1865* (Baton Rouge, LA, 2004), 204; Lee to Davis, Dec. 5, 1864, *OR*, vol. 42, pt. 3:1254–1255.

36. Davis to Bragg, Dec. 13, 1864, *OR*, vol. 42, pt. 3:1271; General Orders No. 12, Hdqrs. Dept. of North Carolina, Dec. 17, 1864, *OR*, vol. 42, pt. 3:1278; Jones, *A Rebel War Clerk's Diary*, 2:341, 356–57.

37. Jones, *A Rebel War Clerk's Diary*, 2:360, 368; Whiting to Hébert, Dec. 9, 1864, *OR*, vol. 42, pt. 3:1264.

38. Patricia L. Faust, ed., *Historical Times Illustrated Encyclopedia of the Civil War* (New York, 1986), 594; William N. Still Jr., "Porter . . . Is the Best Man," *Civil War Times Illustrated* (May 1977), 46.

39. Fonvielle, *The Wilmington Campaign*, 129–72.

40. Chris E. Fonvielle Jr., *To Forge a Thunderbolt: Fort Anderson and the Battle for Wilmington* (Carolina Beach, NC, 2015), 71.

41. Bragg to Sale, Dec. 29, 1864, *OR*, vol. 42, pt. 3:1344.

42. A Late Confederate Officer, "Wilmington During the Blockade," 502; Parker to Whiting, Dec. 25, 1864, *OR*, vol. 42, pt. 3:1307.

43. *Richmond Dispatch*, Jan. 4, 1865; Whiting to Seddon, Jan. 1, 1865, *OR*, vol. 46, pt. 2:1001; Report of David D. Porter, Jan. 17, 1865, U.S. Navy War Records Office, *Official Records of the Union and Confederate Navies in the War of the Rebellion*, 31 vols. (Washington, DC, 1894–1922), 11:441 (hereafter cited as

ORN); Report of Spyers Singleton, Dec. 30, 1864, *OR*, vol. 42, pt. 1:1007–1009; Report of Louis Hébert, Jan. 3, 1865, *OR*, vol. 42, pt. 1:1001; Report of W. H. C. Whiting, Dec. 30, 1864, *OR*, vol. 46, pt. 1:996; Extract from the Official Diary of William Lamb, *ORN*, vol. 11:746–47.

44. *Wilmington Daily Journal*, Dec. 31, 1864 and Jan. 6, 1865; Jones, *A Rebel War Clerk's Diary*, 2:373.

45. Whiting to Seddon, Jan. 1, 1865, and Lee to Seddon, Jan. 8, 1865, *OR*, vol. 46, pt. 2:1000, 1023.

46. Lamb, "Fort Fisher. The Battles Fought There," 276; Lamb, *Colonel Lamb's Story of Fort Fisher*, 22; George H. Moffett to wife, Jan. 2, 1865, George Hall Moffett Papers, South Carolina Historical Society, Charleston; Walter Clark, ed., *Histories of the Several Regiments and Battalions From North Carolina in the Great War, 1861—'65*, 5 vols. (1901; repr., Wilmington, NC, 1982), 2:802, 4:541.

47. Hébert to Whiting, Dec. 31, 1864; Whiting to Anderson, Dec. 30, 1864; Anderson to Whiting, Dec. 31, 1864; Whiting to Anderson, Dec. 31, 1864, all in *OR*, vol. 42, pt. 3:1356, 1359, 1361.

48. Whiting to Seddon, Jan. 1, 1865, *OR*, vol. 46, pt. 2:1001; Report of Porter, Jan. 17, 1865, *ORN*, vol. 11:441; Reports of Louis Hébert, Jan. 3, 1865, and Spyers Singleton, Dec. 30, 1864, *OR*, vol. 42, pt. 1:1001, 1007–1009; Report of W. H. C. Whiting, Dec. 30, 1864, *OR*, vol. 46, pt. 1:996; Extract from the Official Diary of William Lamb, *ORN*, vol. 11:746–47.

49. Ulysses S. Grant, *The Papers of Ulysses S. Grant*, ed. John Y. Simon and David L. Wilson, vol. 13, *November 16, 1864—February 20, 1865* (Carbondale, IL, 1985), 168–69.

50. Fonvielle, *The Wilmington Campaign*, 192–99.

51. Bragg to Lee, Jan. 12, 1865, *OR*, vol. 46, pt. 2:1042; Report of Braxton Bragg, Jan. 13–15, 1865, *OR*, vol. 46, pt. 1:431; A Late Confederate Officer, "Wilmington During the Blockade," 503.

52. Denson, "William Henry Chase Whiting," 162.

53. Lamb, "Fort Fisher. The Battles Fought There," 277.

54. Fonvielle, *To Forge a Thunderbolt*, 74–75.

55. Whiting to Bragg, Jan. 15, 1865, *OR*, vol. 46, pt. 2:1064–65.

56. Bragg to Taylor, Jan. 15, *OR*, vol. 46, pt. 2:1062; "Defence and Fall of Fort Fisher," *Southern Historical Society Papers* 10 (1882): 348.

57. "Defence and Fall of Fort Fisher," 346, 349.

58. Davis to Lee, Jan. 16, 1865, *OR*, vol. 46, pt. 2:1073; William Calder to Mother, Feb. 10, 1865, William Calder Papers, Southern Historical Collection, University of North Carolina Library, Chapel Hill.

59. Denson, "William Henry Chase Whiting," 170, 173.

60. Jones, *A Rebel War Clerk's Diary,* 2:389; *Wilmington Daily North Carolinian,* Jan. 22, 1865; Alexander H. Stephens, *A Constitutional View of the Late War Between the States: Its Causes, Character, Conduct and Results. Presented in a Series of Colloquies at Liberty Hall,* 2 vols. (Chicago, 1868—70), 2:619; William Stanley Hoole, *Lawley Covers the Confederacy* (Tuscaloosa, AL, 1964), 109.

61. Sherman to Grant, Jan. 29, 1865, *OR,* vol. 47, pt. 2:154.

62. Confederate soldier to Kate, Jan. 21, 1865, Catherine Jane Buie Papers, William R. Perkins Library, Duke University, Durham, NC; William Badham Jr. to wife, Feb. 8 and 20, 1865, William Badham Jr. Papers, William R. Perkins Library, Duke University, Durham, NC; Fonvielle, *The Wilmington Campaign,* 309–12; William Henry Tripp to Araminta Guilford Tripp, Jan. 19, 1865, Tripp Family Papers, Southern Historical Collection, University of North Carolina Library, Chapel Hill.

63. Fonvielle, *The Wilmington Campaign,* 313–15.

64. *Wilmington Daily North Carolinian,* Feb. 18, 1865; Bragg to Taylor, Jan. 27, 1865, *OR,* vol. 46, pt. 2:1154.

65. Abstract log of USS *Malvern,* Jan. 28, 1865, *ORN,* vol. 11:740; Grant to Sherman, *OR,* vol. 47, pt. 2:193; Welles to Lanman, Jan. 25, 1865, *ORN,* vol. 12:697; Fox to Trenchard, Jan. 26, 1865, *ORN,* vol. 12:702; Cyrus B. Comstock, *The Diary of Cyrus B. Comstock,* ed. Merlin E. Sumner (Dayton, OH, 1987), 308; James Lee McDonough, *Schofield: Union General in the Civil War and Reconstruction* (Gainesville, FL, 1972), 150; Grant to Schofield, Feb. 19, 1865, *OR,* vol. 47, pt. 2:492. Grant and his entourage departed Hampton Roads, Virginia, on the USS *Rhode Island,* bound for the Cape Fear River, at 10:00 A.M. on January 27, 1865. See Lanman to the Secretary of the Navy, *ORN,* vol. 12:703.

66. Sherman to Palmer, Jan. 21, 1865; Sherman to Foster, Jan. 29, 1865; Sherman to Grant, Jan. 29, 1865, all in *OR* 47, pt. 2:111, 154, 155–56, 163; William T. Sherman, *Memoirs of W. T. Sherman* (1875; repr., New York, 1990), 272; Jacob D. Cox, *Military Reminiscences of the Civil War,* 2 vols. (New York: Charles Scribner's Sons, 1900), 2:395.

67. Cox, *Military Reminiscences,* 2:395; Schofield to Grant, Feb. 15, 1865; Sherman to Grant, Feb. 19, 1865; Grant to Schofield, Feb. 19, 1865; Grant to Sherman, Mar. 16, 1865, all in *OR,* vol. 47, pt. 2:154–56, 436–37, 492, 859; Report of U. S. Grant, *OR,* vol. 46, pt. 1:45.

68. Porter to Welles, Jan. 31, 1865, Feb. 12, 1865, *ORN,* vol. 11:721, vol. 12:16–17; David D. Porter Memoir, 884–85, David D. Porter Papers, Library of Congress, Washington, D.C.; Grant to Sherman, Feb. 1, 1865, *OR,* vol. 47, pt. 2:193.

69. James M. Merrill, "The Fort Fisher and Wilmington Campaign: Letters from Rear Admiral David D. Porter," *North Carolina Historical Review* 35 (Oct.

1958): 469; Grant to Stanton and General Orders No. 12, War Department, both Jan. 31, 1865, *OR*, vol. 47, pt. 2:179; Grant, *Papers of Ulysses S. Grant*, 13:336.

70. Abstract from journal of Jacob D. Cox, Feb. 4, 1865, *OR*, vol. 47, pt. 2:927; Halleck to Grant, Schofield to Palmer, and Scott to Halleck, all Feb. 5, 1865, OR, vol. 47, pt. 2:306, 316; Cox, *Military Reminiscences*, 2:399–400; Jacob D. Cox, *The March to the Sea: Franklin and Nashville* (New York, 1882), 147.

71. Bragg to Vance, Feb. 7, 1865, *OR*, vol. 47, pt. 2:1114; Bragg to Vance, Feb. 7, 1865, Zebulon B. Vance Papers, Division of Archives and History, Raleigh, NC; *Wilmington Daily North Carolinian*, Jan. 26, 1865.

72. Sale to Bragg, Jan. 26, 1865, Feb. 2, 1865; Bragg to Davis, Feb. 3, 1865; Bragg to Lee, Feb. 9, 1865, all in *OR*, vol. 47, pt. 2:1142, 1083, 1088, 1138; Don C. Seitz, *Braxton Bragg: General of the Confederacy* (Columbia, SC, 1924), 507; Judith Lee Hallock, *Braxton Bragg and Confederate Defeat, Vol. 2* (Tuscaloosa, AL, 1991), 246–47.

73. *Charleston Mercury*, Jan. 21, 1865; Zaccheus Ellis to Sister, Feb. 12, 1865, Miscellaneous Confederate Letters, Brunswick Town/Fort Anderson State Historic Site, Winnabow, NC.

74. *Philadelphia Inquirer*, Feb. 21, 1865; Abstract from journal of Jacob D. Cox, Feb. 10, 1865, *OR*, vol. 47, pt. 1:927; Cox, *Military Reminiscences*, 2:405–6; Foster to Schofield, Feb. 4, 1865, Schofield to Grant, Feb. 8, 1865, *OR*, vol. 47, pt. 2:302, 356.

75. Chris E. Fonvielle Jr., "Closing Down the Kingdom: Union Combined Operations Against Wilmington," in *Union Combined Operations in the Civil War*, ed. Craig L. Symonds (New York, 2010), 110–11.

76. Jones, *A Rebel War Clerk's Diary*, 2:430; Edmondston, *"Journal of a Secesh Lady,"* 674.

77. *Fayetteville (NC) Observer Semi-Weekly*, Mar. 2, 1865.

78. Fonvielle, "Closing Down the Kingdom," 112.

79. Davis, *The Papers of Jefferson Davis*, 11:469–70.

Appendix

Confederate Departments of the Western Theater

LEADING A NATION, PARTICULARLY ONE IN ITS INFANCY, IS DIFFICULT UNDER THE BEST OF circumstances. Having to fight a war across a nation the size of the Confederacy from the capital in Richmond, which was situated in the most exposed corner of the country, made the task almost insurmountable. President Jefferson Davis and his secretaries of war attempted to fight the Confederacy's war by following the traditional example of organization by geographical departments, which were frequently subdivided into districts and even subdistricts.[1] Ideally, each department would have its own army to defend it and produce sufficient provisions to support its troops and their horses. The goal of the organization structure was to increase efficiency by reducing the oversight required of the authorities in Richmond. But Federal incursions devastated the system, one which many scholars have concluded was inherently flawed.

Those historians have long criticized President Davis for his dispersal of soldiers early in the war in an attempt to defend all Confederate territory and for his departmentalization of those forces, which hindered cooperation between the commanders of these geographically independent entities. Virginia was divided into the departments or armies of Alexandria, Fredericksburg, Harper's Ferry, Henrico, Kanawha, Norfolk, and the Peninsula. Beyond Virginia, however, Davis handled things differently. Though there was the Army of Pensacola, defense of the Mississippi Valley was divided between two departments, No. 1 (Vicksburg and below) and No. 2, and states such as South Carolina and Georgia were departments unto themselves. Part of this difference between Virginia and the rest of the Confederacy can be attributed to where the enemy threat appeared most imminent. However, part resulted from President Davis's faith in one general in particular—Albert Sidney Johnston. In charge of Department No. 2, he was responsible for defending the Confederacy's northern frontier from the Virginia–Kentucky border westward into Indian Territory, including the entire states of Tennessee and Arkansas, portions of Alabama, Mississippi, and Louisiana, and any operations in Kentucky, Missouri, and Kansas.

Davis would begin consolidating the commands in Virginia in the fall of 1861 and continue to do so the following year. In the Western Theater, however, the trend was just the opposite following Johnston's death at Shiloh in April 1862. His successor was officially relieved of responsibility for anything west of the Mississippi and East Tennessee, and military events had already removed Kentucky and the remainder of Tennessee from his control. Within six months, however, Secretary of War George W. Randolph saw the need for a super department to deal with the three departments stretching from the Appalachian Mountains to the Mississippi River, and created the Department of the West. Though brilliant in concept, it lasted less than a year and largely came to naught because of the personalities involved and because its commander had no authority west of the Mississippi. A second super department was created a year later, but it mattered little by the fall of 1864 and was more of a political ploy than a functioning bureaucratic organization.

The following departmental summaries reflect the almost ceaseless advance of Union forces in the Western Theater, Davis's failure to realize the need for unified command on both sides of the Mississippi River, and occasionally the influence a particular general had on the process. Rather than being arranged alphabetically, the departments are listed in the chronological order in which they were established to provide more insight into the actions of the Richmond authorities as the war progressed.

Lastly, one would think that if nothing else the War Department in Richmond would at least have had a chalkboard showing the boundaries of the various departments. But even a cursory read of the following makes it clear that no "big board" existed. Departmental boundaries set forth in General Orders issued by the Adjutant and Inspector General's Office (A&IGO) could be vague, incomplete, and even contradictory, and on at least one occasion the A&IGO's correction confused the issue even more.

Department of Louisiana

Commanders:

Colonel Paul O. Hébert: assumed April 16, 1861
Major General David E. Twiggs: assigned April 17, 1861; assumed May 31

Established April 16, 1861, to consist "of the C. S. troops in the State of Louisiana." Amended April 17: "New Orleans and its defenses will constitute the Military District of Louisiana, and the senior officer of the troops in service of the Confederate States there will take command of that district, headquarters New Orleans." Twiggs designated it a department when he assumed command. Merged into Department No. 1 by the A&IGO on May 27, but the change did not occur in the field until May 31.

Department No. 1

Commanders:

Colonel Paul O. Hébert: acting May 27–31, 1861

Major General David E. Twiggs: assigned May 27, 1861; assumed May 31; ordered relieved October 7

Major General Mansfield Lovell: assigned October 7, 1861; assumed October 18[2]

Established May 27, 1861, to consist of "the State of Louisiana, together with the southern portion of Mississippi and Alabama, including Fort Morgan." On July 4, "the [Mississippi] river parishes of Louisiana north of Red River" were transferred to Department No. 2. The A&IGO extended Major General Braxton Bragg's command beyond western Florida "to include the coast and State of Alabama" on October 7, and on October 14 that portion of Alabama formerly belonging to Department No. 1 officially became part of the Department of Alabama and West Florida. On December 12 Pascagoula Bay and that part of Mississippi east of the Pascagoula River was transferred to the Department of Alabama and West Florida. The remainder of Louisiana north of the Red River was transferred to the Trans-Mississippi District of Department No. 2 on January 10, 1862. Revised May 26, to "hereafter embrace that portion of the State of Mississippi south of the thirty-third parallel and west of Pascagoula and Chickasawha [*sic*] Rivers, including also that part of the State of Louisiana east of the Mississippi River"; that portion of Louisiana west of the Mississippi transferred to the Trans-Mississippi Department. Merged into Department No. 2 on June 25, 1862.

Department No. 2 (also known as Western Department)

Commanders:

Major General Leonidas Polk: offered command with rank of major general June 25, 1861; assigned July 4; assumed July 13

General Albert Sidney Johnston: assigned September 10, 1861; assumed September 15; killed April 6, 1862

General Pierre G. T. Beauregard: assumed April 6, 1862; temporarily relinquished June 17

General Braxton Bragg: temporarily assumed June 17, 1862; assigned permanently June 20; assumed July 2; temporarily relinquished October 24

Lieutenant General Leonidas Polk: temporarily assigned October 24, 1862

General Braxton Bragg: resumed November 3, 1862

Though conceived on or before June 25, 1861, it was not officially established until July 4 to embrace

> that portion of Alabama north of the Tennessee River, beginning at Waterloo and running thence east with the river to Decatur, as well as the portion of the State lying north of the Memphis and Charleston Railroad from Decatur to Stevenson, together with that portion of Tennessee west and south of the Tennessee River; the [Mississippi] river counties of Arkansas and Mississippi, including Corinth, Mississippi, and the country adjacent thereto, and extending to Eastport, on the Tennessee River; the [Mississippi] river parishes of Louisiana north of Red River, and that portion of Arkansas, besides the river counties above mentioned, lying north and east of White and Black Rivers, . . . headquarters at Memphis, Tenn.

On September 2 it was expanded to include the entire "State of Arkansas and all military operations in the State of Missouri" and on September 10 further amended to "embrace the States of Tennessee and Arkansas, and that part of the State of Mississippi west of the New Orleans, Jackson, and Great Northern and Central Railroad; also, the military operations in Kentucky, Missouri, Kansas, and the Indian country immediately west of Missouri and Arkansas." The September 10 revision also removed the four Louisiana parishes north of the Red River that bordered on the Mississippi River. On October 7, "the state of Alabama," which included part of Department No. 2, was transferred to Major General Braxton Bragg's command which became the Department of Alabama and West Florida. The Indian country was transferred to the Department of Indian Territory on November 22, but the A&IGO reversed itself on January 10, 1862, when it created the Trans-Mississippi District of Department No 2. That district consisted of the "part of the State of Louisiana north of Red River, the Indian Territory west of Arkansas, and the States of Arkansas and Missouri, excepting therefrom the tract of country east of the Saint Francis, bordering on the Mississippi River, from the mouth of the Saint Francis to Scott County, Missouri."

On February 25, 1862, the A&IGO ordered Major General Edmund Kirby Smith to "proceed to Knoxville, and assume command of the troops in East Tennessee, reporting by letter to General A. S. Johnston." No record of the boundary between the two departments has been found, but on March 21, the A&IGO announced "the department under the command of Maj. Gen. E. K. Smith is extended so as to embrace within its limits Chattanooga, Tenn., and the troops in its vicinity." It appears that the intention of Richmond authorities was to convert the former District of East Tennessee in Department No. 2 into an independent department that, should it be cut off from the remainder of Department No. 2 by the advancing Federals, which appeared imminent, it could then report directly to Richmond. It also appears that Richmond wanted to make such an arrangement in a timely manner while at the same time not reflecting negatively on Johnston's reputation or hindering his immediate command of the troops in East Tennessee.

On May 26, 1862, "extended south to the thirty-third parallel east of the Mississippi River and extending on that parallel to the eastern boundary of Alabama," but all territory west of the Mississippi River was transferred to the Trans-Mississippi Department. Redefined on June 25 to "embrace that portion of its former limits which is east of the Mississippi River, and in addition thereto shall comprise Department No. 1, and have its eastern boundary extended to the line of railroad from Chattanooga via Atlanta to West Point, on the Chattahoochee River, and thence down the Chattahoochee and Apalachicola Rivers to the Gulf of Mexico." On June 29, Secretary of War George W. Randolph wrote Bragg "your department is extended so as to embrace that part of Louisiana east of the Mississippi, the entire States of Mississippi and Alabama, and the portion of Georgia and Florida west of the Chattahoochee and Apalachicola Rivers." One reason for merging the Department of Alabama and West Florida into the department was to enable Bragg to "take charge of the Selma and Meridian connection," a railroad construction project. On July 2, Bragg assumed "command of Department No. 2, as extended by the President, and embracing, in addition to the limits already announced, all of Department No. 1, the entire State of Alabama, and eastward to the line of railroad from Chattanooga via Atlanta to West Point, Ga., on the Chattahoochee River, and thence down that stream and the Apalachicola to the Gulf of Mexico." It should be noted that Bragg only claimed authority over that part of Georgia authorized by the A&IGO on June 25, rather than everything "west of the Chattahoochee" as written by Randolph on June 29.

Either in an attempt to clarify "its former limits which is east of the Mississippi River" for the benefit of Bragg or in anticipation of the loss of Chattanooga, on July 18 the A&IGO announced in G.O. No. 50: "II. Military Department No. 2 will embrace the States of Mississippi, Alabama, East Louisiana, and part of Florida which is west of the Chattahoochee and Apalachicola Rivers. III. The Department of East Tennessee will include that part of the State of Georgia which is north of the railroad leading from Augusta via Atlanta to West Point, and so much of North Carolina as is west of the Blue Ridge Mountains in that State." By making it clear that Kirby Smith was to retreat toward Atlanta following the fall of Chattanooga and failing to mention West and Middle Tennessee and operations in Kentucky regarding Department No. 2, this document clearly shows the War Department's perception of future operations in the Western Theater. Mississippi and eastern Louisiana was transferred to the newly created Department of Mississippi and East Louisiana on October 1, and on October 14 the commander of that department was to "assume command of the forces intended to operate in Southwestern Tennessee," effectively transferring West Tennessee from Department No. 2 as well. On November 4, the A&IGO transferred that part of Florida east of the Choctawhatchee River to the newly created Department of Middle Florida. On January 30, 1863, on his own authority, General Joseph E. Johnston extended Department No. 2 to embrace "the line of railroad from Chattanooga to West Point, Ga., with the towns, villages, and stations on it, including the post of Atlanta, Ga., and as much adjacent territory as may be necessary for military purposes," which had been transferred from the Department of East Tennessee to the Department of South Carolina and Georgia on October 7, 1862. On June 8, 1863, the A&IGO announced that "the following will hereafter be the western limits of the Department of East Tennessee, viz: Following the Little Tennessee and Tennessee Rivers to Kingston, thence up Clinch River to mouth of Emery Creek, up Emery Creek to the Cumberland Mountains, and following said mountains to Cumberland Gap. All the country in Tennessee west of this line will be added to the command of General Bragg." No record of the earlier boundary between the two departments has been discovered, but this would indicate that the line had been shifted east with territory being transferred west to Bragg. Abolished on July 25, 1863, and its territory divided between the newly created Department of Tennessee and Johnston's command.

Department of South Carolina

Commander:

Brigadier General Roswell S. Ripley: assigned August 21, 1861

Established August 21, 1861, to consist of that state. On November 5 the coastal defenses of the state were put under the Department of South Carolina, Georgia, and East Florida to be commanded by General Robert E. Lee, who assumed command on November 8. Precisely what constituted the coast remained in question, and on November 9 Secretary of War Judah P. Benjamin informed South Carolina Governor Francis Pickens that "General Lee is in command of the department embracing South Carolina and Georgia, as well as Eastern Florida. This was done in order to enable him to concentrate all our forces at any point that might be attacked." The matter was clarified on December 10 when Lee divided South Carolina's coast into five districts and retained control of the interior of the state himself; Ripley was placed in charge of the Second District.

Department of North Carolina

Because of its proximity to the Confederate capital and President Davis's ever-growing reliance on General Robert E. Lee, the military administration of North Carolina was unlike any other region of the Western Theater. For much of the war, most of the state constituted a department within the

Department of North Carolina and Southern Virginia. Moreover, whether directly or through the commander of that department, from June 1, 1862, until April 9, 1865, Lee, as head of the Department of Northern Virginia, commanded all troops in the Department of North Carolina.

Commanders (Department of North Carolina):

Brigadier General Richard C. Gatlin: officially assigned August 21, 1861, but had been telegraphed to do so on August 19 and he did so on August 20; ordered relived for ill health on March 15, 1862; relieved March 19

Brigadier General Joseph R. Anderson: assigned March 15, 1862; assumed March 19

Major General Theophilus H. Holmes: assigned March 24, 1862; assumed March 25; assigned to command the Trans-Mississippi Department on July 16

Brigadier General Samuel G. French:[3]

Major General Daniel Harvey Hill: assigned July 17, 1862; relinquished command of his division in the Army of Northern Virginia on July 21; assumed command July 29; left to rejoin his division on August 21[4]

Major General Samuel G. French: probably assumed command August 21, 1862, but definitely in command by September 8;[5] nothing indicates he gave up this command when he temporarily commanded the Department of North Carolina and Southern Virginia January 27–February 25, 1863

Major General Daniel Harvey Hill: assigned February 7, 1863; assumed February 25; ordered to Mississippi July 14, but President Davis, who had visited him around July 10, informed him of his promotion to lieutenant general and of his pending transfer and as a consequence Hill departed on July 13[6]

Major General William Henry Chase Whiting: already on duty in department when assigned on July 14, 1863; relieved September 24

Major General George E. Pickett: assigned September 23, 1863; assumed September 24

Not a distinct department between May 5 and November 11, 1864

General Braxton Bragg: assigned November 11, 1864; assumed November 17; ordered to Augusta, Georgia, by President Davis on November 22

Major General William Henry Chase Whiting: temporarily assumed November 23, 1864

General Braxton Bragg: resumed December 17, 1864

Commanders (Department of North Carolina and Southern Virginia):

Major General Gustavus W. Smith: assigned and assumed on September 19, 1862; served as acting secretary of war November 17–21, and remained another week clearing a backlog of paperwork, but there is no indication he turned over command of the department, which was headquartered in Richmond;[7] called from Goldsborough, North Carolina, to Richmond, Virginia, January 27, 1863; submitted his resignation on February 7, which was accepted effective February 17[8]

Major General Samuel G. French: assigned temporarily January 27, 1863; assumed January 28; relieved February 25

Lieutenant General James Longstreet: assigned February 25, 1863; assumed February 26

Department did not exist between May 28, 1863, and April 23, 1864

General Pierre G. T. Beauregard: assigned April 18, 1864; assumed April 23; though he traveled beyond the limits of the department a week previously to meet with President Davis, he apparently remained in charge of the department until he was assigned to command the Military Division of the West on October 3 and the department ceased to exist

Established August 21, 1861, to consist of that state. Roanoke Island, however, had already been occupied by Brigadier General Benjamin Huger with troops from his Department of Norfolk, and Gatlin was in no hurry to change the situation. Finally, on November 26, the A&IGO ordered Gatlin to relieve Huger's troops and take responsibility for the island. Then the A&IGO reversed itself on December 21, declaring "that part of North Carolina east of the Chowan River, together with the counties of Washington and Tyrrell" was removed from the Department of North Carolina and established as a district of the Department of Norfolk. On February 25, 1862, the North Carolina counties of Martin, Bertie, Halifax, Northampton, and Hertford were also transferred to the Department of Norfolk. On May 7, 1862, General Robert E. Lee ordered Holmes to take charge of that portion of North Carolina formally belonging to the Department of Norfolk because of "the withdrawal of General Huger's command" from the Department of Norfolk. On June 1, Lee was assigned to and assumed command of the troops in Virginia and North Carolina; the A&IGO announced the assignment on June 2. On June 3, the A&IGO ordered that "that part of North Carolina west of the Blue Ridge, and adjoining East Tennessee, will be embraced within the Department of East Tennessee," probably to ease the burden on Lee.

The A&IGO officially extended the northern boundary of the Department of North Carolina on June 21 "to the south bank of the James River, including Drewry's Bluff." Headquarters, previously located at Goldsborough, was moved to Petersburg, Virginia.

On September 19, 1862, the A&IGO declared that "hereafter the command of Maj. Gen. G. W. Smith will embrace that part of the country south of the line of operations under General R. E. Lee, including the Department of North Carolina. All commanders within these geographical limits will report to and receive their orders from Major-General Smith." On October 20 this ill-defined "command" included the Department of North Carolina, Department of Henrico, and troops as far north as Fredericksburg, Virginia. The A&IGO announced on April 1, 1863, that

> the geographical limits of the command of Lieutenant-General Longstreet, embracing the defenses of Richmond and extending south to include the State of North Carolina—the whole under the general direction of General R. E. Lee—will be divided into three military departments, as follows: All north of the James River for the defense of Richmond will constitute the Department of Richmond, under Major-General Elzey, headquarters Richmond; all that portion of Virginia south of the James River and east of the county of Powhatan will constitute the Department of Southern Virginia, under Major-General French, headquarters at some central point near Blackwater; the State of North Carolina will constitute the Department of North Carolina under Maj. Gen. D. H. Hill, headquarters Goldsborough.

On May 28, the A&IGO relieved French and declared that the department "will hereafter include the Department of southern Virginia as far north as to embrace the city of Petersburg and its environs, and including the Appomattox River." Headquarters was transferred to Wilmington on July 14. On September 24, Pickett defined the department as embracing "all the district between the Appomattox and Cape Fear Rivers." He obviously received advance notice of the A&IGO's announcement on September 26, that the District of the Cape Fear was removed from the department. On April 18, 1864, the A&IGO consolidated "the Departments of North Carolina and the Cape Fear," which combined embraced "that portion of the State of North Carolina east of the mountains and that section of the State of Virginia south of the James and Appomattox Rivers." Rather than continue as the Department of North Carolina, of which the Cape Fear had formerly been a district, Beauregard resumed using Department of North Carolina and Southern Virginia on April 23, 1864. On May 5, Beauregard divided the Department of North Carolina and Southern Virginia into three districts, with that portion of North Carolina lying north of the Roanoke River combined with southern Virginia constituting the First District with headquarters at Petersburg, Virginia. Consequently, that part of North Carolina remaining under his command was not even contained in a single district. On May 14 the department was extended "to include all that portion of Virginia lying south of James River, including Drewry's Bluff and its defenses."

Military operations had brought the department under the immediate control of General Robert E. Lee before Beauregard was reassigned on October 3. The latter's troops in the vicinity of Petersburg were assigned to

Lieutenant General Richard H. Anderson and the district commanders reported directly to Lee. The A&IGO reestablished it on November 11, 1864, to consist of "the State of North Carolina east of the Blue Ridge Mountains. . . . It will continue a part of the command of General R. E. Lee."

Department of Middle and Eastern Florida

Commanders:

Brigadier General John B. Grayson: assigned August 21, 1861; ordered relieved due to illness October 10

Brigadier General Edmund Kirby Smith: assigned October 10, 1861; countermanded October 22

Brigadier General James H. Trapier: assigned October 22, 1861. At that time he was serving in Charleston, South Carolina, and was not ordered to be relived until November 17. Though he was listed as commanding the department on a monthly report for December, on January 2, 1862, he was at Coosawhatchie, South Carolina, signing as "Commanding, &c., Fernandina." Despite his being present in the department and issuing orders at the time, on March 14, the War Department officially assigned him a second time to command the department. Five days later he was relieved and ordered to report to General Albert Sidney Johnston, commanding Department No. 2.

Florida Governor John Milton: assumed at the request of Grayson prior to October 29, 1861, and sanctioned by Secretary of War Judah P. Benjamin

Colonel W. S. Dilworth: temporarily assigned March 19, 1862

Brigadier General Joseph Finegan: assigned April 8, 1862; assumed April 18

Established August 21, 1861, to include that part of the state east of the Choctawhatchee River. Between November 8, 1861, and April 9, 1862, the commander of the Department of South Carolina, Georgia, and East Florida was responsible for the coastal defense of East Florida.

Merged into Department of South Carolina and Georgia on April 7, 1862, but reestablished on April 9 with headquarters at Tallahassee. On June 25 that part of the department west of the Apalachicola River was transferred to Department No. 2. Merged into the Department of South Carolina and Georgia to be a separate district on October 7, 1862.

Department of Alabama and West Florida

Commanders:

Major General Braxton Bragg: assigned October 7, 1861; assumed October 14; relinquished February 28, 1862

Brigadier General Samuel Jones: assigned by Bragg February 28, 1862[9]

Major General Braxton Bragg: resumed March 4, 1862, by order of General Albert Sydney Johnston, with headquarters at Jackson, Tennessee, "but [Bragg] subsequently explained that he did not intend thereby to take the command from [Jones], but only to attach the department to his command in Tennessee and Mississippi."

Major General Samuel Jones: ordered to Corinth, Mississippi, March 24, 1862; ordered from Corinth to Mobile on March 31

Brigadier General Thomas J. Butler, 9th Brigade, Alabama Militia: assumed temporarily March 29, 1862[10]

Major General Samuel Jones: resumed command April 2, 1862[11]

Brigadier General John H. Forney: assigned April 28, 1862[12]

On October 7, 1861, the War Department issued orders extending Major General Bragg's command in western Florida "to include the coast and State of Alabama…[with] headquarters, near Pensacola." No record of the eastern boundary of Bragg's jurisdiction has been found, but on August 21, 1861, the Choctawhatchee River was designated the western boundary of the newly created Department of Middle and Eastern Florida. If not before, certainly at the time Bragg's command was converted into a department, the Choctawhatchee River would have been its eastern boundary. Bragg did not announce the creation of the new department until October 14. On December 12, it was extended westward to include Pascagoula Bay and that part of Mississippi east of the Pascagoula River. Headquarters moved to Mobile January 27, 1862, but was located temporarily in Pensacola February 28–March 13. On May 26, that part of Mississippi south of the thirty-third parallel and east of the Chickasawhay River was apparently added by default, as it was specifically excluded from the departments bordering the area to the north and west. Ordered merged into Department No. 2 by the A&IGO on June 25, Bragg assumed command of the combined departments on July 2.

Department of Norfolk (VA):

Commander:

Major General Benjamin Huger: already in command on Oct. 15, 1861

Though not officially established by the A&IGO until Oct. 15, 1861, Brigadier General Benjamin Huger had been in charge of the troops in the immediate area around Norfolk since late May. No record of its initial boundaries within Virginia has been located.

During the first year of the war, the A&IGO's most troublesome location to merge into a workable geographical command was Roanoke Island. Shortly after taking command in Norfolk, Brigadier General Huger occupied the island with one of his regiments and continued to support the garrison even after the establishment of the Department of North Carolina on August 21,

1861. On November 26, the A&IGO ordered Brigadier General Richard C. Gatlin, commanding the Department of North Carolina, to relieve Huger's troops and take responsibility for the island. The A&IGO reversed itself on December 21, declaring "that part of North Carolina east of the Chowan River, together with the counties of Washington and Tyrrell" removed from the Department of North Carolina and established as a district of the Department of Norfolk. On February 25, 1862, the North Carolina counties of Martin, Bertie, Halifax, Northampton, and Hertford were transferred to the department as well. On April 12, 1862, General Robert E. Lee ordered Huger to begin reporting to General Joseph E. Johnston, commanding the Department of Northern Virginia. On May 7, 1862, Lee ordered Major General Theophilus H. Holmes, commanding the Department of North Carolina, to take charge of that portion of North Carolina formally belonging to the Department of Norfolk because of "the withdrawal of General Huger's command from the Department."

Department of Georgia

Commander:

Brigadier General Alexander R. Lawton: already commanding at Savannah when assigned October 26, 1861

"The State of Georgia" was established as a separate department on October 26, 1861, with headquarters at Savannah. On November 5 the coastal defenses of the state were put under the Department of South Carolina, Georgia, and East Florida, and the A&IGO never distinguished between those defenses and the entire state. Though Lawton continued to sign as commanding the "Department of Georgia" as late as April 14, 1862, after November 8, 1861, he reported to the commander of the Department of South Carolina, Georgia, and East Florida, General Robert E. Lee, who addressed Lawton as "Commanding District of Georgia." If the Department of Georgia did not cease to exist on December 10, 1861, when Lee announced the District of Georgia, certainly after April 7, 1862, when Georgia became part of the Department of South Carolina and Georgia, no doubt could remain—except in Lawton's mind.

Department of South Carolina, Georgia, and East Florida

Commanders:

General Robert E. Lee: assigned November 5, 1861; assumed November 8; left March 3, 1862

Major General John C. Pemberton: temporarily assigned March 3, 1862; assumed March 4; assigned permanently March 14; assumed March 19

Established November 5, 1861, to consist of "the coasts of South Carolina, Georgia, and East Florida." The South Carolina and Georgia coasts were divided into districts, but East Florida remained part of the Department of Middle and Eastern Florida whose commander reported to Lee. Precisely what constituted the coast remained in question. On November 9, 1861, Secretary of War Judah P. Benjamin informed South Carolina Governor Francis Pickens that "General Lee is in command of the department embracing South Carolina and Georgia, as well as Eastern Florida. This was done in order to enable him to concentrate all our forces at any point that might be attacked." Whatever the original intention, Lee functioned as commander of the entire states of South Carolina and Georgia. Merged into the Department of South Carolina and Georgia on April 7, 1862.

Department of East Tennessee

Commanders:

Major General Edmund Kirby Smith: assigned February 25, 1862; assumed March 8

Major General John P. McCown: temporarily assigned August 24, 1862; assumed September 1; ordered relieved September 19; relieved September 23; reassigned by General Braxton Bragg on September 27 but overruled by the A&IGO

Major General Samuel Jones: assigned September 19, 1862; assumed September 23; ordered transferred by Bragg on September 27; declined to vacate command until confirmed by the A&IGO who overruled Bragg. On October 10 the A&IGO instructed Jones that "in the absence of other orders from General Bragg you will for the present exercise command over the country between the Tennessee and Cumberland Rivers," while remaining in Knoxville. Consequently, Jones was to command the District of Middle Tennessee as Bragg desired, but he was to do so while remaining in and continuing to command the Department of East Tennessee.

Major General Edmund Kirby Smith: announced on October 20, 1862, at Flat Lick, Kentucky, that he was resuming command of the department and as such issued orders between October 20 and November 1.[13]

Major General Samuel Jones: initially unaware of Kirby Smith's actions, Jones continued to run the department from Knoxville. When Richmond learned of this ridiculous situation, Secretary of War George W. Randolph notified Kirby Smith on October 26: "You are second on the list of lieutenant-generals, and of course command by virtue of your rank; but until the plan of the fall campaign in Tennessee is determined General Jones will remain in the department. Such measures as you deem necessary may be immediately taken for the defense of Cumberland

Gap. Show this dispatch to General Jones." Consequently, Jones remained in command of the department. On November 4, 1862, he was ordered to report for duty in the Department of Mississippi and East Louisiana, but remained in command of the Department of East Tennessee until November 9.[14]

Lieutenant General Edmund Kirby Smith: it appears he resumed command on November 9, 1862, only to depart again to resume command of his corps of the Army of Tennessee on November 20[15]

Brigadier General Henry Heth: temporarily assigned by Kirby Smith November 18, 1862; definitely in command by November 20 but did not claim pay for commanding the department prior to November 25;[16] relieved December 23

Lieutenant General Edmund Kirby Smith: after most of his corps was ordered transferred to Vicksburg on December 15, he resumed command of the department on December 23, 1862; apparently issued his last order on January 6 but drew pay for commanding the department through January 31, 1863, but was ordered to the Trans-Mississippi on January 14[17]

Brigadier General Henry Heth: in command on January 17, 1863; ordered relived by the A&IGO January 17;[18] relieved February 4

Brigadier General Daniel S. Donelson: assigned January 17, 1863; relieved from duty with the Army of Tennessee January 30; assumed February 4; became too ill to command sometime between March 30 and April 9, and died April 17[19]

Brigadier General William G. M. Davis: in temporary command by April 10, 1863; commanding on April 23,[20] and undoubtedly relieved on April 25

Major General Dabney H. Maury: assigned April 15, 1863; assumed April 25; relieved May 12

Major General Simon Bolivar Buckner: assigned April 27, 1863; assumed May 12; traveled to Richmond, Virginia, the first week of June but did not relinquish command; in Knoxville June 24; departed on June 27 with reinforcements for General Braxton Bragg

Brigadier General John Pegram: temporarily assumed June 27, 1863

Major General Simon Bolivar Buckner: resumed July 9, 1863; remained in command even while commanding a division and corps in the Army of Tennessee

Lieutenant General James Longstreet: apparently by default, Longstreet took command on November 5, 1863, when he marched from Chattanooga toward Knoxville; relieved April 12, 1864

Major General Simon Bolivar Buckner: assumed April 12, 1864; ordered to the Trans-Mississippi Department on April 28 and relinquished command on May 2

Brigadier General William E. "Grumble" Jones: assigned May 1, 1864;[21] assumed May 2

Colonel George B. Crittenden: assigned by Brigadier General William E. Jones May 31, 1864; relieved June 22

Brigadier General John Hunt Morgan: assumed June 22, 1864; relieved August 30 pending an investigation of his recent expedition into Kentucky

Brigadier General John Echols: assigned August 22, 1864; assumed August 30[22]

Major General John C. Breckinridge:[23] assigned September 27, 1864; assumed command on October 1;[24] in command on January 6, 1865, but by January 19 he was in Richmond, where he would remain as secretary of war

Brigadier General John Echols: assumed command upon Breckinridge's departure[25]

Lieutenant General Jubal A. Early: assigned by General Robert E. Lee on February 25, 1865, to command in addition to the Valley District, Department of Northern Virginia; relieved by Lee on March 29

Brigadier General John Echols: assigned March 29, 1865

Formerly the District of East Tennessee, Department No. 2. On February 25, 1862, the A&IGO ordered Kirby Smith to "proceed to Knoxville, and assume command of the troops in East Tennessee, reporting by letter to General A. S. Johnston." No record of the original boundary between the two departments has been found but on March 21, the A&IGO announced "the department under the command of Maj. Gen. E. K. Smith is extended so as to embrace within its limits Chattanooga, Tenn., and the troops in its vicinity." Based on subsequent A&IGO orders, it appears that Richmond authorities intended to convert the former District of East Tennessee of Department No. 2 into an independent department that, should it be cut off from the remainder of Department No. 2 by the advancing Federals, could then report directly to Richmond, and to make such an arrangement in a manner that would not reflect negatively on Johnston's reputation. Though no written record has been found, the actions of Johnston's successor, General Pierre G. T. Beauregard, and Kirby Smith indicate that Kirby Smith was authorized to report directly to Richmond following Johnston's death. On June 3, the A&IGO ordered that "that part of North Carolina west of the Blue Ridge, and adjoining East Tennessee, will be embraced within the Department of East Tennessee." On July 18, the department was further expanded to "include that part of the State of Georgia which is north of the railroad leading from Augusta via Atlanta to West Point," as the loss of Chattanooga appeared imminent and Richmond authorities wanted Kirby Smith to retreat south, rather than east, should that occur.

Confederate fortunes in the Western Theater quickly turned, however, and, on October 7, with Kirby Smith in Kentucky, the A&IGO transferred all of Georgia into the Department of South Carolina and Georgia. Apparently this order failed to reach Kirby Smith because on November 20, Adjutant and Inspector General Samuel Cooper directly notified Kirby Smith "Atlanta is not within the Department of East Tennessee, but will probably be added to it soon." Cooper's bizarre speculation proved unfounded but no doubt reflected the thinking of many following the Confederate abandonment of Kentucky. With Kirby Smith in Kentucky and Beauregard being assigned to command the Department of South Carolina and Georgia, the transfer of northern Georgia was logical, especially in light of the other command problems regarding Jones, Bragg, and Kirby Smith. On December 6, 1862, the town of Bristol, Virginia, was added to the department, which was further expanded on January 17, 1863, to "include within its limits the counties of Washington, Russell, Buchanan, Wise, Scott, and Lee, in Virginia. The command of Brig. Gen. Humphrey Marshall will be considered as embraced within this department." On June 8, 1863, the A&IGO announced that "the following will hereafter be the western limits of the Department of East Tennessee, viz: Following the Little Tennessee and Tennessee Rivers to Kingston, thence up Clinch River to mouth of Emery Creek, up Emery Creek to the Cumberland Mountains, and following said mountains to Cumberland Gap. All the country in Tennessee west of this line will be added to the command of General Bragg." Abolished on July 25 and its territory merged with part of Department No. 2 to form the Department of Tennessee under Bragg, at least in part because of the recommendation of Buckner.[26]

On August 6, however, Bragg announced that "the administration of that district [East Tennessee] will remain with Major-General Buckner." Then, on August 28, the A&IGO reversed itself, announcing that "the Department of East Tennessee will be continued in its former limits so far as the administrative duties of the command are regarded. In strategic operations it will be subordinate to and a part of the Department of Tennessee."[27] On September 2, Buckner acknowledged that Bragg had made the Hiwassee River the boundary between the two departments. Boundary redefined on February 1, 1864, to "include, on the east, the counties of Russell, Buchanan, Wise, Scott, Lee, and Washington, in Virginia, and that part of North Carolina west of the Blue Ridge; on the south, the country north of the Little Tennessee River; and on the west the country east of the Tennessee and Clinch Rivers and Emory's Creek." On May 23, Jones was assigned to command of the Department of Southwestern Virginia as well, which he assumed on May 25. Combining the two departments resulted from the commander of the Department of Southwestern Virginia, Major General John C. Breckinridge, having moved east with a sizeable portion of his troops to defend the Valley District of the Department of Northern Virginia and then to reinforce the Army of Northern Virginia. Until February 20, 1865, Jones and his successors commanded the Department of Southwestern Virginia and East Tennessee. On February 20, General Robert E. Lee ordered "the command of Lieutenant-General Early [Valley District, Department of Northern Virginia] is extended to embrace the Department of Southwestern Virginia and East Tennessee, and the department thus formed will hereafter [be] designated the Department of Western Virginia and East Tennessee." Lee had exceeded his authority, as "it is the province of the War Department alone to make and unmake commands." Following Early's relief on March 29, Echols's command did not include the Valley District.

Department of South Carolina and Georgia

Commanders:

Major General John C. Pemberton: in command on April 7, 1862; on September 17, ordered to report to Richmond upon being relieved by Beauregard; relieved September 24

General Pierre G. T. Beauregard: assigned August 29, 1862; assumed September 24

Established April 7, 1862, by merging the Department of South Carolina, Georgia, and East Florida and the Department of Middle and Eastern Florida. Two days later the Department of Middle and Eastern Florida was reestablished as an independent command. On June 25, that portion of Georgia west of "the line of railroad from Chattanooga via Atlanta to West Point, on the Chattahoochee River," was transferred to Department No. 2. On July 18, "that part of the State of Georgia which is north of the railroad leading from Augusta via Atlanta to West Point" was transferred to the Department of East Tennessee. On October 7, the A&IGO abolished the Department of Middle and Eastern Florida and made it a district of the Department of South Carolina and Georgia, which consisted of "the States of South Carolina, Georgia, and that part of Florida east of the Apalachicola River." On November 4, the A&IGO established "the Departments of East and Middle Florida; the former to comprise that part of Florida east of the Suwanee River; the latter west of the Suwanee River to the Choctawhatchee River." The commanders of each of these departments would report to Beauregard. Renamed the Department of South Carolina, Georgia, and Florida in December by Beauregard.

Department of Southern Mississippi and East Louisiana

Commander:

Major General Earl Van Dorn: assigned June 20, 1862; assumed June 24

Announced by the War Department on June 20, 1862, its boundary was set forth by Van Dorn on June 26 as consisting of that part of Louisiana east of the Mississippi River and those counties of Mississippi lying south of the thirty-third parallel. On July 2, however, Bragg still considered it part of his Department No. 2, calling it the District of the Mississippi, and describing it as "embracing all the country west of Pearl River from its mouth to Jackson, Miss., and the line of the Mississippi Central Railroad to Grand Junction." On July 18, the A&IGO ordered that "Military Department No. 2 will embrace the States of Mississippi, Alabama, East Louisiana, and part of Florida which is west of the Chattahoochee and Apalachicola Rivers." It is likely that this is but another example of the A&IGO's inability to be precise and that the intention was for Van Dorn to command an independent department but to report to the commander of Department No. 2 rather than Richmond. Whether department or district, on October 1 it became part of the newly created Department of Mississippi and East Louisiana.

Department of South Carolina, Georgia, and Florida

Commanders:

General Pierre G. T. Beauregard: already in command in December 1862; temporarily reassigned April 20, 1864

Major General Samuel Jones: temporarily assumed April 20, 1864

Lieutenant General William J. Hardee: assigned September 28, 1864, by General John Bell Hood by order of President Davis (A&IGO issued official order October 28); assumed October 5; relieved February 16, 1865

General Pierre G. T. Beauregard: assumed February 16, 1865; relieved February 25

General Joseph E. Johnston: assigned by General-in-Chief Robert E. Lee on February 22, 1865; assumed February 25

Beginning about December 2, 1862, some of Beauregard's correspondence and orders for the Department of South Carolina and Georgia have the headline Department of South Carolina, Georgia, and Florida. In G. O. No. 127, Headquarters Department of South Carolina, Georgia, and Florida, December 19, 1862, Beauregard announces his staff members as "commander of the department." He followed up on December 28 by announcing the "existing sub-divisions of this department," which included four military districts of South Carolina; the District of Georgia that embraced "the State of Georgia, excluding the defenses of the Apalachicola River and its main affluents"; the District of East Florida "including all that portion of the State of Florida lying east of the Suwanee River"; and the District of Middle Florida embracing "that portion of Florida between the Suwanee and Choctawhatchee Rivers, and including all works for the defense of the Apalachicola and its main affluents." Though the commanders in Florida went along with Beauregard's change and no evidence has been found that the War Department called Beauregard on it, the A&IGO continued to refer to the two Florida districts as departments, and on at least one occasion referred to the Department of Middle Florida as the Department of West Florida.[28] On the authority of General Joseph E. Johnston, Department No. 2 was extended on January 30, 1863, to embrace "the line of railroad from Chattanooga to West Point, Ga., with the towns, villages, and stations on it, including the post of Atlanta, Ga., and as much adjacent territory as may be necessary for military purposes." On July 25, 1863, that part of Georgia west of a line running south from the Blue Ridge Mountains in North Carolina "to the Georgia Railroad; thence along the lines of railroad, via Atlanta, to West Point, and from that place north to the Tennessee River" was transferred to the newly created Department of Tennessee. As later clarifications would make clear, when the A&IGO ran a line in a given direction it was not meant literally. In this case, the line running north from West Point followed the Georgia–Alabama state line. Referencing an August 12, 1863, letter that noted orders issued on July 25, the A&IGO issued an order on February 13, 1864, describing the line running south from North Carolina as "a line south from the source of the Little Tennessee River to Greensborough, Ga.," which left extreme northeastern Georgia as well as that part of the state south of the railroad running from Greensborough via Atlanta to West Point within this department. On February 23, 1864, the A&IGO ordered that "the Districts of East and Middle Florida will be united into a district to be known as the District of Florida, and will be embraced in the command of the Department of South Carolina, Georgia, and Florida." On August 15, 1864, the A&IGO created the Department of Tennessee and Georgia "to include all the State of Georgia north and west of the following line: Commencing at Augusta and running along the line of the Augusta and Savannah Railroad to Millen, thence along the western boundary lines of the counties of Bulloch and Tattnall, thence along the south bank of the Ocmulgee River to the northeast corner of Irwin County, thence south to the Florida line, thence along the Florida line to the Appalachicola [*sic*] River." One source claims the department was expanded on November 17 to embrace all of Georgia south of the Chattahoochee, and that on January 4, 1865, it was extended "to west of Augusta and Millen, embracing approaches."[29] If the former were true, the latter would have been unnecessary. While the latter would have made sense militarily, the A&IGO failed to mention it on January 6 when it announced that the department included "besides the States of South Carolina and Florida, that portion of Georgia embraced in the following lines: Commencing at Augusta and running along the Georgia Railroad to Warrenton; thence, via Sparta and Milledgeville, following the line of the railroad, to the Ocmulgee River, but not including Macon; down the Ocmulgee to Coffee County, following the western boundary of that county to the Allapaha [*sic*] River, and down that river and the Suwanee to the Gulf." Headquarters was located in Charleston until that city was evacuated.

Department of Mississippi and East Louisiana

Commanders:

Major General John C. Pemberton: assigned October 1, 1862; assumed October 14

General Joseph E. Johnston, as commander of the Department of the West: assigned May 9, 1863; assumed May 13

Lieutenant General William J. Hardee: assumed as temporary commander of the Department of the West: July 24, 1863[30]

Established on October 1, 1862, to include Mississippi and that portion of Louisiana east of the Mississippi River. Almost immediately promoted to lieutenant general, Pemberton's responsibilities were expanded on October 14 to "assume command of the forces intended to operate in Southwestern Tennessee," the same day he established his headquarters at Jackson. Contrary to popular belief, the department ceased to exist on July 25, 1863, when it was merged with territory formerly belonging to Department No. 2 to create an actual Department of the West, rather than one that was only supervisory in nature. As this goes against current belief, please refer to the Department of the West for a detailed explanation.

Department of East Florida

Commander:

Brigadier General Joseph Finegan: assigned November 4, 1862

Established November 4, 1862, to comprise that part of Florida "east of the Suwanee River...[with] habitual headquarters at Lake City." Rather than Richmond, the commander was to report to General Pierre G. T. Beauregard, commanding the Department of South Carolina and Georgia. On December 28, Beauregard announced the "existing sub-divisions of this department [South Carolina, Georgia, and Florida]," including the District of East Florida, which "included all that portion of the State of Florida lying east of the Suwanee River." Though Finegan went along with Beauregard's change and no evidence has been found that the War Department called Beauregard on it, the A&IGO continued to refer to the two Florida districts as departments. On February 23, 1864, however, the A&IGO ordered that "the Districts of East and Middle Florida will be united into a district to be known as the District of Florida, and will be embraced in the command of the Department of South Carolina, Georgia, and Florida. Maj. Gen. Patton Anderson is assigned to the command of the District of Florida. He will proceed to that district and report to General Beauregard."

Department of Middle Florida

Commanders:

None assigned November 4, 1862

Brigadier General Howell Cobb: assigned by General Pierre G. T. Beauregard on November 11, 1862

Brigadier General Joseph Finegan: assigned temporarily August 7, 1863; assumed August 12

Brigadier General Howell Cobb: resumed prior to being "assigned to the duty of organizing, at Atlanta, the Georgia militia" on September 8, 1863

Brigadier General Joseph Finegan: assigned temporarily and assumed September 8, 1863

Brigadier General William M. Gardner: assigned October 6, 1863; assumed by November 1

Established November 4, 1862, to comprise that part of Florida "west of the Suwanee River to the Choctawhatchee River...whose habitual headquarters will be at Quincy." Rather than Richmond, the commander was to report to General Beauregard, commanding the Department of South Carolina and Georgia. On December 28, Beauregard announced the "existing subdivisions of this department [South Carolina, Georgia, and Florida]," including the District of Middle Florida embracing "that portion of Florida between the Suwanee and Choctawhatchee Rivers, and including all works for the defense of the Apalachicola and its main affluents." Though Cobb went along with Beauregard's change and no evidence has been found that the War Department called Beauregard on it, the A&IGO continued to refer to the two Florida districts as departments, and on at least one occasion they referred to the Department of Middle Florida as the Department of West Florida.[31] According to a letter by Adjutant and Inspector General Samuel Cooper on August 12, that portion of Florida between the Choctawhatchee and Apalachicola Rivers was transferred to the Department of the West. On February 23, 1864, the A&IGO ordered that "the Districts of East and Middle Florida will be united into a district to be known as the District of Florida, and will be embraced in the command of the Department of South Carolina, Georgia, and Florida. Maj. Gen. Patton Anderson is assigned to the command of the District of Florida. He will proceed to that district and report to General Beauregard."

Department of the West

Commanders:

General Joseph E. Johnston: assigned November 24, 1862; assumed December 4

Lieutenant General William J. Hardee: assumed temporary command July 24, 1863;[32] relieved August 6[33]

General Joseph E. Johnston: resumed August 6, 1863; relinquished December 22

Lieutenant General Leonidas Polk: assigned December 22, 1863; assumed December 23[34]

Established on November 24, 1862, to embrace the Departments of East Tennessee, No. 2, and Mississippi and East Louisiana in order to have someone in the Western Theater, rather than the authorities in Richmond, coordinate troop movements between the three departments. Its original boundary, however, is significant, because it included the area east of the Mississippi River to a line "commencing with the Blue Ridge range of mountains running through the western part of North Carolina, and following the line of said mountains through the northern part of Georgia to the railroad south from Chattanooga; thence by that road to West Point, and down the west or right bank of the Chattahoochee River to the boundary of Alabama and Florida; following that boundary west to the Choctawhatchee River, and down that river to Choctawhatchee Bay (including the waters of that bay) to the Gulf of Mexico." That portion of Georgia it included had been transferred from the Department of East Tennessee to the Department of South Carolina and Georgia on October 7. Rather than a mistake by the A&IGO, however, it appears that Johnston's authority was deliberately extended beyond the geographical limits of the three departments he was to coordinate because of the need to use the railroad running from West Point via Atlanta to Chattanooga to shuttle troops between Tennessee and Mississippi. The A&IGO reiterated Johnston's authority over part of Georgia on November 29 when it announced "the city of Atlanta, Ga., will be included within the department under the command of General Joseph E. Johnston."

Extended by the expansion of the Department of East Tennessee to include the town of Bristol, Virginia, on December 6, 1862, and the Virginia counties of Washington, Russell, Buchanan, Wise, Scott, and Lee, in Virginia, along with "the command of Brig. Gen. Humphrey Marshall," on January 17, 1863. When the Department of the Gulf was created in the spring from territory formerly contained in Department No. 2, it was specified that it "will constitute a department within the geographical command of General J. E. Johnston."

On May 9, 1863, Secretary of War James A. Seddon instructed Johnston: "Proceed at once to Mississippi and take chief command of the forces, giving to those in the field, as far as practicable, the encouragement and benefit of our personal direction. Arrange to take for temporary service with you, or to be followed without delay, 3,000 good troops.... Acknowledge receipt." Not only did this message contradict the reason for the department's creation, it portended its imminent dismantling. When Vicksburg fell on July 4, there was no longer a need for someone closer than Richmond to supervise troop movements between Tennessee and Mississippi. Consequently, on July 25, the A&IGO abolished two of the four departments Johnston oversaw, combined them to form the Department of Tennessee, and failed to mention Johnston's role concerning the new department. With his relationship already extremely strained with President Davis at the time, Johnston probably realized that this was not an oversight by the A&IGO. Needing to clarify the matter in any case, he immediately queried the War Department. On August 12, Adjutant and Inspector General Samuel Cooper responded by letter:

> The limits of your department, on the east and north, seem settled by Special Orders, copies of which are herein inclosed; but as you request a more explicit statement defining them, I reply by letter. It is contemplated that your command should embrace the country west of the Apalachicola and Chattahoochee Rivers, and of the Alabama and Georgia State line, until it strikes the southeastern corner of Calhoun County, in the former State; thence along the southern line of the following tier of counties in Alabama, to wit: Calhoun, Saint Clair, Blount, Morgan, Lawrence, and Franklin; thence along the Alabama and Mississippi State line to the Tennessee River, and along that river to its confluence with the Ohio River.
>
> The Counties named above, and all the country north of them, come within the limits of General Bragg's department.

Contrary to current belief, it was not the Department of the West but the Department of Mississippi and East Louisiana that was abolished on July 25. In the late nineteenth century the editorial staff of the *Official Records* understood the A&IGO's actions and for that reason indexed Johnston's orders issued during this period under the Department of the West. Sometime during the twentieth century historians began misinterpreting these events[35] and, admittedly, they were aided by Johnston and Hardee who headed their orders as coming from "Headquarters" without referencing any department.

Even though Johnston had been ordered into the field on May 9, it was the fall of Vicksburg that brought about a formal change regarding Johnston's responsibilities. Rather than merely a supervisor between Richmond and department commanders in the Western Theater, he was now directly responsible for a sizeable portion of that theater as well as being the intermediator for the commander of the Department of the Gulf. On July 25, the department was bounded on the west by the Mississippi River, on the north by the Ohio and Tennessee Rivers, and on the east by a line running south along the Alabama and Georgia border, thence down the Chattahoochee to the northern boundary of Florida. Cooper's letter of August 12 indicates that Florida west of the Apalachicola River was also added to the Department of the West on July 25. On August 4, Franklin, Lawrence, Morgan, Blount, Saint Clair, Calhoun, Cherokee, De Kalb, and Marshall counties in northern Alabama were transferred to the Department of Tennessee. On November 14, the Department of West Tennessee was established; its boundaries were never defined, but its commander reported to Johnston rather than directly to Richmond. When Polk took over he continued to follow Johnston's habit of only using "Headquarters," but in a circular issued on January 11, 1864, he referenced "East Louisiana, Mississippi, and Western Tennessee." The A&IGO was quick to set him straight on the name, if not the boundary of his department, ordering on January 28, that "that portion of the Confederate States now under the command of Lieut. Gen. Leonidas Polk" will be known as the Department of Alabama, Mississippi, and East Louisiana. With Johnston gone, there was no reason to retain the former name.

Department of the Gulf

Commander:

Major General Dabney H. Maury: assigned April 27, 1863; assumed May 19[36]

Previously a district of Department No. 2, the A&IGO was quicker to get the Department of the Gulf's first commander there than to announce its establishment which, on June 8, 1863, defined it as "Mobile, and the country containing the approaches to it, as well as that immediately around it, will constitute a department within the geographical command of General J. E. Johnston." It remained an independent department following the creation of the equally geographically ill-defined Department of Alabama, Mississippi, and East Louisiana on January 28, 1864. To settle the boundary between the two, the A&IGO announced on February 7 that "the boundaries of the Department of the Gulf are thus defined: Beginning on the west at the mouth of Pearl River and running north with said river to the 32d parallel of latitude; thence along that parallel eastward to its intersection with the Georgia State line; thence southward with the eastern boundary line of the Department of Alabama, Mississippi, and East Louisiana to the Gulf." By this description, all of the department was west of the eastern boundary of the Department of Alabama, Mississippi, and East Louisiana. Most likely the A&IGO intended for the Department of the Gulf to be independent but have its commander report to the commander of the Department of Alabama, Mississippi, and East Louisiana as he had to General Johnston, whom Lieutenant General Leonidas Polk had succeeded, rather than directly to Richmond. Apparently Polk, commander of the Department of Alabama, Mississippi, and East Louisiana, was not satisfied with this arrangement, and on April 6, 1864, the A&IGO revoked the June 8,

1863, order and designated the Department of the Gulf "as the District of the Gulf, in the Department of Alabama, Mississippi, and East Louisiana."

Department of Tennessee

Commanders:

General Braxton Bragg: in command of Department No. 2 on July 25, 1863, when department renamed; took a ten-day leave to visit his ailing wife, which apparently ended on August 6 when he assumed command of the new department[37]

Lieutenant General Leonidas Polk: temporarily in command July 26–August 5, 1863

General Braxton Bragg: assumed August 6, 1863; relinquished command December 2

Lieutenant General William J. Hardee: assumed temporary command December 2, 1863[38]

General Joseph E. Johnston: assigned December 16, 1863; assumed command December 27; relieved July 18, 1864

General John Bell Hood: assigned July 18, 1864

Established on July 25, 1863, by merging the Department of East Tennessee with part of Department No. 2 and embracing "the country now included in the Department of East Tennessee and west of the Blue Ridge Mountains in North Carolina, and a line running south to the Georgia Railroad; thence along the lines of railroad, via Atlanta, to West Point, and from that place north to the Tennessee River, and down that stream to its mouth." As later clarifications would make clear, when the A&IGO ran a line in a given direction it was not meant literally. In the case of the above, the line running north from West Point followed the Georgia–Alabama state line. Referencing an August 12, 1863, letter which noted orders issued on July 25, the A&IGO issued an order on February 13, 1864, describing the line running south from North Carolina as "a line south from the source of the Little Tennessee River to Greensborough, Ga." The following counties in Alabama were added on August 4: Franklin, Lawrence, Morgan, Blount, Saint Clair, Calhoun, Cherokee, De Kalb, and Marshall. On August 28, the A&IGO modified previous orders, announcing that "the Department of East Tennessee will be continued in its former limits so far as the administrative duties of the command are regarded. In strategic operations it will be subordinate to and a part of the Department of Tennessee." On September 2, Major General Simon Bolivar Buckner acknowledged that Bragg has made the Hiwassee River the boundary between the Department of Tennessee and the Department of East Tennessee. The boundary between the two departments was defined by the A&IGO on February 1, 1864, as the "Tennessee and Clinch Rivers and Emory's Creek."

On February 13, 1864, the A&IGO ordered that "the Department of Tennessee will be bounded on the north and east by the western limits of the Department of East Tennessee, as described in paragraph XIII, Special Orders, No. 26, current series, and a line south from the source of the Little Tennessee River to Greensborough, Ga., on the south and west by the Georgia Railroad from that place to Atlanta, Ga., and the Montgomery and West Point Railroad to West Point, Ga., and on the west by the eastern and northern limits of the Department of Mississippi [Alabama, Mississippi, and East Louisiana], as described in a letter from this office dated August 12, 1863, addressed to General Joseph E. Johnston." On March 25, 1864, the western boundary was redefined as running "from Gunter's Landing on the Tennessee River, in a direct line to Gadsden, on the Coosa River; thence down that river to the junction with the Tallapoosa River; thence in a direct line to the intersection of the northern boundary of Florida with the Chattahoochee River, and down that river and bay to the Gulf." On August 15, 1864, the department was merged into the newly created Department of Tennessee and Georgia.

Department of the Cape Fear

Commander:

Major General William Henry Chase Whiting: already in command on September 26, 1863

Formerly a district of the Department of North Carolina, on September 26, 1863, it was separated from that department and its commander was ordered to report directly to the War Department. On April 18, 1864, it was reunited with the Department of North Carolina.

Department of West Tennessee

Commander:

Brigadier General Nathan Bedford Forrest: assigned November 14, 1863; assumed by December 6

By order of President Davis, established by General Joseph E. Johnston on November 14, 1863. No geographical boundary was set, rather, Forrest "will, on arriving there, immediately proceed to raise and organize as many troops for the Confederate States service as he finds practicable." By December 6 he had established his headquarters at Jackson and raised about five thousand men. It is clear from the manner in which the department was established and by a letter written on December 6 by Forrest to Johnston, commander of the Department of the West, that Forrest was to report to him rather than directly to Richmond. After he replaced Johnston, Lieutenant General

Leonidas Polk issued a circular on January 11, 1864, announcing that "East Louisiana, Mississippi, and Western Tennessee, are hereby organized into two cavalry departments. The dividing line between these two cavalry departments will run so as to include in the northern department the counties of Monroe, Chickasaw, Calhoun, Yalobusha, and Tallahatchie, and that part of Sunflower and Boliver lying north of a line drawn from the southwest corner of Tallahatchie County to the town of Prentiss, on the Mississippi River." Forrest was given command of the northern department. Forrest responded by signing as commanding "Cavalry Department of West Tennessee and North Mississippi." This resulted in Assistant Adjutant General H. L. Clay endorsing one such document: "The Cavalry Department of West Tennessee and North Mississippi is not known at this office. North Mississippi and West Tennessee are within the limits of General Polk's command," which led to a second endorsement: "An inspection of this command has been ordered." Before Forrest learned of his bureaucratic misstep, however, he began signing as commanding "Forrest's Cavalry Department," which apparently was acceptable to the War Department. Based on the A&IGO's overruling General Robert E. Lee's attempt to alter departmental boundaries in February 1865 (see Department of East Tennessee), it is surprising that there is no official recognition of this department being abolished.

Department of Alabama, Mississippi, and East Louisiana

Commanders:

Lieutenant General Leonidas Polk: already in command on January 28, 1864; relieved May 4; relinquished "temporarily" May 9

Major General Stephen D. Lee: assigned May 4, 1864; assumed May 9; ordered to Army of Tennessee July 26 where he assumed command of Hood's Corps on July 27

Major General Dabney H. Maury: assumed temporary command July 26, 1864

Lieutenant General Richard Taylor: assigned August 15, 1864; assumed September 6, with headquarters at Meridian, Mississippi; having received orders on November 16 from General Pierre G. T. Beauregard to take charge of the forces opposing Major General William T. Sherman's march to the sea, he arrived at Macon, Georgia, at dawn on November 22; on December 1 President Davis telegraphed him in Savannah to return to his department[39]

Major General Dabney H. Maury: temporarily assumed November 22, 1864[40]

Lieutenant General Richard Taylor: resumed December 12, 1864;[41] relieved January 23, 1865, to take temporary command of the Army of Tennessee;

though Beauregard wanted the assignment made permanent, Taylor objected, and was relieved on January 26; there is no record he relinquished temporary command of the department during these four days

Established on January 28, 1864, to include "that portion of the Confederate States now under the command of Lieut. Gen. Leonidas Polk." Hardly surprising with such a description, Polk was quick to stretch the limits of his department (see the Department of the Gulf and the Department of West Tennessee for his actions regarding those departments, both of which were commanded by officers he outranked, which was not the case with General Joseph E. Johnston). On March 25, the A&IGO had to specify the line between Polk and Johnston's Department of Tennessee as running "from Gunter's Landing on the Tennessee River, in a direct line to Gadsden, on the Coosa River; thence down that river to the junction with the Tallapoosa River; thence in a direct line to the intersection of the northern boundary of Florida with the Chattahoochee River, and down that river and bay to the Gulf." On May 8, 1864, in a departmental circular, Polk defined the boundaries as "beginning at the confluence of Tennessee and Ohio Rivers; thence along the Tennessee to Gunter's Landing; thence in a direct line to Gadsden, on Coosa River; thence down that river to its junction with Tallapoosa River; thence in a direct line to intersection of northern boundary of Florida with the Choctawhatchee River, and down that river and bay to the Gulf; south by the Gulf of Mexico and west by the Mississippi River to mouth of Ohio; thence up the Ohio to mouth of Tennessee River." On October 1, the A&IGO redefined the eastern boundary as "the Appalachicola [*sic*] River, thence along the Chattahoochee River north and following the boundary line between Georgia and Alabama to the Tennessee River." Apparently this order failed to reach Taylor, who wrote the A&IGO on October 30: "Please send orders establishing Alabama and Georgia State line as eastern boundary of my department, according to the verbal instructions received by me from the President." Became a part of the Military Division of the West on October 3, 1864.

Department of Tennessee and Georgia

Commanders:

General John Bell Hood: already in command on August 15, 1864; relieved at own request January 23, 1865

Lieutenant General Richard Taylor: temporarily assumed January 23, 1865, on own authority following Hood's departure but officially ordered to do so later that day by Beauregard; ended January 26[42]

Lieutenant General Alexander P. Stewart: in other instances of the war, command of the Army of Tennessee equated to command of its department as well, and he was in charge of taking that army from Mississippi to South Carolina. Consequently, he should be considered commander of the department from January 26, 1865, until relieved by Beauregard

General Pierre G. T. Beauregard: by February 19, 1865, Stewart had returned to command of his corps and Beauregard was in command of the army

General Joseph E. Johnston: assigned by General-in-Chief Robert E. Lee on February 22, 1865; assumed on February 25[43]

Major General Howell Cobb: assigned by Johnston on March 27, 1865, and assumed same day

Established August 15, 1864, by expanding the Department of Tennessee "to include all the State of Georgia north and west of the following line: Commencing at Augusta and running along the line of the Augusta and Savannah Railroad to Millen, thence along the western boundary lines of the counties of Bulloch and Tattnall, thence along the south bank of the Ocmulgee River to the northeast corner of Irwin County, thence south to the Florida line, thence along the Florida line to the Appalachicola [*sic*] River." On October 1, the A&IGO redefined the western boundary as "commencing at the southwestern boundary between Georgia and Florida on the Appalachicola [*sic*] River, thence along the Chattahoochee River north and following the boundary line between Georgia and Alabama to the Tennessee River" and its southern boundary being the northern boundary of Florida. Became a part of the Military Division of the West on October 3, 1864. On January 6, 1865, extended to include that part of Georgia north and west of a line "commencing at Augusta and running along the Georgia Railroad to Warrenton; thence, via Sparta and Milledgeville, following the line of the railroad, to the Ocmulgee River, but not including Macon; down the Ocmulgee to Coffee County, following the western boundary of that county to the Allapaha [*sic*] River, and down that river and the Suwanee to the Gulf."

Department of Western Kentucky

Commanders:

Brigadier General Adam R. Johnson: assigned September 6, 1864

Brigadier General Hylan B. Lyon: assigned September 26, 1864

Established September 6, 1864, "to wit: Commencing at the mouth of Salt River, Ky., and extending through Elizabethtown, Glasgow, and Tompkinsville, Ky., to Carthage, Tenn.; thence along the Cumberland River to Nashville; thence with the line of the Northwestern railroad to the Tennessee River; thence west to Hickman, Ky.; thence along the Mississippi River to the mouth of the Ohio River; thence along the Ohio River to the beginning of the line." It is worth noting that on February 4, 1865, Lyon signed as commanding the department at Aberdeen, Mississippi. It appears that at least part of the reason for creating this department was to enhance the legality of enforcing the conscription act within its boundaries, and its abolishment was never considered, though, on March 23, Lyon was ordered to report to Lieutenant General Richard Taylor so long as he remained within the limits of Taylor's Department of Alabama, Mississippi, and East Louisiana.

Military Division of the West

Commander:

General Pierre G. T. Beauregard: assigned October 3, 1864; assumed October 17

Established October 3, 1864, to enable Beauregard to coordinate operations in the Department of Tennessee and Georgia and the Department of Alabama, Mississippi, and East Louisiana, and especially to provide close supervision of General John Bell Hood. The move aided President Davis politically following the fall of Atlanta, and also pleased Generals Robert E. Lee and Beauregard, because it provided Beauregard with an independent command outside of Virginia. Ceased to exist on February 16, 1865, when Beauregard "assume[d] command of all the troops operating in the State of South Carolina."

Notes

1. In addition to the essays on the generals, from the conception of this series it was our desire to also aid researchers interested in the Confederate high command in the Western Theater. To fulfill that goal we planned an appendix for volumes two, three, and four, respectively dealing with the generals, the armies, and the geographical departments. Arthur W. Bergeron Jr. gathered almost all of the information this appendix is based on and drafted most of the text as well; unless otherwise noted, the information is from the *Official Records*. His research included a careful perusing of bound volumes of the original orders issued by the A&IGO. Unfortunately, he found they contained nothing pertinent that had not been published in the *Official Records*.
2. *New Orleans Bee*, Oct. 19, 1861.
3. Holmes assumed command of the Trans-Mississippi Department on July 30, so he must have departed his former command before being relieved by Hill. As senior brigadier, temporary command would have devolved upon French.
4. As the ranking North Carolinian behind Holmes, Davis selected Hill for political reasons. General Lee chose not to assign another major general to command Hill's Division and was successful in convincing Davis to allow Hill to temporarily return to the Army of Northern Virginia. Hal Bridges, *Lee's Maverick General: Daniel Harvey Hill* (New York, 1961), 87–89.

5. On the return for September 1862, French called his new command under Major General Gustavus W. Smith the Department South of James River; however, the territorial boundary had not changed and he quickly dropped the name.

6. Bridges, *Lee's Maverick General*, 193–94.

7. Leonne M. Hudson, *The Odyssey of a Southerner: The Life and Times of Gustavus Woodson Smith* (Macon, GA, 1998), 135–36

8. Hudson, *The Odyssey of a Southerner*, 148, 150.

9. A footnote in the *OR* states that "Jones seems to have assumed command, under this order [February 28], March 3, 1862." *OR*, vol. 6:836n.

10. *Mobile (AL) Advertiser and Register*, March 30, 1862.

11. On April 9, 1862, General Robert E. Lee ordered Jones to report to Corinth, Mississippi, as soon as Forney relieved him. Forney arrived in Mobile by April 17 but was unable to relieve Jones because of "his wound and general health." *OR*, vol. 6:881.

12. It is likely Forney assumed command on April 28

13. Edmund Kirby Smith, Compiled Service Records of Confederate General and Staff Officers and Nonregimental Enlisted Men, Roll 228, M331, National Archives and Records Service, Washington DC (hereinafter cited as NA).

14. Samuel Jones, Compiled Service Records of Confederate General and Staff Officers and Nonregimental Enlisted Men, Roll 144, M331, NA.

15. William Frayne Amann, *Personnel of the Civil War*, Vol. 1, *The Confederate Armies* (New York, 1961), 345.

16. Henry Heth, Compiled Service Records of Confederate General and Staff Officers and Nonregimental Enlisted Men, Roll 125, M331, NA.

17. Kirby Smith, Compiled Service Records of Confederate General and Staff Officers and Nonregimental Enlisted Men, Roll 228, M331, NA.

18. Heth, Compiled Service Records of Confederate General and Staff Officers and Nonregimental Enlisted Men, Roll 125, M331, NA.

19. Confirmed as major general April 22, 1863, to rank from January 17, 1863. Daniel S. Donelson, Compiled Service Records of Confederate General and Staff Officers and Nonregimental Enlisted Men, Roll 77, M331, NA.

20. Wm. G. M. Davis, Compiled Service Records of Confederate General and Staff Officers and Nonregimental Enlisted Men, Roll 73, M331, NA.

21. Amann, *Personnel of the Civil War*, 1:296.

22. Ibid., 252.

23. One source states that on September 17, 1864, the A&IGO ordered Breckinridge to resume his former command of the Department of Southwestern Virginia. If true, then the A&IGO forgot that department had ceased to exist when Breckinridge had left it four months before. Ibid., 228.

24. William C. Davis, *Breckinridge: Statesman, Soldier, Symbol* (Baton Rouge, LA, 1974), 458.

25. John Echols, Compiled Service Records of Confederate General and Staff Officers, and Nonregimental Enlisted Men, Roll 83, M331, NA.

26. Arndt M. Stickles, *Simon Bolivar Buckner: Borderland Knight* (1910; repr., Wilmington, NC, 1987), 219–24.

27. This division of administrative responsibilities was violated on at least two occasions regarding who was to command the Western District of North Carolina, Department of East Tennessee. *OR*, vol. 30, pt. 4:656, and vol. 31, pt. 3:711.

28. *OR*, vol. 28, pt. 2:397.

29. Amann, *Personnel of the Civil War*, 1:197.

30. William J. Hardee, Compiled Service Records of Confederate General and Staff Officers and Nonregimental Enlisted Men, Roll 117, M331, NA.

31. *OR*, vol. 28, pt. 2:397.

32. Hardee, Compiled Service Records of Confederate General and Staff Officers and Nonregimental Enlisted Men, Roll 117, M331, NA.

33. Based on orders and correspondence of both Johnston and Hardee headed "Morton, August 6, 1863."

34. Leonidas Polk, Compiled Service Records of Confederate General and Staff Officers and Nonregimental Enlisted Men, Roll 199, M331, NA.

35. Craig L. Symonds, *Joseph E. Johnston: A Civil War Biography* (New York, 1992), 219.

36. *Mobile (AL) Daily Tribune*, May 23, 1863.

37. Samuel J. Martin, *General Braxton Bragg, C.S.A.* (Jefferson, NC, 2011), 271.

38. Hardee, Compiled Service Records of Confederate General and Staff Officers and Nonregimental Enlisted Men, Roll 117, M331, NA.

39. T. Michael Parrish, *Richard Taylor: Soldier Prince of Dixie* (Chapel Hill, NC, 1992), 423–27.

40. Amann, *Personnel of the Civil War*, 1:173.

41. Ibid.

42. Richard Taylor, Compiled Service Records of Confederate General and Staff Officers and Nonregimental Enlisted Men, Roll 243, M331, NA.

43. On March 16, 1865, Johnston ordered Lieutenant General Alexander P. Stewart to take command of the Army of Tennessee, but it appears he retained command of the Department of Tennessee and Georgia.

Bibliography

Manuscripts

Allen, Captain Theodore F. Diary. Special Collections, The Filson Historical Society, Louisville, KY.

Badham, William, Jr. Papers. William R. Perkins Library, Duke University, Durham, NC.

Barksdale, William R. Papers. Mississippi Department of Archives and History, Jackson.

Bragg, Braxton. Papers. Library of Congress, Washington, DC.

———. Papers. William P. Palmer Collection, Western Reserve Historical Society, Cleveland, OH.

Brent, George W. Papers. William R. Perkins Library, Duke University, Durham, NC.

Buie, Catherine Jane. Papers. William R. Perkins Library, Duke University, Durham, NC.

Bullitt, Thomas W. "Some Recollections of the War." Bullitt Family Papers. Special Collections, The Filson Historical Society, Louisville, KY.

Calder, William. Papers. Southern Historical Collection, University of North Carolina Library, Chapel Hill.

Chilton, Robert H. Collection. Library of the Museum of the Confederacy, Richmond, VA.

Compiled Military Service Records of Volunteer Union Soldiers Belonging to the 56th through 138th Infantry Units, United States Colored Troops (USCT), 1864–1865. Record Group 109, National Archives and Records Service, Washington, DC.

Compiled Service Records of Confederate General and Staff Officers and Nonregimental Enlisted Men. M331. National Archives and Records Service, Washington, DC.

Compiled Service Records of Confederate Soldiers Who Served in Organizations from the State of Georgia. M266. National Archives and Records Service, Washington, DC.

Compiled Service Records of Confederate Soldiers Who Served in Organizations from the State of Kentucky. M319. National Archives and Records Service, Washington, DC.

Compiled Service Records of Confederate Soldiers Who Served in Organizations from the State of Mississippi. M269. National Archives and Records Service, Washington, DC.

Confederate Collection. Tennessee State Library and Archives, Nashville.

Cooper Family. Papers. Tennessee State Library and Archives, Nashville.

Dixon, William D. Diary. Georgia Historical Society, Savannah.

"Farmers Bank vs. Jacob T. Cassell," Case Nos. 19594 and 19595. Jefferson County Circuit Court. Kentucky Department for Libraries and Archives, Frankfort.

"Farmers Bank vs. James F. Witherspoon," Case No. 483. Kentucky Court of Appeals. Kentucky Department for Libraries and Archives, Frankfort.

"Farmers Bank vs. Thomas Johnson," Case No. 1971. Kentucky Court of Appeals. Kentucky Department for Libraries and Archives, Frankfort.

Garrett, Jill K. "General Gideon J. Pillow and the Pillow Family." Unpublished manuscript in possession of Jill K. Garrett, Columbia, TN.

Guerrant, E. O. Papers. Archives, Special Collections Research Center, University of Kentucky, Lexington.

Helm, Benjamin Hardin. Biographical File. Kentucky Historical Society Library, Frankfort.

Helm, Emilie Todd. Papers. Kentucky Historical Society Library, Frankfort.

Hughes, Archelaus M. Diary. Tennessee State Library and Archives, Nashville.

Hunter-Taylor Papers. Confederate Military Manuscripts. Series B: Holdings of the Louisiana State University. Reel 9. University Microfilms Publications.

Jones, C. C. Collection. Manuscripts Division, Howard-Tilton Memorial Library, Tulane University, New Orleans, LA.

Jones, Joseph. Collection. Manuscripts Division, Howard-Tilton Memorial Library, Tulane University, New Orleans, LA.

Jones, Rev. C. C. Papers. Hargrett Rare Book and Manuscript Library, University of Georgia, Athens.

Knott, Maria I. Diary. Knott Collection. Manuscripts Division, Kentucky Library, Western Kentucky University, Bowling Green.

Letters Received by the Confederate Secretary of War, 1861–1865. Record Group 109, War Department Collection of Confederate Records. National Archives and Records Service, Washington, DC.

Letters Sent, Gen. W. H. C. Whiting's Command. Record Group 109, War Department Collection of Confederate Records. National Archives and Records Service, Washington, DC.

Lincoln, Abraham. Papers. Library of Congress. Washington, DC.

Lowndes, James. Papers. South Caroliniana, University of South Carolina, Columbia.

Manigault, Gabriel. "Memoirs." South Carolina Historical Society, Charleston.

Mattingly, George R. "Reminiscences of the Nelson Grays." Transcript. Kentucky Historical Society Library, Frankfort.

McBride, Robert M. "The Gideon J. Pillow Everybody Knows." Unpublished manuscript in possession of Jill K. Garrett, Columbia, TN.

Minor, Hubbard T. Papers. U.S. Army Military History Institute, Carlisle, PA.

Miscellaneous Confederate Letters. Brunswick Town/Fort Anderson State Historic Site, Winnabow, NC.

Moffett, George Hall. Papers. South Carolina Historical Society, Charleston.

Pillow, Brig. Gen. Gideon J. Command Special Order Book. Record Group 109, War Department Collection of Confederate Records. National Archives and Records Service, Washington, DC.

Pillow, Gideon J. Military Service Record. Record Group 109, War Department Collection of Confederate Records. National Archives and Records Service, Washington, DC.

———. Papers. Record Group 109, War Department Collection of Confederate Records. National Archives and Records Service, Washington, DC.

Pillow, Gideon Johnson. Letter. Special Collections, University of Tennessee Libraries, Knoxville.

Pirtle, Alfred. Journal, 1859–62. Special Collections, The Filson Historical Society, Louisville, KY.

Porter, David D. Papers. Library of Congress, Washington, DC.

Porter, Nimrod. Diary. Southern Historical Collection. University of North Carolina Library, Chapel Hill.

Records of Commissioned Officers of Mississippi Militia, 1848–1861. Registers of Military Commissions, Series 224. Mississippi Department of Archives and History, Jackson.

Reynolds, Daniel H. Diary. Daniel H. Reynolds Papers. Special Collections Department, University of Arkansas Libraries, Fayetteville.

Simpson, John W. "A Boy's Story of the Battle of Fishing Creek and Other Incidents of the Civil War." Unpublished handwritten manuscript. Mill Springs National Battlefield Library, Nancy, KY.

Smith, D. Howard. Papers. Special Collections, Kentucky Historical Society Library, Frankfort.

Soldiers Who Served in Organizations from the State of Ohio, Indexes to the Carded Records of Soldiers Who Served in Volunteer Organizations During the Civil War, compiled 1899–1927, documenting the period 1861–1866. M552. National Archives and Records Service, Washington, DC.

Tripp Family Papers. Southern Historical Collection, University of North Carolina Library, Chapel Hill.

Vance, Zebulon B. Papers. Division of Archives and History, Raleigh, NC.

Walthall, E. C. Papers. Department of Archives and Special Collections, J. D. Williams Library, University of Mississippi, Oxford.

Walthall, Edward C. Papers. Library of Congress, Washington, DC.

Walthall, Edward Cary. Papers. Mississippi Department of Archives and History, Jackson.

Zollicoffer, Felix K. Letter. Archives and Manuscripts, Chicago History Museum.

———. General and Special Orders Book, Aug. 21, 1861—Jan. 2, 1862. Manuscripts Department, Eleanor S. Brockenbrough Library, Museum of the Confederacy, Richmond, VA.

Government Documents

Barnes, Joseph K. *The Medical and Surgical History of the Rebellion, 1861–65.* 6 vols. Washington, DC: Government Printing Office, 1870–88.

Buell, Don Carlos. Statement of Major General Buell *in Review of the Evidence before the Military Commission Appointed by the War Department.* Washington, DC: n.p., 1863.

Journal of the House of Representatives of the Commonwealth of Kentucky [1855–1856]. Frankfort: A. G. Hodges, 1856.

Memorial Addresses on the Life and Character of Edward C. Walthall Delivered in the Senate and House of Representatives, Fifty-Fifth Congress, Second and Third Sessions. Washington, DC: Government Printing Office, 1899.

Official Register of the Officers and Cadets of the U.S. Military Academy, West Point, New York. n.p., 1838.

Official Register of the Officers and Cadets of the U.S. Military Academy, West Point, New York. n.p., 1841.

Ohio Roster Commission, *Official Roster of the Soldiers of the State of Ohio in the War of the Rebellion.* 12 vols. Cincinnati: Ohio Valley Press, 1886.

Register of the Officers and Cadets of the U.S. Military Academy, West Point, New York. n.p., 1839.

Register of the Officers and Cadets of the U.S. Military Academy, West Point, New York. n.p., 1840.

Report of the Adjutant General of the State of Kentucky. 2 vols. Frankfort: Public Printer, 1867.

U.S. Census Office. *Eighth Census of the United States, Free Schedule.* Washington, DC, 1860. Yalobusha County, MS.

———. *Eighth Census of the United States, Slave Schedule.* Washington, DC, 1860. Yalobusha County, MS.

U.S. Navy War Records Office. *Official Records of the Union and Confederate Navies in the War of the Rebellion*. 31 vols. Washington, DC. 1894–1927.

U.S. War Department. *The War of the Rebellion: A Compilation of the Official Records of the Union and Confederate Armies*. 128 vols. Washington, DC, 1880–1901.

Newspapers and Periodicals

Aberdeen (MS) Examiner

Atlanta Constitution

Atlanta Journal Magazine

Augusta (GA) Constitutionalist

Barbour County Index (Medicine Lodge, KS)

Charleston Mercury

Columbus (GA) Daily Sun

Dodge City (KS) Times

Fayetteville (NC) Observer Semi-Weekly

Frankfort (KY) Tri-Weekly Yeoman

Harper's New Monthly Magazine

Jackson Weekly Mississippian

Lexington (KY) Observer and Reporter

Louisville (KY) Daily Journal

Maysville (KY) Daily Evening Bulletin

Memphis Appeal

Memphis Commercial Appeal

Memphis Daily Appeal

Memphis Public Ledger

Mobile (AL) Advertiser and Register

Mobile (AL) Daily Tribune

Nashville Daily Union and American

National Tribune (Washington, DC)

New Orleans Bee

New York Times

Newnan (GA) Herald

Opelousas (LA) Courier

Pascagoula (MS) Democrat-Sun

Philadelphia Inquirer

Point Pleasant (WV) Weekly Register

Richmond Daily Dispatch

Richmond Dispatch

Richmond Sentinel

Richmond Whig

Stanford (KY) Semi-Weekly Interior Journal

Walker County (GA) Messenger

Wilmington Daily Journal

Wilmington Daily North Carolinian

Printed Primary Sources

Alderson, William T., ed. "The Civil War Reminiscences of John Johnston." *Tennessee Historical Quarterly* 13, no. 4 (Dec. 1954): 329–54.

Beatty, John. *The Citizen-Soldier: The Memoirs of a Civil War Volunteer.* 1879. Reprint, Lincoln, NE: Bison Books, 1998.

Black, Roy W. Sr., ed. "William J. Rogers' Memorandum Book." *Papers of the West Tennessee Historical Society* 9 (1955): 59–92.

Broun, Thomas L. "General R. E. Lee's War-Horses, Traveller and Lucy Long." *Southern Historical Society Papers* 18 (1890): 388–91.

———. "General R. E. Lee's War-Horses." *Southern Historical Society Papers* 19 (1891): 333–35.

Buford, A. *Church and Turf. Lecture by Gen'l. A. Buford. Delivered in Campbell-Street Church, Louisville, Ky., April 30th, 1882.* Louisville, KY: Courier-Journal, 1882.

Cannon, J. P. *Bloody Banners and Barefoot Boys: A History of the 27th Regiment Alabama Infantry CSA; The Civil War Memoirs and Diary Entries of J. P. Cannon M.D.* Edited by Noel Crowson and John V. Brogden. Shippensburg, PA: White Mane, 1997.

Cobb, Thomas R. R., "Extracts from Letters to his Wife, February 3, 1861–December 10, 1862." *Southern Historical Society Papers.* 28 (1900): 280–301.

Chesnut, Mary. *Mary Chesnut's Civil War.* Edited by C. Van Woodward. New Haven, CT: Yale Univ. Press, 1981.

Clark, Walter A. *Under the Stars and Bars, or Memories of Four Years Service with the Oglethorpes, of Augusta, Georgia*. Augusta, GA: Chronicle Print, 1900.

Comstock, Cyrus B. *The Diary of Cyrus B. Comstock.* Edited by Merlin E. Sumner. Dayton, OH: Morningside, 1987.

Cox, Jacob D. *Military Reminiscences of the Civil War.* 2 vols. New York: Charles Scribner's Sons, 1900.

Cumming, Joseph B. *Address of Joseph B. Cumming at the Unveiling of the Monument to Maj. Gen'l. William Henry Talbot Walker on the Battle Field of Atlanta, July 22, 1902.* Augusta, GA: n.p., 1902.

Cumming, Kate. *Kate: The Journal of a Confederate Nurse.* Edited by Richard B. Harwell. Baton Rouge, LA: Louisiana State Univ. Press, 1959.

———. *A Journal of Hospital Life in the Confederate Army of Tennessee, From the Battle of Shiloh to the End of the War.* Louisville, KY, n. d.

Dacus, Robert H. *Reminiscences of Company "H," First Arkansas Mounted Rifles.* Dardanelle, AR: Post-Dispatch, 1897.

Davis, Jefferson. *The Papers of Jefferson Davis.* Vol. 10, *October 1963—August 1864.* Edited by Lynda L. Crist, Kenneth H. Williams, and Peggy L. Dillard. Baton Rouge, LA: Louisiana State Univ. Press, 1999.

———. *The Papers of Jefferson Davis.* Vol. 11, *September 1864—May 1865.* Edited by Lynda Lasswell Crist, Barbara J. Rozek, and Kenneth H. Williams. Baton Rouge, LA: Louisiana State Univ. Press, 2004.

———. *The Rise and Fall of Confederate Government.* 2 vols. New York: D. Appleton, 1881.

"Defence and Fall of Fort Fisher." *Southern Historical Society Papers* 10 (1882): 346–68.

Denson, C. B. "William Henry Chase Whiting: An Address Delivered in Raleigh, N.C. on Memorial Day (May 10), 1895, Containing a Memoir of the Late Major-General William Henry Chase Whiting of the Confederate Army." *Southern Historical Society Papers* 26 (1898): 129–81.

Dinkins, James. *1861 to 1865, by an Old Johnnie: Personal Recollections and Experiences in the Confederate Army.* Cincinnati: Robert Clarke, 1897.

Dodge, Grenville M. *The Battle of Atlanta and Other Campaigns, Addresses, etc.* Council Bluffs, IA: Monarch, 1910.

Dowd, William F. "Lookout Mountain and Missionary Ridge." *Southern Bivouac* 4, no. 4 (Dec. 1885), 399.

Duke, Basil W. *History of Morgan's Cavalry.* Cincinnati: Miami, 1867. Reprint, New York: Kraus Reprint, 1969. Page references are to both editions as indicated.

Du Pont, Samuel Francis. *Samuel Francis Du Pont, a Selection from His Letters.* Edited by John D. Hayes. 3 vols. Ithaca, NY: Cornell Univ. Press, 1969.

Edmondston, Catherine Ann Devereux. *"Journal of a Secesh Lady": The Diary of Catherine Ann Devereux Edmondston, 1860–1866.* Edited by Beth B. Crabtree and James W. Patton. Raleigh: North Carolina Division of Archives and History, 1979.

Ewell, Richard S. *The Letters of General Richard S. Ewell: Stonewall's Successor.* Edited by Donald C. Pfanz. Knoxville: Univ. of Tennessee Press, 2012.

Ewing, G. D. "Morgan's Last Raid into Kentucky." *Confederate Veteran* 31 (July 1923): 254–56.

French, Samuel G. *Two Wars: The Autobiography and Diary of Gen. Samuel G. French, CSA.* Nashville, TN: *Confederate Veteran,* 1901.

Fuller, John W. "A Terrible Day: The Battle of Atlanta, July 22, 1864." In vol. 5 of *Battles & Leaders of the Civil War,* edited by Peter Cozzens, 546-58. Urbana: Univ. of Illinois Press, 2002.

Galloway, Laura. Autograph book. In 1994 catalog of *Southern Historical Showcase.* Nashville, TN.

Grainger, Gervis D. *Four Years with the Boys in Gray.* Franklin, KY: n.p., 1909.

Grant, Ulysses S. *The Papers of Ulysses S. Grant.* Edited by John Y. Simon and David L. Wilson. Vol. 13, *November 16, 1864—February 20, 1865.* Carbondale: Southern Illinois Univ. Press, 1985.

Green, John W. *Johnny Green of the Orphan Brigade: The Journal of a Confederate Soldier.* Edited by A. D. Kirwan. Lexington: Univ. Press of Kentucky, 1956.

Guerrant, Edward O. *Bluegrass Confederate: The Headquarters Diary of Edward O. Guerrant.* Edited by William C. Davis and Meredith L. Swentor. Baton Rouge: Louisiana State Univ. Press, 1999.

Hancock, R. R. *Hancock's Diary: or a History of the Second Tennessee Confederate Cavalry, with Sketches of First and Seventh Battalions; also Portraits and Biographical Sketches.* Nashville, TN: Brandon, 1887.

Handerson, Henry E. *Yankee in Gray: The Civil War Memoirs of Henry E. Handerson, with a Selection of His Wartime Letters.* Cleveland, OH: Press of Western Reserve Univ., 1962.

Headley, John W. *Confederate Operations in Canada and New York.* New York: The Neale Publishing Co., 1906.

Helm, Emilie Todd. "President Lincoln and the Widow of General Helm." *Century Magazine* 52, no. 2 (June 1896): 318.

Hewett, Janet E., ed. *Supplement to the Official Records of the Union and Confederate Armies.* 100 vols. Wilmington, NC: Broadfoot, 1994–2004.

Hill, Daniel Harvey. "Chickamauga–The Great Battle of the West." In vol. 3 of *Battles and Leaders of the Civil War: Being for the Most Part Contributions by Union and Confederate Officers based upon "The Century War Series,"* edited by Robert Underwood Johnson and Clarence Clough Buel, 638-62. 1884–88. Reprint, New York: Thomas Yoseloff, 1956.

Hood, John Bell. *Advance and Retreat: Personal Experiences in the United States and Confederate States Armies.* New Orleans: Hood Orphan Memorial Fund, 1880. Reprint, New York: Da Capo, 1993. Page references are to both editions as indicated.

Hord, Henry Ewell. "Brice's X Roads From a Private's View." *Confederate Veteran* 12, no. 11 (Nov. 1904): 529–30.

———. "Pursuit of Gen. Sturgis." *Confederate Veteran* 13, no. 1 (Jan. 1905): 17-18.

———. "Scouting About Memphis," *Confederate Veteran* 20, no. 5 (May 1912): 207–9.

Jackman, John S. *Diary of a Confederate Soldier: John S. Jackman of the Orphan Brigade.* Edited by William C. Davis. Columbia, SC: Univ. of South Carolina Press, 1990.

Johnson, Robert Underwood, and Clarence Clough Buel, eds. *Battles and Leaders of the Civil War: Being for the Most Part Contributions by Union and Confederate Officers Based upon "The Century War Series."* 4 vols. New York: D. Appleton, 1884—88. Reprint, New York: Thomas Yoseloff, 1956. Page references are to both editions as indicated.

Jones, Charles C. *The Siege of Savannah in December 1864 and the Confederate Operations in the Third Military District of South Carolina during General Sherman's March to the Sea.* Albany, NY: Joel Munsell, 1874.

Jones, Charles C., Jr. *Historical Sketch of the Chatham Artillery during the Confederate Struggle for Independence.* Albany, NY: Joel Munsell, 1867.

Jones, J. B. *A Rebel War Clerk's Diary at the Confederate States Capital.* 2 vols. Philadelphia: J. B. Lippincott, 1866.

Jones, Martha McDowell Buford. *Peach Leather and Rebel Gray: Bluegrass Life and the War, 1860–1865. Farm and Social life, Famous Horses, Tragedies of War. Diary and Letters of a Confederate Wife.* Edited by Mary E. Wharton and Ellen F. Williams. Lexington, KY: Helicon, 1986.

Joy, Charles G. "The Stampede at LaFayette, Ga." *Confederate Veteran* 20, no. 10 (Oct. 1912): 473–77.

Kelly, R. M. "A Brush with Pillow." In vol. 3 of *Sketches of War History, 1861–1865: Papers Read Before the Ohio Commandery of the Military Order of the Loyal Legion of the U.S.* 319–33. Cincinnati: Commandery, 1888–1908.

Kendall, John Smith, ed. "Recollections of a Confederate Officer." *Louisiana Historical Quarterly* 29 (Oct. 1946): 1041–1228.

Lamb, William. *Colonel Lamb's Story of Fort Fisher.* Carolina Beach, NC: Blockade Runner Museum, 1966.

———. "The Defense of Fort Fisher." In vol. 4 of *Battles and Leaders of the Civil War: Being for the Most Part Contributions by Union and Confederate Officers based upon "The Century War Series,"* edited by Robert Underwood Johnson and Clarence Clough Buell, 642–54. New York: D. Appleton, 1884–88.

———. "Fort Fisher. The Battles Fought There in 1864 and '65." *Southern Historical Society Papers* 21 (1893): 257–90.

Lee, Robert E. *Lee's Dispatches: Unpublished Letters of General Robert E. Lee to Jefferson Davis and the War Department of the Confederate States of America, 1862–65.* Edited by Douglas Southall Freeman. New York: G. P. Putnam's Sons, 1915.

———. *The Wartime Papers of R. E. Lee.* Edited by Clifford Dowdey. Boston: Little, Brown, 1961.

Liddell, St. John Richardson. *Liddell's Record.* Edited by Nathaniel Cheairs Hughes Jr. Dayton, OH: Morningside, 1985.

Lincoln, Abraham. *Collected Works of Lincoln.* Edited by Roy Basler. 8 vols. New Brunswick, NJ: Rutgers Univ. Press, 1953.

Mackall, William W. *A Son's Recollection of His Father.* New York: E. P. Dutton, 1930.

Manigault, Arthur Middleton. *A Carolinian Goes to War: The Civil War Narrative of Arthur Middleton Manigault.* Edited by R. Lockwood Tower. Columbia, SC: Univ. of South Carolina Press, 1983.

Mason, F. H. *The Twelfth Ohio Cavalry…in the War of the Rebellion.* Cleveland, OH: Nevins, 1871.

McNeilly, James H. "Franklin—Incidents of the Battle." *Confederate Veteran* 26, no. 3 (Mar. 1918): 116-18.

———. Untitled article. *Confederate Veteran* 22, no. 2 (Feb. 1914): 60.

———. "With the Rear Guard." *Confederate Veteran* 26, no. 8 (Aug. 1918): 338–40.

Merrill, James M. "The Fort Fisher and Wilmington Campaign: Letters From Rear Admiral David D. Porter." *North Carolina Historical Review* 35 (Oct. 1958): 461–75.

Morton, John Watson. *The Artillery of Nathan Bedford Forrest's Cavalry.* Nashville, TN: M. E. Church, South, 1909.

———. "Battle of Tishomingo Creek or Brice's Cross-Roads." *Southern Bivouac* 1, nos. 9–10 (May–June 1883): 366-83.

Mosgrove, George Dallas. *Kentucky Cavaliers in Dixie: The Reminiscences of a Confederate Cavalryman.* 1895. Reprint, Jackson, TN: McCowat-Mercer, 1957.

Myers, Robert Manson, ed. *The Children of Pride: A True Story of Georgia and the Civil War.* New Haven, CT: Yale Univ. Press, 1972.

Nisbet, James Cooper. *Four Years on the Firing Line.* Jackson, TN: McCowat-Mercer, 1963. Reprint edited by Bell Irwin Wiley. Wilmington, NC: Broadfoot, 1987. Page references to both editions as indicated.

Olmstead, Charles H. *The Memoirs of Charles H. Olmstead.* Edited by Lilla Mills Hawes. In *Collections of the Georgia Historical Society.* Vol. 14. Savannah: Georgia Historical Society, 1964.

Osborn, George C., ed. "Civil War Letters of Robert W. Banks: Atlanta Campaign." *Georgia Historical Quarterly* 27, no. 2 (June 1943): 208–16.

Patrick, Robert. *Reluctant Rebel: The Secret Diary of Robert Patrick, 1861–1865.* Edited by F. Jay Taylor. Baton Rouge, LA: Louisiana State Univ. Press, 1959.

Quintard, Charles Todd. *Doctor Quintard, Chaplain, C.S.A., and Second Bishop of Tennessee: The Memoir and Civil War Diary of Charles Todd Quintard.* Edited by Sam Davis Elliott. Baton Rouge, LA: Louisiana State Univ. Press, 2003.

Roy, T. B. "General Hardee and the Military Operations Around Atlanta." *Southern Historical Society Papers* 8 (Sept. 1880): 337–87.

Sanders, David W. "Autobiography of Maj. D. W. Sanders." *Confederate Veteran* 18, no. 8 (Aug. 1910): 370-72.

———. "Hood's Tennessee Campaign." *Confederate Veteran* 15, no. 9 (Sept. 1907): 401-7.

Seaton, Benjamin M. *The Bugle Softly Blows: The Confederate Diary of Benjamin M. Seaton.* Edited by Harold B. Simpson. Waco, TX: Texian Press, 1965.

Sherman, William T. *Memoirs of W. T. Sherman.* 1875. Reprint, New York: Library of America, 1990.

Smith, Daniel P. *Company K, First Alabama Regiment, or Three Years in the Confederate Service*. 1885. Reprint: Baltimore, MD: Butternut, 1984.

Smith, Robert D. *Confederate Diary of Robert D. Smith*. Edited by Jill K. Garrett. Columbia, TN: United Daughters of the Confederacy, 1997.

Stephens, Alexander H. *A Constitutional View of the Late War Between the States: Its Causes, Character, Conduct and Results. Presented in a Series of Colloquies at Liberty Hall*. 2 vols. Chicago: National, 1868–70.

Stephenson, Philip Daingerfield. *The Civil War Memoir of Philip Daingerfield Stephenson, D.D.* Edited by Nathaniel C. Hughes Jr. Conway, AR: Univ. of Central Arkansas Press, 1995.

Sykes, E. T. *Walthall's Brigade: A Cursory Sketch, with Personal Experiences of Walthall's Brigade, Army of Tennessee, C.S.A., 1862–1865*. Publications of the Mississippi Historical Society, Centenary Series. Vol. 1, pt. 2. Jackson: Mississippi Historical Society, 1916.

Tarrant, Edward W. "With Walthall at Nashville." *Confederate Veteran* 13, no. 2 (Feb. 1905): 66.

Taylor, Richard. *Destruction and Reconstruction: Personal Experiences of the Late War in the United States*. Edinburgh and London: William Blackwood and Sons, 1879.

Tyler, H. A. "Forrest Covers Hood's Retreat." *Confederate Veteran* 12, no. 9 (Sept. 1904): 436.

Welles, Gideon. *Diary of Gideon Welles, Secretary of the Navy under Lincoln and Johnson*. 3 vols. Boston: Houghton Mifflin, 1911.

White, Robert H., ed. *Messages of the Governors of Tennessee*. Vol. 5, *1857–1869*. Nashville: Tennessee Historical Commission, 1959.

Wise, Henry A. "The Career of Wise's Brigade." *Southern Historical Society Papers* 25 (1897): 1-22.

Young, Lot D. *Reminiscences of a Soldier of the Orphan Brigade*. n.p., n.d.

Secondary Sources

Published Secondary Sources

Allardice, Bruce S., and Lawrence Lee Hewitt, eds. *Kentuckians in Gray: Confederate Generals and Field Officers of the Bluegrass State*. Lexington: Univ. Press of Kentucky, 2008.

Amann, William Frayne. *Personnel of the Civil War*. Vol. 1, *The Confederate Armies*. New York: Thomas Yoseloff, 1961.

Ashe, Samuel A'Court. *History of North Carolina*. 2 vols. Raleigh, NC: Edwards and Broughton, 1925.

Baker, Jean H. *Mary Todd Lincoln: A Biography*. New York: W. W. Norton, 1987.

Banks, Robert W. *The Battle of Franklin, November 30, 1864.* 1908 Reprint, Dayton, OH: Morningside, 1982.

Bauer, K. Jack. *The Mexican War, 1846–1848.* New York: Macmillan, 1974.

Bearss, Edwin. "Edward Cary Walthall." In vol. 6 of *The Confederate General,* edited by William C. Davis and Julie Hoffman, 104-7. Harrisburg, PA: National Historical Society, 1991.

Bergeron, Arthur W., Jr. "William Andrew Quarles." In vol. 5 of *The Confederate General,* edited by William C. Davis and Julie Hoffman, 66-67. Harrisburg, PA: National Historical Society, 1991.

Berry, Stephen. *House of Abraham: Lincoln and the Todds, A Family Divided By War.* New York: Houghton Mifflin, 2007.

The Biographical Cyclopedia of the Commonwealth of Kentucky. Chicago: John M. Gresham, 1896.

The Biographical Encyclopaedia of Kentucky of the Dead and Living Men of the Nineteenth Century. Cincinnati: J. M. Armstrong, 1878.

Boatner, Mark M., III. *The Civil War Dictionary.* New York: McKay, 1959. Revised edition, New York: David McKay, 1988. Page references are to both editions as indicated.

Bradley, Mark. *Last Stand in the Carolinas: The Battle of Bentonville.* Campbell, CA: Savas Woodbury, 1996.

Bradley, Michael R. *Tullahoma: The 1863 Campaign for Control of Middle Tennessee.* Shippensburg, PA: Burd Street, 2000.

———. "Tullahoma: The Wrongly Forgotten Campaign." *Blue & Gray* 27, no. 1 (2010): 6–25, 40–65.

Bridges, Hal. *Lee's Maverick General: Daniel Harvey Hill.* New York: McGraw-Hill, 1961. Reprint, Lincoln, NE: Univ. of Nebraska Press, 1991. Page references are to both editions as indicated.

Brown, Russell K. *To the Manner Born: The Life of General William H. T. Walker.* Macon, GA: Mercer Univ. Press, 2005.

Buck, S. H. "First Kentucky Confederate Cavalry." *Confederate Veteran* 21, no. 9 (Sept. 1913): 449.

Castel, Albert. *Decision in the West: The Atlanta Campaign of 1864.* Lawrence, KS: Univ. Press of Kansas, 1992.

Chalmers, General [James R.]. "Forrest and His Campaigns." *Southern Historical Society Papers* 7 (1879): 451–86.

Clark, Walter, ed. *Histories of the Several Regiments and Battalions from North Carolina in the Great War, 1861–'65.* 5 vols. 1901. Reprint, Wilmington, NC: Broadfoot, 1982.

Coleman, J. Winston, Jr. *Historic Kentucky.* Lexington, KY: Henry Clay, 1967.

Collins, Lewis. *History of Kentucky.* 2 vols. Covington, KY: Collins, 1874.

Connelly, Thomas L. *Army of the Heartland: The Army of Tennessee, 1861–1862*. Baton Rouge, LA: Louisiana State Univ. Press, 1967.

———. *Autumn of Glory: The Army of Tennessee, 1862–1865*. Baton Rouge, LA: Louisiana State Univ. Press, 1971.

Cooling, Benjamin F. *Forts Henry and Donelson: The Key to the Confederate Heartland.* Knoxville, TN: Univ. of Tennessee Press, 1987.

Coulter, E. Merton. *The Confederate States of America, 1861–1865*. Baton Rouge: Louisiana State Univ. Press, 1950.

Cox, Jacob D. *The March to the Sea: Franklin and Nashville.* New York: Charles Scribner's Sons, 1882.

Cozzens, Peter. *This Terrible Sound: The Battle of Chickamauga*. 1992. Reprint, Urbana, IL: Univ. of Illinois Press, 1996.

———. *No Better Place to Die: The Battle of Stone's River.* Urbana, IL: Univ. of Illinois Press, 1990.

Crooks, Daniel J., Jr. *Lee in the Low Country: Defending Charleston and Savannah 1861–1862*. Charleston, SC: History Press, 2008.

Cummings, Charles. *Yankee Quaker, Confederate General: The Curious Career of Bushrod Rust Johnson.* Rutherford, NJ: Fairleigh Dickinson Univ. Press, 1971.

Current, Richard N., ed. *Encyclopedia of the Confederacy*. 4 vols. New York: Simon and Schuster, 1993.

Dalton, C. David. "Zollicoffer, Crittenden, and the Mill Springs Campaign: Some Persistent Questions." *Filson Club History Quarterly* 60 (Oct. 1986): 463–71.

Daniel, Larry J. *Shiloh: The Battle that Changed the Civil War.* New York: Simon and Schuster, 1997.

Davis, Burke. *To Appomattox: Nine April Days, 1865.* New York: Rinehart, 1959.

Davis, Stephen. *Atlanta Will Fall: Sherman, Joe Johnston, and the Yankee Heavy Battalions*. Wilmington, DE: SR Books, 2001.

———. "A Georgia Firebrand: Major General W. H. T. Walker, C.S.A." *Georgia Historical Quarterly* 64, no. 4 (Winter 1979): 447–60.

Davis, William C. *Breckinridge: Statesman, Soldier, Symbol*. Baton Rouge, LA: Louisiana State Univ. Press, 1974.

———. *The Orphan Brigade: The Kentucky Confederates Who Couldn't Go Home*. Garden City, NY: Doubleday, 1980.

Davis, William C., and Julie Hoffman, eds. *The Confederate General*. 6 vols. Harrisburg, PA: National Historical Society, 1991.

"Dedication of the Gen. Zollicoffer Tablet." *Confederate Veteran* 18, no. 7 (July 1910): 335.

Donald, David Herbert. *Lincoln*. London: Jonathan Cape, 1995.

Duncan, Richard R. *Lee's Endangered Left: The Civil War in Western Virginia, Spring of 1864*. Baton Rouge, LA: Louisiana State Univ. Press, 1998.

Eicher, John H., and David J. Eicher. *Civil War High Commands*. Stanford, CA: Stanford Univ. Press, 2001.

Elliott, Charles. "Brig. Gen. Benjamin Hardin Helm." In *Kentuckians in Gray: Confederate Generals and Field Officers of the Bluegrass State*, edited by Bruce S. Allardice and Lawrence Lee Hewitt, 138-44. Lexington: Univ. Press of Kentucky, 2008.

Elliott, Sam D. *Soldier of Tennessee: General Alexander P. Stewart and the Civil War in the West*. Baton Rouge, LA: Louisiana State Univ. Press, 1999.

Evans, Clement A., ed. *Confederate Military History*. 12 vols. Atlanta: Confederate, 1899.

Faust, Patricia L., ed. *Historical Times Illustrated Encyclopedia of the Civil War*. New York: Harper and Row, 1986.

Fletcher, R. D. "Burial Place of Gen. B. R. Johnson." *Confederate Veteran* 15, no. 12 (Dec. 1907): 551.

Fonvielle, Chris E., Jr. "Closing Down the Kingdom: Union Combined Operations Against Wilmington." In *Union Combined Operations in the Civil War*, edited by Craig L. Symonds, 96-114. New York: Fordham Univ. Press, 2010.

———. *To Forge a Thunderbolt: Fort Anderson and the Battle for Wilmington*. Carolina Beach, NC: SlapDash, 2015.

———. *The Wilmington Campaign: Last Rays of Departing Hope*. Campbell, CA: Savas, 1997.

Fortier, Alcée. *A History of Louisiana*. 4 vols. New York: Manzi, Joyant & Co., Successors, 1904.

Frazer, Robert W. *Forts of the West: Military Forts and Presidios and Posts Commonly Called Forts West of the Mississippi River to 1898*. Norman, OK: Univ. of Oklahoma Press, 1972.

Freeman, Douglas S. *R. E. Lee*, 4 vols. New York: Charles Scribner's Sons, 1934-35. Reprint, New York: Charles Scribner's Sons, 1949. Page references are to both editions as indicated.

"Gen. E. C. Walthall." *Confederate Veteran* 6, no. 7 (July 1898): 305-7.

George, Henry. *History of the 3d, 7th, 8th, and 12th Kentucky, C.S.A.* Louisville, KY: C. T. Dearing, 1911. Reprint, Melber, KY: Simmons Historical, 1987. Page references are to both editions as indicated.

Goodrich, John T. "Gregg's Brigade in the Battle of Chickamauga." *Confederate Veteran* 22, no. 6 (June 1914): 264-65.

Goodspeed Brothers. *Biographical and Historical Memoirs of Mississippi, Embracing an Authentic and Comprehensive Account of the Chief Events in the History of the State and a Record of the Lives of Many of the Most Worthy and Illustrious Families and Individuals*. 2 vols. Chicago: Goodspeed, 1891.

Goodwin, Doris Kearns. *Team of Rivals: The Political Genius of Abraham Lincoln*. New York: Simon and Schuster, 2005.

Gott, Kendall D. *Where the South Lost the War: An Analysis of the Fort Henry–Fort Donelson Campaign, February 1862*. Mechanicsburg, PA: Stockpole, 2002.

Green, Maureen Helm. "Emilie." *Kentucky Ancestors* 44, no. 1 (Autumn 2008): 4-16.

Hafendorfer, Kenneth A. *Mill Springs: Campaign and Battle of Mill Springs, Kentucky.* Louisville, KY: KH, 2001.

Hallock, Judith Lee. *Braxton Bragg and Confederate Defeat, Vol. 2.* Tuscaloosa, AL: Univ. of Alabama Press, 1991.

Harrison, Lowell H. *The Civil War in Kentucky.* Lexington, KY: Univ. Press of Kentucky, 1975.

———. "Kentucky-born Generals in the Civil War." *Register of the Kentucky Historical Society* 64 (Apr. 1966): 129–60.

———. *Lincoln of Kentucky.* Lexington, KY: Univ. Press of Kentucky, 2000.

Hattaway, Herman. *General Stephen D. Lee.* Jackson, MS: Univ. Press of Mississippi, 1976.

Hay, Thomas Robson. "The Atlanta Campaign [pt. 1]." *Georgia Historical Quarterly* 7, no. 1 (Mar. 1923): 19–43.

Head, Thomas A. *Campaigns and Battles of the Sixteenth Regiment, Tennessee Volunteers.* Nashville, TN: Cumberland Presbyterian, 1885.

Helm, Katherine. *The True Story of Mary, Wife of Lincoln.* 1928. 3rd ed., Rutland, VT: Academy Books, 2001.

Henry, Robert Selph. *"First With the Most" Forrest.* Indianapolis: Bobbs-Merrill, 1944.

Herr, W. W. "Kentuckians at Chickamauga." *Confederate Veteran* 3, no. 10 (Oct. 1895): 294-95.

Hewitt, Lawrence L. "Daniel H. Reynolds." In vol. 5 of *The Confederate General,* edited by William C. Davis and Julie Hoffman, 84-85. Harrisburg, PA: National Historical Society, 1991.

Hoole, William Stanley. *Lawley Covers the Confederacy.* Tuscaloosa, AL: Confederate, 1964.

Horn, Stanley F. *The Army of Tennessee.* 1941. Reprint, Wilmington, NC: Broardfoot, 1987.

Hudson, Leonne M. *The Odyssey of a Southerner: The Life and Times of Gustavus Woodson Smith.* Macon, GA: Mercer Univ. Press, 1998.

Hughes, Nathaniel C., Jr., and Roy P. Stonesifer Jr. *The Life and Wars of Gideon J. Pillow.* Chapel Hill, NC: Univ. of North Carolina Press, 1993. Reprint, Knoxville, TN: Univ. of Tennessee Press, 2011. Page references are to both editions as indicated.

Hughes, Nathaniel Cheairs, Jr. *The Battle of Belmont: Grant Strikes South.* Chapel Hill, NC: Univ. of North Carolina Press, 1991.

———. *Bentonville: The Final Battle of Sherman and Johnston.* Chapel Hill, NC: Univ. of North Carolina Press, 1996.

———. *General William J. Hardee: Old Reliable.* Baton Rouge, LA: Louisiana State Univ. Press, 1965.

———. *Brigadier General Tyree H. Bell, C.S.A.: Forrest's Fighting Lieutenant.* With Connie Walton Moretti and James Michael Browne. Knoxville: Univ. of Tennessee Press, 2004.

Jacobson, Eric A., and Richard A. Rupp. *For Cause and For Country: A Study of the Affair at Spring Hill and the Battle of Franklin.* Franklin, TN: O'More, 2006.

Jenkins, Kirk C. *The Battle Rages Higher: The Union's Fifteenth Kentucky Infantry.* Lexington, KY: Univ. Press of Kentucky, 2003.

Johnston, William Preston. *The Life of General Albert Sidney Johnston: Embracing His Services in the Armies of the United States, the Republic of Texas, and the Confederate States.* New York: D. Appleton, 1879.

Jones, Eugene W. Jr. *Enlisted for the War: The Struggles of the Gallant 24th Regiment, South Carolina Volunteers, Infantry, 1861–1865.* Hightstown, NJ: Longstreet House, 1997.

Jordan, Thomas, and J. P. Pryor. *The Campaigns of General Nathan Bedford Forrest and of Forrest's Cavalry.* 1868. Reprint, New York: Da Capo, 1996.

———. *The Campaigns of Lieut.-Gen. N. B. Forrest, and of Forrest's Cavalry, with Portraits, Maps, and Illustrations.* New Orleans, LA: Blelock, 1868.

Joyce, Fred. "Orphan Brigade at Chickamauga." *Southern Bivouac* 3, no. 1 (Sept. 1884): 29-32.

———. "The Mother and Two Sons." *Southern Bivouac* 2, no. 7 (Mar. 1884): 314–15.

"Judge Horatio Washington Bruce." *Confederate Veteran* 11, no. 2 (Feb. 1903): 79–80.

Kelly, R. M. "Holding Kentucky for the Union." In vol. 1 of *Battles and Leaders of the Civil War: Being for the Most Part Contributions by Union and Confederate Officers based upon "The Century War Series,"* edited by Robert Underwood Johnson and Clarence Clough Buel, 373–92. 1884–88. Reprint, New York: Thomas Yoseloff 1956.

Kiser, William S. *Dragoons in Apacheland: Conquest and Resistance in Southern New Mexico, 1846–1861.* Norman, OK: Univ. of Oklahoma Press, 2012.

Kleber, John E., ed. *The Kentucky Encyclopedia.* Lexington: Univ. Press of Kentucky, 1992.

Kolakowski, Christopher L. *The Stones River and Tullahoma Campaigns.* Charleston, SC: History Press, 2011.

Krick, Robert E. L. *Staff Officers in Gray: A Biographical Register of the Staff Officers in the Army of Northern Virginia.* Chapel Hill, NC: Univ. of North Carolina Press, 2003.

Krick, Robert K. "Three Confederate Disasters on Oak Ridge: Failures of Brigade Leadership on the First Day of Gettysburg." In *The First Day at Gettysburg: Essays on Confederate and Union Leadership,* edited by Gary W. Gallagher, 92–139. Kent, OH: Kent State Univ. Press, 1992.

Krolick, Marshall D. "Brig. Gen. Abraham H. Buford. In *Kentuckians in Gray: Confederate Generals and Field Officers of the Bluegrass State,* edited by Bruce S.

Allardice and Lawrence Lee Hewitt, 49–55. Lexington: Univ. Press of Kentucky, 2008.

Kurtz, Wilbur G. "The Death of Major General W. H. T. Walker, July 22, 1864." *Civil War History* 6, no. 2 (June 1960): 174–79.

Lawrence, Alexander A. *A Present for Mr. Lincoln: The Story of Savannah from Secession to Sherman.* Macon, GA: Ardivan, 1961.

Levin, H., comp. *The Lawyers and Lawmakers of Kentucky.* Chicago: Lewis, 1897.

Lindsley, John B., ed. *The Military Annals of Tennessee.* 2 vols. 1896. Reprint, Wilmington, NC: Broadfoot, 1995.

Long, E. B. *The Civil War Day by Day, An Almanac 1861–1865.* Garden City, NY: Doubleday, 1971.

Losson, Christopher. *Tennessee's Forgotten Warriors, Frank Cheatham and His Confederate Division.* Knoxville, TN: Univ. of Tennessee Press, 1989.

Malone, Dumas, ed. *Dictionary of American Biography.* 20 vols. New York: Charles Scribner's Sons, 1926–36.

Martin, Samuel J. *General Braxton Bragg, C.S.A.* Jefferson, NC: McFarland, 2011.

McDonough, James Lee. *Schofield: Union General in the Civil War and Reconstruction.* Tallahassee: Florida State Univ. Press, 1972.

———. *Shiloh: In Hell Before Night.* Knoxville, TN: Univ. of Tennessee Press, 1977.

McMorries, Edward Y. *History of the First Regiment Alabama Volunteer Infantry C.S.A.* Montgomery, AL: Brown, 1904.

McMurry, Richard M. *John Bell Hood and the War for Southern Independence,* Lexington, KY: Univ. Press of Kentucky, 1982.

McMurtry, R. Gerald. *Ben Hardin Helm.* Chicago: Civil War Round Table of Chicago, 1943.

———. "Zollicoffer and the Battle of Mill Springs." *Filson Club History Quarterly* 29 (Oct. 1955): 303–19.

McWhiney, Grady. *Braxton Bragg and Confederate Defeat.* Vol. 1, *Field Command.* Tuscaloosa, AL: Univ. of Alabama Press, 1969.

———. "Controversy in Kentucky: Braxton Bragg's Campaign of 1862." *Civil War History* 6 (Mar. 1960): 5–42.

"Miscellany." *Southern Bivouac* 1, no. 7 (Mar. 1883): 314.

Mobley, Joe A. *War Governor of the South: North Carolina's Zeb Vance in the Confederacy.* Gainesville: Univ. Press of Florida, 2005.

Moore, Frank, ed. *The Rebellion Record: A Diary of American Events with Documents, Narratives, Illustrative Incidents, Poetry, Etc.* 12 vols. New York: D. Van Nostrand, 1861–68.

Morrison, James L. Jr. *"The Best School in the World": West Point in the Pre-Civil War Years, 1833–1866.* Kent, OH: Kent State Univ. Press, 1986.

Mosser, Jeffrey. "I Shall Make Him Remember This Insult." *Civil War Times Illustrated* 32, no. 1 (Mar.–Apr. 1993): 24, 49, 52–57, 60–62.

"Mr. Lincoln and Ben Hardin Helm." *Confederate Veteran* 4, no. 3 (Mar. 1896): 72.

Myers, Raymond E. *The Zollie Tree.* Louisville, KY: Filson Club Press, 1964.

Myrick, Susan. *White Columns in Hollywood: Reports from the Gone With the Wind Sets.* Macon, GA: Mercer Univ. Press, 1994.

Newton, Steven H. *Lost for the Cause: The Confederate Army in 1864.* Mason City, IA: Savas, 2000.

Nicholas, Ron. "Mill Springs: The First Battle for Kentucky." In *The Civil War in Kentucky: Battle for the Bluegrass State,* edited by Kent Masterson Brown, 47-77. Mason City, IA: Savas, 2000.

Nye, W. S. "The Battle of LaFayette." *Civil War Times Illustrated* 6 (June 1966): 34–40.

Otey, Mercer. "The Story of Our Great War." *Confederate Veteran* 9, no. 3 (Mar. 1901): 107–10.

Paden, Rebecca Nash, and Joe McTyre. *Images of America: Cobb County.* Charleston, SC: Arcadia, 2005.

Parks, Edd Winfield. "Zollicoffer: Southern Whig." *Tennessee Historical Quarterly* 11 (Dec. 1952): 346–55.

Parrish, T. Michael. *Richard Taylor: Soldier Prince of Dixie.* Chapel Hill, NC: Univ. of North Carolina Press, 1992.

Parson, Thomas E. *Work for Giants: The Campaign and Battle of Tupelo/Harrisonburg, Mississippi, June–July 1864.* Kent, OH: Kent State Univ. Press, 2014.

Penn, William A. *Rattling Spurs and Broad Brimmed Hats: the Civil War in Cynthiana and Harrison County, Kentucky.* Midway, KY: Battle Grove Press, 1995.

Perrin, W. H., J. H. Battle, and G. C. Kniffin. *Kentucky, A History of the State.* Louisville, KY: E. A. Battey, 1888.

Pirtle, John B. "The Defense of Vicksburg in 1862 and the Battle of Baton Rouge." *Confederate Veteran* 32, no. 7 (July 1924): 264–66.

Porter, James D. *Tennessee.* Vol. 10. *Confederate Military History Extended Edition,* edited by Clement A. Evans. Wilmington, NC: Broadfoot, 1987.

Powell, David A. *The Chickamauga Campaign—Glory or the Grave: The Breakthrough, the Union Collapse, and the Defense of Horseshoe Ridge, September 20, 1863.* El Dorado Hills, CA: Savas Beatie, 2015.

———. *Failure in the Saddle: Nathan Bedford Forrest, Joe Wheeler, and the Confederate Cavalry in the Chickamauga Campaign.* New York: Savas Beattie, 2010.

Purcell, Douglas C. "Military Conscription in Alabama during the Civil War." *Alabama Review* 34 (Apr. 1981): 94–106.

Ramage, James A. *Rebel Raider: The Life of General John Hunt Morgan.* Lexington, KY: Univ. Press of Kentucky, 1986.

"Record of Walthall's Division at Franklin and Nashville in late 1864." *Confederate Veteran* 7, no. 6 (June 1899): 265.

Reid, Whitelaw. *Ohio in the War: Her Statesmen, Her Generals, and Soldiers.* 2 vols. Cincinnati: Moore, Wilstach and Baldwin, 1868.

Robertson, Jno., comp. *Michigan in the War.* Rev. ed., Lansing, MI: W. S. George, 1882.

Sanders, Stuart. *The Battle of Mill Springs, Kentucky*. Charleston, SC: Arcadia, 2013.

Sartain, James A. *History of Walker County Georgia*. Vol. 1. Dalton, GA: A. J. Showalter, 1932.

Seitz, Don C. *Braxton Bragg: General of the Confederacy.* Columbia, SC: State, 1924.

Shortridge, Wilson P. "Kentucky Neutrality in 1861." *Mississippi Valley Historical Review* 9 (Mar. 1923): 283–301.

Simpson, Henry Clay, Jr. *Josephine Clay: Pioneer Horse Woman of the Bluegrass.* Louisville, KY: Harmony House, 2005.

"Sketch of General B. H. Helm." *The Land We Love* 3 (June 1867): 163–67.

Smith, A. F. Untitled article. *Confederate Veteran* 6, no. 7 (July 1898): 307–8.

Smith, Derek. *Civil War Savannah*. Savannah, GA: Frederic C. Beil, 1997.

Smith, Timothy B. *Champion Hill: Decisive Battle for Vicksburg.* New York: Savas Beatie, 2004.

Speed, Thomas. *The Union Cause in Kentucky, 1860–1865.* New York: G. P. Putnam's Sons, 1907.

Speer, William S. *Sketches of Prominent Tennesseans.* Nashville, TN: Albert B. Tavel, 1888.

Stamper, James C. "Felix K. Zollicoffer: Tennessee Editor and Politician." *Tennessee Historical Quarterly* 28 (Winter 1969): 356–76.

Stephens, Larry. *Bound for Glory: A History of the 30th Alabama Infantry Regiment, C.S.A.* Ann Arbor, MI: Sheridan, 2005.

Stickles, Arndt M. *Simon Bolivar Buckner: Borderland Knight.* 1940. Reprint, Wilmington, NC: Broadfoot, 1987.

Still, William N. Jr. "Porter…Is the Best Man." *Civil War Times Illustrated* (May 1977): 4–9, 44–47.

Sword, Wiley. *Embrace an Angry Wind*. New York: Harper Collins, 1992.

Symonds, Craig L. *Joseph E. Johnston: A Civil War Biography.* New York: W. W. Norton, 1992.

———. *Stonewall of the West: Patrick Cleburne and the Civil War.* Lawrence, KS: Univ. Press of Kansas, 1997.

Tansill, Robert. *A Free and Impartial Exposition of the Causes which Led to the Failure of the Confederate States to establish their Independence*. Washington, DC: n.p., 1865.

Tennessee Civil War Commission. *Tennesseans in the Civil War,* 2 vols. Nashville: Tennessee Civil War Centennial Commission, 1964–65.

"Third Reunion of the Kentucky Brigade." *Southern Bivouac* 3, no. 3 (Nov. 1884): 116-21.

Thompson, Ed Porter. *History of the Orphan Brigade*. 1868. Reprint, Dayton, OH: Morningside, 1973.

Thompson, Illene D. and Wilbur E. Thompson. *The Seventeenth Alabama Infantry: A Regimental History and Roster.* Bowie, MD: Heritage, 2001.

Townsend, William H. *Lincoln and His Wife's Home Town*. Indianapolis: Bobbs-Merrill, 1929.

———. *Lincoln and the Bluegrass: Slavery and Civil War in Kentucky*. Lexington: Univ. Press of Kentucky, 1955.

Tucker, Glenn. *Chickamauga: Bloody Battle in the West*. New York: Bobbs-Merrill, 1961. Reprint, Dayton, OH: Morningside, 1992. Page references are to both editions as indicated.

Turchin, John Basil. *Chickamauga.* 1888. Reprint, Charleston, SC: Nabu Press, 2010.

The Union Army: A History of Military Affairs in the Loyal States 1861–65—Records of the Regiments in the Union Army—Cyclopedia of Battles—Memoirs of Commanders and Soldiers. Vol. 6, *Cyclopedia of Battles—Helena Road to Z*. Madison, WI: Federal, 1908.

Union Soldiers and Sailors Monument Association, Louisville. *Union Regiments of Kentucky.* Louisville, KY: Courier-Journal, 1897.

Van Horne, Thomas B. *History of the Army of the Cumberland: its Organization, Campaigns, and Battles written at the request of Major-General George H. Thomas chiefly from his private military journal and official and other documents furnished by him,* 3 vols. Cincinnati: Robert Clarke, 1875.

Wakelyn, Jon L. *Biographical Dictionary of the Confederacy*. Westport, CT: Greenwood, 1977.

Ward, Andrew. *River Run Red: The Fort Pillow Massacre in the American Civil War.* New York: Viking, 2005.

Warner, Ezra J. *Generals in Gray: Lives of the Confederate Commanders*. Baton Rouge, LA: Louisiana State Univ. Press, 1959.

Wells, John B. III, and James M. Prichard. *10th Kentucky Cavalry, C.S.A.* Baltimore: Gateway, 1996.

Welsh, Jack D. *Medical Histories of Confederate Generals*. Kent, OH: Kent State Univ. Press, 1995.

Williams, Hunter B. "Military Operations in the Jackson Purchase Area of Kentucky, 1862–1865, Part II." *Register of the Kentucky Historical Society* 63 (July 1965): 240–67.

Wills, Brian S. *A Battle from the Start: The Life of Nathan Bedford Forrest.* New York: HarperCollins, 1992.

Wright, Marcus J. "Sketch of General Felix K. Zollicoffer." *Southern Bivouac* 2 (July 1884): 485–99.

Wyeth, John Allan. *Life of General Nathan Bedford Forrest*. New York: Harper and Brothers, 1899.

———. *Life of Lieutenant-General Nathan Bedford Forrest*. New York: Harper and Brothers, 1908.

Wynne, Ben. *A Hard Trip: A History of the 15th Mississippi Infantry, CSA*. Macon, GA: Mercer Univ. Press, 2003.

Young, Bennett H. "Zollicoffer's Oak." *Southern Historical Society Papers* 31 (1903): 165–72.

Thesis

Hardin, Paul D. "Edward Cary Walthall: A Mississippi Conservative." Master's thesis, Duke University, 1940.

Internet Resources

Barlow, Captain Edward C. Diary. Accessed June 21, 2015. http://www.barlowgenealogy.com/BOB/ECBarlowDiary.html.

Hopkins, Craig. "John Jacob Zollicoffer Family." Accessed Sept. 27, 2016. http://www.rootsweb.ancestry.com/~tnmaury/biotext.htm.

Lambert, Audrey June (Denny). "General Felix K. Zollicoffer." Accessed Apr. 1, 2008. http://www.ajlambert.com/history/zollicof.pdf.

Walden, Geoffrey R. "Death of Gen. Felix K. Zollicoffer." Accessed Apr. 1, 2008. http://www.geocities.com/Pentagon/Quarters/1864/zolldeath.htm.

Wood, E. Thomas. "Nashville now and then: Fightin' words." Accessed Jan. 16, 2009. http://www.nashvillepost.com/home/article/20401180nashville-now-and-then-fightin-words

Personal Communications

William K. Scarborough to Nathaniel C. Hughes, Jr., Jan. 3, 1993.

Contributors

Editor's Note: The institution granting the contributor's highest degree is given in parentheses following his or her name.

STEWART L. BENNETT (Maine) is the Department Chair of Social and Behavior Sciences and Associate Professor of History at Blue Mountain College in Blue Mountain, Mississippi. A 2010 recipient of the Mississippi Humanities Council: Humanities Teacher Award, Bennett is the author of *The Battle of Brice's Crossroads* (2012) and essays in *The Chattanooga Campaign* (2012) and *The Tennessee Campaign of 1864* (2016). He is also coeditor of *The Struggle for the Life of the Republic: A Civil War Narrative by Brevet Major Charles Dana Miller, 76th Ohio Volunteer Infantry* (2004).

KEITH S. BOHANNON (Pennsylvania State) is a professor of history at the University of West Georgia. He is coeditor of *A Georgian with Old Stonewall in Virginia: The Letters of Ujanirtus Allen, Company F, 21st Georgia Volunteer Infantry* (1998), as well as being the author of numerous essays and articles including "John Bell Hood" in *Leaders of the Lost Cause: New Perspectives on the Confederate High Command* (2004).

MICHAEL R. BRADLEY (Vanderbilt) taught United States history for thirty-six years at Motlow College until his retirement in 2006. A prolific writer, his publications dealing with the Civil War include books about the Tullahoma Campaign of 1863, guerilla warfare in Middle Tennessee, and subordinates of Nathan Bedford Forrest, as well as articles in *Blue & Gray* and *North & South* magazines. He also served as a member of the Tennessee Civil War Sesquicentennial Commission.

C. DAVID DALTON (Kentucky) holds the Elizabeth Hoyt Clark Chair of Humanities and is Professor of History at College of the Ozarks, Point Lookout, Missouri. He has received fellowships from the Virginia Historical

Society and Gilder Lehrman Institute, the 2000 Missouri Governor's Award for Excellence in College Teaching, and the 2009 Eugene Charles Wittick Teaching Excellence Award from his institution. He is most recently published in *Kentuckians in Gray* (2008) and *The Encyclopedia of the American Civil War* (2002).

ROGER S. DURHAM (Georgia Southern) is a native of Illinois and a veteran of U.S. Army service in Vietnam. He worked in the museum and historic site profession for forty years, being employed by the states of Georgia and Texas, the Department of the Army, the National Park Service, and the Department of the Interior. In 2012 he retired as the director of the U.S. Army Heritage Museum at Carlisle Barracks, Pennsylvania. He has authored or edited numerous books and articles including *The Blues in Gray: The Civil War Journal of William Daniel Dixon and the Republican Blues Daybook* (2000) and *A Confederate Yankee: The Journal of Edward William Drummond, a Confederate Soldier from Maine* (2004).

CHRIS E. FONVIELLE JR. (South Carolina) is a native of Wilmington, North Carolina. Formerly the curator of the Blockade Runners of the Confederacy Museum, he has taught at the University of North Carolina Wilmington since 1996 where he is currently an associate professor in the Department of History. A prolific author on Civil War North Carolina, his books include *The Wilmington Campaign: Last Rays of Departing Hope* (1997), *Louis Froelich: Arms-Maker to the Confederacy* (2008), and *Fort Fisher 1865: The Photographs of T. H. O'Sullivan* (2011). Chris and his wife Nancy live in Wilmington with their two daughters, Mary and Anne.

NATHANIEL CHEAIRS HUGHES JR. (North Carolina), a native Tennessean, had two careers: as a teacher, coach, and headmaster at Webb School in Bell Buckle, Tennessee, at St. Mary's Episcopal School in Memphis, at Girls Preparatory School in Chattanooga, and at the University of Memphis, and as a writer of history. Before his death in 2012, Hughes published twenty-three books, from *General William J. Hardee: Old Reliable* (1965) to *Yale's Confederates: A Biological Dictionary* (2009). He also served in the Marine Corps as leader of an armored amphibian platoon and took great pride in his three sons also becoming Marine officers.

JAMES M. PRICHARD (Wright State University) supervised the Kentucky State Archives Research Room from 1985 to 2008 and is currently employed at The Filson Historical Society in Louisville. He authored *Embattled Capital: Frankfort, Kentucky in the Civil War* (2014) and, with John B. Wells III, *10th Kentucky Cavalry, C.S.A.* (1996). His essays appear in *Virginia at War:*

1863 (2010), *Confederate Generals in the Western Theater: Vol. 2* (2010), and *Kentuckians in Gray* (2008), his articles in *Civil War Times, North & South* and *True West* magazines, and he contributed entries to both *The Encyclopedia of the American Civil War* (2002) and *Biographical Dictionary of the Union* (1995).

STUART W. SANDERS (Centre) is the former executive director of the Perryville Battlefield Preservation Association and is currently a public history administrator in the Commonwealth of Kentucky. He is the author of *Perryville Under Fire: The Aftermath of Kentucky's Largest Civil War Battle* (2012), *The Battle of Mill Springs, Kentucky* (2013), and *Maney's Confederate Brigade at the Battle of Perryville* (2014), and his articles have appeared in *Kentuckians in Gray* (2008), *Confederate Generals in the Western Theater: Vol 2* (2010), *Confederate Generals in the Western Theater: Vol. 3* (2011), *Confederate Generals in the Trans-Mississippi: Vol. 1* (2013), *MHQ: The Quarterly Journal of Military History, Civil War History, Civil War Times Illustrated, America's Civil War, Blue & Gray, Civil War Quarterly, The Journal of America's Military Past,* and *The Register.*

BRIAN S. WILLS (Georgia) is the Director of the Center for the Study of the Civil War Era and Professor of History at Kennesaw State University in Kennesaw, Georgia. In addition to leading tours, offering lectures, and conducting programs, Wills is the author of numerous works relating to the American Civil War, including biographies of Confederate generals Nathan Bedford Forrest and William Dorsey Pender, and an award-winning study of Union general George Henry Thomas. He has also written about the Civil War in Virginia and in the movies. When not teaching and working in Kennesaw, he spends time on his farm in Virginia.

Index

Page numbers in **boldface** refer to illustrations. Units above the regimental level are listed under their commander's name. Unless obvious or otherwise noted, all named military officers, government officials, units, forts, camps, naval vessels, geographical districts, and departments are Confederate.